UPHOLSTERY
A Practical Guide

UPHOLSTERY
A Practical Guide

DESMOND GASTON

Illustrated by Tig Sutton

HarperCollins*Publishers*

First published in 1982
by William Collins Sons & Co Ltd
London, Glasgow, Sydney,
Auckland, Johannesburg
Reprinted 1983, 1986, 1989, 1991

Designed by Caroline Hill
Illustrated by Tig Sutton

ISBN 0 00 411671 2

Text set in Century Schoolbook 227
by Advanced Filmsetters (Glasgow) Ltd.
Printed and bound in Great Britain by
William Collins Sons & Co Ltd.

Preface

You might expect that it would be very easy for me to dash down a few instructions on upholstery, a craft that I have studied and practised nearly all my working life. But after plying this trade for such a long time, my fingers perform many actions so automatically that no conscious thought seems to govern their movements. It is only since I have been teaching at our local Adult Education Centre that I realise how foreign and sometimes difficult these movements are to newcomers to upholstery. I am frequently taken aback when requested to show, in slow motion, some process or technique, and I suddenly ask myself: 'how ever do I do this?'. But I find that it is good for me to become aware again of movements that I have been accustomed to performing automatically.

It was with surprise and happiness that I realized how 'hooked' on the craft of upholstery people seem to become, judging by the reaction of the folk in my upholstery classes, and it is my hope that perhaps you will be able to catch some of the enthusiasm that comes from working with twines, webbing, soft fillings and woven fabrics. Most of the attraction, I suppose, is the thrill of being able to transform a ragged wreck into an exciting and comfortable piece of upholstered furniture. Also, when you build up the upholstery starting from nothing but the bare frame of a settee, easy chair or couch, you are not bound by a set form or shape that has to be reproduced exactly. A lot of your own ideas of shapes, sizes, softness, firmness and trimmings can be incorporated so that you can produce something that really contains a lot of you and your own style.

However, when you begin to do traditional upholstery work yourself you must be prepared for shocks, thrills and a lot of precise, time-consuming work—I'm afraid you can't cut corners if you want to produce long lasting, high quality upholstery in the traditional way. The first shock will be to discover just how much dust accumulates inside old upholstered furniture. And then, when all the old materials have been stripped off, you will be appalled by the number of holes left in the frame by tacks. Often these tacks have been used to fasten the previous upholstery of two or maybe three refurbishings. The holes always make the frame look in a worse condition than it really is—remember that tacks are wedge-shaped and so the largest part of each hole is on the surface and the interior of the wood is usually sound.

Then, when you come to build up your own new upholstery you will be amazed at the number of layers that constitute traditional work. Let's take an easy chair seat, for instance. If we count the layers from the bottom to the top you will have webbing on which springs are fastened; the springs themselves which are overlaid with stout hessian; then the first layer of stuffing, usually horse hair, which in turn is covered with a lighter weight hessian. Another thickness of hair or wool is added as a second stuffing and this is covered by a calico cloth. Over the calico goes a thickness or two of wadding to prevent the prickly horse hair from working through, and lastly, the covering material is stretched over. So, all in all, there will be about nine different layers! It is not my intention to put you off by telling you all this but to give you an idea of just what is involved in a piece of fine, traditional upholstery work.

You will find in this book a chapter on basic skills, where I have given full instructions for the fundamental tasks which are repeated in the majority of upholstery jobs. This is followed by detailed work projects in order of increasing difficulty, and at the end of the book is an A to Z of upholstery tasks that have peculiarities and problems additional to those already mentioned. My ardent wish is to contribute to keeping alive the old tried and trusted ways handed down by upholsterers over the years, and it is the traditional aspects of the craft of upholstery that I have emphasized in these pages.

A note about tools and materials: most upholstery suppliers only deal direct with the trade, so I suggest that first of all you consult the yellow pages in your telephone directory to find a local upholsterer or upholsterer's warehouseman for your tools and materials. However, many do-it-yourself shops and the larger department stores now stock certain upholstery sundries and soft furnishings. Also, D. L. Forster Ltd, 17 Tramway Avenue, Stratford, London E15 4PG, although they do not supply the public direct, are pleased to send a list of stockists in your area on receipt of written enquiries.

Acknowledgements

I am most grateful to my friend Ted Collins to whom I am indebted for much guidance, many suggestions and a great deal of practical help and encouragement in writing this book. The students in my upholstery classes have also helped in unexpected ways by asking questions and making me explain many of the simple aspects of upholstery which I had presumed were common knowledge. When you have been doing upholstery work for as long as I have many of the techniques and actions become automatic and it is so helpful to be asked questions in this way. I would also like to express my thanks to Caroline Hill, my designer, and to Cathy Gosling for being a most understanding, patient and thorough editor.

Desmond Gaston

Contents

1 Tools, Equipment and Materials

Anyone who takes up the trade of the upholsterer initially has one small advantage over those entering many other trades, in that the hand tools required are comparatively simple and inexpensive. For those of you who are beginners I will list the necessary tools and describe their uses.

As the first task we face when reupholstering is undoing, unpicking and ripping off the old materials, let us start with the instruments of destruction.

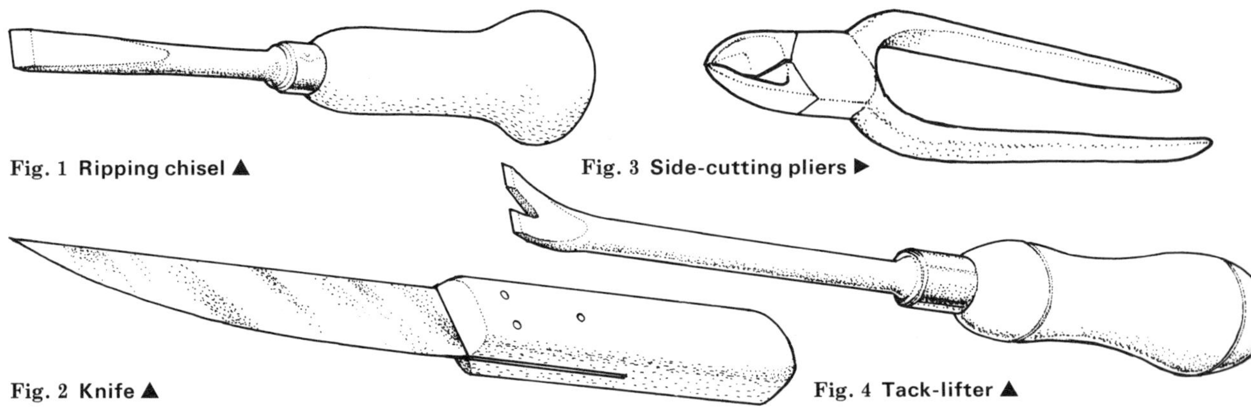

Fig. 1 Ripping chisel ▲

Fig. 3 Side-cutting pliers ▶

Fig. 2 Knife ▲

Fig. 4 Tack-lifter ▲

TOOLS

Ripping Chisel

This is a tool exclusive to the upholsterer. It is used for getting out all the old tacks easily and quickly. I have two, one with a wide blade, the other with a narrow one. The ripping chisel (**fig. 1**) is used with a small mallet.

Knives

A collection of sharp—and I do mean sharp—knives is essential to enable you to slash away all the old coverings, hessians and twines (**fig. 2**).

Pair of Pincers

Thinking again about removing tacks—a small pair of pincers is very handy. Try and get some with the jaws ground from the underside with no bevel on the top faces so that they will remove tacks, nails and pins that are close in to the wood.

Side-Cutting Pliers

I have a small pair of side-cutting pliers that I have adapted by grinding the jaws to more of a point when closed (**fig. 3**). You would be surprised how useful these are for removing awkward tacks. You can dig the points into the wood round a tack head and extract the tack with ease. I always keep my pliers in my pocket when circulating among students in the class and lend them out for removing wrongly positioned tacks.

Tack-Lifter

This needs to have a well defined crook, as illustrated (**fig. 4**), and although not a lot of use for removing ordinary tacks, it is essential for extracting the dome-headed decorative chair nails that are frequently used in leather upholstery. And now to tools of construction.

Scissors

These come under both headings, as they are needed for unpicking as well as refurbishing.

Cutting-out shears: these are used for making long, straight cuts in covering cloths, hessians, linings, etc.

Small pointed trimmers: are for small cuts, trimming surplus fabric, fitting upholstery cloth and unpicking.

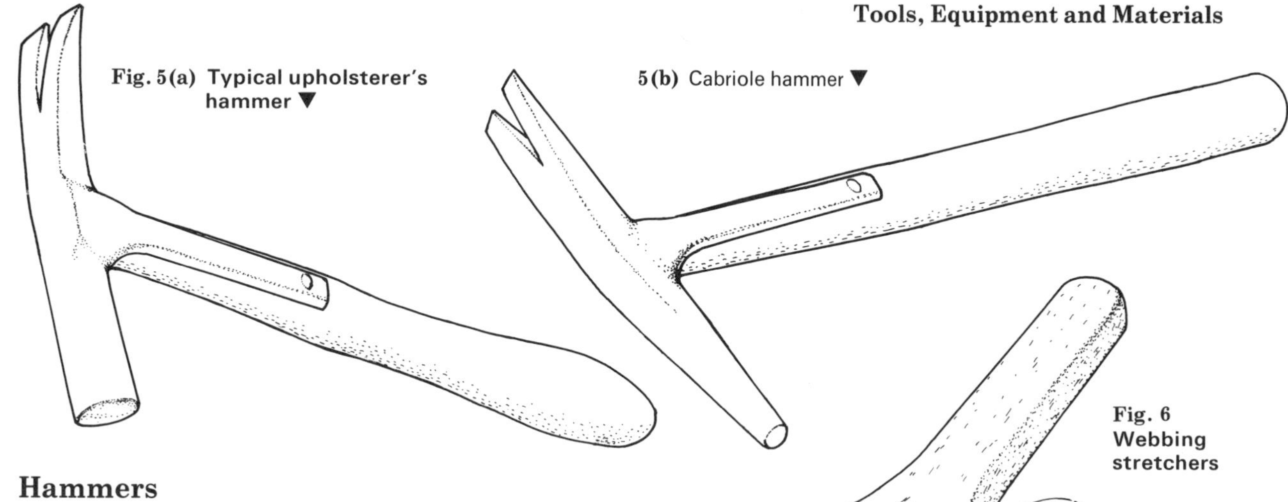

Fig. 5(a) Typical upholsterer's hammer ▼

5(b) Cabriole hammer ▼

Hammers

You will need several different types of hammer.

Upholsterer's hammer: with a head and claw for general purposes (**fig. 5a**).

Magnetic hammer: this will hold a tack on its face, and is useful for those places where fingers cannot reach. It is also invaluable for picking up dropped tacks.

Cabriole hammer: a rare specimen nowadays, this is used for fine tacking work around and near show wood and into tacking rebates where a larger-headed hammer would cause damage to the woodwork (**fig. 5b**).

Two-headed hammer: combines the general purpose with the cabriole but, of course, does not have the very useful claw for removing temporary tacks.

Heavy hammer: I like a slightly heavier, larger-faced hammer to use with large tacks when webbing. With this hammer tacks can be driven well home, a very important point to remember, especially when fastening the webbing.

Webbing Stretchers

There are three types.

Slot and peg: the webbing is pushed down through the slot and the peg inserted in the loop of webbing which protrudes underneath (**fig. 6a**).

Hinged bar: this is the sort I favour. The webbing is looped beneath the bar and the hinge action pinches and grips the webbing (**fig. 6b**).

Pincer-type: these webbing stretchers are also known as wide-jawed hide strainers (**fig. 6c**). They are much more costly and rely upon a hard grip to hold the webbing, but they are useful for short ends of webbing.

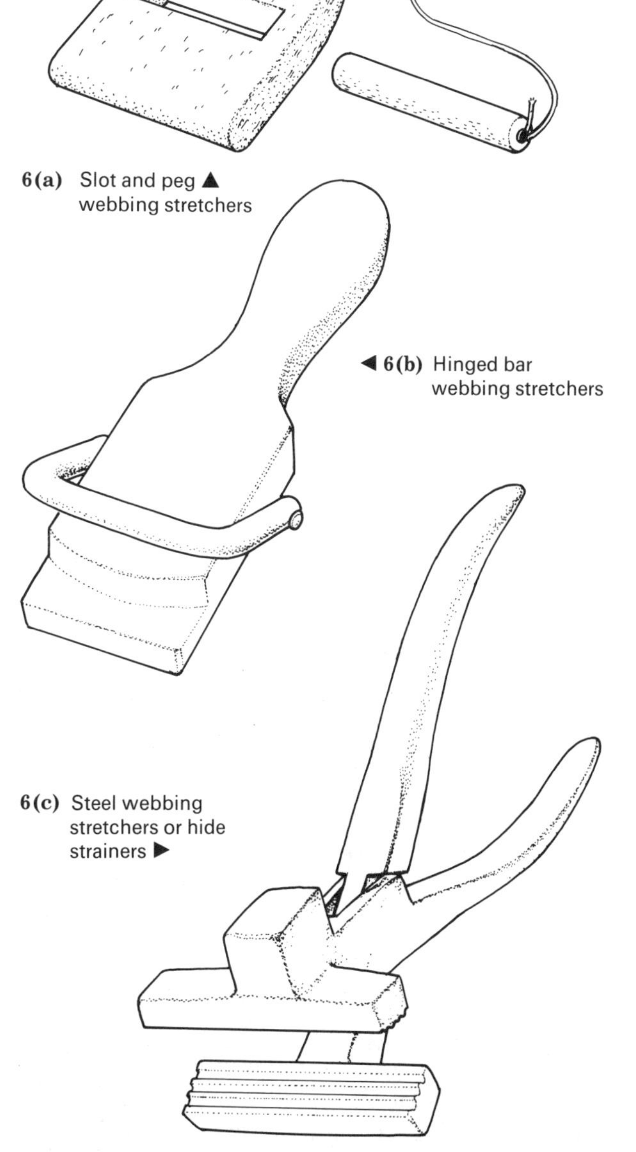

Fig. 6 Webbing stretchers

6(a) Slot and peg ▲ webbing stretchers

◀ 6(b) Hinged bar webbing stretchers

6(c) Steel webbing stretchers or hide strainers ▶

Fig. 7 Needles (all drawn approximately half size)

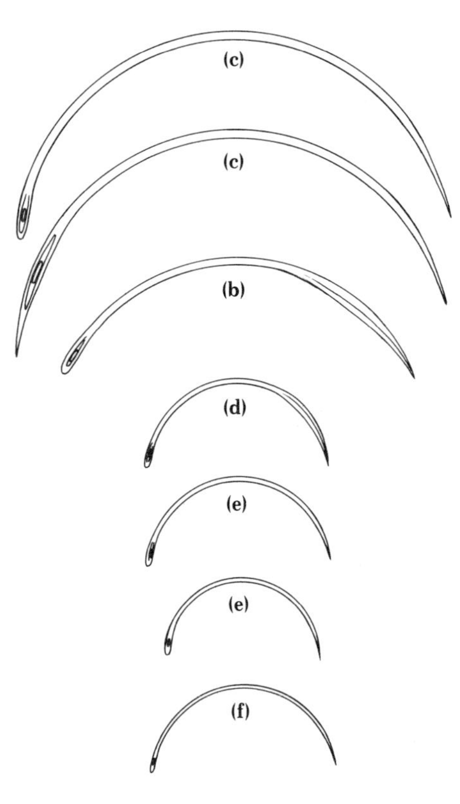

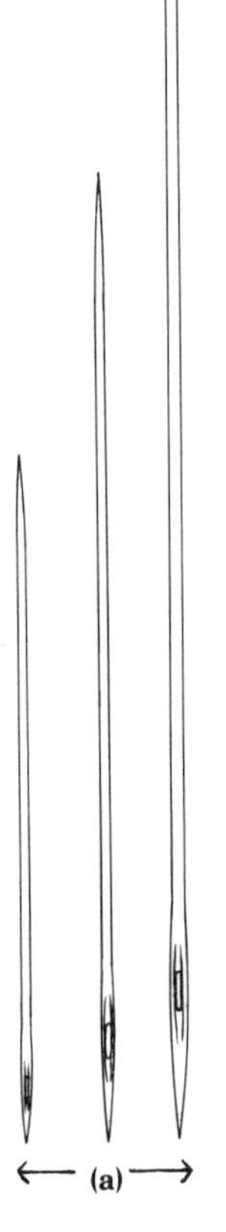

7(a) Mattress needles
7(b) Spring needle
7(c) Semi-circular needles
7(d) Bayonet point needle
7(e) Round point needles
7(f) Cording needle

Needles

The different needles required for sewing with twine are illustrated in **fig. 7a–f**.

Mattress needles: you will need three sizes of these double-pointed needles: a very long one, 350 mm (14 in), 12 gauge thickness; one of medium length, 250 mm (10 in), 13 gauge thickness; and a short one, 180 mm (7 in), 14 gauge thickness (**fig. 7a**).

Spring needle: the slightly curved spring needle has what we call a bayonet point (**fig. 7b**). It is used for sewing or fastening springs to webbing or hessian. You will need one that measures 125 mm (5 in) or 150 mm (6 in).

Semi-circular needles: these are used for sewing with twine. Their size is determined by the length of the needle measured round the curve (**fig. 7c**), and if you can also buy one with a point at each end, so much the better. If not, you can modify the one-pointed curved needle for a certain type of work, as I will describe later (page 185).

For use with thread or cotton much smaller curved needles are required.

Bayonet point needle: you need one 75 mm (3 in) length, 17 gauge thickness, for use on tough materials such as leather (**fig. 7d**).

Round point needles: for general upholstery work you need one 75 mm (3 in), 17 gauge, and one 60 mm ($2\frac{1}{2}$ in), 17 gauge (**fig. 7e**).

Cording needles: get two or three in 75 mm (3 in) length, 19 gauge (**fig. 7f**). These fine needles are used for sewing on decorative chair cord and for sewing on braid and fringe. They tend to break easily but they are not expensive.

Regulators

These instruments (**fig. 8**) have a number of uses—packing and distributing stuffing, marking, and in buttonwork. Also, if you are like me and have rather large fingers, the regulator is very useful as an extra finger for holding covering material while fixing.

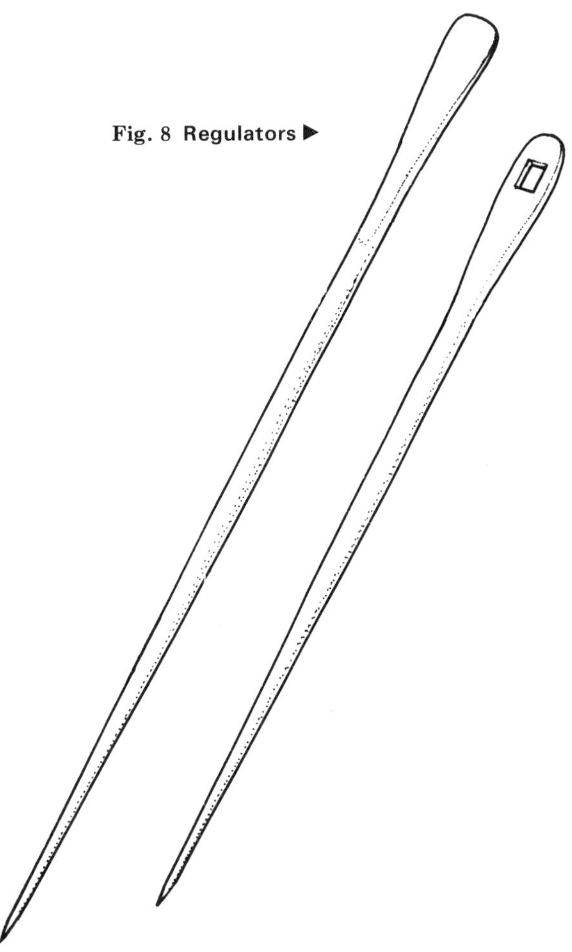

Fig. 8 Regulators ▶

Pins and Skewers

Upholsterer's pins and skewers are items unique to the trade. The pins look like dressmakers' pins but are at least 38 mm ($1\frac{1}{2}$ in) long. The skewers are 75 mm (3 in) or 100 mm (4 in) long. Pins and skewers are used for temporarily holding and fixing coverings, hessians and in cushion work.

Rules and Measures

Rules, measures and straight edges will all be used in your upholstery work.

Steel tape: the most important measuring tool. Nearly all measurements in upholstery involve distances round and over curved surfaces, so the tape must be flexible.

Yardstick: most of the new yardsticks measure one metre but also include imperial measurements. As well as a yardstick's obvious purpose for measuring or checking lengths of cloth, webbing, hessian and so on, it is very useful for setting out, and as a straight edge.

Upholstery gauge—'Gaston's special': This is a tool that you can make yourself: I designed it to gauge guide lines on the first stuffing upholstery scrim for lines of stitches and ties. It can be cut from wood 2 cm ($\frac{3}{4}$ in) thick, with a small coping saw, fret saw or a band saw. The notches at each end are made with a rat-tail file or cut as Vs with a small saw. In **fig. 9** I have shown the dimensions for this particular gauge which will serve most purposes.

Fig. 9 Gaston's special upholstery gauge ▼

notch for marker
notch for marker
10.25 cm (4")
3.25 cm (1¼")
27cm (10⅝")
2cm (¾")

Staple gun

The staple gun is a tool which has proved popular with upholsterers during the last few years and is used a great deal in modern upholstery. However, I hesitate to use staples on antique work, except in certain special circumstances, which I will detail later on. A staple gun is a great time-saver. It can be bought at most hardware stores but, when purchasing one, do take a piece of hardwood with you in your pocket to try out the stapler. Some have very light springs which are of no use except on softwood—and, of course, it is softwood that the shop assistant will offer you to try out this weapon! Fire a staple into your piece of hardwood and, if the gun is a good one, the staple will be driven well and truly home. The gun should take the thin 6 mm (¼ in) staples.

Button-Fold Sticks

'Gaston's specials': you can make button-fold sticks (**fig. 10**) for yourself from thin, smooth hardwood. Being made of wood they are kinder to covering fabric than the flat rounded end of a steel regulator and are used to make the folds between buttons in Victorian buttonwork.

Tubular Cutter

You will find a good use in buttonwork for a 25 mm (1 in) diameter tubular cutter for making holes in foam and stuffing (**fig. 11**). This can be made from a piece of steel cycle frame tubing cut to about 150 mm (6 in) long, which can then be ground at one end to a sharp edge.

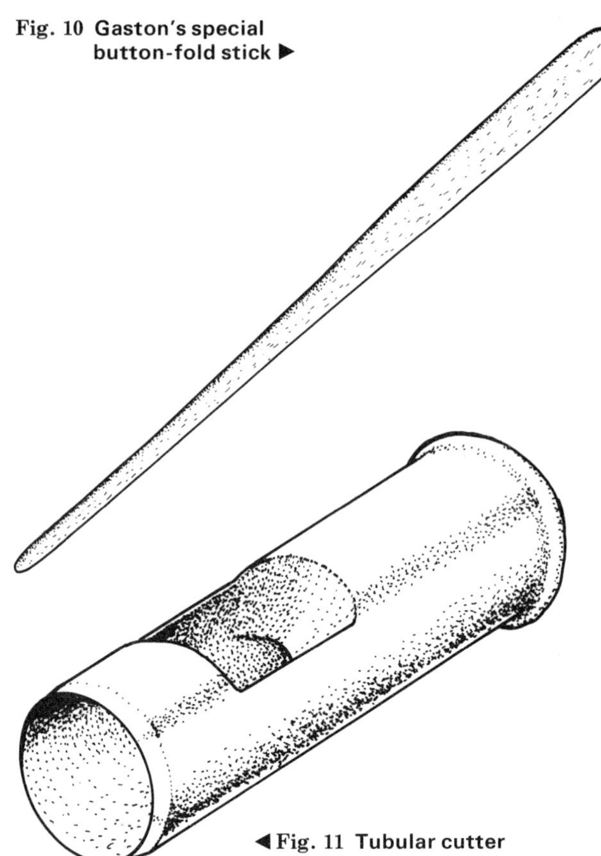

Fig. 10 Gaston's special button-fold stick ▶

◀ Fig. 11 Tubular cutter

EQUIPMENT

Trestles

It is always important for both comfort and efficiency to have your work at the right height, so trestles of different heights are necessary. I have three sizes: a pair of high trestles for working on seats of easy chairs; a medium-size pair for doing arms; and a pair of low ones for working on backs and wings. Each trestle has a groove or trough in the top. This takes the castors and legs, thus preventing the chair or settee from moving while you are working on it.

A Workmate

I have a Workmate that is in constant use and I have made a table top that can be clamped to the top. This is very useful for working on single chair seats or stools, as the legs can be adjusted to two heights. The lower position is used when ripping off, webbing and putting on stuffing, while the higher level makes edge stitching, covering and trimming easier.

Cutting-Out Table

A sheet of 12 mm (½ in) plywood 2.4 × 1.2 m (8 × 4 ft) screwed to a framework of 25 × 50 mm (1 × 2 in) and set on the top of the high trestles will prove a boon for cutting out, setting out and other table jobs. It will be much more convenient and comfortable than using the floor.

Softening

A builders' word for protective padding or cushioning to help spread the weight load over fragile surfaces. For your softening save some old foam cushions that you can use to rest the backs of easy chairs on when they are inverted for webbing and so on.

MACHINERY

Carding Machine

The carding machine is the upholsterer's most expensive piece of machinery, but it is not so necessary for an amateur as, these days, you can buy ready-carded stuffings and fillings—at a price. However, if you intend to do a fair bit of upholstery and you spot an old carding machine in a sale or junk yard, buy it—that is, if you have room to set it up, for it needs a shed of its own. It will soon pay for itself. Another idea is to get together a group of people as keen on upholstery as yourself, and set up a carding and machining centre in someone's garden shed. You can all take your stuffings there and rejuvenate them, for that is what a carding machine does. The lumps of matted horsehair or other types of filling are fed into a hopper and passed between opposing spiked rollers which separate and comb the fibres while all the dust is sucked out by an extractor fan at the back. The filling then comes out all clean, soft and springy, ready to be re-used. If you cannot get access to a carding machine, the other alternative is to get to know your friendly neighbourhood upholsterer, who, for a fee, may do your carding for you.

Sewing Machine

This is the next largest piece of machinery. You can probably get by with an ordinary domestic model to begin with, but this will not deal with the very heavy fabrics, such as tapestry and thick modern leathercloths. These may have to be fed through in four or more thicknesses when making piped cushion covers, for example. Later on you may be able to purchase second-hand a tailor's or industrial sewing machine but meanwhile if you have to manage with your domestic machine fit it with the thickest gauge needle it will take.

Button Presses

I mention these in passing just in case you see any for sale second-hand, perhaps in an auction sale. Since most people would never be able to guess their purpose, you might be able to buy them cheaply. They can be bought new, but they are quite expensive now—however, again, perhaps they could be acquired by your upholstery group for a joint machining centre. There are two types of press.

Cutting press: the cutting press (**fig. 12a**) has as accessories circular cutters to cut discs of cloth for covering button moulds.

Fly press: this press (**fig. 12b**) can be fitted with appropriate dies and when operated it compresses a disc of covering material and a two-part button mould together. In this way it makes an upholstery button very quickly and easily.

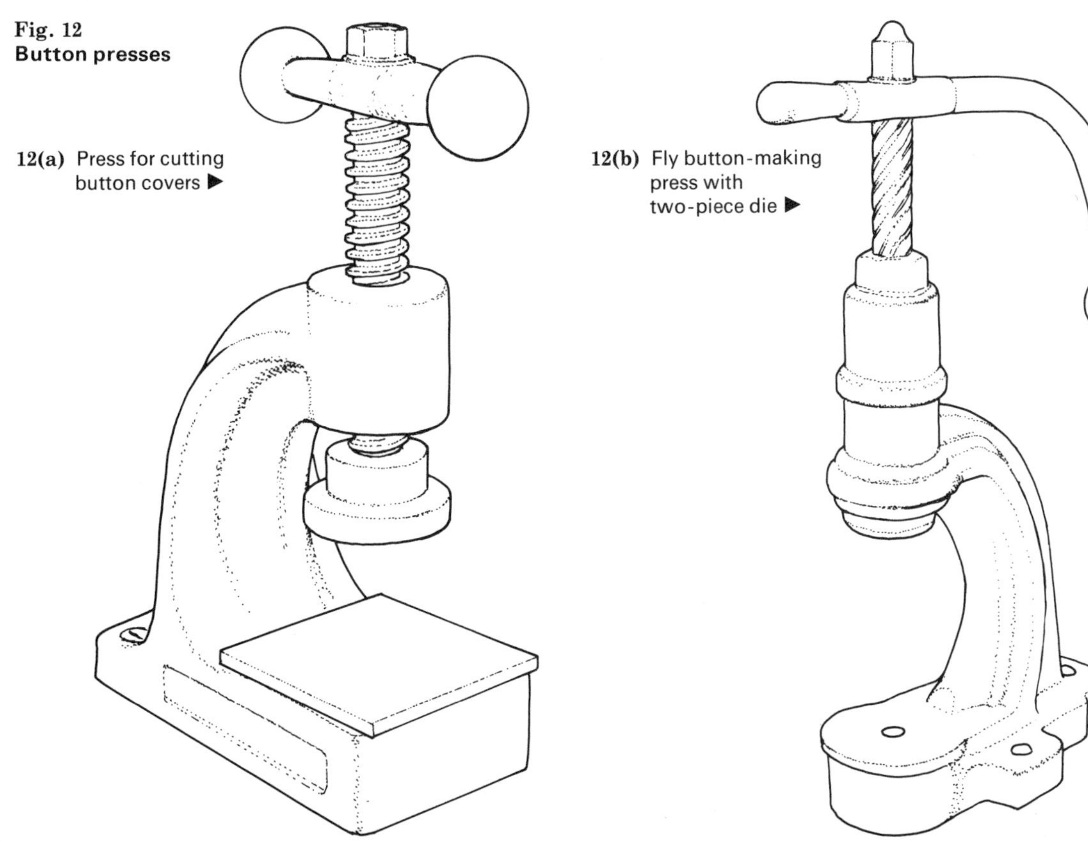

Fig. 12
Button presses

12(a) Press for cutting button covers ▶

12(b) Fly button-making press with two-piece die ▶

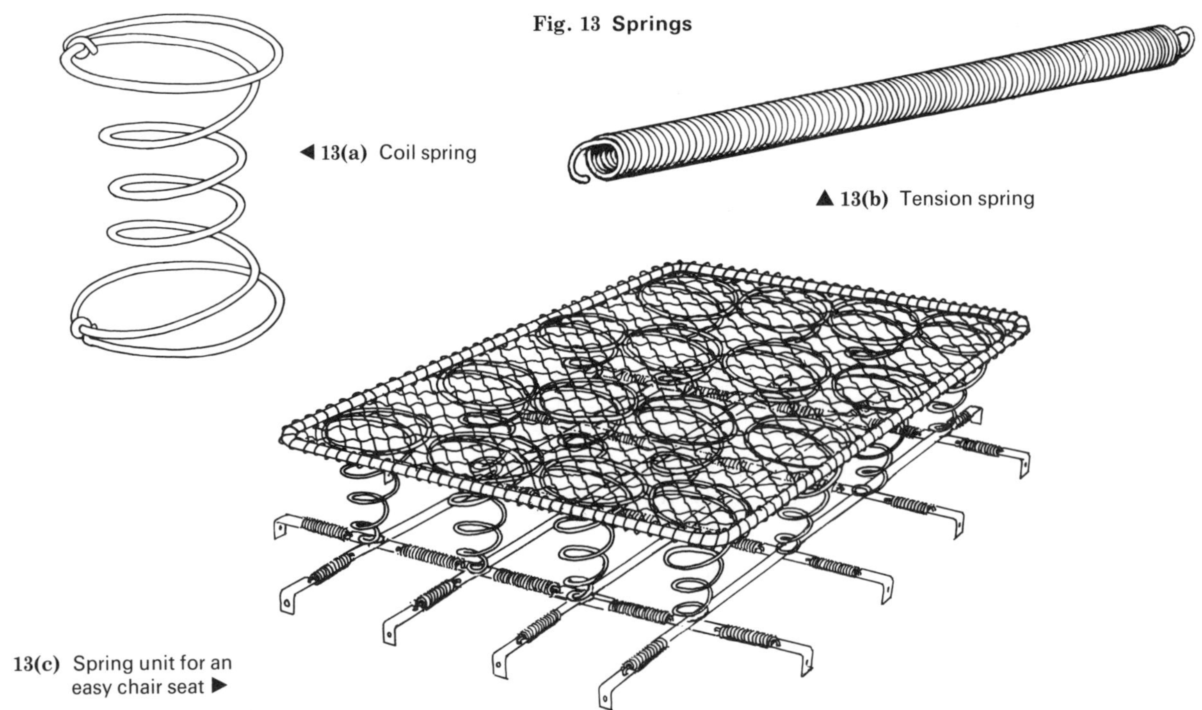

Fig. 13 Springs

◀ 13(a) Coil spring

▲ 13(b) Tension spring

13(c) Spring unit for an easy chair seat ▶

MATERIALS

Let us look at the materials and sundries used in upholstery, some of which, if you are tackling a number of jobs, might to advantage be bought in quantity.

Supports

Webbing: I find the best and longest lasting webbing is English 50 mm (2 in) black and white. It pays always to use the best, because webbing is a basic support and it needs to be strong enough to bear the weight of springs or filling, which are sometimes compressed by large persons descending on them at speed.

Rubber webbing: many modern upholstered chairs have rubber webbing for their seat platforms and usually this is 50 mm (2 in) in width. Rubber webbing makes a comfortable and efficient base for a cushioned seat but will need replacing after three to five years of use. When buying rubber webbing get a good thick type—they do vary considerably in quality. Metal clips are supplied for fastening to the ends of the webbing straps, and this makes for easier fixing.

Heavy hessian or tarpaulin: is a thick and strong hessian and you will be using this as a platform over webbing or to cover upholstery springs. I usually buy the 450 g (16 oz) tarpaulin.

Springs

There are three main forms as illustrated:

Upholstery coil spring: is the most common and the earliest type of spring. The form of these springs has changed little since the early nineteenth century when they were first introduced into upholstery (**fig. 13a**).

Tension spring: is used mostly in seats of fireside chairs. These springs (**fig. 13b**) are attached to the frame by webbing with eyelets, rings or hardened steel pins.

Spring units: modern spring unit assemblies for seats (**fig. 13c**), backs and arms can be obtained in many sizes. The best seat units have small tension springs between the steel base laths and the frame, and have a woven mesh top covering and holding the springs.

Other Hessian and Undercovering Cloth

In addition to tarpaulin hessian there are other lighter-weight hessians. For first stuffing coverings you will need a strong scrim hessian, which is a very pliable canvas for forming edge shapes. Then 280 g (10 oz) hessian is used for bottom coverings and for reinforcing outside arm and back panels. A cheap but strong black cotton lining is sometimes preferred for bottom covering, while for upholstery undercoverings you will need a good quality unbleached calico.

Twines, Cords and Threads

(a) **Laid cord** is the name in the trade for a thickish cord, usually made from hemp or jute. This is used for lacing upholstery springs together.
(b) **Twine**: the stoutest twine, usually called **No. 1**, is used for tying springs to webbing and hessian, and for fastening tufts or buttons. **No. 2** and **No. 3** are finer twines used for edge stitching and for sewing hessians. Keep a lump of beeswax with your twines and use it to dress them. This will preserve and strengthen them.
Nylon tufting twine: nylon twine is the best cord to use for buttonwork. It is expensive but very strong.
Cotton piping cords: the two sizes that I use are the 6 mm ($\frac{1}{4}$ in) for making piping for large proportioned upholstery and a thinner cord 4 mm ($\frac{1}{8}$ in) wide for fine work on smaller chairs and cushions.
Threads and cottons: for ladder or slip stitching two sizes of thread are needed. **No. 18** is a stout thread and **No. 25** a thinner one. I find a **No. 24** cotton is the best general purpose thread for the sewing machine but there are available many nylon and other man-made yarns which are very strong and are suitable for stitching nylon and other cloths made of man-made fibres.

Tacks

There are two varieties in most sizes of upholstery tack. The stouter tack with a large head is called 'improved' and those with smaller heads are called 'fine'. All these are termed 'cut tacks' and are available from hardware stores in 500 g (just over 1 lb) packets. There is another kind called 'bayonet' tacks but these are little used by upholsterers as they are more akin to nails, with square, parallel shanks, (**fig. 14**).
16 mm ($\frac{5}{8}$ in) improved tacks: the largest tacks, used mostly for fastening webbing.
16 mm ($\frac{5}{8}$ in) fine tacks: can be used for fastening webbing and heavy support hessian when the wood of the frame is liable to split if stouter tacks are used.
13 mm ($\frac{1}{2}$ in) improved tacks: used for fastening support hessians.
13 mm ($\frac{1}{2}$ in) fine tacks: for general tacking through thick covering cloth or multi-thicknesses of cloth.
10 mm ($\frac{3}{8}$ in) fine tacks: the smallest generally used in upholstery, although 6 mm ($\frac{1}{4}$ in) tacks can be obtained for especially delicate work.
Gimp pins: like very fine tacks. They are not merely for fixing gimp or braid but are also useful for general tacking purposes on delicate woodwork. These come in japanned black, white and various colours. Black are the most useful.

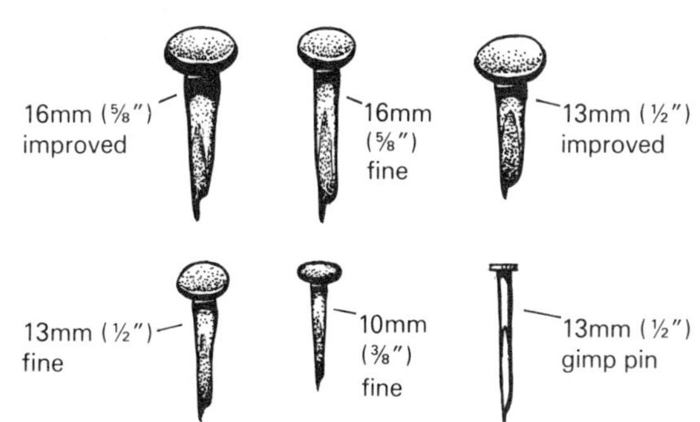

Fig. 14 Tacks and gimp pins

Adhesives

There are two fields in upholstery where adhesives are used. An impact adhesive is used for joining and building up rubber and plastic foam. This is not quite the same adhesive as that used for fixing plastic laminates—it is modified to give a soft bond—so that when it is used to join pieces of foam, say to make up a shaped cushion, hard ridges of dried adhesive will not form along the joins. Another type of impact adhesive is used for fastening braids and trimmings. The impact fastness of this glue is retarded so that trimmings can be adjusted before they become firmly fixed. The adhesive is also thixotropic (jelly-like) for easy application.

Fillings

You will learn most about upholstery filling or stuffings when you are stripping and ripping off your chair, settee or couch but I will try to give you a guide to help you recognize the various substances, so that you will know which to save or discard. Let us start with the types of filling to throw away or burn; by the way, most are good to put on your compost heap.

In some poorly upholstered chairs you will find woodwool (shavings) or 'best Italian hair', as it is known to the trade. Then there is brown seaweed and where this has been used as a first stuffing the salt that it contains usually causes the springs to rust through the hessian covering them. Flock is made of old woollen clothes carded up, and mill puff or mill seed is a whitish cotton stuffing resembling cold rice pudding. When this is used it makes a real pudding of a seat—hard and ungiving. Now for the ones that you can save and re-card.

Horsehair and sheep's wool: the best fillings, so take great care of them when you find them, for nowadays they are rare and if you should be lucky enough to find them new the price is prohibitive. Treat animal fibre fillings such as these with a spray to discourage moths. Several of the students in our evening institute class have experimented by washing their horsehair fillings before re-carding them. They either washed small quantities at a time by hand in a bowl, or placed the hair in an old but sound pillow case and washed it in a washing machine. Do be careful if you try this, though, for I shudder to think what would happen to the machine if the hair should escape. I must say that, although the process seems laborious, the resulting super-clean, sweet-smelling horsehair is a joy to work with.

Vegetable fibres: there are vegetable fibres worth saving too, among them Algerian fibre, a curly grass-like filling, usually green or black in colour, and coconut fibre, also known as coir fibre. Both are very durable stuffings and can be re-carded successfully. However, if they show signs of becoming dry, brittle and short, they are best thrown out or burnt. Cotton and wool-and-cotton felt fillings can also be re-carded and used as top stuffings.

Upholstery foam: polyether plastic foam can be obtained in thicknesses from 6 mm ($\frac{1}{4}$ in) to 100 mm (4 in). To comply with legislation for safety this must be flame-retardant foam. For cushion interiors I use rubber block foam, 50 mm (2 in), 75 mm (3 in) or 100 mm (4 in) thickness. This has more resilience than the plastic variety, and lasts longer.

Waddings, felts, acrylic wool: upholstery is rather like road building—the coarser stuff goes underneath and is topped by something finer to make a smooth and even surface. To get the smoother, softer surface we need cotton wadding. Here again, buy the best quality, which should have been manufactured evenly with none of the lumps or foreign bodies that are frequently found in cheaper wadding. It comes in 10 m (33 ft) rolls and is about 48 cm (19 in) in width, but the best quality wadding can be split or opened up still further, giving a thickness of wadding which will then be about 90 cm (36 in) wide.

Rolls of white cotton felt or wool-and-cotton mixtures can be obtained in sheet form up to 25 mm (1 in) thick. This is useful for top filling as it remains soft and does not consolidate too much.

If you want to add even more richness to the feel of your upholstery, acrylic wool is good. This again comes in rolls, and in various thicknesses but it is much more expensive than the vegetable waddings.

Coverings (Furnishing Fabrics)

Upholstery covering materials are many and varied, some cheap, some expensive and, as with everything, you pay the most for the best quality cloth. I will list the names of the different cloths that you are most likely to come across and try to describe them but if you want to become familiar with the various weaves my advice is that you try to visit as many fabric shops as you can and study, feel and compare the different cloths at close quarters. Also study the different fibres that go into the make-up of each cloth.

To my mind, cloths that contain real wool are definitely the most durable but many man-made fibres are strong, soft and wear well.

Tapestry: the best is made of wool or a cotton and wool mixture and a good quality tapestry is a very durable, thick, closely woven cloth. It is made in both traditional and modern designs.

Quilted tapestry: the cloth is woven in two layers which are then interwoven at places in the design, to give an embossed look.

Brocatelle: this is a type of brocade cloth with a design woven in relief using both glossy and dull yarns to highlight or shade the pattern.

Damask: many damasks are plain one-colour cloths with the design created by clever changes in the weaving. You will probably remember grandmother's beautiful white damask table cloths. There are also striped damasks, such as those in Regency stripe.

Cotton velour: is a type of velvet with a very closely woven cotton pile. It has a rich, luxurious look, but some 'shade' badly after a little use, especially on chair seats.

Dralon velvet: this ever-popular furnishing fabric now comes in many textures and finishes from a bright sheen to a dull suede leather look. There are dralon velvets in ribbed pile, corduroy, slub pile and some with beautifully embossed and colourful patterns. Dralon is a very durable, easy-to-clean cloth.

Mohair velvet: this usually has a shaggy look but is lovely and soft to touch.

Real velvet: there is nothing to rival the look and the feel of real silk velvet. But what a price!

Uncut moquette: this tends to be derided nowadays and brings to mind old railway carriage upholstery. Nevertheless, made in 100 per cent wool it is a most durable fabric.

Tweeds: these have burst upon the market in recent years in many forms and designs and are good value when closely woven and substantial. Tweeds are made up in many of the man-made fibres but the best are the pure wool tweeds.

Leathercloths: these are now a far cry from the early oil cloth imitation leathers. There are a variety of different grains and effects available and they are often difficult to tell from real leather.

These are just a few of the large variety of furnishing fabrics available; there are many more for your choice. Choose carefully because quality is important so try to learn how to recognize good cloths by their feel, their weight, their texture and the closeness of the weave (hold them up to the light).

For instructions on measuring fabric refer to the sections on pages 27 and 91.

Trimmings

To finish this chapter I will illustrate a few of the popular trimmings used to give a good finish to upholstery work (**fig. 15a–n**). I'm afraid however, that these names are not universally used and sometimes trimmings are given different names. Banding and studs, *Hidem* piping and *Flexibead* trimmings are for leatherwork only.

Fig. 15 Trimmings

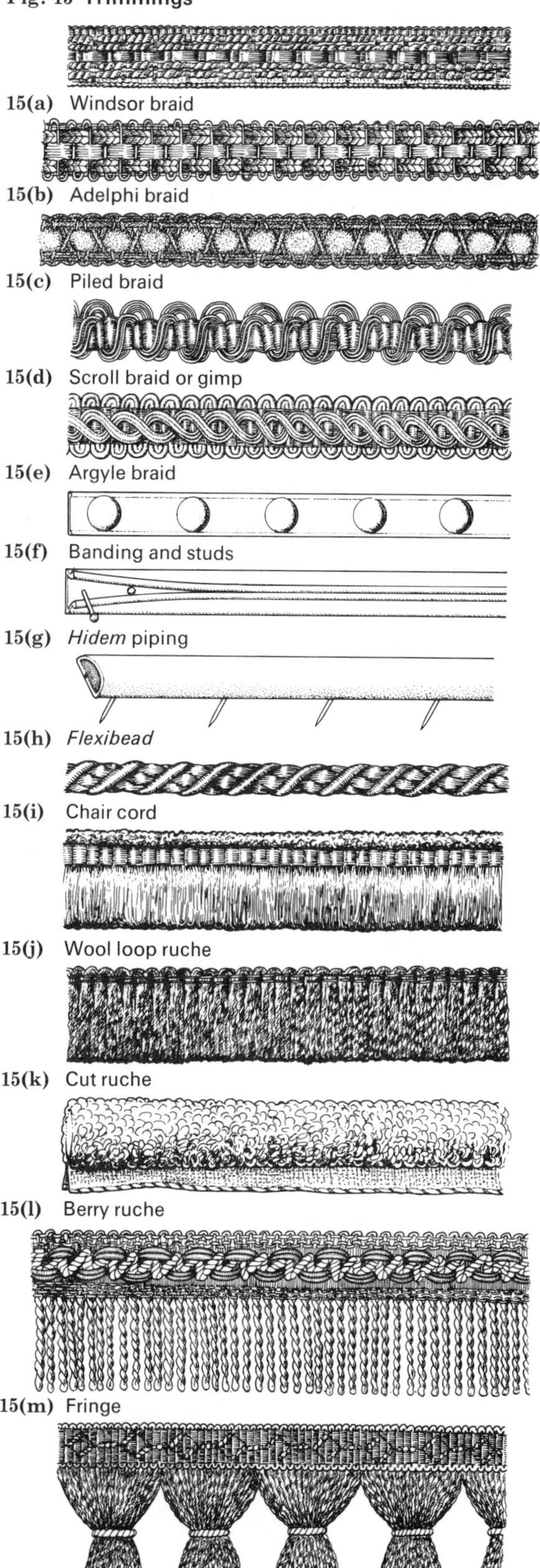

15(a) Windsor braid
15(b) Adelphi braid
15(c) Piled braid
15(d) Scroll braid or gimp
15(e) Argyle braid
15(f) Banding and studs
15(g) *Hidem* piping
15(h) *Flexibead*
15(i) Chair cord
15(j) Wool loop ruche
15(k) Cut ruche
15(l) Berry ruche
15(m) Fringe
15(n) Tassel fringe

2 Buying Upholstered Furniture

It is no easy task when looking at upholstered furniture to tell good quality from bad, because everything is stuffed over and covered up; and so the unwary often end up buying a 'pig in a poke' and paying large sums of money for nothing but a very poorly made frame. Experience is dearly bought in this field so I thought it might be useful if I jotted down a few hints, pointers and guides to help when you go hunting in sale-rooms or junk shops for those bargains.

Fig. 16 A crinoline chair

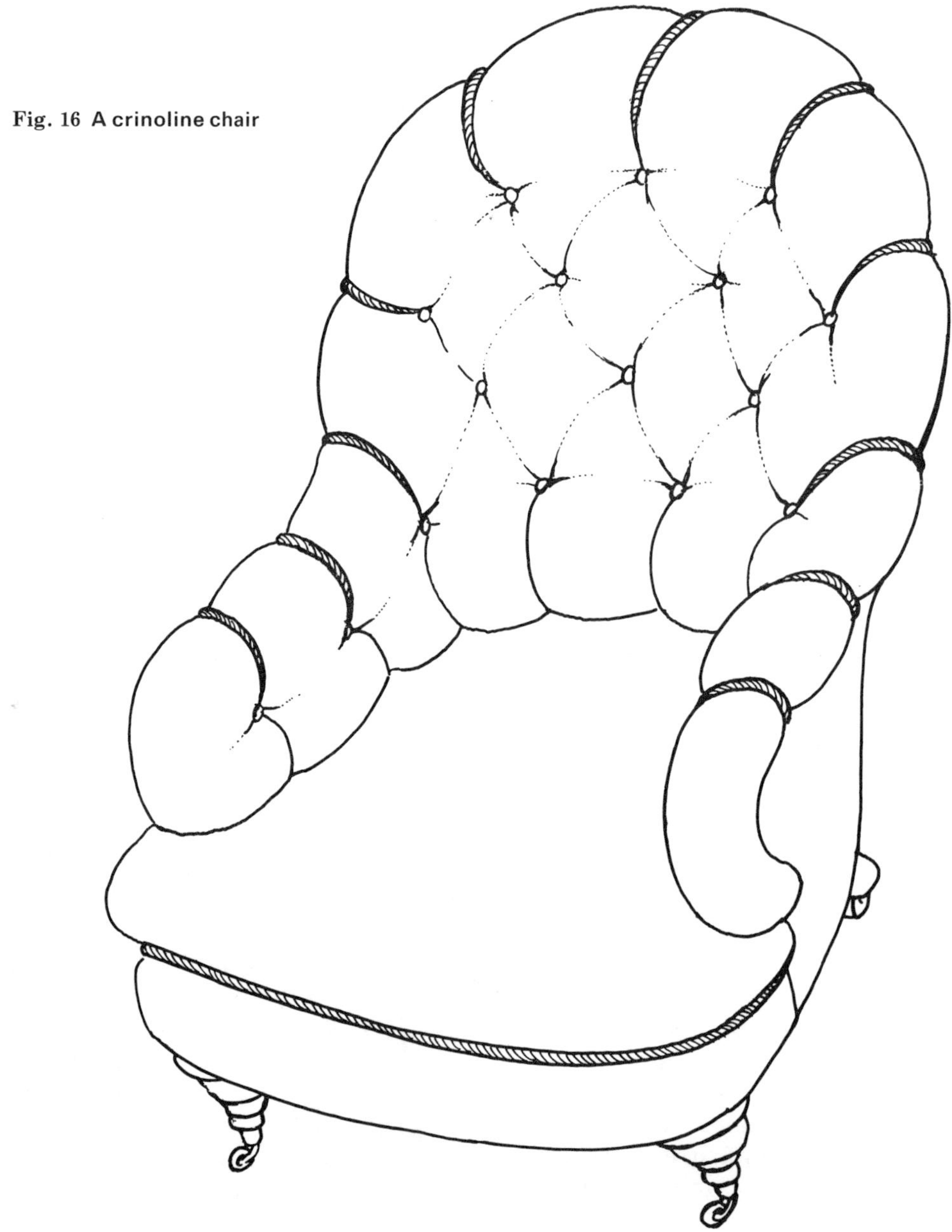

WHAT TO LOOK FOR

You can get caught out so easily. Someone I know came to me with a wing easy chair that he had just bought. When I first set eyes on it I was puzzled—there was something about it that did not ring true. It certainly looked old if one could go by the leg assembly, which was mahogany with stretchers between square section legs, and seemed to date from the 1760s. But the upholstered top part seemed a little unbalanced somehow. The shape of the wings had more than a hint of years later than 1760. So, with my curiosity stirred, I stripped the chair of its upholstery. My suspicions were well founded, for I discovered that this was a two-in-one chair. Yes, I reckon the legs and stretchers were early but a cleverly adapted frame, probably of a chair dating from about 1830, had been set on top. This was not all, because it was clear that the wings and the scroll arm fronts had pieces of even newer wood added to alter their shape. It always amazes me the lengths to which some people will go in order to deceive, but may be I am being uncharitable for it could be that originally it just seemed a good idea to make two wrecks into one useful chair. However, although the original intention may have been honourable, a chair like this is not what it seems and so the moral of the story is that you must look carefully and suspiciously at old pieces of furniture and examine them well before paying out large sums of money.

You will, of course, ask how you can examine furniture thoroughly when everything is covered with upholstery. I think I can help you here: let's take a walk around an imaginary antique shop and pretend that we want to buy an easy chair.

Examining the Frame

Now, here is a comfortable-looking chair, one that we call a Crinoline chair (**fig. 16**).

Some say the chairs came to be called Crinoline chairs because they were designed for ladies wearing crinoline dresses. My own theory is that the term crinoline is perhaps related to the construction of the chair, which is made with a hoop iron and rod upper structure built upon a circular or part-circular wooden seat frame with legs. This construction reminds me of the hooped support for a crinoline skirt.

Some chairs of the same shape are made with wooden frames, now how can we tell the difference when everything is covered? You can usually feel if it is wood if you press your hand into the top or sides of the back, but a more reliable way of checking is to take hold of the top of the chair as you face it from the front, hold the seat front with your other hand and gently pull the back forward. If the frame is iron there will be considerable give here as the iron rod and hoop frame bends under your gentle pressure. A wooden frame should be firm and unmoving. I say, should be, because with this test you can also tell the state of the frame and if you hear creaks and groans when you pull, then this indicates that the joints are loose or broken. Or, in the case of an iron frame, if you find too much movement here or a decided looseness between the back and the arms, this probably indicates that the ironwork has broken; this most often occurs where the back meets the arms.

Before I go any further, let me say that you will probably give offence to the owner of the shop if you go round pulling his chairs about. But these tests can be done quite gently and unobtrusively, so that no one notices.

Signs of Good Quality

Let's move over to the easy chair in the corner; this is completely stuffed over, with nothing showing in the way of wood but the legs (**fig. 17**). However, we can deduce a lot from just these legs. Firstly, the design and turning of the legs are clues to the age of the chair but, as well as denoting the period, the legs also indicate quality or lack of it. Now, this chair we are looking at has elegant, well turned legs and they are made of walnut.

It helps a lot if you can get to know the various woods, for the type of wood used is a sure sign of quality. The better chairs have legs made from hardwoods such as mahogany, walnut, oak or the finer birch wood. On cheaper chairs beech-turned legs were often used, coloured and polished to look like more expensive wood.

If you look at the back legs of this chair you will notice that the wood is the same as that of the front legs; this is good. Some back legs are made of beech, which means that the

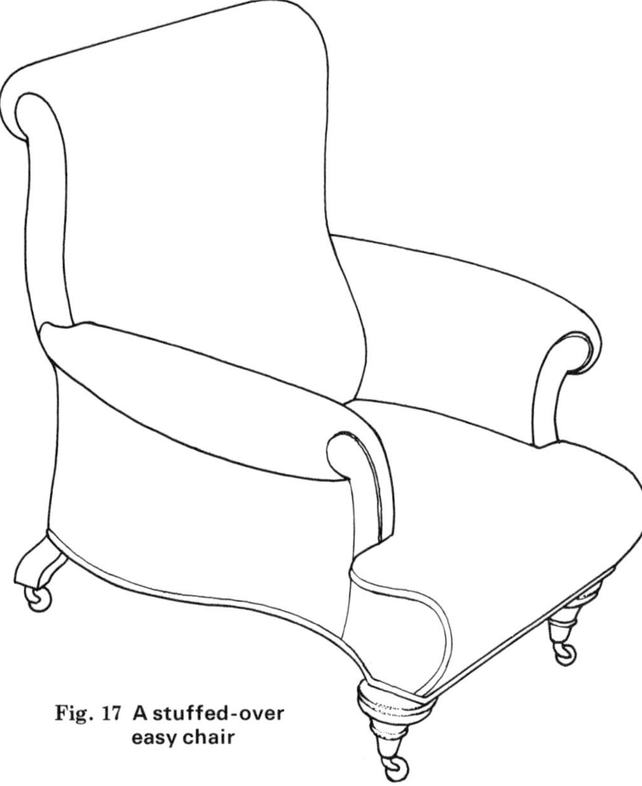
Fig. 17 A stuffed-over easy chair

maker just used the extension of the back upright of the chair and did not take the trouble to join on the hardwood for the legs. The shape of the back legs is important too; you will notice that these have a well defined curve. Examine the castors; a proud manufacturer would always fit the legs with good quality brass castors with brass or porcelain bowls—but check that they are the originals. You can do this by inspecting the screws that fasten the castors to the legs to see if they have been disturbed or if there are any new screw holes.

It is also a good idea to examine—surreptitiously—the size of the wood of the frame, especially the seat frame; just place your hand under one side of the bottom and judge the size of the wood here. It should be at least 45 to 50 mm ($1\frac{3}{4}$ to 2 in) square in section, for this is where the strength of the frame needs to be.

Now the chair may look bonny, and you have established that it is of good quality, but I wonder what state the frame is in? There are a couple of tests that you can do to tell if all is well here. Face the chair and take hold of the left-hand side of the top of the back and the right arm front, then gently pull diagonally; do the same with the opposite corners and, if there is a lot of movement, this means that the frame joints are loose. Place your hands on the arms and pull these towards each other and you can then tell whether the joints here are loose or not.

Examining for Woodworm

One question that is difficult to answer is, whether there is any woodworm in the frame inside? Woodworm in the confines of the inside of an easy chair can spread rampantly with very little, if any, signs from the outside that anything is amiss, especially if the legs are of mahogany, which woodworm does not often attack. On the chair that we are looking at the walnut legs would most probably show signs of infestation—just one or two holes could mean that the inside was riddled. If woodworm had been making a real meal of the frame, then the frame test described earlier should give an indication of this.

Let us leave the antique shop and make our way to the local auction sales-rooms. It is viewing day and you will be allowed much more freedom to examine the merchandise thoroughly. This is the best place to buy a chair or other upholstered furniture if you want to refurbish it yourself. In antique shops every piece will be reupholstered or smartened up to look good, but inside you will often find just the old upholstery plus a lot of wadding which has been added to fill up hollows in the seat and back and the whole lot has been covered with new material. All this is done as cheaply as possible for a quick sale. I hasten to add that not all antique shops sell goods of this description; some have reputable craftsmen to do their upholstery.

POINTS TO LOOK FOR IN A VICTORIAN SPOONBACK CHAIR

A Victorian spoonback chair catches your eye in the sales-room. That will fetch a good price, I bet. But is it of good quality? There is a lot more to see on a chair like this, with so much wood on show (**fig. 18**). You can do the usual tests for the robustness of the frame and joints. Observe the sweep of the moulded show wood round the back, is it evenly curving and do the two sides match? If the chair is carved, you can look for delicacy of carving.

Fig. 18 A Victorian spoon-back chair

The front legs and front facing wood to the arms should be elegantly turned or carved. The size and appearance of the back legs are good indicators of quality. The back legs of the best chairs will have a well defined curved or ogee (double curved) shape, and will be about 50 mm (2 in) square in section. The legs on poorer chairs look skimpy and weak.

Checking for Bad Repairs

The wood, be it mahogany, oak, walnut, satinwood or satin birch, should be examined for splits and for bad repairs, such as nails or screws driven through joints. Look at the tops of the front legs; if there are any large holes filled with wax filler, the filler probably conceals a large screw—which could be the only thing holding a front joint together. Look in the vicinity of joints for smaller holes which have been disguised with filler or wax. They could indicate nails that have been punched in and filled over and in this case it will be difficult to dismantle the joint without causing damage to the woodwork.

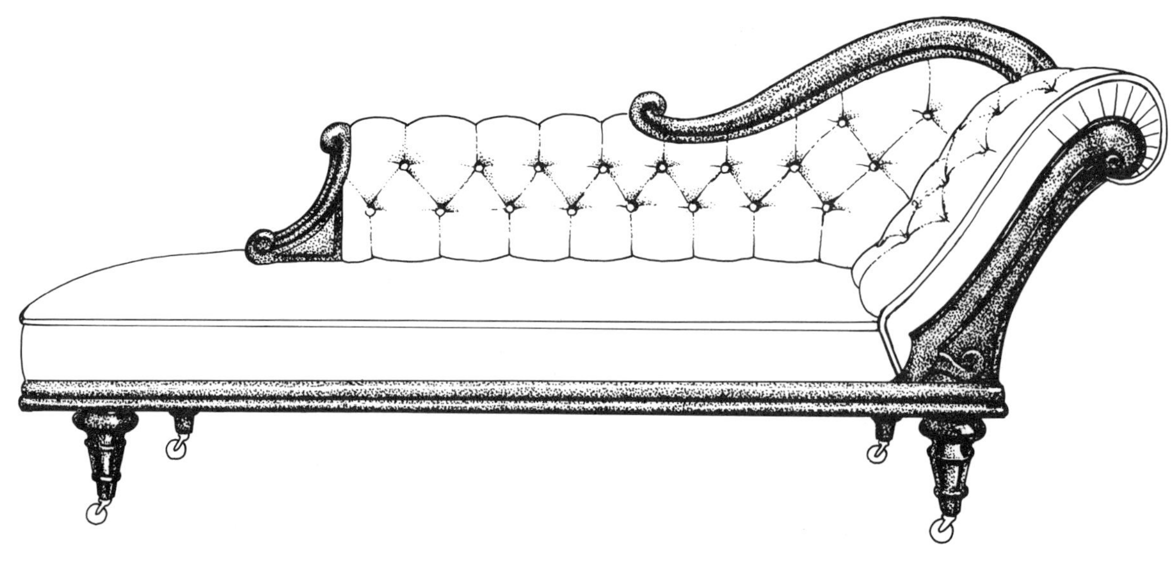

Fig. 19 A high quality Victorian couch

LOOKING AT COUCHES

The forms and shapes of the Victorian couch or chaise-longue are many and varied. Here are two in the sales-room, and how convenient for us, they are side by side so we will be able to compare them. They are of about the same period but at opposite ends of the scale of quality. One (**fig. 19**), in mahogany, has smooth and exactly carved show wood on the front scroll of the head, surrounding the back and in the form of moulding all round the seat. If we look at the legs, there is plenty of wood in them but they have been delicately turned to give them an elegant look. And they are set off really well with solid brass cup castors. The show wood has been deeply and crisply carved and the polish, although well worn, still has a bit of a shine to it.

Its sale-room neighbour is very different. This couch (**fig. 20**) also has a lot of show wood, but it is of rather dingy walnut—or could it be birch or beech? It is difficult to tell, because the wood has obviously been

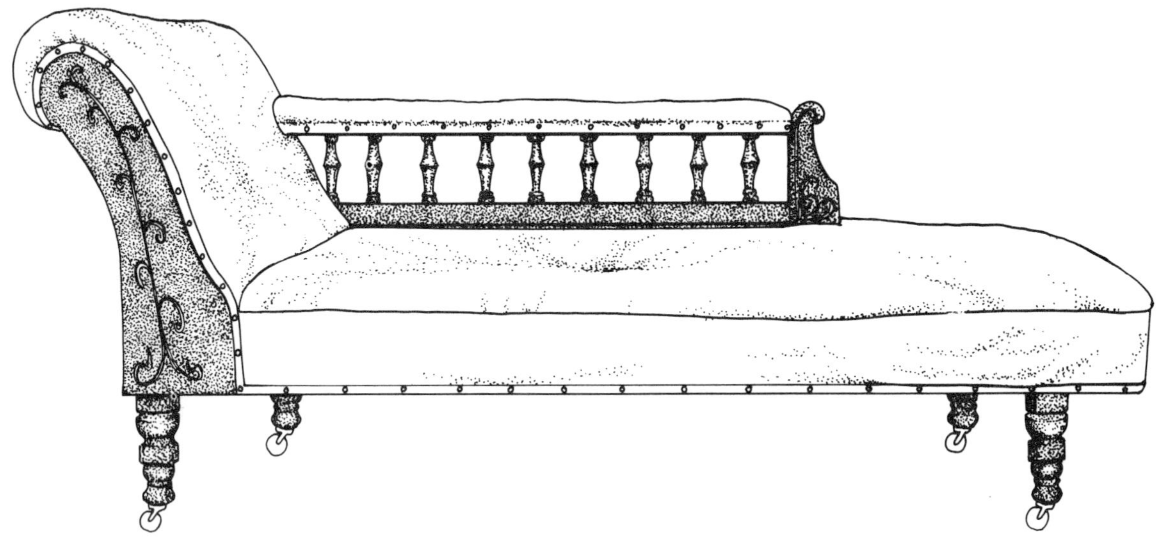

Fig. 20 A couch of inferior quality

varnished and the varnish has perished, cracked and blistered. The show wood facing on the head front is flat and the carving not much more than scratched in. The back consists of a row of turned spindles, each one just slightly different in shape from its neighbour, and topped by a long upholstered pad. No moulded show wood round the seat on this one, although I suspect that at one time there was some but it has fallen off or broken. The last covering has been taken right down to the bottom. But oh dear, the legs . . . not much imagination or art in these! The poor things are only half the thickness they should be to lend a good balance of design to the whole; and the castors are the small cast iron and red china sort.

So there you have the good and the bad in a simple Victorian couch. There are many types, forms and designs of couch but I hope that the description of these two will start you looking in detail at all those you come across.

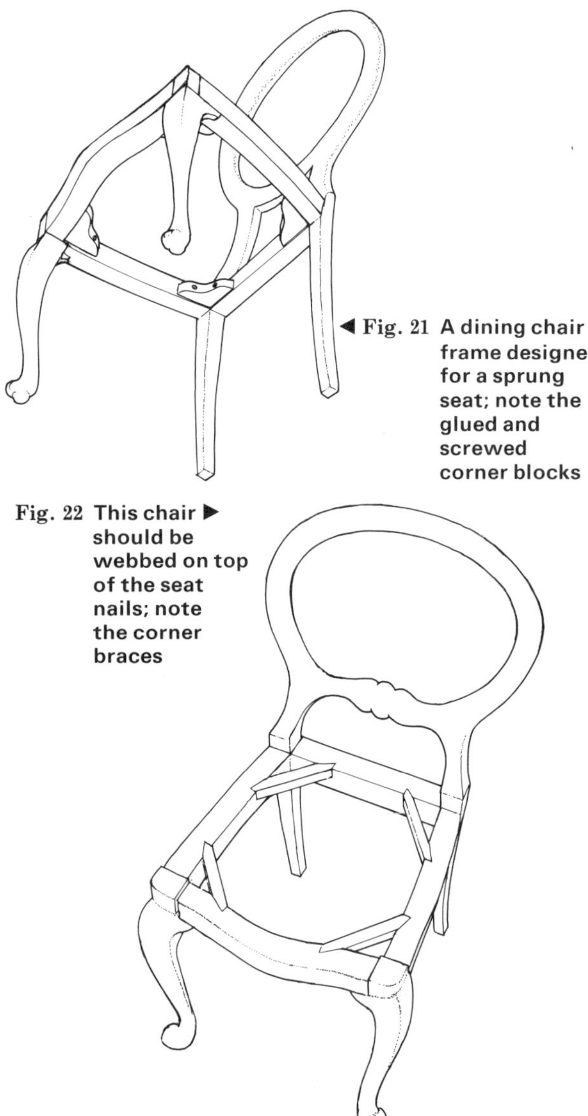

◀ Fig. 21 A dining chair frame designed for a sprung seat; note the glued and screwed corner blocks

Fig. 22 This chair ▶ should be webbed on top of the seat nails; note the corner braces

DINING CHAIRS

Over there is a set of Victorian dining chairs with balloon backs and stuffed-over seats, shall we have a look at those? The first thing to do when examining a chair is to turn the chair upside down and look at the bottom of the seat. These chairs have no springs in the seats and yet they have a black lining covering the bottom. This is most suspicious, for whoever last upholstered these chairs seems to have had something to hide. Ah, here is one of the set with the bottom lining half off, so let's have a peep inside. Just as I thought, the seat rails are so full of woodworm that pieces are dropping off. We can now see that this seat originally had springs—there are all the tack holes where the webbing had been fastened on the underside of the rails. Another indication of a sprung seat is the glued and screwed corner blocks (**fig. 21**). A stuffed-over seat intended to be just top-stuffed without springs would have corner braces notched into the rails in order to give the rails the corner strength needed when webbing was stretched across the top of the seat frame (**fig. 22**). With this chair we are looking at, obviously the upholsterer could not fix the webbing to the underside because the wood there had perished under the ravages of the woodworm, so he top-webbed it, doing away with the springs, and covering up this awful mess, saying to himself, what the eye doesn't see, etc.

But here is a completely different story . . . When viewing Victorian furniture, you must not only have eyes for the better class things; many of the less expensive pieces are well worth considering, even if they look total wrecks. If you have an eye open you can spot pieces that, with a lot of care, can be brought back to serve a useful existence and look quite beautiful again. In fact, some chairs can be made to look far better than they did when they were new. This brings to mind the two little Victorian servants' hall balloon back chairs that Flora found (**fig. 23**).

For several years Flora has been an ardent student, not only of upholstery but also of furniture restoration. I looked with a very cynical eye at these two white-painted chairs with greasy, threadbare leathercloth seats which were shedding awful dirty grey flock through several large rents. But despite my expression of doubt, she set to work, taking off the terrible upholstery and with great patience stripping off all the layers of paint. One seat frame had to be renewed—it was too full of woodworm—and we found a nice piece of hornbeam for this. But what an amazing revelation when all the paint was off, for the wood, an attractively grained birch, came up beautifully under Flora's skilful French polishing. After reupholstering, the little banjo-shaped seats, built up this time with proper stitched roll edges and covered in a delicate blue velvet, looked really expensive. So here are two chairs that began life rather humbly, but with a bit of love and care have now become objects of beauty as well as usefulness.

Fig. 23 A Victorian balloon-back chair

◀ 23(a) Before

23(b) After ▶

3 Basic Skills in Upholstery

In this chapter I intend to describe the techniques and methods that are common to most upholstery jobs. I hope that you will then be able to use the chapter like a pocket book of upholstery; something that you can constantly refer back to when tackling different work projects in order to refresh your memory on such basic subjects as knots, fixing webbing, which hessians to use, and so on.

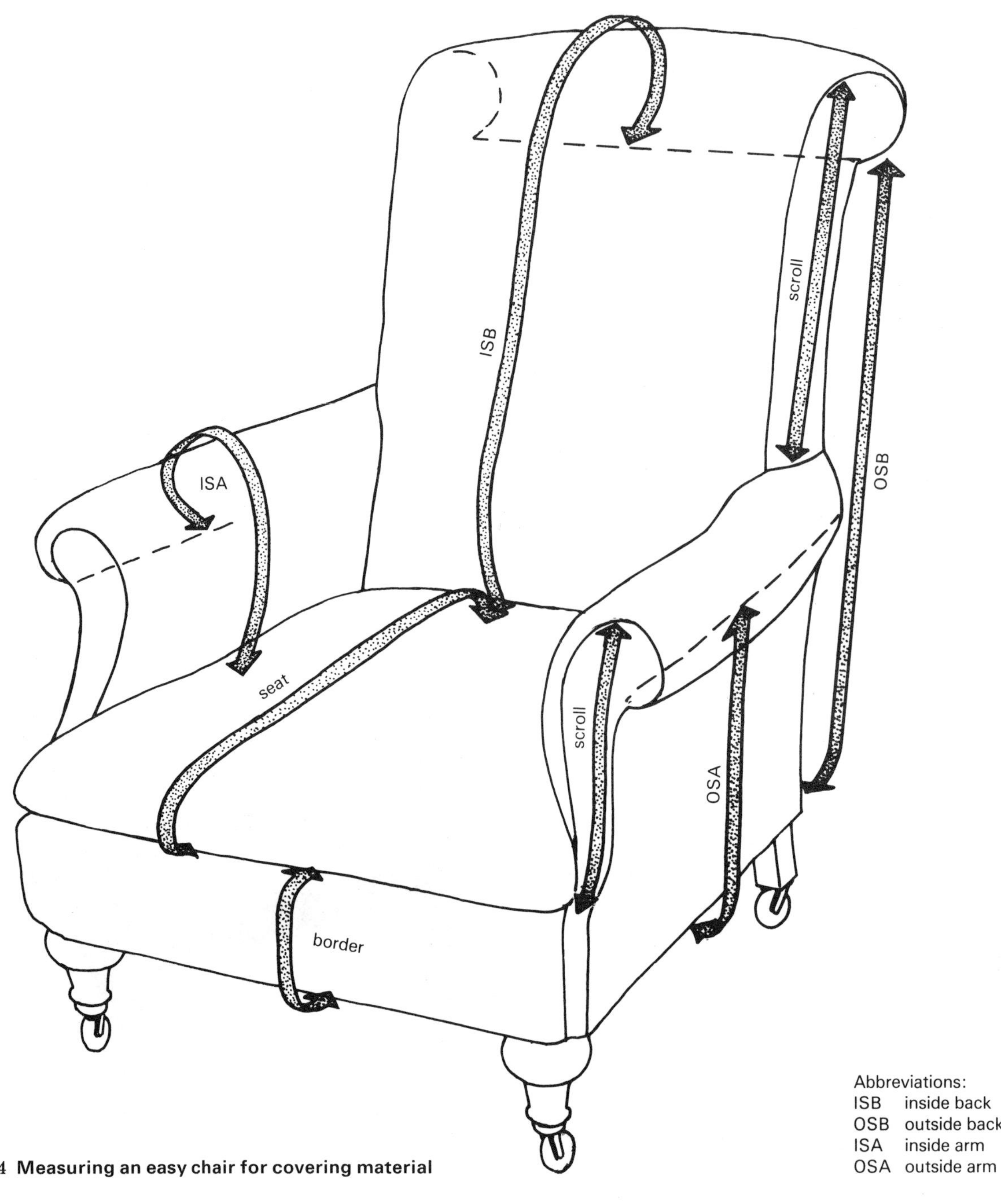

Fig. 24 Measuring an easy chair for covering material

MEASURING UP FOR THE NEW COVERING MATERIAL

Let us imagine that you have in front of you an easy chair of about 1900 vintage (**fig. 24**)—a chair that has an excellent frame and originally had very good upholstery.

So there you stand viewing this poor old chair all in rags and tatters and I know you are itching to rip off all the old upholstery, but hold on a while. The first thing to do is to measure up for your new covering material while there is still some semblance of shape to the chair. So get your flexible spring steel rule and begin drawing out a table (**fig. 25**) on which to jot down your measurements.

Before starting to measure, check the way the material should run. With a patterned cloth it is usually easy to see the top and bottom of the design, although some are pretty obscure. Some flowery designs are difficult, but remember, buds at the top, stalks at the bottom. With piled fabrics, such as velvet, the pile or nap should always run downwards. On the arms and inside back it should run down towards the seat; on the seat it should run from back to front. The direction of the pile for the other cuts is obvious.

Most furnishing fabrics are made 132 to 137 cm (52 to 54 in) in width. Your upholstery will be fuller than it is at present so in all your measurements make allowance for this by holding the tape a little away from the present surface. Now, begin by measuring the inside back of the chair; measure the width to determine whether a half width will reach across. On the chair depicted it will, which means that the inside and the outside back coverings will both come from one complete width, so those two headings can be bracketed together and whichever measurement is the greater entered against them.

On this chair the inside arms also take only half a width each, but on a larger chair a full width may have to be allowed for each arm. Any off-cuts should be noted. Do not entertain the thought of joining arm coverings to make them wide enough—some upholsterers do, but this practice does not make for a good job and very little material is saved in the process. When you are taking your arm measurements, tuck your tape well down into the seat side crevice, so that it touches the

Fig. 25 Chart for measuring covering material

Cut	Length	Off cuts	
		Length	Width
inside back			
outside back			
inside arms			
outside arms			
seat			
front border			
cushion			
scroll fronts			
piping			
Total			

tacking bar. Allow a couple of centimetres beyond this. Under the top roll-over of the back and of the arms allow 25 mm (1 in) more than where the outside panel joins. For the outside arms, allow 50 mm (2 in) more than the exact measurement. Here again, a full width may be necessary for each outside arm—if so, note down the off-cuts.

Then measure the seat from back to front. Tuck your tape well into the back crevice, and at the front, allow for the fact that this old seat front has been pushed back considerably through years of use and also that it is nowhere near the height that it should be. There will be nearly half a width left over from the seat—enter this in the 'off-cuts' column. The seat border will also have to come from a full width; for this measurement allow for turning in at the top and plenty for tacking beneath the front rail.

It is time now to look at the sizes of the off-cuts. I think you will find that there is enough to cover the front arm scroll facings and the two scrolls on each side of the back. The rest will do for making piping for the cushion and the scrollwork. Measure for the cushion, allowing 25 mm (1 in) for seams. The top and bottom panels will cut from one full width. The cushion border will need two pieces, full width, to the measure of the depth of the cushion plus 25 mm (1 in) for seams.

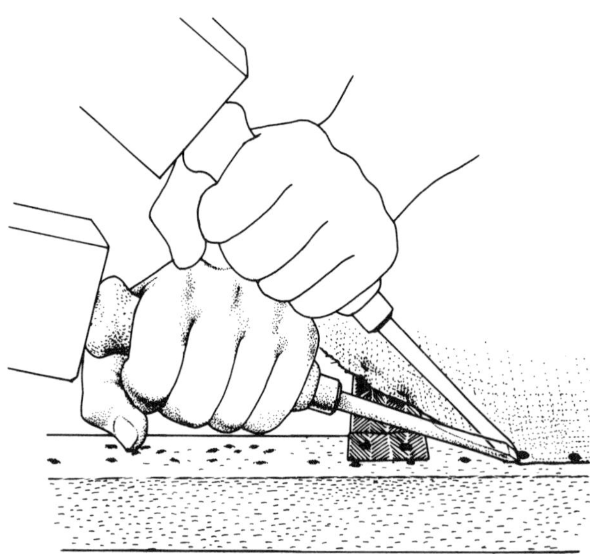

Fig. 26 Using the ripping chisel

Allowing for Pattern Matching
If your material has a design that needs continuity, you should allow an extra 50 cm (20 in). If you choose a material with a large pattern that necessitates keeping the design central on the back, seat and arms, then you will have to make an extra allowance. Most pattern books show the distance of the repeat of the design, or if you buy from the roll you can get the shop assistant to tell you, or measure for yourself. Usually 75 cm (just under 30 in) is an adequate allowance.

RIPPING OFF

Ripping off is the trade term for taking off the old material and upholstery from the frame. Not much skill in this, you say? Perhaps you are right, but I can endeavour to make this rather boring job more interesting and speedy by pointing out the best ways of doing it.

The tools you will need are a sharp knife and some scissors, a ripping chisel, a small mallet and side-cutting pliers (adapted).

Stripping and Observing
Cut away the covering and remove the filling with your knife and scissors. When I am stripping a chair I like to cut away most of the old hessian, webbing, twines and ties at once, to give easier access to the ripping chisel, but when you are beginning, my advice is to take everything off layer by layer, for you can learn a lot from the old work. It can be quite exciting when you remove the seat from an old chair such as this one; who knows what treasures you may find among the buttons, tiddlywinks, mottoes from long-pulled Christmas crackers, hair-grips, mouldy nuts and picture postcards of the old chain pier at Brighton. As well as 'treasures' there will be a terrible amount of dust and dirt, so do wear a mask.

Using the Ripping Chisel
The ripping chisel, used with a small mallet, considerably speeds the process of removing tacks, but you must take care with this tool, or you may damage the woodwork. Place the blade of the chisel against a tack head and drive with your mallet. As the tack begins to lift lower the handle of the chisel and continue to drive, but more gently, to remove the tack (**fig. 26**). Keep your eye on the tack being removed and not on the handle of the chisel, but do not hold your face directly over the work—tacks can fly up, and sometimes the heads come off as well. Try to rip in the direction of the grain of the wood to avoid too much damage. Inevitably you will split some pieces from the frame, do save these fragments and stick them back immediately. You will soon get into the swing with your ripping chisel and mallet, but use the adapted side-cutting pliers to clear the tacks from delicate woodwork, such as the wood near the front leg joints of this easy chair.

FIXING WEBBING

Now we turn to the skills involved in re-upholstering. Webbing forms the most important basic support. The illustrations in **fig. 27** show how it should be attached.

Make a 25 mm (1 in) fold at the end of the webbing and place it on the frame with the fold uppermost (**a**).

Fix the webbing to the frame with a staggered row of tacks (**b**). You will have to use your discretion as to the size and number of tacks. For most woods four 15 mm ($\frac{5}{8}$ in) improved tacks will be about right, but a very hard wood may need only 12 mm ($\frac{1}{2}$ in) improved tacks. If the wood splits easily fine tacks will have to be used and, since the fine tacks have smaller heads, more tacks will be required in the row. Be careful how you drive in your tacks. Each should be driven home with the head perfectly flat and level with the surface of the frame. If a tack is driven in crooked, part of the head will cut into the webbing, weakening the fixing. The whole idea of a large-headed tack is to give the maximum frictional surface between wood, webbing and the tack head.

Figs (**c**) and (**d**) show two different types of webbing stretcher in use—a hinged bar stretcher in (**c**) and a slot and peg stretcher in (**d**). You can see how webbing is held and pulled tight on the different models. Black and white cotton webbing has little elasticity and should not be overstrained. Stretch the webbing and fasten at the stretched end with three tacks. Cut off 25 mm (1 in) from the row of tacks and fold it back. A further two tacks are placed between the three tacks underneath to hold the fold down.

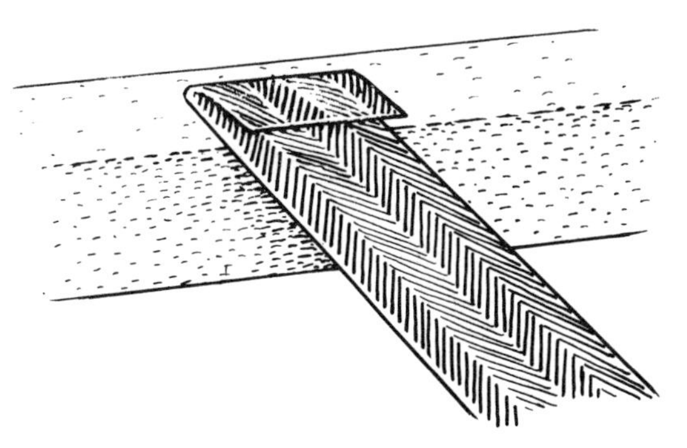

27(a) Folding the webbing over ►

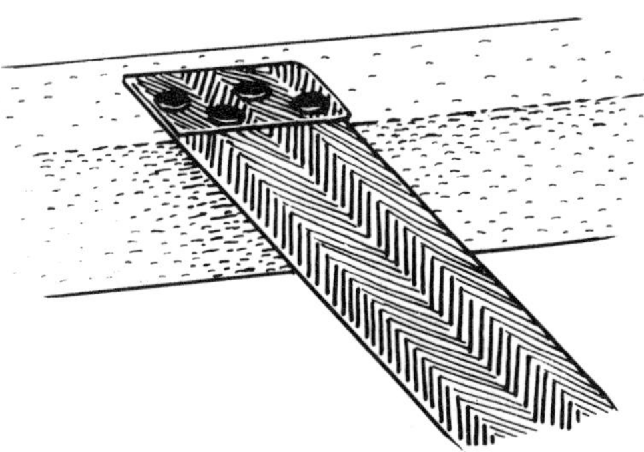

27(b) Four tacks in a staggered row ▲

27(c) Using a hinged bar webbing stretcher ▼

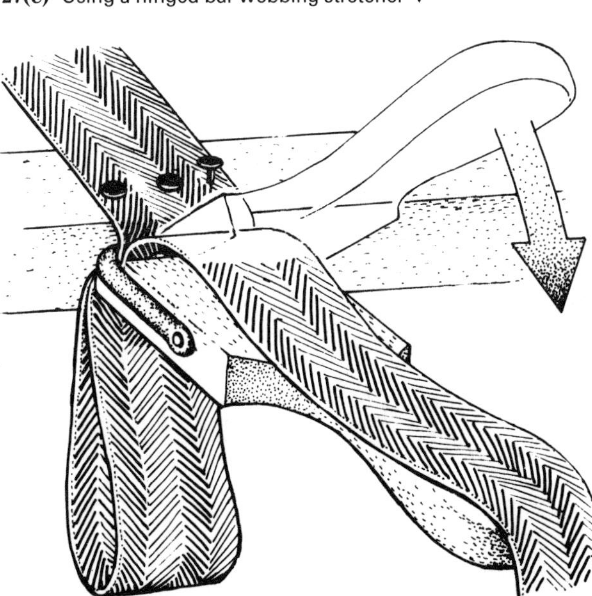

27(d) Using a slot and peg webbing stretcher ▼

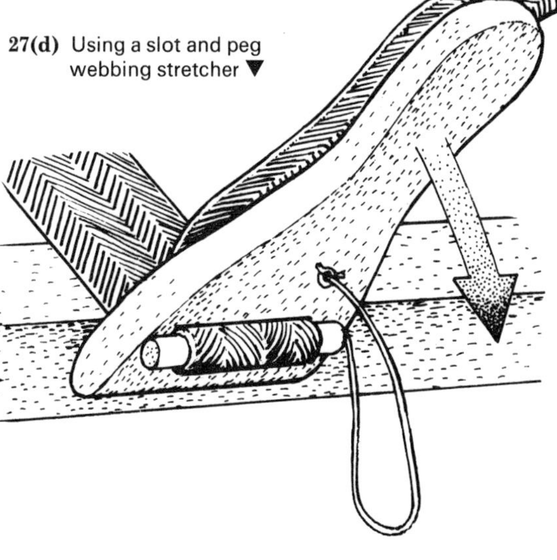

Fig. 27 Fixing webbing

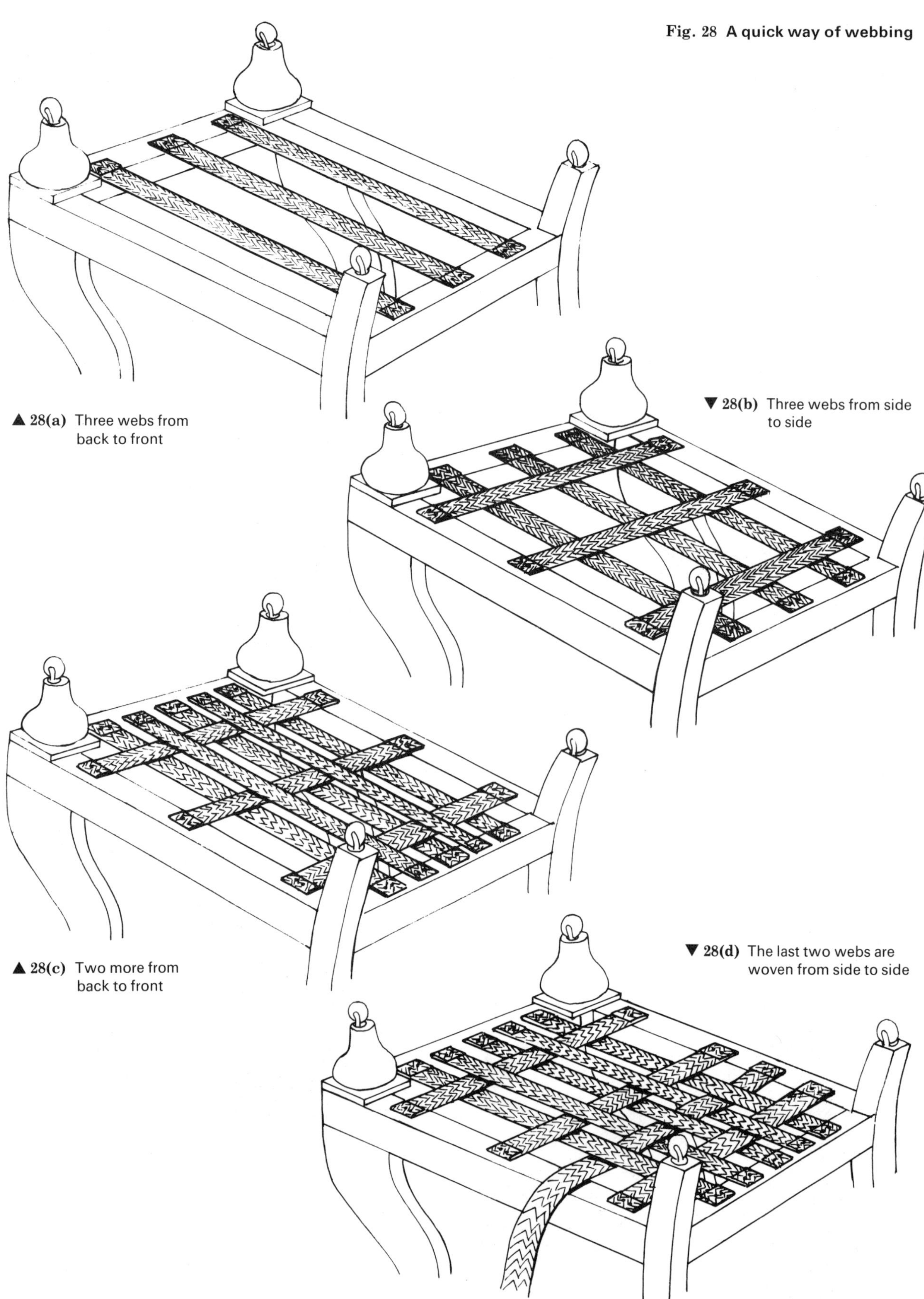

Fig. 28 A quick way of webbing

▲ 28(a) Three webs from back to front

▼ 28(b) Three webs from side to side

▲ 28(c) Two more from back to front

▼ 28(d) The last two webs are woven from side to side

A Quick Way of Webbing

Most people find it easier to stretch and fasten all the webs from back to front and then weave the cross webs in afterwards. But there is a much quicker way of webbing that professional upholsters use and we will employ this method on our easy chair (**fig. 28**). Start by stretching three pieces from back to front as shown (**a**). Place three more across from side to side and on top of the first webs (**b**). On top of these stretch two more pieces from back to front, between the first three (**c**). The remaining two webs, which are passed across from side to side, are the only ones that are actually woven, through the back-to-front webs (**d**).

The Use of Glue

Some seat frames present a problem when it comes to renewing the webbing. Take, for instance, an occasional chair with a pin cushion seat where there is very little width of wood for fastening webbing—let alone the hessian, undercover and covering material which all have to follow. To add to the difficulties, the seat has probably been re-upholstered once or twice before and there are a multitude of old tack holes. In cases like this I like to squeeze a line of P.V.A. glue from one of those small plastic bottles with a pointed nozzle and tack down the webbing on this, using finer tacks. This gives a much greater hold to the fixing.

Using Heavy Hessian

Next in strength to webbing for upholstery supports is the heavyweight hessian, the 450 g (16 oz) tarpaulin. On loose drop-in seats or top-webbed stuffed-over dining chair seats tarpaulin is fixed next to the webbing, to complete a platform on which to build up further upholstery. Tarpaulin may be used alone as a support for a panel of upholstery on a chair back, if the back is too small or the wood too narrow or delicate to take webbing. And tarpaulin is also used to encase springs incorporated into upholstery.

Fastening Tarpaulin Hessian

12 mm ($\frac{1}{2}$ in) improved tacks are generally used for fastening tarpaulin but finer tacks must be used if the wood tends to split easily. As an example of how to fix hessian I shall take a plain and simple square pin cushion stool (**fig. 29**).

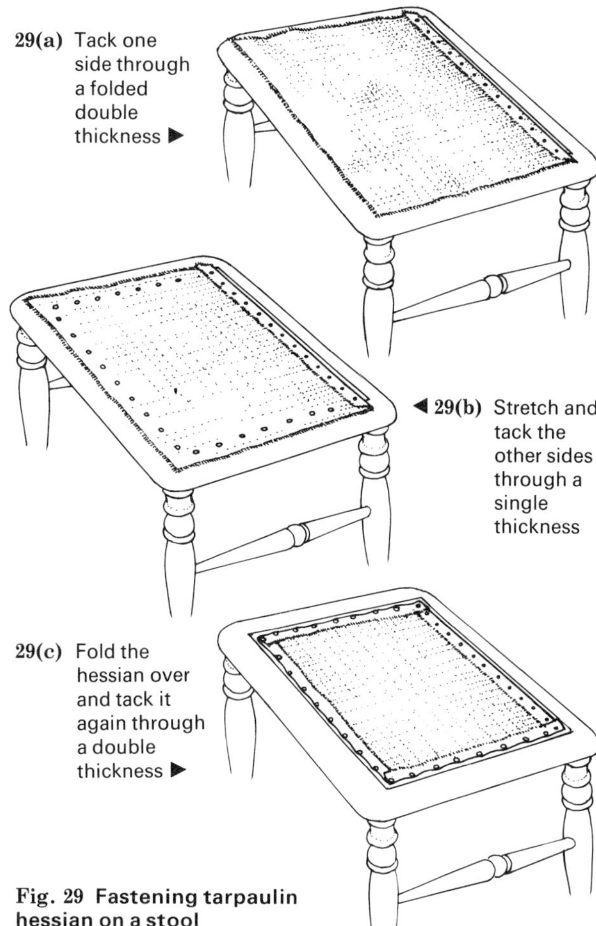

29(a) Tack one side through a folded double thickness ▶

◀ **29(b)** Stretch and tack the other sides through a single thickness

29(c) Fold the hessian over and tack it again through a double thickness ▶

Fig. 29 Fastening tarpaulin hessian on a stool

Cut off your hessian a bit larger all round than the size of the seat and then fold over a turning of about 25 mm (1 in) all along one side. Tack this with permanent tacks about 38 mm ($1\frac{1}{2}$ in) apart on one side of the stool frame (**a**).

Stretch the hessian tightly and tack along the opposite side through a single thickness, placing tacks about 100 mm (2 in) apart. Repeat this on the other two sides (**b**).

Turn over the hessian and tack through the double thickness, placing the tacks between those underneath (**c**). As with webbing, make sure that the tacks are driven well home with the heads perfectly flat.

In cases where the wood of the chair frame on seat or back is poor or much distressed by previous upholstery tack holes, lines of glue can be laid to assist in holding the hessian, and staples can be used instead of tacks to avoid further damage.

▼ **Fig. 30** Tarpaulin hessian as a spring covering

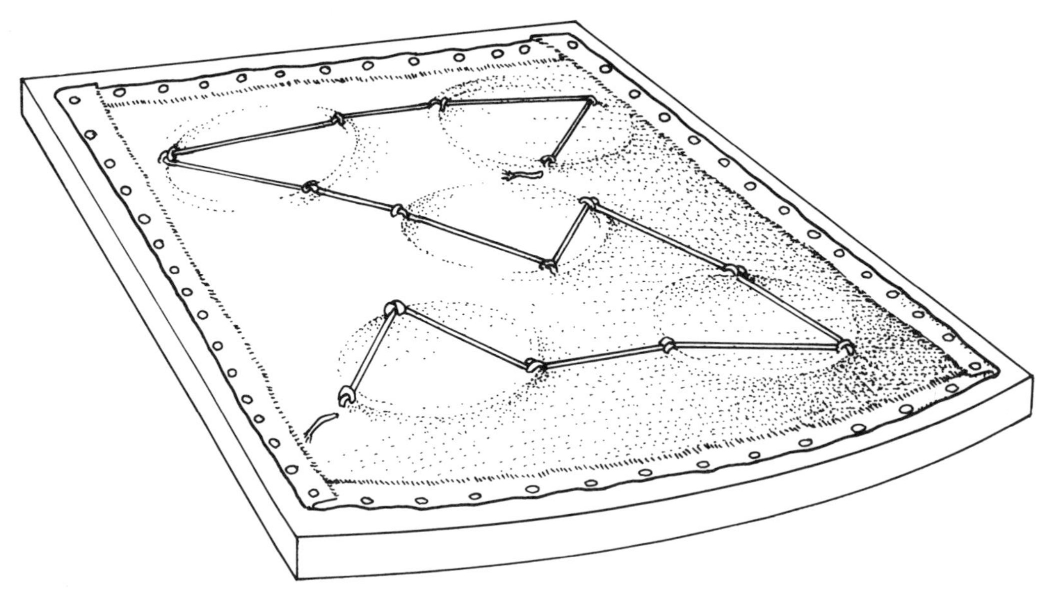

Tarpaulin Hessian as a Spring Covering

A simple chair seat with the springs covered with tarpaulin is shown in **Fig. 30**. You can see that the tacking is done in the same way as on the stool in **fig. 29**, with flanges turned over on the top. A deal of adjustment is necessary to get the springs tensioned evenly, so you should 'temporary tack' through just a single thickness. (In temporary tacking the tacks are driven part way in just so that they hold and can be easily removed.) When all is satisfactory, the tacks can be driven home, the hessian turned back on itself and more tacks placed between the others.

▼ **Fig. 31** A reef knot

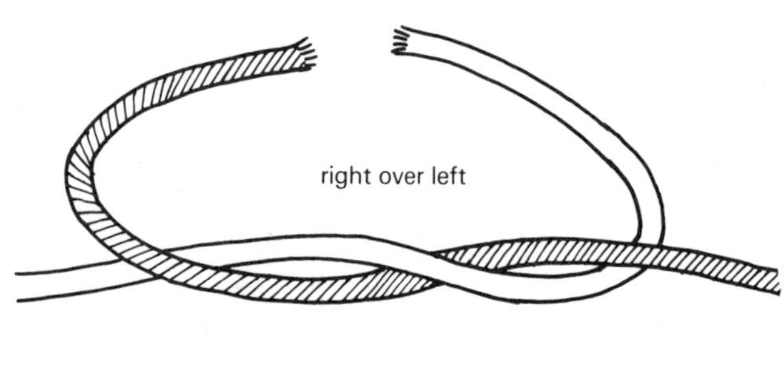

SKILLS WITH CORDS, TWINES AND THREADS

Knots in Upholstery

The diagrams in **figs 31–38** will show you how to tie the knots which are used in upholstery.

The reef knot: this knot is used for joining cords of equal thickness, and the rule is left over right and right over left—pass the left-hand cord over the right-hand cord then the right over the left, repeat and pull to tighten

▼ **Fig. 32 A sheet bend**

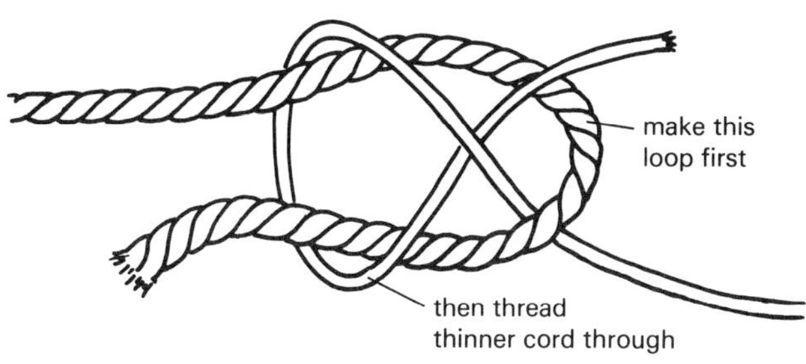

▼ **Fig. 33 Half hitches**

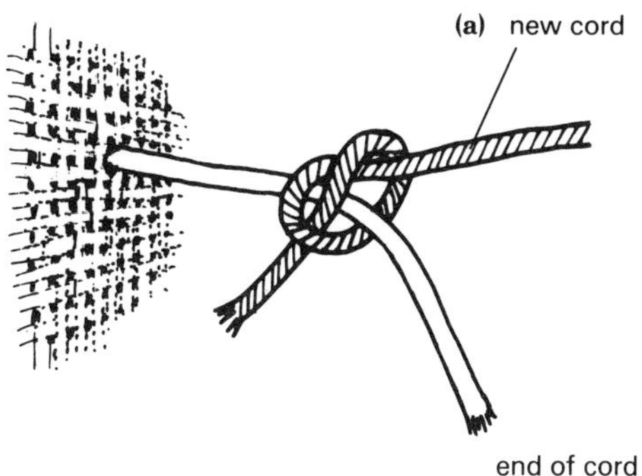

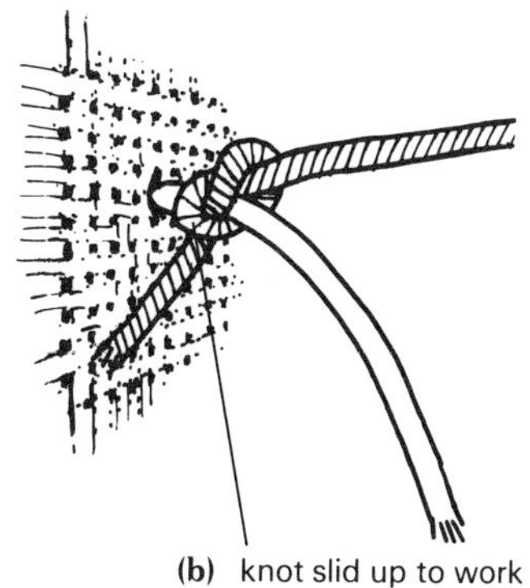

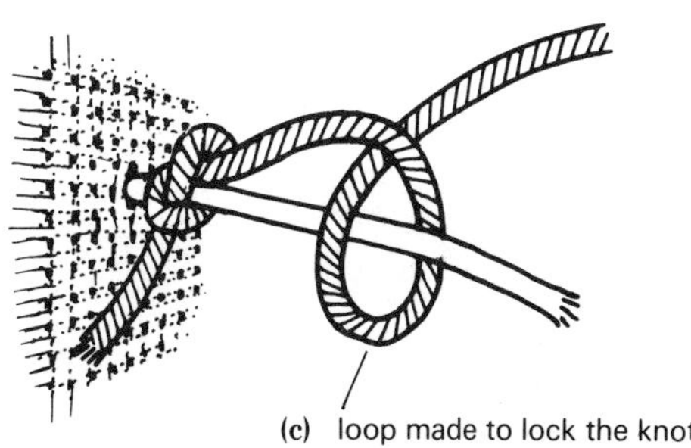

(**fig. 31**). The reef knot is not used very often, but it is useful if you misjudge the length of cord required—say, for lacing springs—and need to join on an extra piece. It can also be used for tying off cottons and twines at the end of a row of stitches.

The sheet bend: this is a knot for joining cords of unequal thicknesses. A loop is formed with the thicker cord and the thinner cord is threaded through the loop, taken round and tucked under (**fig. 32**); the knot is tightened by pulling on the thinner cord.

Half hitches: the half hitch (**fig. 33**) forms part of several knots and can be used for instance when joining on extra twine for blind stitching or roll-edge stitches, or for joining on another length of thread when ladder stitching, when you need to join the new cord close up to the last stitch made. Make a half hitch by looping your new cord round the old short length. Slide it up to the last stitch that you have made. Then tie another half hitch, looping the new length over the old short end, and pull tight. Do this twice or three times for security, and do not cut off the old end too close to the knots—leave at least 25 mm (1 in).

Fig. 34 The upholsterer's slip knot

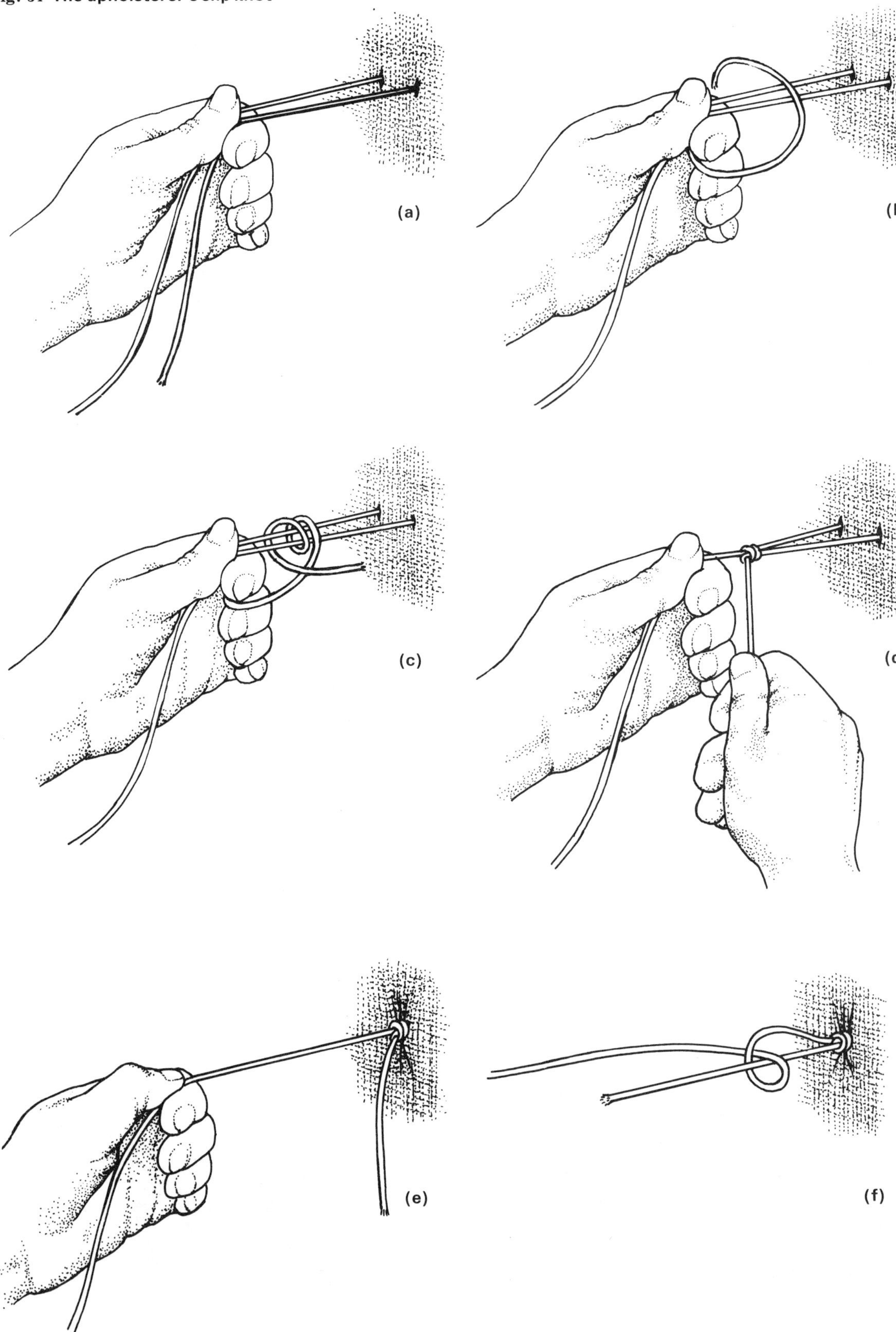

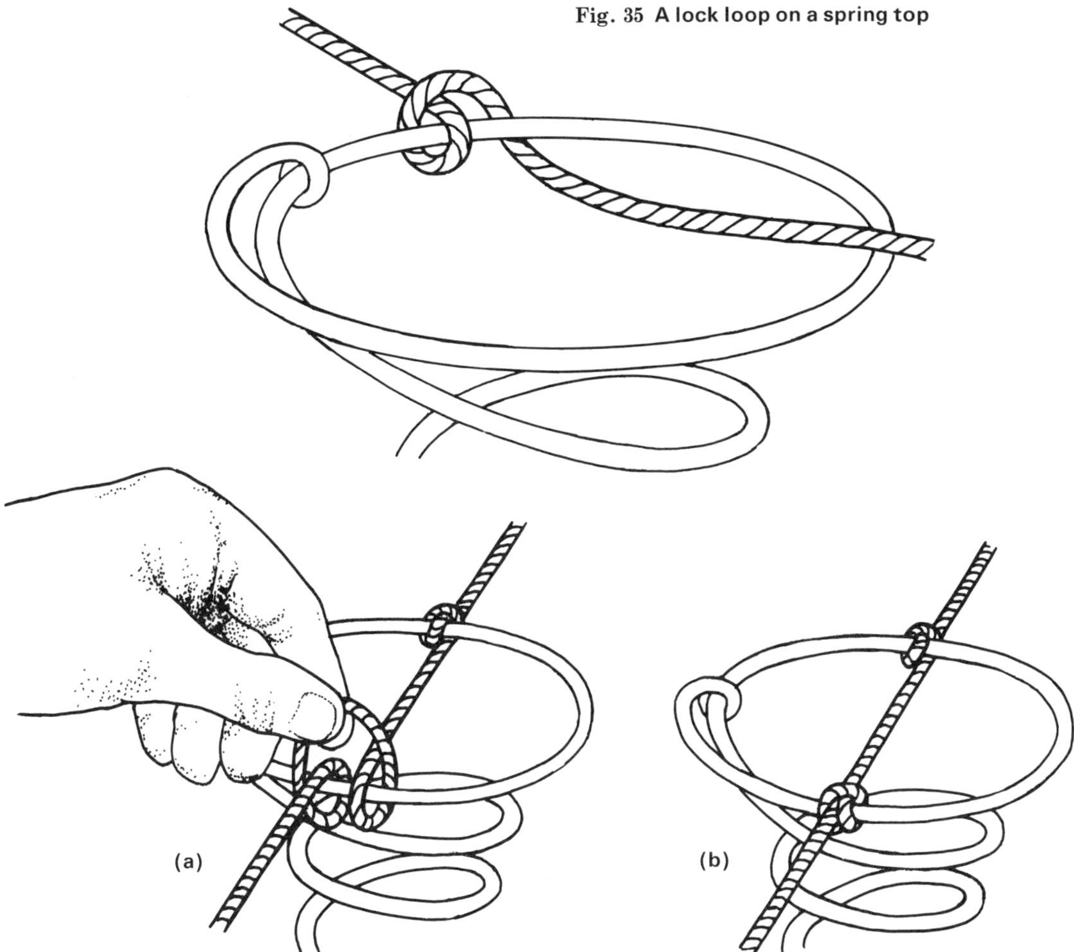

Fig. 35 A lock loop on a spring top

Fig. 36 A clove hitch ▲

The upholsterer's slip knot: this is the knot that is most frequently used by the upholsterer, so you must learn to make it quickly (**fig. 34**). It is used for fastening twine, thread and cotton to begin a line of stitches or ties and also for tying in stuffings, putting in buttons and for many other jobs. Let us say, for instance, that you are about to fasten a button in some button-back upholstery. There are the two ends of the buttoning twine protruding from the back hessian.

Hold the two ends of twine together between the thumb and forefinger of your left hand (**a**). The cord end on the right should be at least 100 mm (4 in) behind the finger and thumb. Take the end on the right forward and bend it across the cords in front of your thumb (**b**). Take the right cord end twice round both cords and through the loop you have made (**c**).

Pull this cord end to form a moderately tight knot (**d**).

Pull the other cord to slip the knot up to the required tension, then give the shorter cord a tug to tighten the knot (**e**).

Lock the knot by looping the longer cord over the shorter one, in three half hitches (**f**).

The lock loop: this is used when lacing springs with laid cord and as its name implies is not really a knot, but a loop that locks itself and is easily adjustable when loosened (**fig. 35**).

The clove hitch: to make a clove hitch (**fig. 36**), which is used on the front part of the coil of a spring, bring the cord over the spring from the back and under, coming up again on the right side of the cord. Hold the cord between the thumb and index finger in a loop (**a**). Then take the cord over the spring again, this time to the left, and through the loop. Take your finger away and pull the knot tight (**b**).

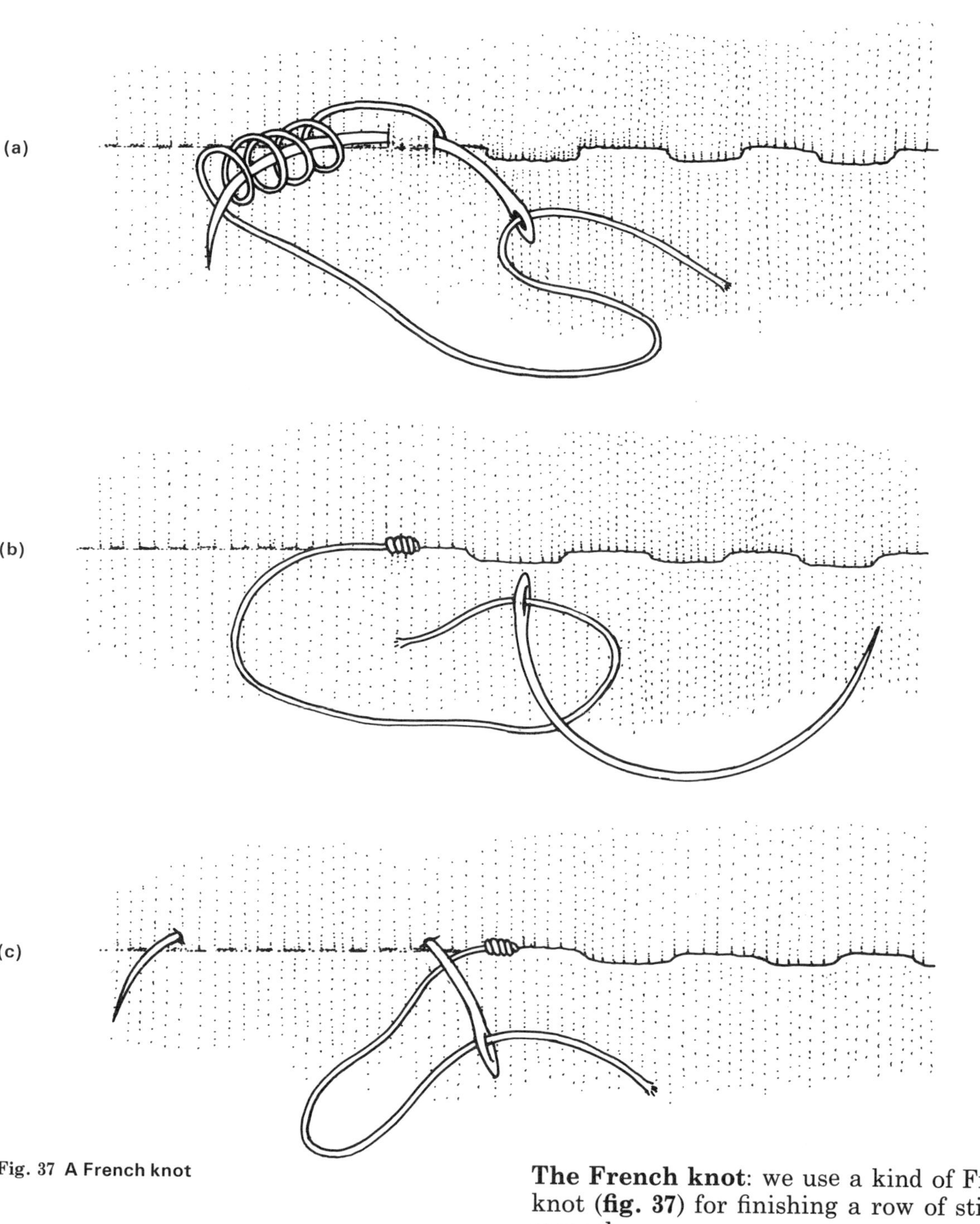

Fig. 37 A French knot

The French knot: we use a kind of French knot (**fig. 37**) for finishing a row of stitches securely.

Make your final stitch very small. Take the trailing thread and wind it round the needle four or five times (**a**).

Pull the needle through and tighten the knot up close to the fabric (**b**).

Make a further two stitches to give length to the end before cutting off so that the knot does not come undone.

(a) (b) (c) (d)

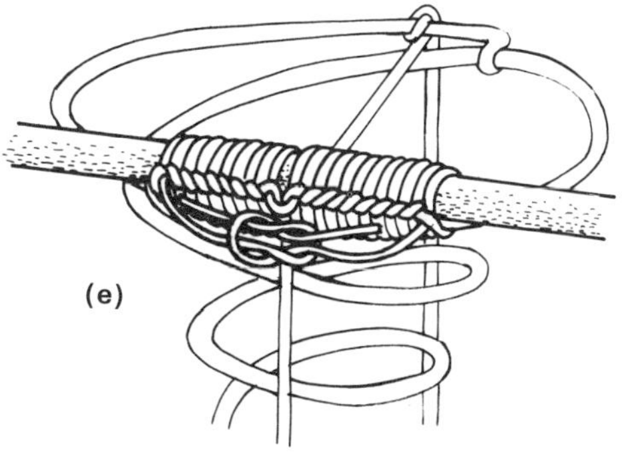

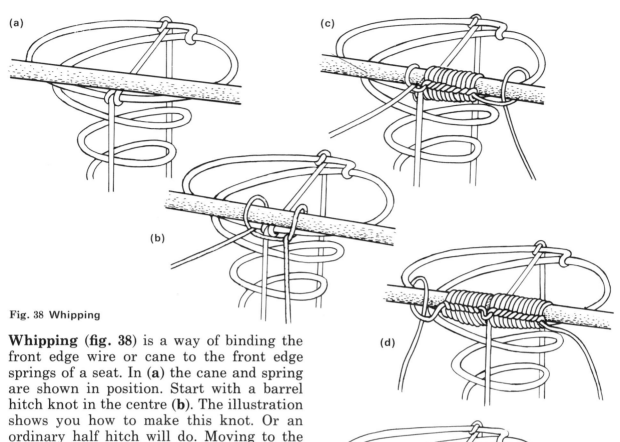

Fig. 38 Whipping

Whipping (fig. 38) is a way of binding the front edge wire or cane to the front edge springs of a seat. In **(a)** the cane and spring are shown in position. Start with a barrel hitch knot in the centre **(b)**. The illustration shows you how to make this knot. Or an ordinary half hitch will do. Moving to the right, make a row about 25 mm (1 in) long of lock loops **(c)**. Do likewise on the left side **(d)**. Finish by tying both ends together in the centre with a reef knot **(e)**.

SPRINGS

The size, gauge and number of springs can be varied according to the size and shape of the seat and also to make it harder or softer. Usually springs of 125 to 150 mm (5 to 6 in) will be required, in 10 or 12 gauge. When I am building a new seat I try to keep the person it belongs to in mind, thinking of their height and approximate weight so that I can choose heavier or lighter springs accordingly.

Fastening Springs

In **fig. 39** you can see how to fasten a spring to the webbing support. Use **No. 1** stout twine, as we want the springs to stay there for a very long time. Make three stitches at equal distances round the spring base, fastening each stitch with a half hitch beneath the webbing.

Springs are fastened through the heavy hessian spring covering in the same way.

Fig. 39 Fastening springs ▼

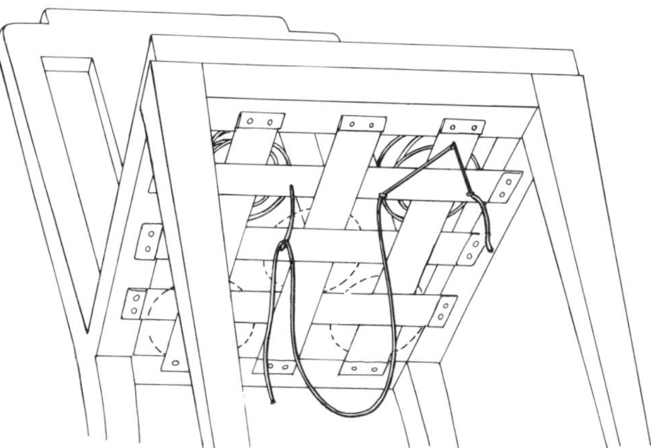

Fig. 40 Lacing springs with laid cord

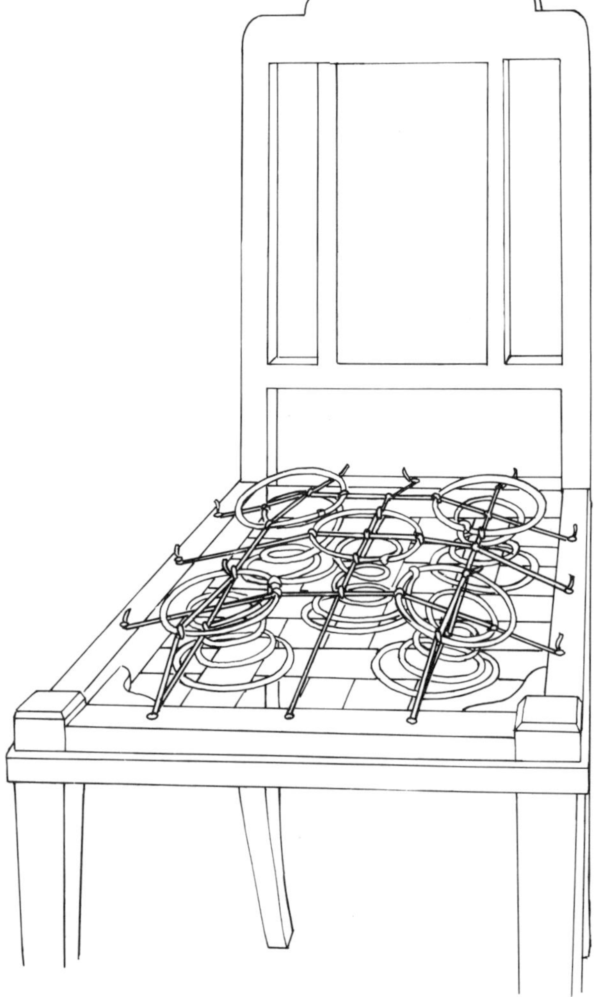

Lacing Springs with Laid Cord

The springs in seats need to be laced down with the stout cord known as 'laid cord'. To measure the length required, stretch the laid cord over the springs from back to front, then add half the length again to allow for knotting. This is a general rule of thumb but obviously it depends on the depth of the built-up edge of the finished seat. For the single chair seat illustrated (**fig. 40**) six pieces of cord are needed.

Tie a single knot in the end of each piece of cord and push a 16 mm ($\frac{5}{8}$ in) improved tack through the knot. Fasten three cords to the back rail and three cords to the left-hand rail opposite the springs. Hammer the tacks into the centre of the wood of each rail.

Hold down the back right-hand spring to the required height—with this chair I would say about 50 mm (2 in) higher than the rails. Tie the cord with a lock loop on the back of the second coil down and a clove hitch on the front of the top coil. This is to keep the spring straighter at the waist; if the cord is tied over the back of the top coil it throws the waist of the spring off-centre and in this position it may buckle after only a short period of use.

Bring the cord forward to the front right-hand spring. Tie a lock loop on the back of the top coil then a clove hitch on the front of the second coil down.

Fasten the cord to the front rail by twisting it round a tack driven half-way in. When you have adjusted the tension correctly drive the tack home and tie a half hitch round the cord to make it secure.

Take the end of the cord back up to the top coil of the front spring. Pull the cord fairly tight, then tie it off with a clove hitch and a half hitch.

Repeat this procedure with the other cords and your seat should end up looking something like the seat in **fig. 40**. Note the position of the laced springs and how they are 'fanned' out. Test each spring by pressing it down; it should go down in an arc to a perfectly upright position when compressed. Notice how the 'knuckles' of the springs are facing inwards and the knuckles on the bases of the springs are positioned on webbing and not over a space between the webs. It is very important for the long life of springs to position them correctly.

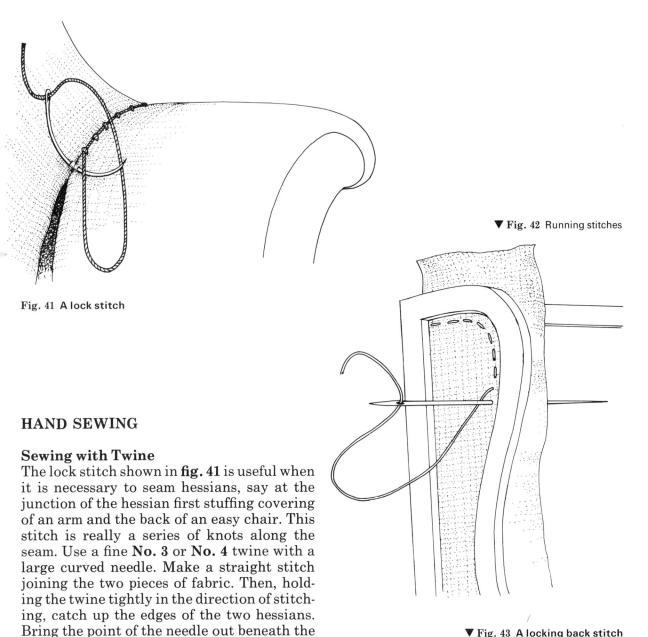

Fig. 41 A lock stitch

▼ **Fig.** 42 Running stitches

HAND SEWING

Sewing with Twine

The lock stitch shown in **fig. 41** is useful when it is necessary to seam hessians, say at the junction of the hessian first stuffing covering of an arm and the back of an easy chair. This stitch is really a series of knots along the seam. Use a fine **No. 3** or **No. 4** twine with a large curved needle. Make a straight stitch joining the two pieces of fabric. Then, holding the twine tightly in the direction of stitching, catch up the edges of the two hessians. Bring the point of the needle out beneath the taut twine so that in fact it is passing through a loop and as you pull the stitch up it forms a half hitch knot.

There are easier stitches that you make with twine. A simple running stitch is used for fastening two layers of hessian (**fig. 42**).

The 'locking back stitch' is similar to the blind edge stitches which I will deal with at the end of this chapter (pages 47–49) and is used when joining the first stuffing covering of scrim hessian to the basic support hessian where stitched edges are to be formed. In **fig. 43** you see it being used on the back of an iron-frame crinoline chair.

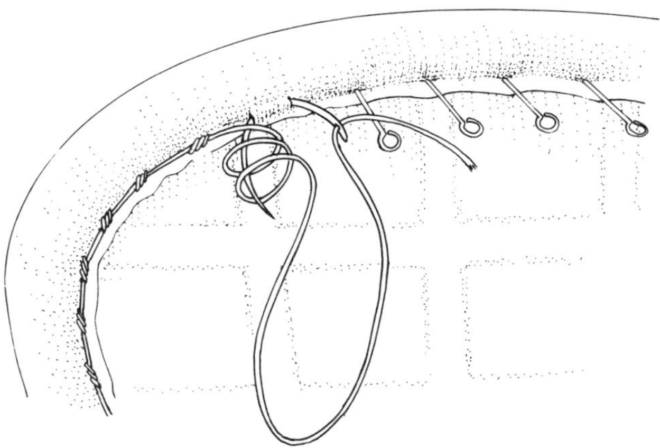

▼ Fig. 43 A locking back stitch

Fig. 44 Ladder or slip stitching

(a)

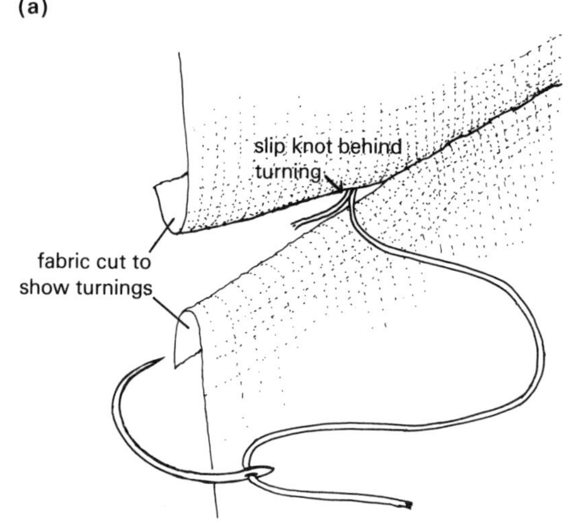

(b)

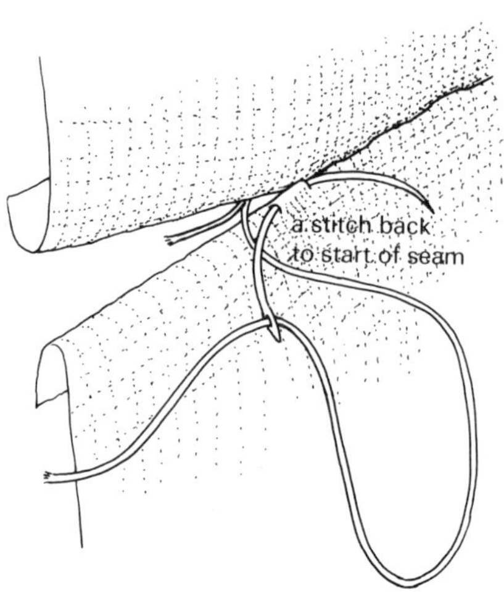

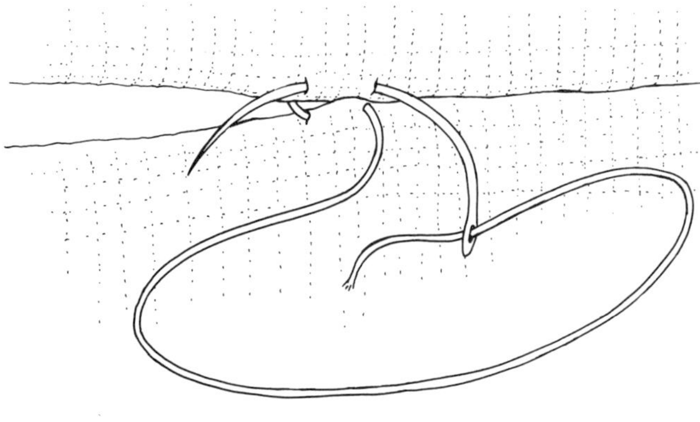

(c)

Sewing with Thread and Cotton

The ladder or slip stitch: modern upholsterers often fasten outside seams with small gimp pins or with 'back tacking strip', a metal band with protruding spikes. But, to my mind, on a quality piece of upholstered furniture all outside seams that cannot be machine stitched should be hand stitched with small, neat, ladder stitches. The method is illustrated in **fig. 44**. For most jobs a 75 mm (3 in) 17 gauge curved needle is the most suitable.

To begin, take a small stitch just beneath the overlapping covering material, 10 mm ($\frac{3}{8}$ in) to the right of the beginning of the seam (**a**). Secure the stitch with an upholsterer's slip knot.

Take a stitch through the line of the fold of the overlapping cloth back to the beginning of the seam (**b**). This makes a secure start to the sewing and also obscures the knot and thread end, which can now be tucked away beneath the fold.

Take the first stitch in the direction of sewing by making the point of your needle enter the opposite fabric a thread or two back from the place where the last stitch emerged (**c**). You can now see the reason for the

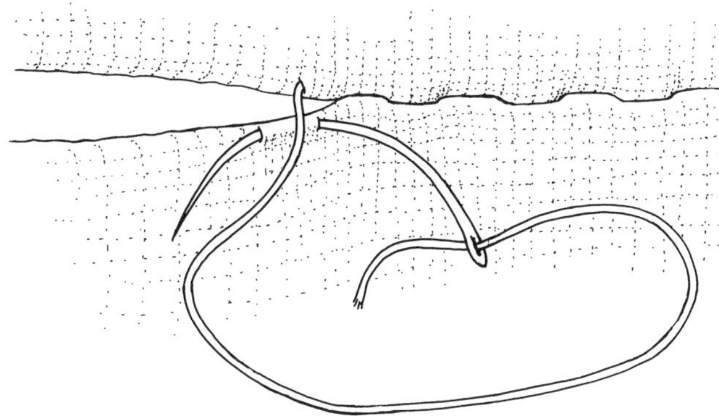

curved needle, for the two pieces of cloth that are to be sewn together are stretched taut, and nearly always there is a part of the wooden frame beneath. Sewing with a straight needle would prove extremely difficult.

The rule that the next stitch should be started a thread or two back from where the needle last emerged applies all the way, so that as you pull the thread tight after each stitch, it disappears completely (**d**). The length of stitch is determined by your cloth. For heavy, coarsely woven fabrics, such as tweed, a stitch of up to 15 mm ($\frac{5}{8}$ in) is acceptable. But for finer fabrics, a 5 to 10 mm ($\frac{3}{16}$ to $\frac{3}{8}$ in) stitch is much neater.

When you come to the end of the seam, the thread must be securely finished off, so use the French knot described earlier. Do not cut off the thread at the knot, or it will soon come undone. With the needle still threaded, take two or three stitches back along the seam (**e**), then cut the thread off close to the surface of the cloth. Alternatively, if your seam ends at the bottom of the chair, you can put in a tack underneath, wind the thread round it and then drive the tack home to hold the thread.

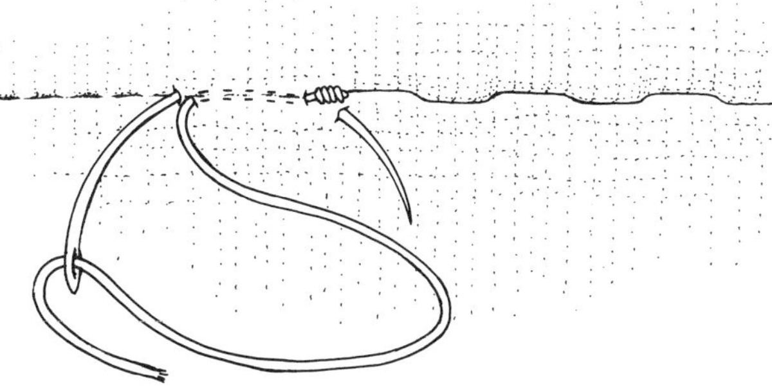

(e)

Fig. 45 Sewing on braid

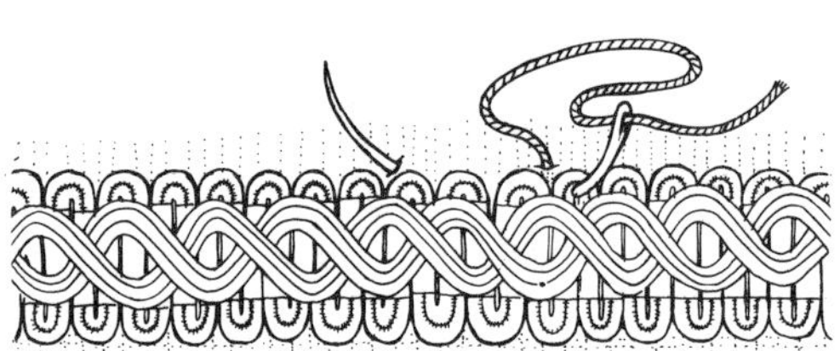

Fig. 46 Sewing on fringe

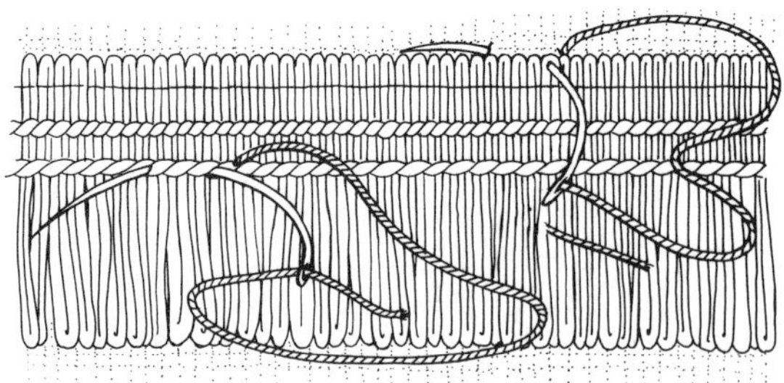

Fig. 47 Sewing on decorative chair cord

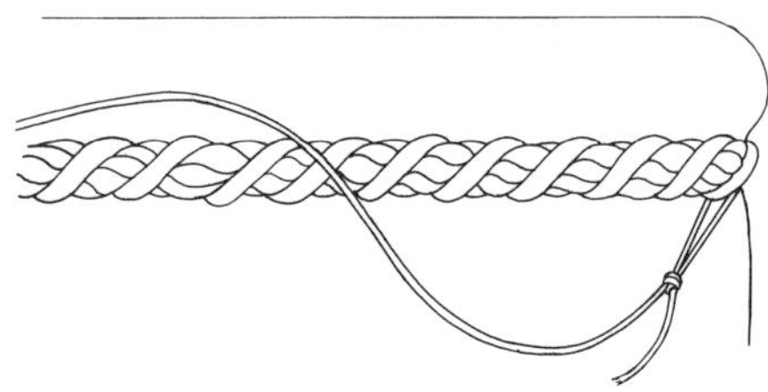

47(a) ▲

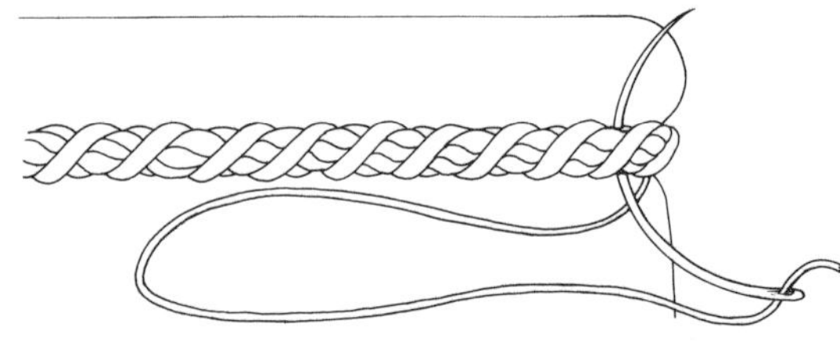

47(b)

Sewing on Braid and Fringe

It is a good idea to fasten braid with adhesive first, and I shall deal with this later in this chapter in the section on using adhesives (pages 50–51). But you must not rely upon adhesive alone for fastening, because after a year or two it very often deteriorates and, at the slightest provocation, your trimming will be hanging off making everything look very tatty. Always sew braid as well, for that extra security.

Stitch the braid as shown in **fig. 45**, catching the top loops of the braid to the fabric underneath. If possible, put another row of stitches along the bottom. Use a matching cotton and make the stitches very small so that they cannot be seen.

I do not use adhesive for fastening fringe but fix it with two rows of stitches, as shown in **fig. 46**. The top stitches are exactly the same as for braid, but the second row consists of simple in-and-out stitches which hold in the lower part of the fringe.

Sewing on Decorative Chair Cord

It is nice to know how to fix decorative chair cord, for as a trimming this always sets off a chair well and gives it a more luxurious look. Chair cord is a silken twisted cord, usually about 6 to 10 mm ($\frac{1}{4}$ to $\frac{3}{8}$ in) in diameter. You can choose cord either to match or to contrast with the colour of your chair covering.

When you intend to trim with this cord, simply ladder stitch the seams in the places where it is to be used—usually the arm scrolls, front border, wings and maybe the top of the outside back. After this, pin the cord in position over the seams and sew on with a fine 75 mm (3 in) 19 gauge curved cording needle (**fig. 47**).

47(c)

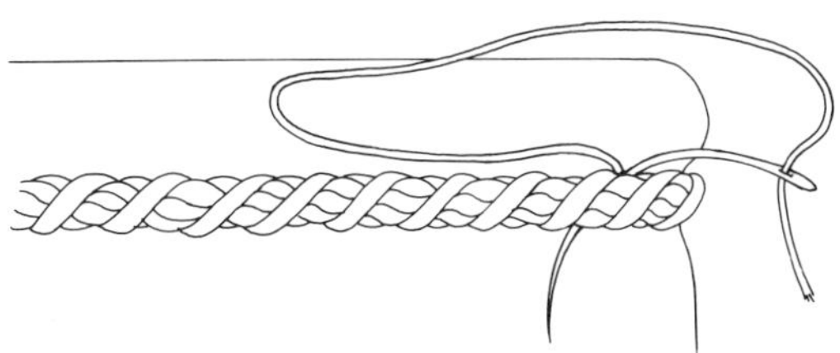

47(d)

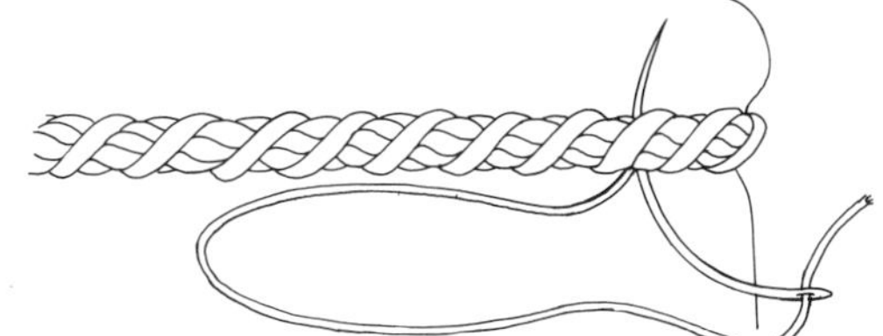

Begin with a small stitch and a slip knot which will be concealed beneath the cord (**a**).

Make a stitch sideways through the centre of the cord (**b**).

Going back from this a fraction, make the next stitch about 10 mm ($\frac{3}{8}$ in) beneath the cord and in line with the ladder stitches (**c**). When it emerges bring the needle to the opposite side of the cord.

Backing again a fraction from the end of the last stitch, make a further stitch at 90 degrees through the centre of the cord (**d**).

Continue in this fashion along the length of the cord. Be particularly careful to fasten the cord securely at the end. And before cutting your cord do wrap it round with a piece of transparent adhesive tape and then cut through the centre of this. If you do not do this the cord will fray out and untwist in no time.

Incorporating Piping into a Seam

Lastly, in this hand-sewing section, let me show you how to sew piping into a seam. For an example I will describe how to fit a facing to an arm front scroll.

First, fix the piping with pins beneath the lip of the scroll's edge.

Next, pad out the facing with suitable stuffing (hair and wadding). Cut the material roughly to shape and fix it on, using the same pins removed one at a time and put back, this time also catching the folded-in edge of the covering.

Finally, sew in the facing cover and the piping together, using a sort of ladder stitch but going through the flange of the piping at the line of machined stitches each time you make a stitch in the facing or the inside of the scroll lip (**fig. 48**).

Fig. 48 Incorporating piping into a seam

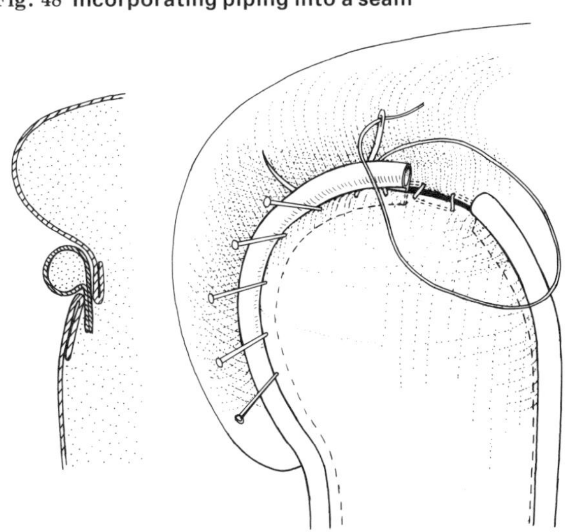

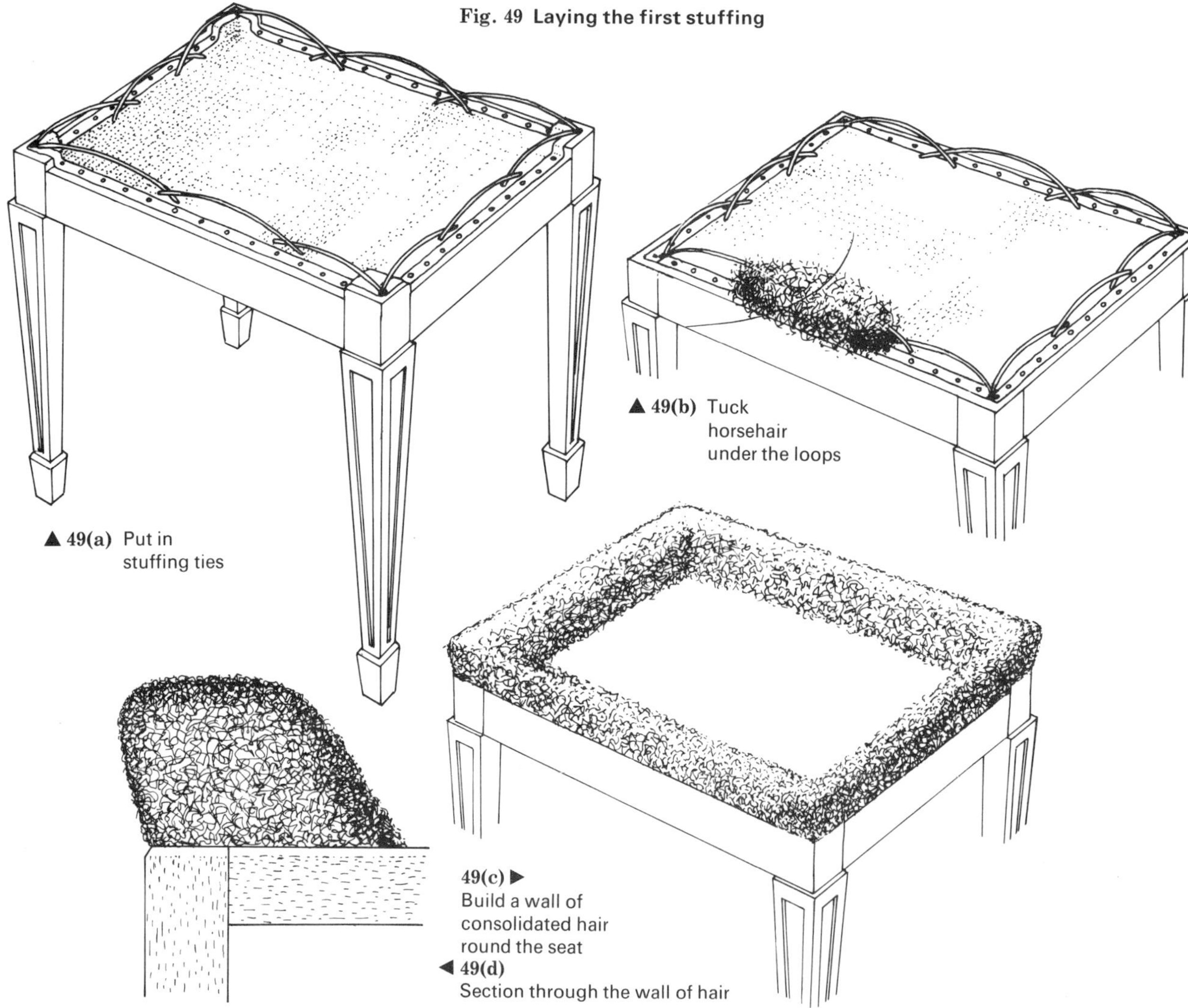
Fig. 49 Laying the first stuffing

▲ 49(a) Put in stuffing ties

▲ 49(b) Tuck horsehair under the loops

49(c) ▶ Build a wall of consolidated hair round the seat

◀ 49(d) Section through the wall of hair

THE TRADITIONAL STITCHED ROLL EDGE

Very occasionally I have had in my workshop ancient chairs on which I have found traces of some of the original upholstery. A Queen Anne period chair had an edge made of rolls of straw bound with twine. An early Georgian chair had gained a little in sophistication, with horsehair instead of straw and the edges sewn rather in the way mattress borders used to be stitched. Then I have found chairs from the late eighteenth century into the late nineteenth century with much improved upholstery foundations and stitched edges to everything, elaborate scrolls on arms and back panels as well as to seat fronts, all done in the way I shall now show you. It is a way of achieving firm upholstery that will retain a shape yet will not be so hard as to be uncomfortable. As an example I will take an ordinary stuffed-over stool seat.

The First Stuffing

When the basic support of webbing and hessian has been put on, the next step is to lay a first stuffing of horsehair (**fig. 49**).

Using your largest 100 or 125 mm (4 or 5 in) curved needle, put in stuffing ties (bridle ties) of **No. 3** twine 25 mm (1 in) from the edge (**a**). Notice the back stitch between the loops.

Tuck well carded horsehair, a small handful at a time, under the loops of twine (**b**), to form a wall of fairly consolidated hair all the way round the seat (**c**). In the enlarged inset (**d**) you will see the shape to aim for. Corners are difficult, but try to get them as firm as the rest of the edge. You can do this by rolling in extra hair, which will bind on to the hair

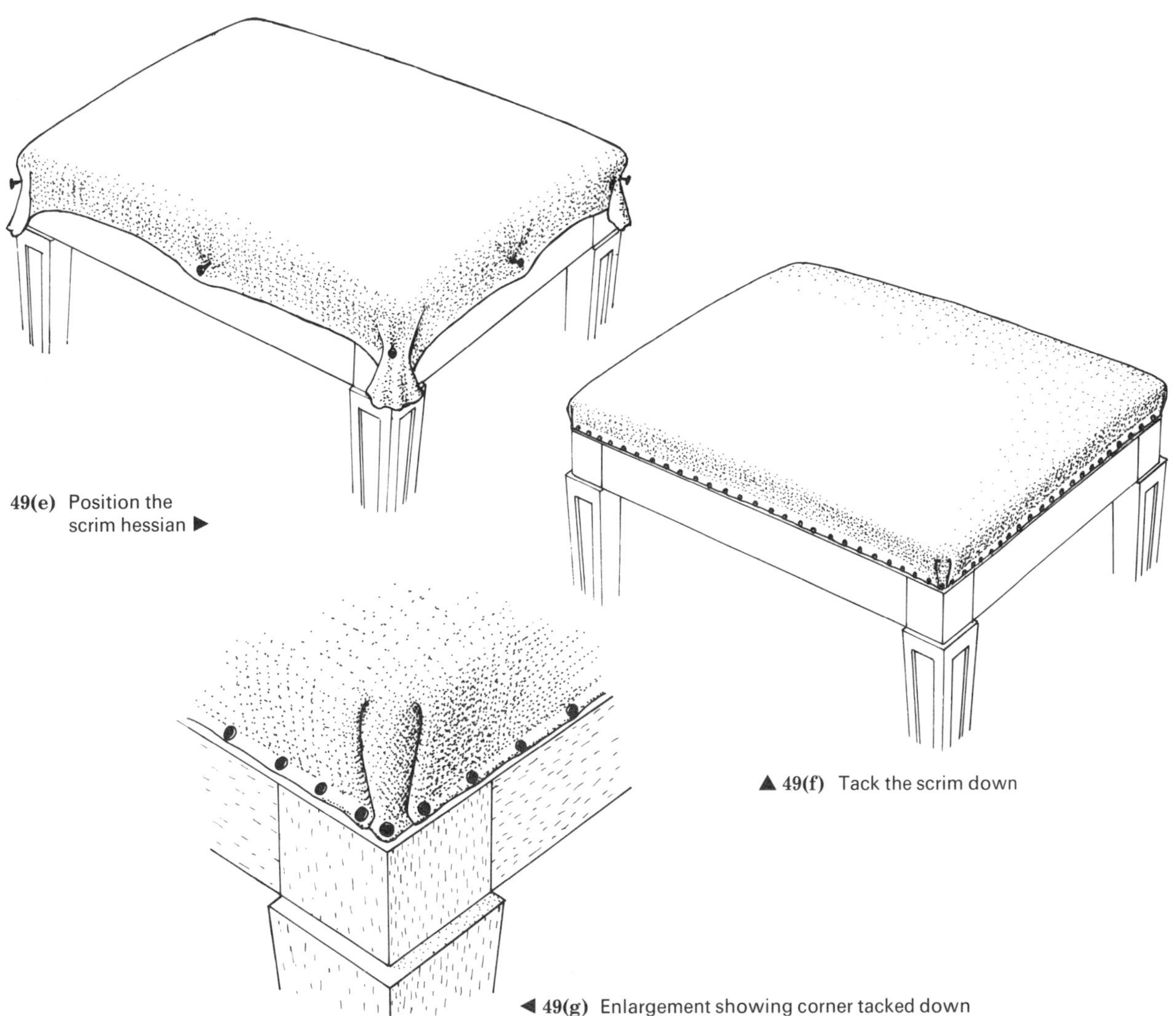

49(e) Position the scrim hessian ▶

▲ 49(f) Tack the scrim down

◀ 49(g) Enlargement showing corner tacked down

already held by the ties. Do a real bit of sculpting to get these edges as close to the shape that you want for the finished job; this means straight, even, slightly overhanging the frame and pretty firm. Fill up the centre now, aiming at a slightly domed shape with the middle about 38 mm ($1\frac{1}{2}$ in) higher than the edges.

Now for the hessian. I think scrim hessian is best for this work, although 280 g (10 oz) will do. Measure and cut off a piece, allowing an extra 25 mm (1 in) all round to turn in. Mark the centre of each side of your stool and the centres of the four sides of your piece of hessian. Lay the hessian over the stuffing and position temporary tacks at the marks. Next, temporarily tack the corners, just one tack in each, pulling the scrim fairly tight to give a little tension (**e**). Now fasten all round the stool with temporary tacks. Be careful to keep the threads of the weave of the scrim running parallel to the edge of the frame.

You will have noticed the chamfer along the edge of the seat rail; it is on this that the scrim is permanently tacked. Drive in the tacks at intervals of about 20 mm ($\frac{3}{4}$ in) carefully aligning the tacks along a thread of the scrim. Your edges will then be the same height all the way round (**f**). Fasten the corners last. The inset (**g**) shows the best way to do it. Tack the centre of the corner, then make a small pleat on each side. You will have to make many adjustments to the corners before you get them right; try to get them to the same height and overhang as the rest of the edge and with the same density of stuffing, even if you have to ram a little more hair in before finally tacking down the scrim.

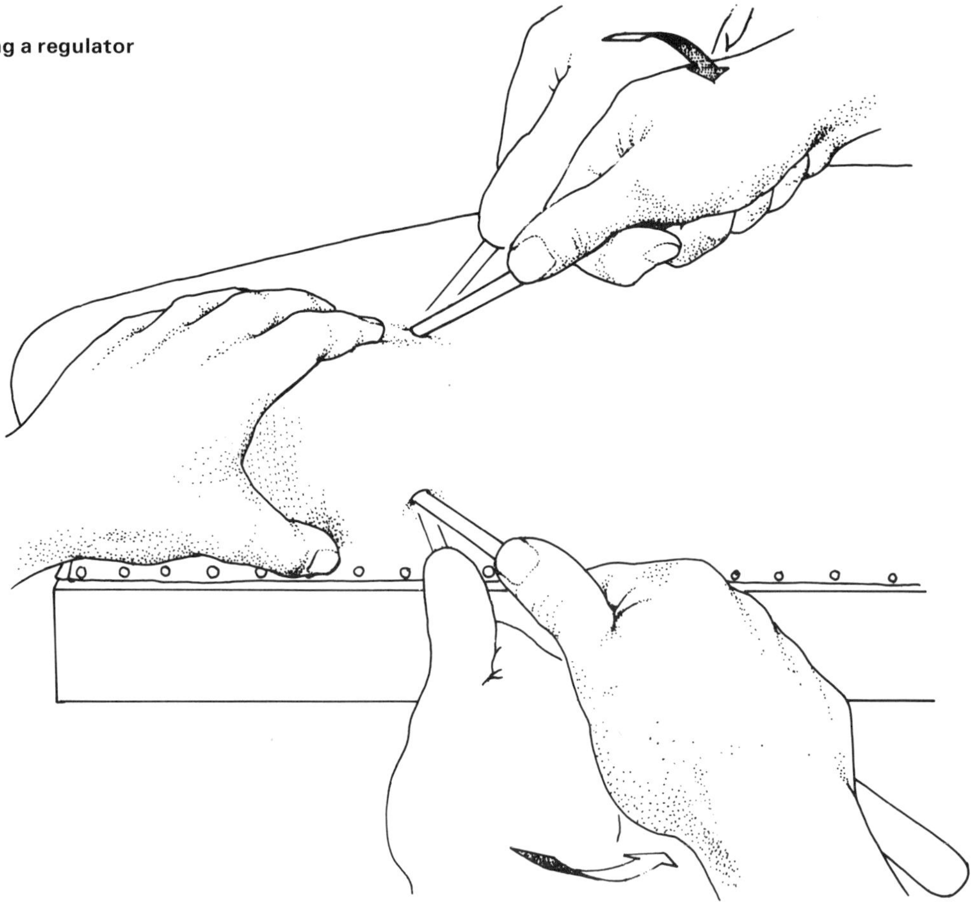

Fig. 50 Using a regulator

Using a Regulator

At this stage of your upholstery you can practise 'regulating'. It looks so simple but I find many folk do not grasp what regulating is all about. With a little practice you should be able to redistribute stuffing that is within the confines of scrim hessian to any shape desired. Of course, you will not have to do this to any great extent as you will already, so cleverly, have got most of the hair in an even and orderly shape. But should there be a hollow or a lump that has missed your dexterous fingers this can now be rectified with the regulator. In the drawing (**fig. 50**) you can see how to use this. Simply push the regulator into the stuffing to about a third of its length and, keeping the fulcrum at the place where the regulator enters the hessian, lever the horsehair filling into the hollow or away from the over-full area, as you will.

Fig. 51 Putting in through stuffing ties

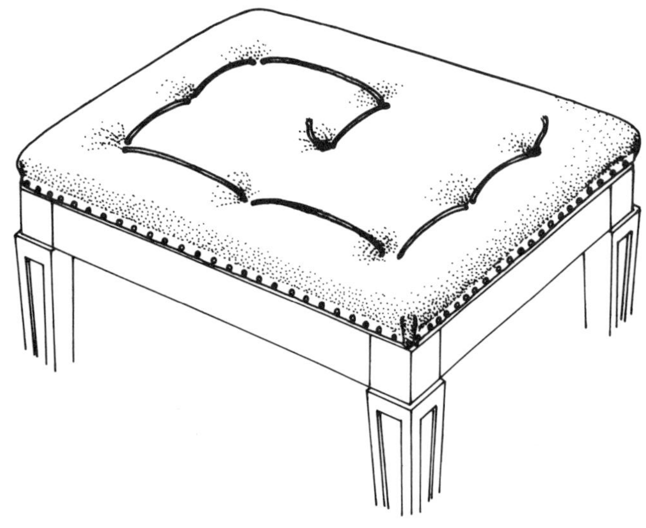

Through Stuffing Ties

Through stuffing ties (**fig. 51**) are used to anchor the top scrim hessian through the stuffing to the hessian and webbing underneath. With a crayon or felt tip pen and an upholstery gauge (page 11), mark the top hessian in the form of a rectangle with the sides 100 mm (4 in) from the seat edges. Take a 250 mm (10 in) double-pointed needle and thread it with **No. 1** stout twine. In one corner of the marked rectangle make a stitch about 15 mm ($\frac{5}{8}$ in) long, taking it through the seat. Tie the stitch off loosely with an upholsterer's slip knot. Proceed as you see in the drawing, finishing up with one stitch in the very centre of the seat. Pull down the ties tightly, holding the slack as you do so with each tie in turn, starting with the first slip knot and ending with the centre stitch. Fasten off this centre stitch with a number of half hitches. Unthread the needle and put it safely away. Nasty accidents can happen with these double-pointed needles—especially when they are left somewhere with twine dangling. If the twine gets caught round a leg or a foot it may pull the sharp needle into a position to inflict a painful wound. I speak from bitter experience.

EDGE-STITCHING

Now you are ready to try your skill at a stitched edge. I shall tell you *how* to do it first, then at the end it will be clearer and more easy to explain *why* we do it. Thread your 250 mm (10 in) double-pointed needle with about 3 m (10 ft) of **No. 3** twine. When edge-stitching work from left to right, or the other way round if you're left handed. On this stool we are going to put in two 'blind' rows and one row of 'through' stitches to form a roll edge.

Describing this method of stitching in words is difficult, but I will do my best to make it clear with the help of the drawings (**fig. 52**).

Face one side of your stool and start by pushing in your needle on the line of tacks 30 mm (about $1\frac{1}{4}$ in) from the left-hand corner. The point should come through the top about 90 mm ($3\frac{1}{2}$ in) back from the edge (**a**).

Pull the needle through just as far as the eye. Give the needle a bit of a twist in an anti-clockwise direction to 'scoop' horsehair inside the seat with the eye-end point of the needle (**b**).

Push the needle back so that it emerges at the far end of the corner, again just on the

Fig. 52 Edge stitching

(a)

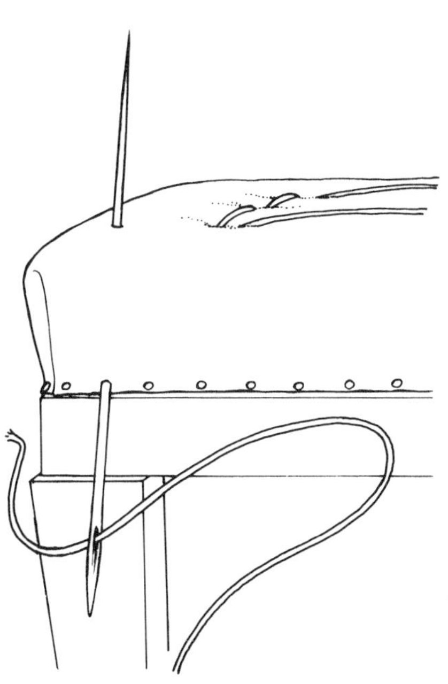

(b)

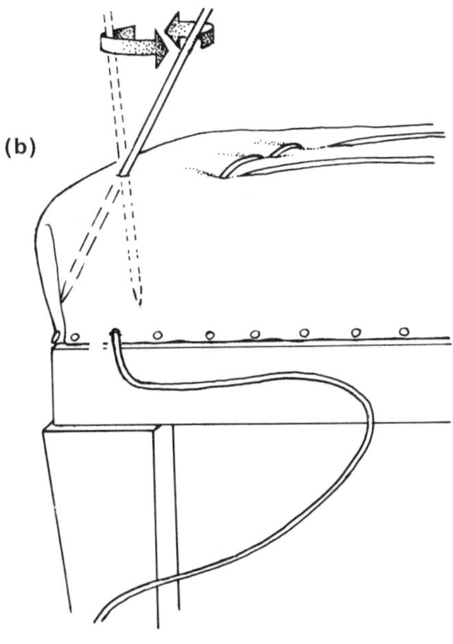

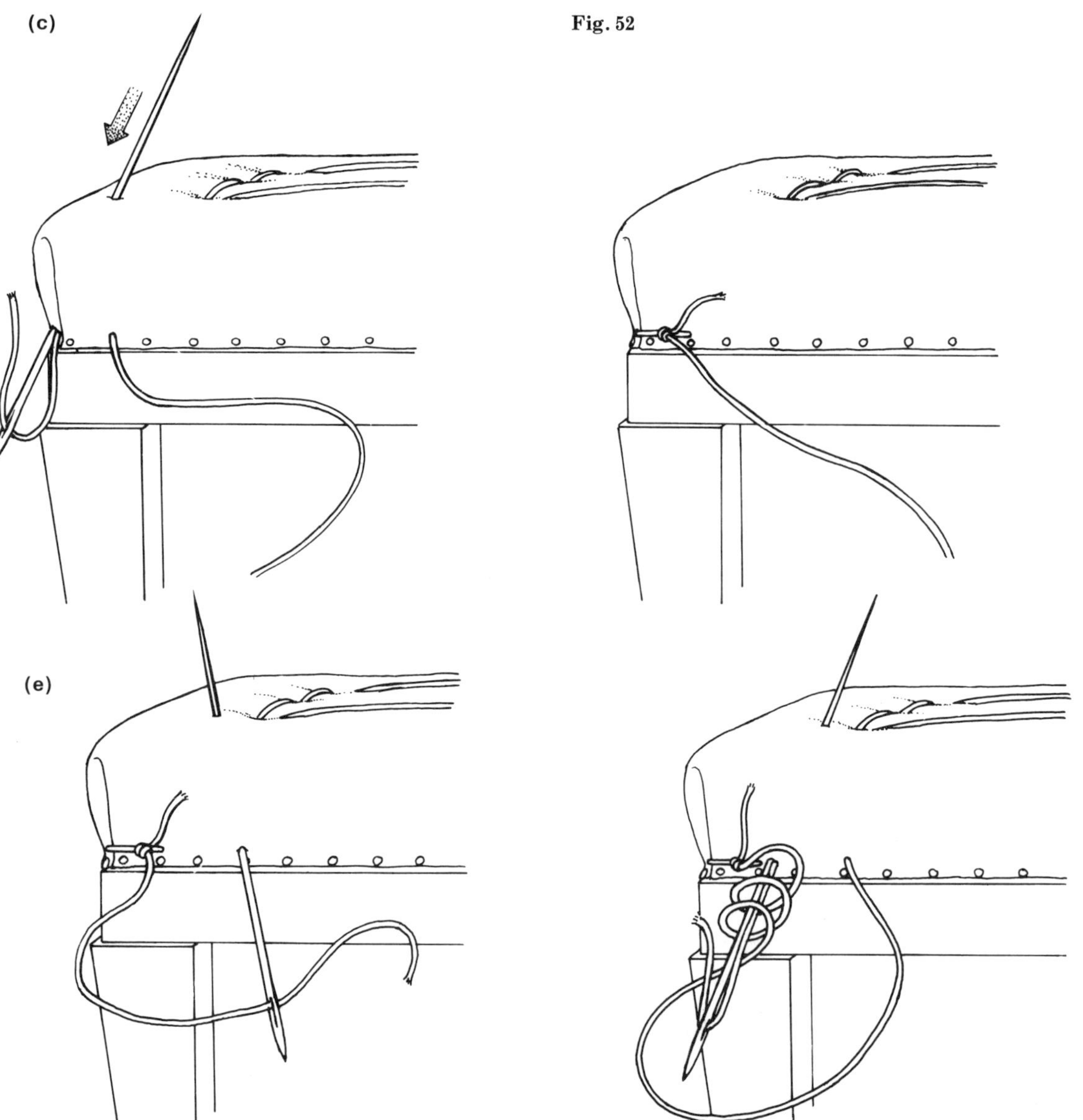

line of tacks (the point of the needle should actually scrape the wood of the frame) (**c**).

Pull the twine through, tie it with an upholsterer's slip knot and pull it tight (**d**).

Push the needle in again 38 mm ($1\frac{1}{2}$ in) to the right of the knot at the angle shown (**e**).

Do the anti-clockwise 'scoop twist' as in (**b**) then return the needle so that about half its length comes out at the front at the point where the first stitch ended. Take the twine leading from this starting stitch and wind it three times, clockwise, round the needle (**f**).

Pull the needle right out and the twine will follow through the windings that you have made round the needle. Pull the whole length of twine through and tighten the stitch.

Carry on stitching in this manner round your stool until you come back to your starting place, then tie off the end of twine to the short end of the starting stitch (**g**). It often happens that you run out of twine before you reach the end of a row. If so, join on more twine with half hitches. By the way, do dress the twine with beeswax—it will be less likely to kink and knot up when you are stitching. Use your regulator now to work up the hair and even out the edge and then put in another row of blind stitches in the same way, this time 12 mm ($\frac{1}{2}$ in) above the first row.

Now we have to put a roll round the seat edge to give it crispness and definition when it is covered. The method is similar to the blind stitching, but it differs in that the stitches go through to the top. Use your regulator once again to bring up the edge and really consolidate the hair inside. Feel with your fingers to see that there are no soft or lumpy places along this edge. If there are, deal with them with the regulator. Now, with your upholstery gauge and felt tip pen mark a line about 23 mm ($\frac{7}{8}$ in) in from the edge on the top (**h**). Draw another line round the sides 23 mm ($\frac{7}{8}$ in) down—or just above the second row of stitches.

With a rectangular seat it is best to put in a single stitch in each corner—just single through loops of twine about 20 mm ($\frac{3}{4}$ in) long tied with a slip knot and fastened off with a couple of half hitches (**i**). These give a good tension along the edges.

Begin again on one side of your stool, 20 mm ($\frac{3}{4}$ in) from a left-hand corner, pushing your needle through the marked line on the front and coming through the line drawn along the top. Take the needle right out, then push it back through as near to the left-hand corner as possible. Guide it so that it comes out on the front line. Tie an upholsterer's slip knot and pull the twine up tightly. For the next stitch, push the needle 25 mm (1 in) to the right of the first stitch. Guide the needle so that it comes through the hessian on the line you have drawn along the top. Now pull the needle right through and pass it back through the edge at the place where the first stitch finished. Wind the twine around the needle three times, just as you did with the blind stitches (**j**), and pull it up very tightly in the direction of stitching, using the fingers of your left hand to squeeze the stitch together as you pull. Carry on round the seat and when you reach your starting place again tie the twine to your first stitch with a reef knot. A section through the edge, illustrating a firm, round roll formed in the manner described is shown in (**k**).

So now you see what we are trying to achieve with edge stitching. With the blind stitches we are gradually bringing forward and binding the horsehair into a dense wall at the edge. We then top this with a neat roll. And here we have an edge strong enough to be sat on and remain in shape and yet not so hard as to cause discomfort to anyone who sits on the stool.

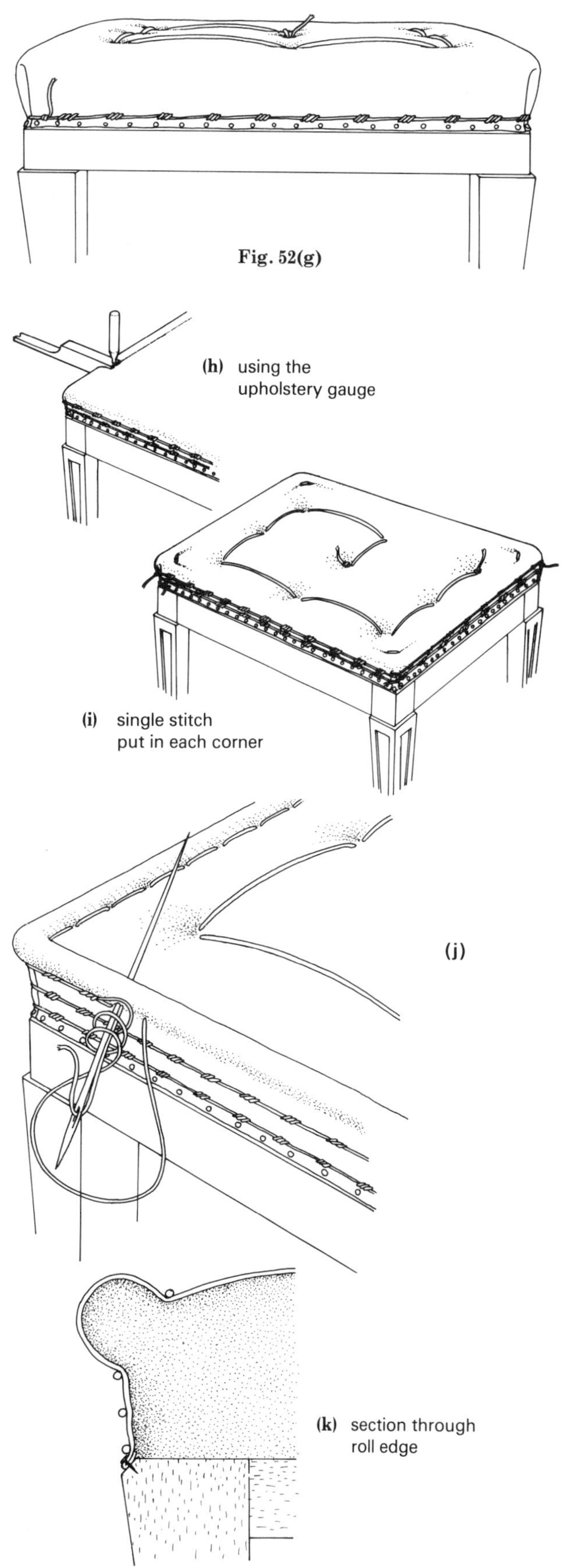

Fig. 52(g)

(h) using the upholstery gauge

(i) single stitch put in each corner

(j)

(k) section through roll edge

Fig. 53 Fastening braid with adhesive

53(a) Secure the end of the braid with gimp pins

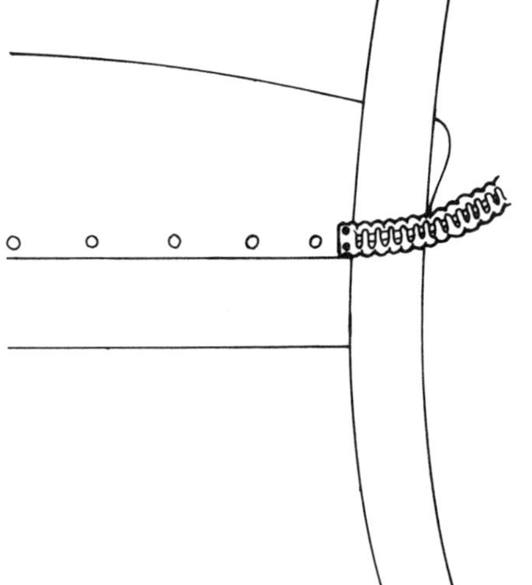

53(b) Apply adhesive to the fabric

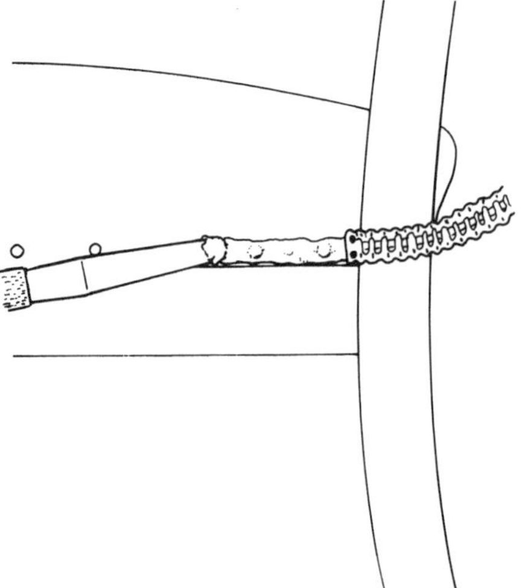

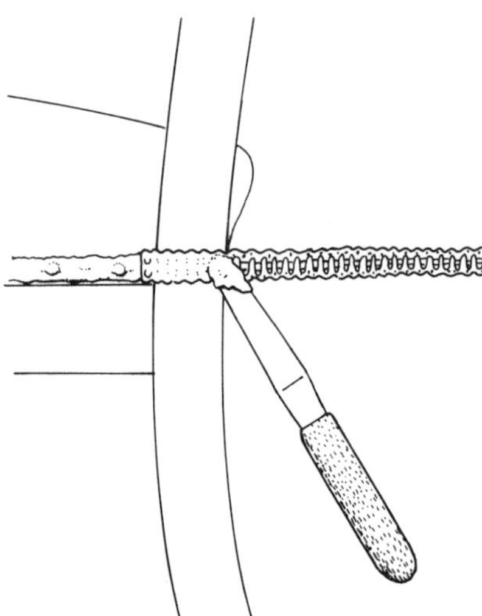

53(c) Spread adhesive along the braid

USING ADHESIVES IN UPHOLSTERY

There are several uses for adhesives in upholstery. Very often a standard-sized rubber cushion made of foam will require pieces added to make it up to the desired size or shape. For building on there is a special impact adhesive with a 'soft bond', which means that you do not end up with a hard line of glue along the join. There are a number of adhesives for fastening braid as a trimming. One of these is a latex preparation which has to be used with great care, for if any is spilt or splashed on the covering it is practically impossible to remove it without making a mark. The adhesive that I favour is a thixotropic impact adhesive. Because it is a jelly, it is easy to dispense and does not come off the spreading knife in long, unmanageable strands, which is what happens with most impact glues. Also, because it only sticks tightly when firm pressure is applied, if you stick the braid lightly at first you will be able

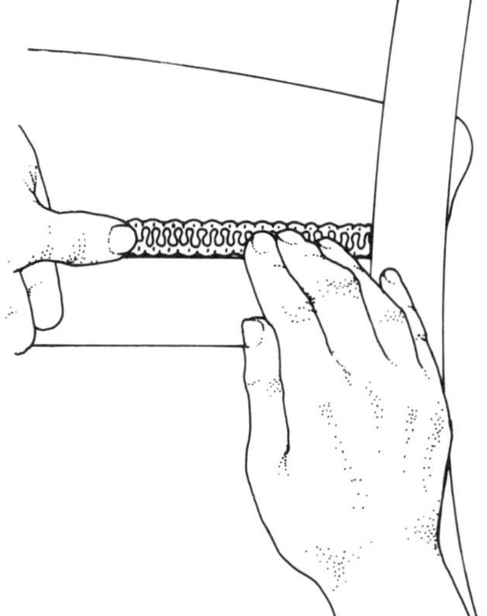

53(d) Press the braid into position with your fingers

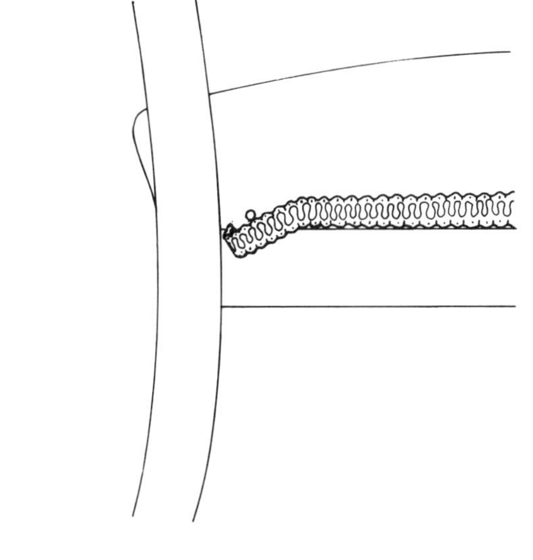

53(e) Fold the end under

to remove it to readjust if necessary. The following instructions apply to both of these adhesives (**fig. 53**).

Secure the end of the braid to the chair fabric with two gimp pins (**a**).

Apply a line of adhesive to the fabric (**b**). Spread the adhesive along the braid, holding the braid taut and scraping the glue along to ensure a thin, even application (**c**). Do not lay the braid down to spread the adhesive—if you do this the adhesive may go through to the face, especially with a thin braid. Coat no more than 50 cm (20 in) of braid at a time.

Stretch the braid along the fabric, gently pressing it down with the fingers (**d**).

To finish off, cut the braid 6 mm ($\frac{1}{4}$ in) too long and fold this extra under. Put another dab of adhesive on the folded piece and press it back into position (**e**).

Leave the adhesive to set for a few minutes, then roll the braid with a small seam roller (**f**) and stitch it as described on page 42.

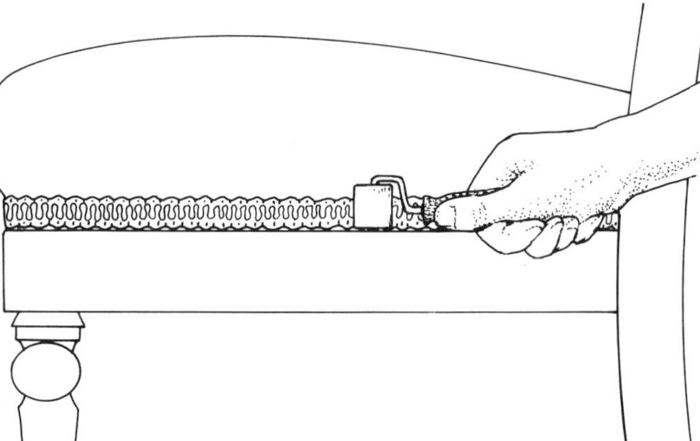

53(f) Press the braid with a roller

MODERN UPHOLSTERY

I do not intend to say a lot here about modern upholstery, except to mention a few hints regarding maintenance and replacements, and to tell you how a modern piece of furniture can be reupholstered in a traditional way. Some other aspects of modern upholstery are covered in Chapter 6 where I show you how to reupholster a wing fireside chair.

Replacing Rubber Webbing

Rubber webbing, which is used a great deal in modern upholstery, needs to be replaced after a few years. The better chairs have webbing straps with metal fixing clips which fit into slots in the seat rails. You can make up new pieces by buying rubber webbing and the end clips.

Before cutting off the lengths of webbing, you must allow for stretching to give a bit of tension. With webbing of average thickness, straps up to 30 cm (1 ft) long should be 25 mm (1 in) shorter than the distance between slots; straps over 60 cm (2 ft) should be shorter by 12 mm ($\frac{1}{2}$ in) for every 30 cm (1 ft). Make the straps a little longer than this if the webbing is particularly thick, a little shorter if it is very thin. The end clips must be very securely clamped on to the webbing. They should be squeezed in an engineer's metal working vice, then hammered down on a piece of thick iron plate so that the metal clip really grips the rubber. Narrow rubber webbing, such as is sometimes used in chair backs, can be fixed with large-headed tacks or by two lines of 10 mm ($\frac{3}{8}$ in) staples, driven in with a staple gun.

Transforming a Modern Chair

I must tell you about Brenda's chair because this shows how it is possible to take an unattractive piece of modern furniture and transform it into something good.

Brenda came for her second year to our class with a tale of woe: she had now reupholstered nearly everything in her flat and had nothing left to do; in her desperation she brought along a small, modern television or sewing chair, just a seat and back job, there it is in the picture (**fig. 54**). Well, she spent an evening stripping it down to the frame and then we got our heads together. Someone said, 'What about a buttoned back?' Then

Fig. 54 A small modern sewing or television chair

54(a) Before

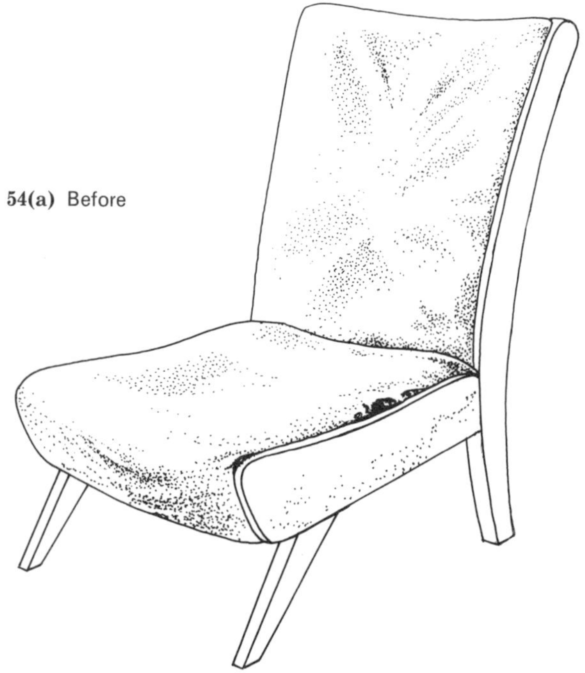

54(b) After

there was a suggestion from someone else about putting in a conventional coil spring seat instead of the unit that it had had before. 'A double-bordered seat?' said Brenda, with a glint in her eye. Then I remembered a pair of cabriole legs that had been lying about in my workshop for at least twenty years—when we tried them they were just the size. So off came the nasty, thin, splayed front legs, and on with the 'Queen Anne's'. These made a stronger job of the frame too, as they had square posts at the top which fitted inside the frame. These legs were well polished by Brenda, who was by now getting very enthusiastic. You can see in the illustration what a transformation she worked on this chair. The back has side scrolls built up with proper stitched edges. And the seat also is built up, with multiple rows of blind stitches and a roll edge. This proved to be a good practice piece for traditional upholstery methods. Covered in a strong, small-patterned cotton print and trimmed with a silken cord it has become a very desirable, expensive-looking sewing chair. I suppose that the lesson to be learnt here is, that we should not look with disdain on all modern furniture when it has reached its life's end, but should try to see what possibilities there are for transformation.

4 The Drop-In Seat

The drop-in seat is an entirely separate removable seat frame upholstered and fitted within the seat rails of a chair or stool. These seats, sometimes known as 'trapseats', are found in dining chairs, footstools, and larger stools such as dressing table and piano stools. This is the ideal task for the beginner. It is something that I like the students in the class that I teach to have for their first job, because it gives a gentle introduction to some of the basic skills of upholstery.

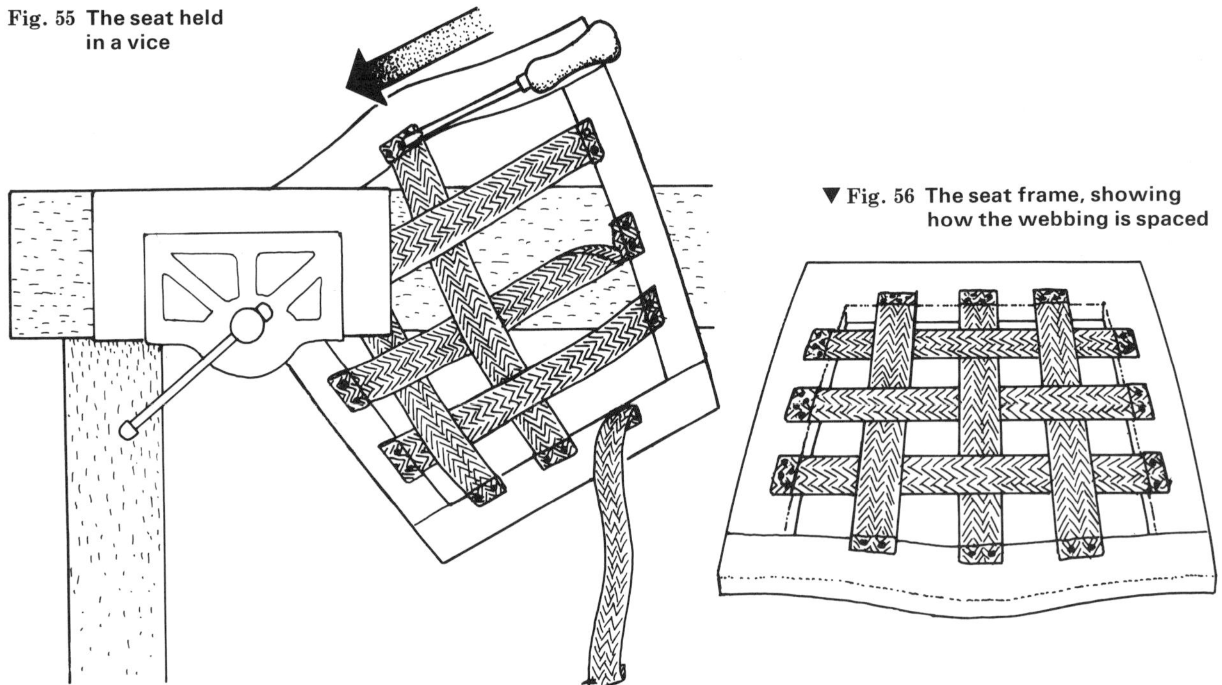

Fig. 55 The seat held in a vice

▼ Fig. 56 The seat frame, showing how the webbing is spaced

Measuring

And so to begin; measure the seat while the old covering and upholstery are still on. With your flexible steel measure take a reading over the seat from back to front. Allow plenty under the seat for turning, for you will be turning in and neatening off the material when you finally tack it down. Many loose seats are finished with a covering of hessian or lining over the underside; I always view these with suspicion and get the feeling that the upholsterer had something to hide. You, on the other hand, are going to be proud of your upholstery and leave to view the facts of good workmanship and best quality materials.

Ripping Off

For directions on ripping off, refer to Chapter 3 (page 28). Stripping a small item like this chair seat will be much easier if you can use a carpenter's vice to hold it as you work (**fig. 55**).

When the frame is bare, examine the joints to make sure they are sound and well glued. It can be very frustrating to get all the new webbing stretched on tightly only to find that the joints are giving way and the whole frame is in danger of coming apart. Test the joints by tapping inside the frame with a mallet to see if they will come apart, or try twisting the frame, for this will also show any give in the joints. There is one more test to do before proceeding further and that is to place the seat frame in the stool or chair to check on the fit. If you are using a thicker covering cloth you may have to plane off some wood to allow for this, or if the cover was originally poorly fitted you may have to glue on thin strips of wood to make up the gaps.

Webbing

Having just read the chapter on basic skills, you will be familiar with the methods of fixing and stretching webbing (pages 29–30). 'Yes, but how many pieces of webbing should I put on?' you ask. Well, webs should be no more than 50 mm (2 in) or the width of the webbing apart (**fig. 56**). An average-sized single chair seat takes three pieces from back to front and two or three pieces from side to side. A large carver chair may perhaps need four strips back to front and three across. Over the webbing is stretched 450 g (16 oz) tarpaulin hessian (**fig. 57**). For directions on fastening I refer you again to Chapter 3 (pages 31–32).

The Stuffing

To anchor the stuffing in place, stuffing ties in the form of large stitches (page 44) must be put into the hessian in lines across the seat (**fig. 58a**). These ties should be fairly taut.

For the best and most lasting results use a good quality horsehair stuffing. Tuck lines of stuffing under the ties, as in **fig. 58b**. If these lines of hair are placed evenly and are of uniform density and size, the even distribution of stuffing over the seat will be assured. The next step is to fill in between these lines of hair. Then tease over a further layer of hair to form a dome-shaped mass, as in **fig. 58c**.

The amount of stuffing required will depend upon the quality of the horsehair, as the shorter hair consolidates under hard pressure, while the better quality long, curled horsehair will stay risen and springy until confined by the undercovering. If you are doing a set of chairs it is a good idea to weigh out equal amounts of stuffing to get all the seats to the same size and shape.

The Undercovering

The next stage is to pull the mass of horsehair down to the desired shape by putting

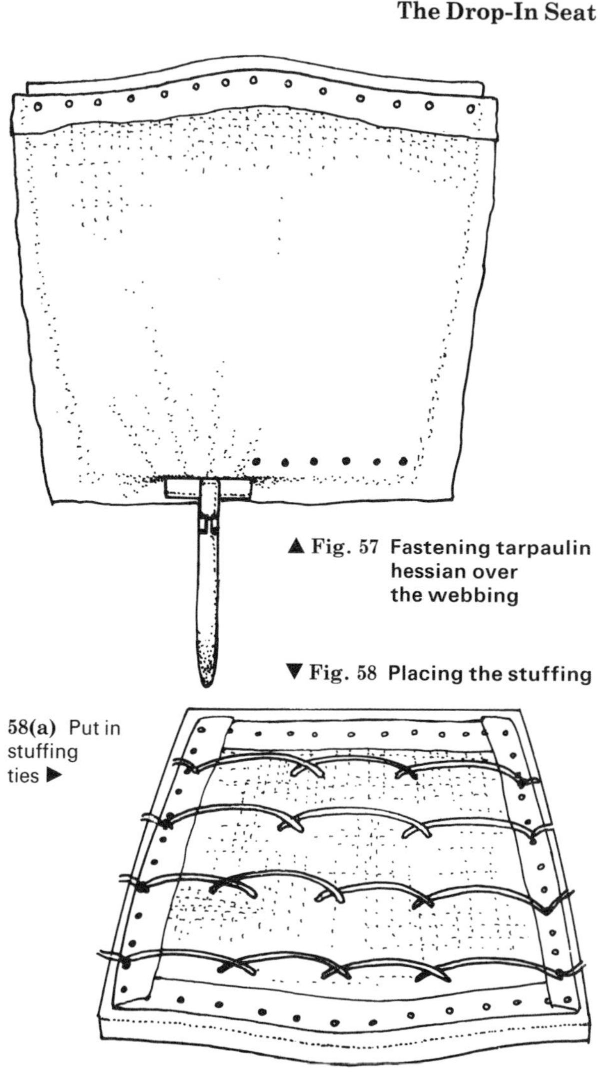

▲ Fig. 57 Fastening tarpaulin hessian over the webbing

▼ Fig. 58 Placing the stuffing

58(a) Put in stuffing ties ▶

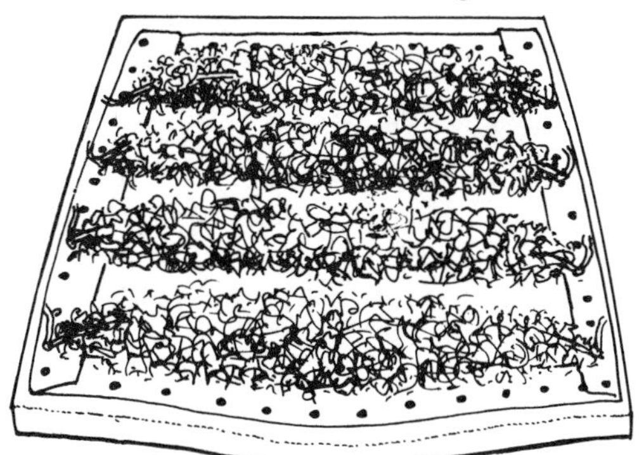

58(b) Tuck horsehair under the stuffing ties ▼

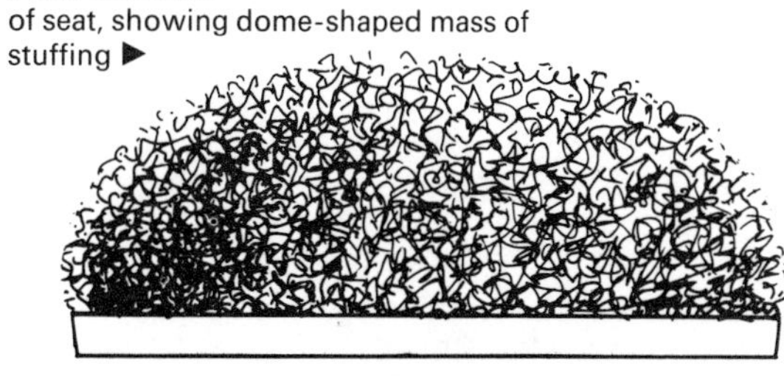

58(c) Front elevation of seat, showing dome-shaped mass of stuffing ▶

Fig. 59 Putting on an undercovering

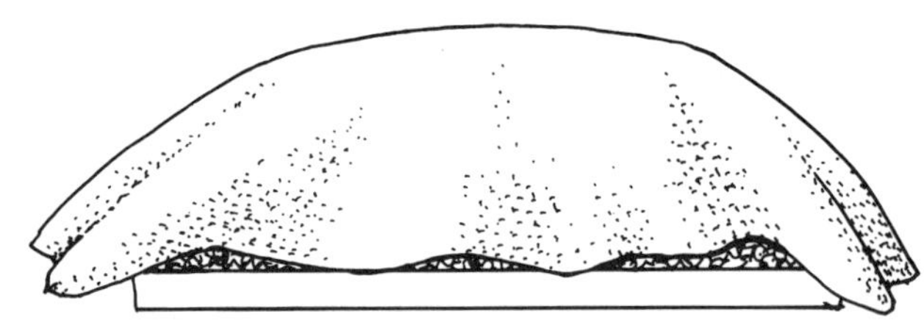

▲ **59(a)** Position the undercovering over the stuffing

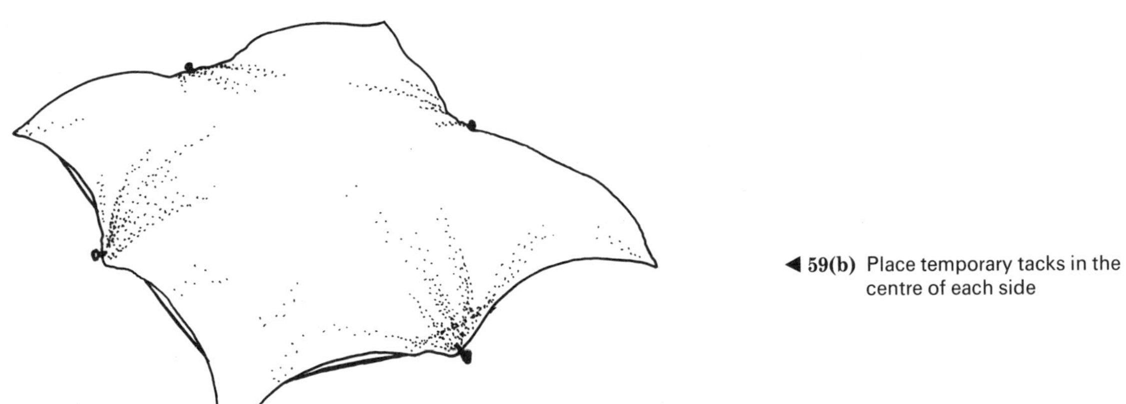

◀ **59(b)** Place temporary tacks in the centre of each side

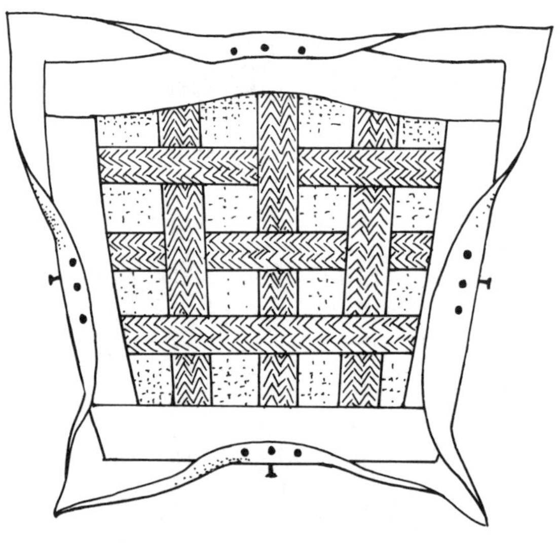

▲ **59(c)** Temporarily tack the undercovering to the underside of the seat rails

on an undercover. Some upholsterers, for reasons of economy and speed, use no undercoverings at all, but with you speed is not so important as quality of workmanship; and, when you consider the high cost of the covering material, it is as well to employ methods that will prolong the life of the fabric. And that is just what an undercover will do—as all the strain of containing the filling and securing the basic shape is taken by a simple, strong but cheap woven fabric. I use a good unbleached calico for undercoverings. Roughly measure the size required and tear off the fabric. Make a small snip and then rip across; the calico will tear along a thread and your piece will be nice and square.

Fig. 59 shows you how to put on the undercover. At **(a)** we see the calico lying loosely over the hair, having been positioned so that there is an equal amount of material hanging down each side. Drive in four temporary tacks—12 mm ($\frac{1}{2}$ in) fine tacks—just far enough to hold, in the centre of each side **(b)**. Turn and hold the seat with its back edge on

▼ **59(d)** Temporarily tack the corners

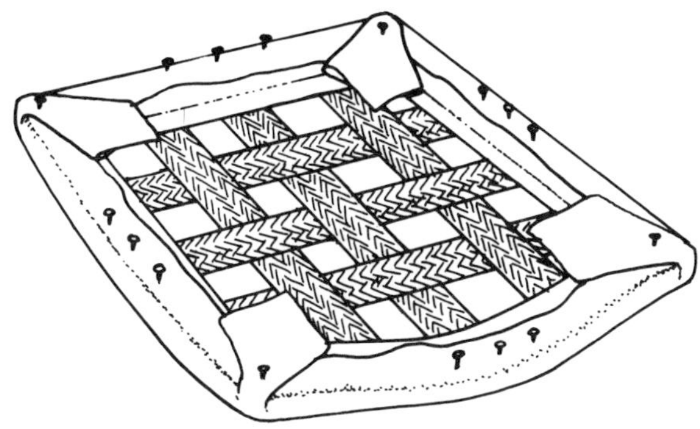

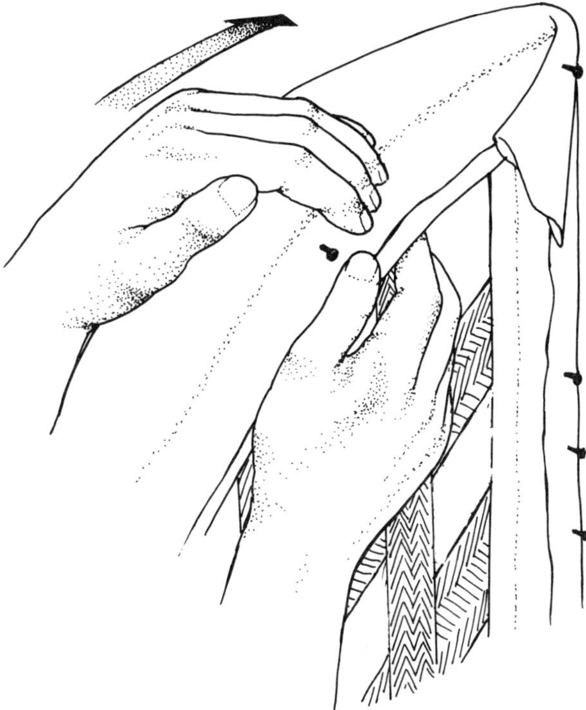

59(e) Stretch and smooth the undercovering ▲▼

the bench and, (if you are right-handed), the left edge towards you. Put three temporary tacks in the centre of the underside of each rail (**c**). Then remove the first temporary tacks. This temporary tacking is very important, allowing you to adjust and position the covering before permanently fixing it. Gently stretch the calico at the corners, pulling diagonally and placing temporary tacks as shown in (**d**). The diagonal stretching at each corner gives tension along all four sides and you can see that it immediately gives the whole seat an even, domed appearance. Keep a constant eye upon the line of threads in the centre of the calico, so that they remain straight from back to front and from side to side. Any deviation indicates that you are stretching too far on one side or the other.

Still holding the seat on its edge, take out the three temporary tacks in the centre of the front edge. Tuck back any hair that has worked over the edge of the wood. Stretch the cloth as in (**e**). If you are right-handed, pull the cloth with your right hand, using your

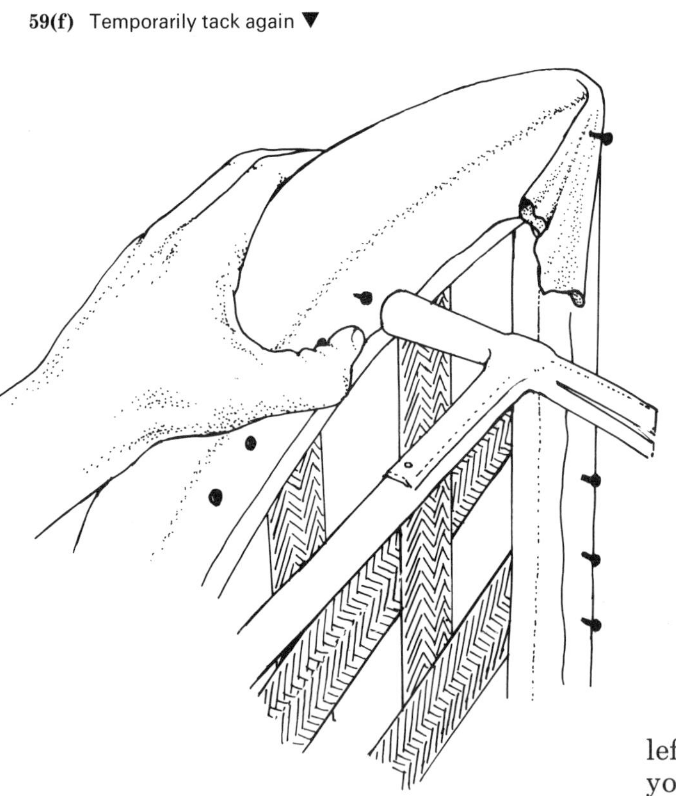

59(f) Temporarily tack again ▼

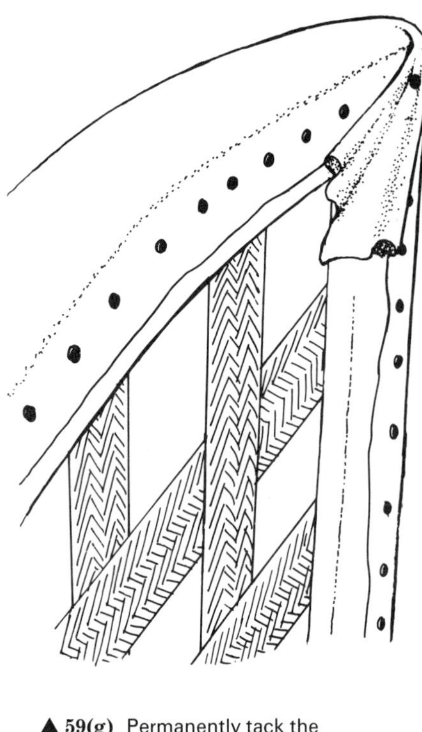

▲ **59(g)** Permanently tack the corners

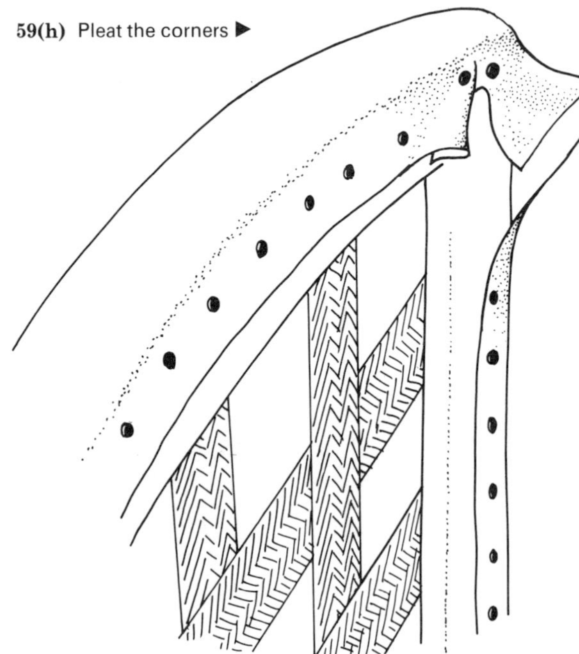

59(h) Pleat the corners ▶

left to smooth and compress the stuffing. As you adjust the cloth, put in temporary tacks again. Stretch the cover and place a tack in the centre and then, work away from yourself, by smoothing and stretching the fabric with your left hand along the front of the seat. This action takes up any fullness and eliminates 'tack marks'—lines which run from the tack, making a small groove over the seat. These will appear if the fabric is pulled very tightly at the point where it is held by the tack while remaining looser between tacks. A couple of strokes, then smooth and stretch from back to front, with your right hand still holding the edge of the cloth. Do not pull—merely anchor the material and take up any slack brought over by the smoothing and stretching.

On the last stroke of your left hand, bring your thumb over and use it to hold the cloth while the right hand picks up the tack and hammer to secure it temporarily (**f**). Repeat this procedure on the other three sides of the seat to a point 70 mm ($2\frac{3}{4}$ in) from the corners.

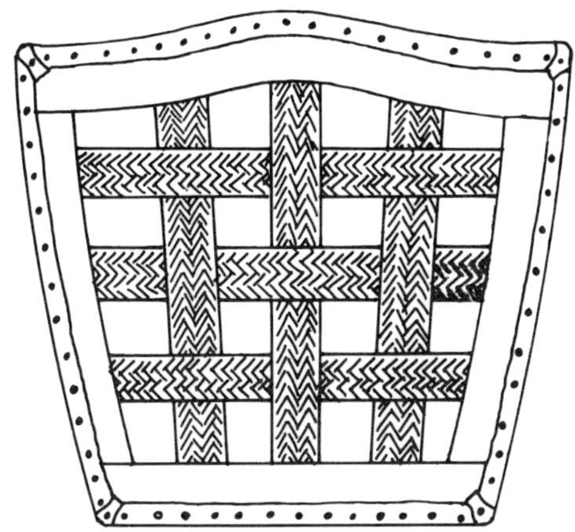

◀ **59(i)** Permanently fix the undercovering

Pull down the corners again (**g**), and this time drive a tack right home in the position shown.

Continue the stretching process right up to the corners, pleating in the corners neatly as in (**h**). Now permanently tack with 10 mm ($\frac{3}{8}$ in) fine tacks all round the seat as in (**i**), keeping within 12 mm ($\frac{1}{2}$ in) of the outside edge. Remove the temporary tacks and trim off surplus calico.

Your seat should now have assumed a good, even, fairly firm shape. But note how the horsehair is working through the weave of the cloth. Hair will work through almost any cloth except the hairproof ticking used for mattresses. So we must arrest its progress with something that it cannot penetrate—cotton wool, cotton felt or wadding.

Cut off two layers of wadding for extra security and lay it on top of the undercover. Trim the wadding around the edges as in (**j**), so that none will extend over the sides—remember that the seat has to fit into the chair frame.

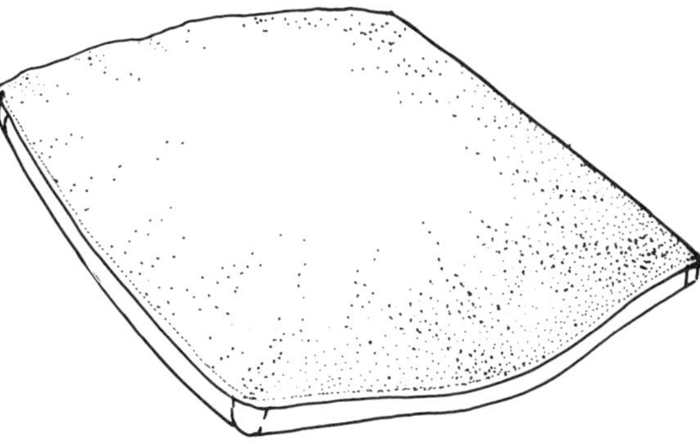

▲ **59(j)** Place cotton wadding over the undercovering

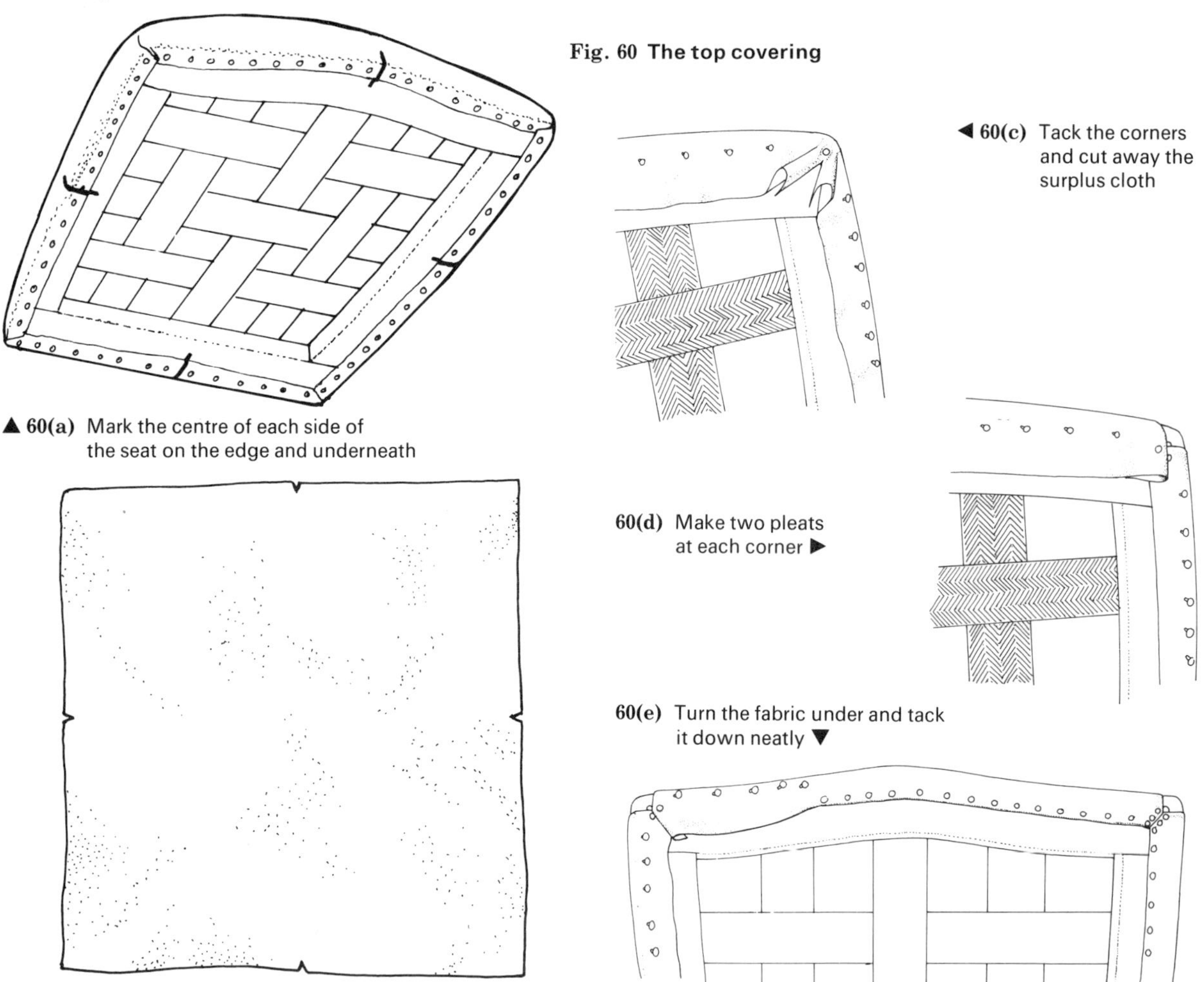

Fig. 60 The top covering

▲ 60(a) Mark the centre of each side of the seat on the edge and underneath

▲ 60(b) Mark the centre of each side of the covering material with a small V

◀ 60(c) Tack the corners and cut away the surplus cloth

60(d) Make two pleats at each corner ▶

60(e) Turn the fabric under and tack it down neatly ▼

The Top Covering

Now we come to the final stage—putting on the furnishing fabric (**fig. 60**). Mark the centre of each side of the seat on the edge and underneath with a soft pencil (**a**). Measure the length and width of the seat, measuring the width at the front, where the seat is widest. Allow a turning of 38 mm ($1\frac{1}{2}$ in) all round. Refer to Chapter 3 (pages 27–28) for directions on cutting the fabric. When you have cut the piece of cloth to size find the centre of each side by folding the cloth in half, first lengthways and then widthways, and nicking the corner of the fold so that a small V is made in the exact centre (**b**).

Lay the cloth over the seat and adjust the position until you are satisfied that the marks on the frame correspond with the V cut in the cloth. If, because of the shape of your seat, the marks on the sides do not meet when the cloth is adjusted properly, make sure that they are the same distance apart on each side. Temporarily tack, just as you did with the undercover, but this time you must take even more care to keep the weave straight back to front and side to side.

The corners must be neatly pleated. Permanently fix a tack in each corner, then cut away the surplus material in the form of a square up to the tack (**c**). You can see at (**d**) how the two pleats on one of the corners are made. These can be permanently fixed as shown. Finally, turn the material under and tack it down neatly all round (**e**).

POST-WAR LOOSE SEATS

Many of the cheaper dining chairs made in the 1950–60s had no webbing in the seats but just a piece of plywood or even hardboard nailed on the frame. The stuffing was either made of cotton wool felt or polyether (polyurethane) foam. This early foam was very

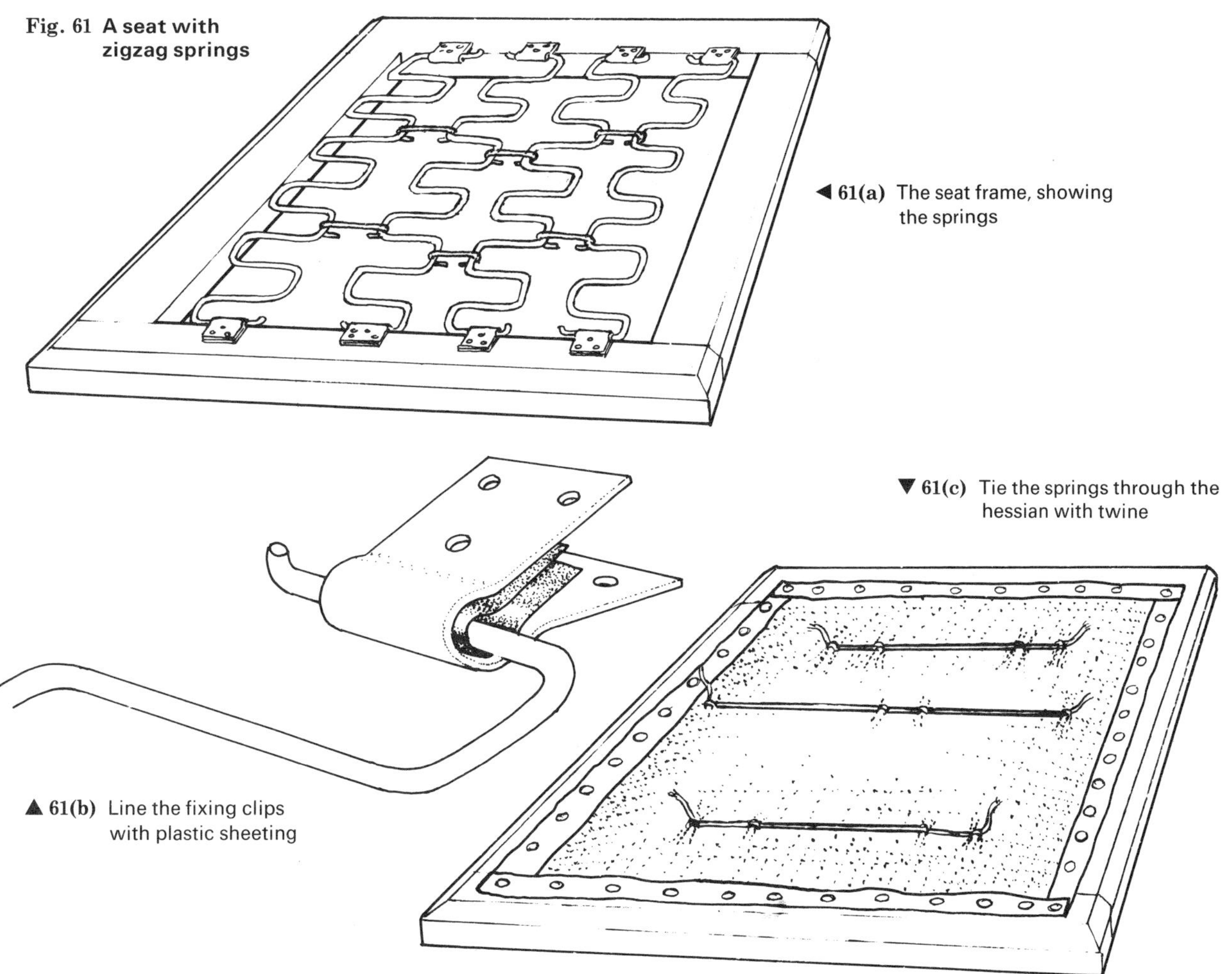

Fig. 61 A seat with zigzag springs

◀ 61(a) The seat frame, showing the springs

▲ 61(b) Line the fixing clips with plastic sheeting

▼ 61(c) Tie the springs through the hessian with twine

unstable and after a year or two would disintegrate into a powder or sticky granules (the modern equivalent, however, is very long-lasting). If the frame of this type of seat is robust, you can remove the plywood board and reupholster it with webbing as described in Chapter 3 (pages 29–31), but if the seat frame relies upon the plyboard for strength, and you want a comfortable seat then perhaps you should consider making up new stouter frames.

SEATS WITH ZIGZAG SPRINGS

Many modern seats have springs of the zigzag strip kind, sometimes called ripple wire springs (**fig. 61a**). Very little can go wrong with these springs so long as they remain linked together laterally. Wire links or small tension springs are used for this purpose. However, these do sometimes get noisy after a year or two and squeak when the chair is sat on. So, when reupholstering, remove the springs and line the fixing clips with a material such as a thick leathercloth or plastic sheeting (**b**).

These seats are very simple to upholster. Just cover the zigzag springs with stout tarpaulin hessian stretched over fairly tightly and tacked in the usual manner—the springs should be tied through at several points along their length (**c**). On top of the hessian place a layer of thick cotton felt and secure it with a few through ties of twine. Then add a layer of 25 mm (1 in) thick polyether foam to make a very comfortable seat.

To cut the foam, lay the seat on top of the foam sheet and cut round it with a very sharp knife, keeping about 10 mm ($\frac{3}{8}$ in) outside the frame. With some shears or scissors, chamfer the top edges of the foam and then cover it with a calico undercover as described on pages 56–59.

Fig. 62 A drop-in seat with coil springs

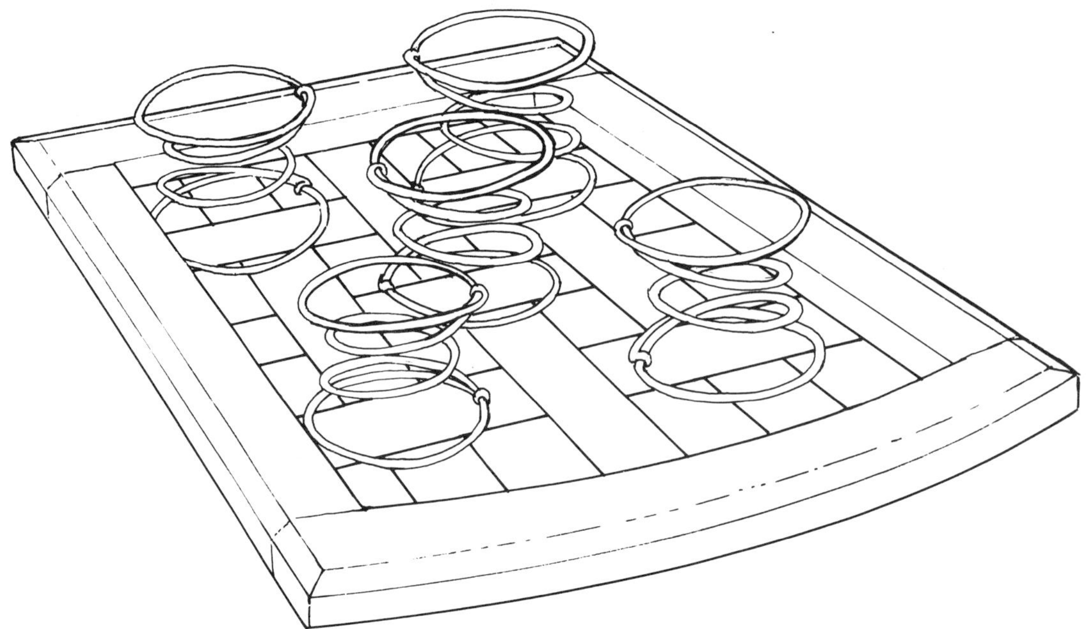

▲ **62(a)** The five springs in position

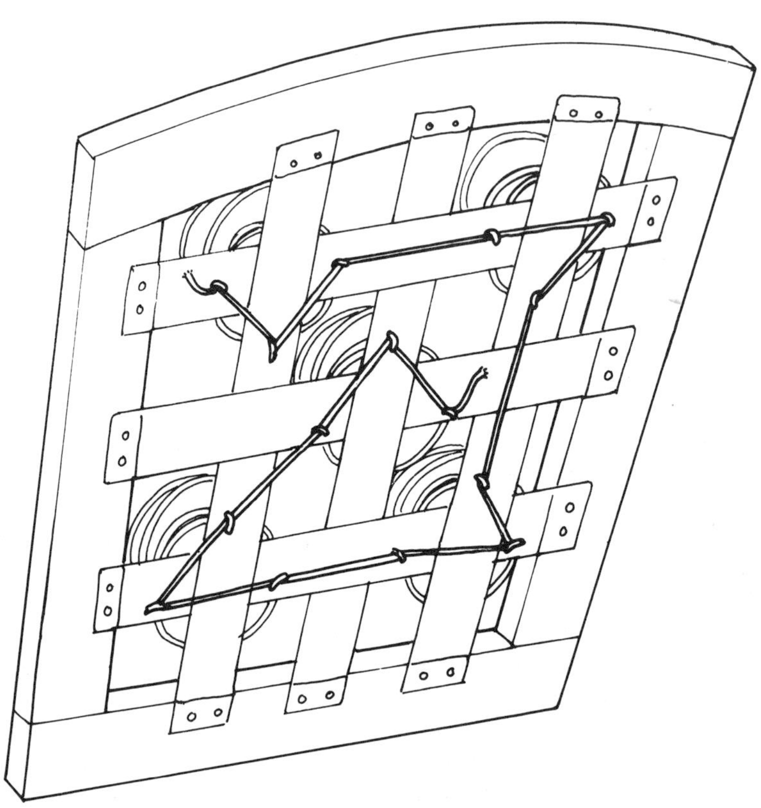

62(b) Fasten the springs to the webbing

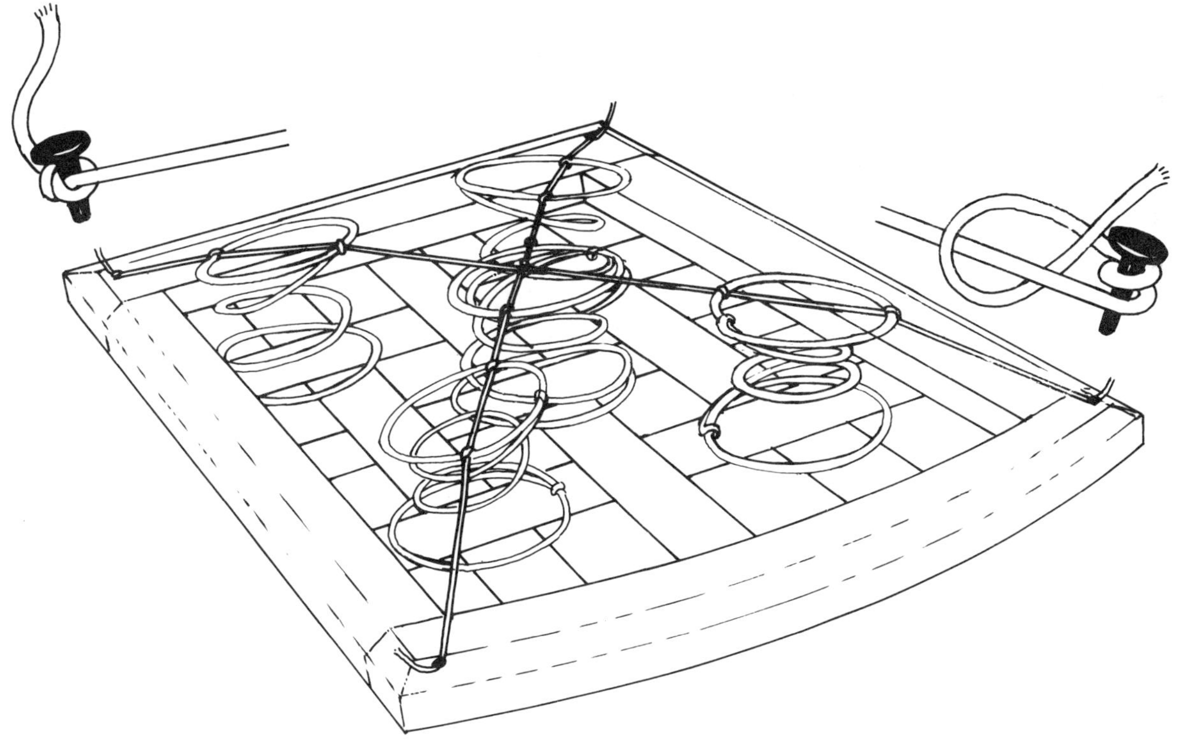

62(c) Lace the springs with two diagonal ties

DROP-IN SEATS WITH COIL SPRINGS

Some good class dining chairs made before the Second World War had small coil springs in the loose seats (**fig. 62**). The springs are usually four or five in number, about 75 to 100 mm (4 to 5 in) high and gauge 12. When working on a chair of this type, you can either dispense with the springs and re-upholster it as just described, or re-make it as a spring seat. The springs will need renewing. Place the webbing under the frame and tie the springs to the webbing at the usual three points on each spring base (page 37). If there are five springs, place the first in the centre and fasten it. Then sew on the other springs mid-way between the frame and the centre spring to form a square round it (**a**) and (**b**). If only four springs are used these are placed in the form of a square but closer together in the centre of the seat. Pull the springs down well with laid cord using two diagonal ties (**c**). Again, I refer you to Chapter 3, pages 37–38, but note that the cord is knotted on the top coils of all the outside springs with these seats and not on the second coil down as previously described. Because the springs are very short there will be little or no distortion at the centre waist of the springs. When you have finished lacing, the centre spring should be no more than 75 mm (3 in) high.

Stretch 450 g (16 oz) tarpaulin hessian over the springs and tack it down in the same way as you did with your loose seat. Then, with stout twine, stitch the tops of the springs to the hessian in the same way as you fixed the bottoms of the springs—so that they are attached at three points round the top coil, secured by a single knot on each stitch (**c**).

From this point, the procedure is the same as for a seat without springs, except that when you have finished you will need to cover the underside with hessian or lining to hide the webbing and make a neat finish.

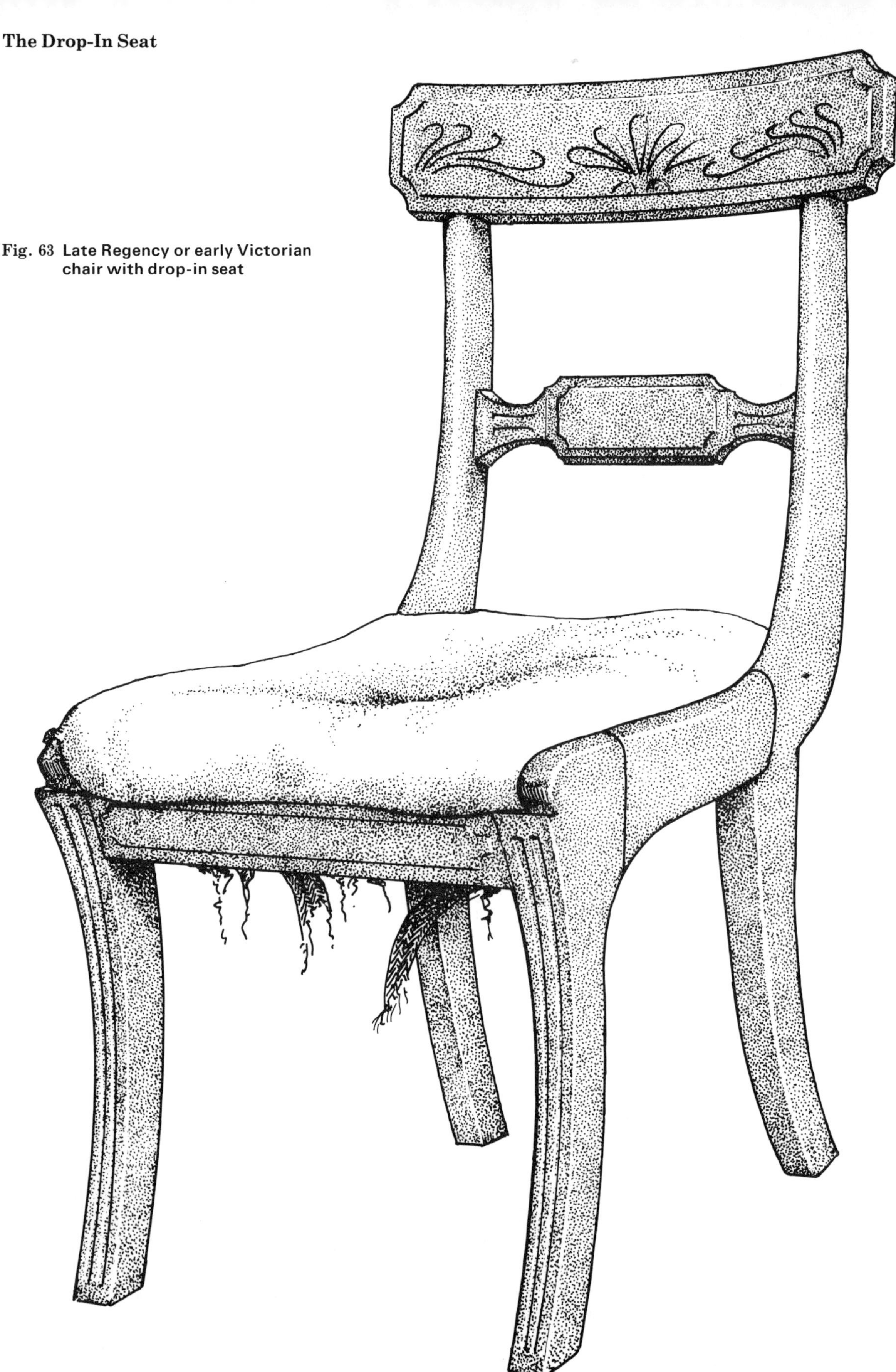

Fig. 63 Late Regency or early Victorian chair with drop-in seat

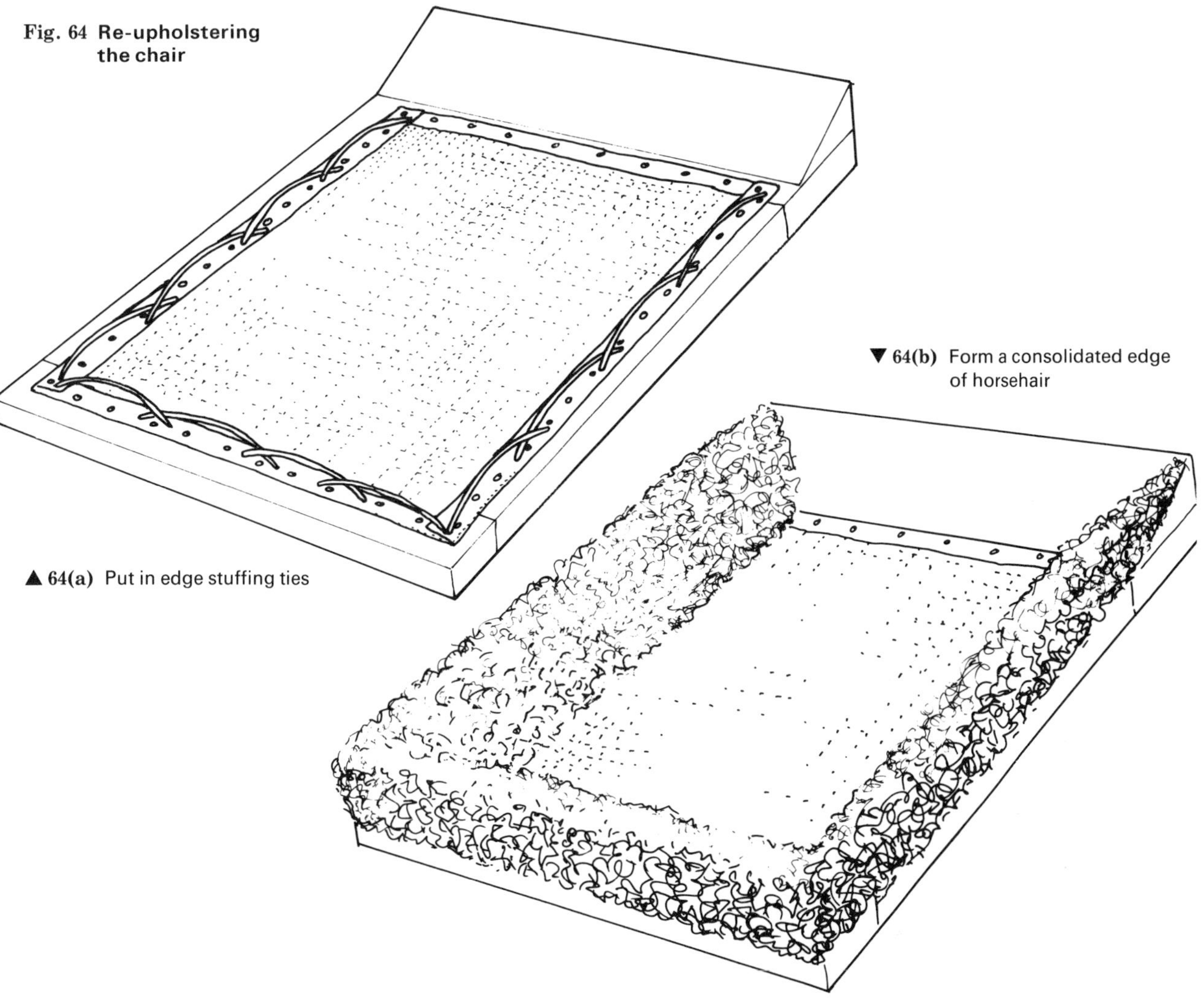

Fig. 64 Re-upholstering the chair

▲ **64(a)** Put in edge stuffing ties

▼ **64(b)** Form a consolidated edge of horsehair

REGENCY AND EARLY VICTORIAN LOOSE SEATS

There is one more form of loose seat that I would like to mention—the type found on dining chairs of the Regency, William IV and early Victorian periods. The seats fit between raised side rails and are prevented from slipping forward on the chair seat frame by a peg which protrudes from the centre of the front rail of the chair and fits into a corresponding hole in the frame of the loose seat. These seats are a little more complicated to upholster, as the front and sides are built up with stitched edges.

Let us examine a typical example (**fig. 63**), one which looks as if the seat is about to fall through. The black shiny material with which it is covered—probably the original covering—is made of horsehair interwoven with cotton or linen and is called hair seating. This is a very strong, durable material and is, I believe, still made to this day.

The job is quite straightforward at the start—you can call on your previous experience to take you to the stage where you cover the new webbing with tarpaulin hessian. Once you have done that, the next step is to put some stuffing ties in with your large circular needle along the two sides and the front, approximately 20 mm ($\frac{3}{4}$ in) from the front edge (**fig. 64a**). These ties are to hold and retain the roll of horsehair which will form the core of your edges. On some seats you will find that the back has already been built up to edge height with a triangular section piece of wood; if this is not present, put in stuffing ties along the back edge also.

Now tuck horsehair under the stuffing ties to form a dense roll (**b**). Then fill the centre of the seat with hair to just over the height of

▼ **64(c)** Fasten the first stuffing covering

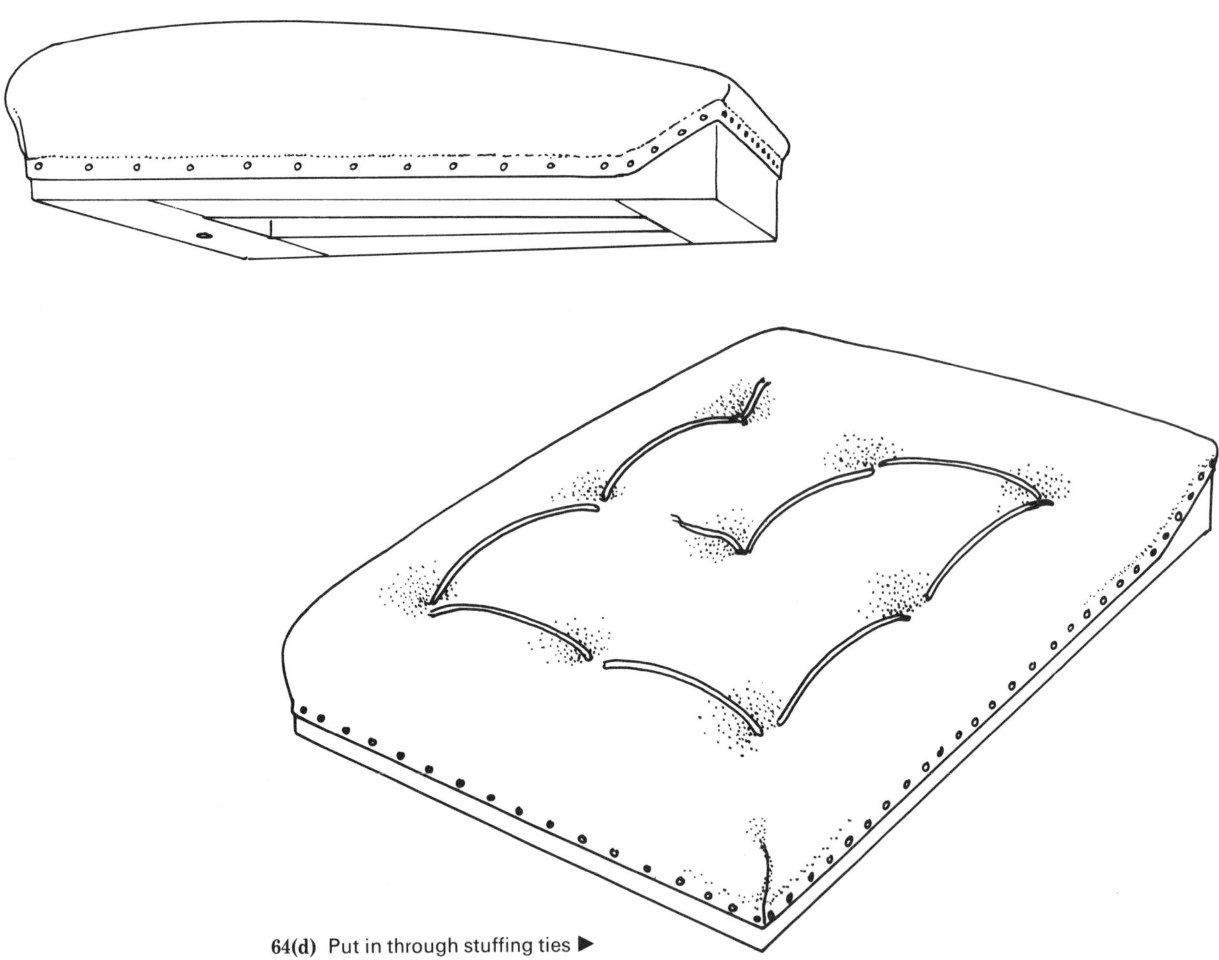

64(d) Put in through stuffing ties ▶

the edges. Tack on the first stuffing covering of scrim hessian (**c**). Hold on, you say, what height does this edge and seat need to be? If you place the loose frame in the chair seat, the raised side rails will give a good indication of the thickness of the seat needed because the finished height should be just above these rails. And if there is a wooden raised edge at the back of the seat frame, this will also show the intended height.

The method of covering the first stuffing is as follows. Measure and cut off a piece of scrim hessian large enough to cover the seat. Mark the centres of each side of the seat frame and the centres of the four sides of the hessian and temporarily tack the hessian, matching the marks just as you did when covering the other loose seat. There is usually a small chamfer along the top edges of the frame—if there is not, it is a good idea to make one with a plane or rasp—and it is along this chamfer that the line of permanent tacks is placed. Use 10 mm ($\frac{3}{8}$ in) tacks and place them about 20 mm ($\frac{3}{4}$ in) apart. Start in the centre of the back and when you are tacking the front and the back follow a thread of the hessian with the row of tacks. Slight adjustments must be made at the corners, a thread or two being taken up here. Do not try to follow a thread when tacking along the sides—the seat is narrower at the back. The front edge should overhang the frame by about 15 mm ($\frac{5}{8}$ in) (**c**). The sides should also overhang, but to a smaller degree. Remember, the seat must fit between the side rails of the chair. Use your regulator at this stage to adjust the stuffing beneath the hessian and manipulate the corners into sharp, square shapes.

When your first stuffing is adjusted and

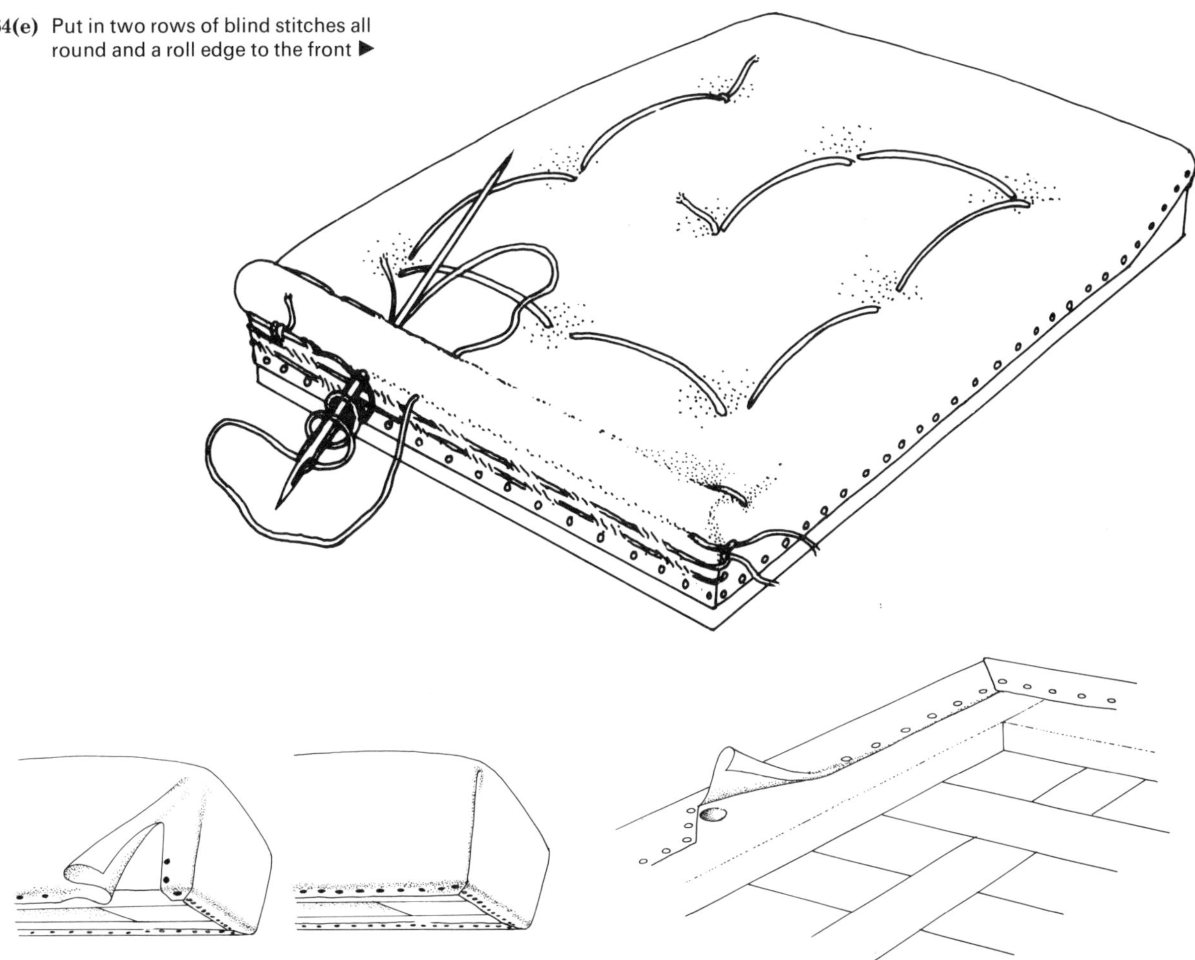

64(e) Put in two rows of blind stitches all round and a roll edge to the front ▶

▲ **64(f)** Pleat the material neatly at the corners

▲ **64(g)** Cut away the fabric to leave the peg hole uncovered

regulated so that all the edges are straight and true, put in the through stuffing ties (**d**), this time going right through the seat and anchoring the scrim hessian to the webbing and hessian beneath. Using an upholstery gauge and a felt tip pen, mark a rectangle 100 mm (4 in) from the seat edges. Put in your through ties with stout **No. 1** twine, starting at a back corner and finishing in the centre (pages 46–47).

Follow the procedure for edge stitching outlined in Chapter 3 (pages 47–49) putting in two rows of blind stitches all round but making a rolled edge to the front only (**e**).

On a seat like this, roll edges are not needed on the sides as the side edges are protected within the confines of the chair rails. If you have a carpenter's vice you can use it to hold the chair seat while you work. But this aid is not essential.

Put on the top stuffing, undercover, wadding and covering fabric in exactly the same way as you did on the dining chair seat—with the exception of the corner pleats, which on this seat must be single. At (**f**), you can see exactly how they are made. The material is pulled diagonally towards the corner and fixed at the front with two tacks. The surplus material is then cut away up to the tacks and the pleat is folded neatly and squarely up to the corner. With some materials, the pleat may be sewn up to make an even neater job, using the ladder stitch described on pages 40–41.

There is one final point. When you are neatly turning in and finishing off the material under the seat, do not forget to leave the hole for the peg uncovered. At (**g**), you can see how to cut the fabric in a V up to the hole.

5 The Stuffed-Over Seat

The term 'stuffed-over' is used to describe an upholstered chair seat which is built permanently on to the chair frame. The covering is stretched over the seat and either fixed along the sides up to facings or beads of wood or turned under and fixed beneath the seat rails.

This is a good task for a beginner as upholstering the stuffed-over seat of a dining chair is a job small enough to undertake even if work space is limited or time is at a premium; yet it includes almost all the basic tasks of traditional upholstery. I have noticed with students that after completing a stuffed-over dining chair seat, if they have achieved a good standard of craftsmanship, they begin to sail through more complicated jobs.

In our class there are two students who have, during most of one term, specialized in the dining chair stuffed-over seat and have achieved near perfection. Michael and Paul, working slowly and very painstakingly, have produced work that looks quite professional and each has put his own interpretation into the shaping.

Michael's dining chair seats have a classical, late eighteenth century look with vertical stitched edges and just a slight dome to the top. Paul, on the other hand, has interpreted his seats in the early twentieth century way, with the edges shallower and extending well out from the frame. These examples show that there is a lot of scope, even with a small upholstery task like this stuffed-over seat, for you to put your own stamp on the work.

Preparation

There is such variety among the shapes, sizes and types of stuffed-over seats, but we shall begin with a simple, straight-edged dining chair seat like the Regency chair in **fig. 65**. The seat of this chair looks quite hollow—it has reached a stage where it might collapse and fall through at any moment. Take off the old upholstery in the usual way with the ripping chisel and mallet (page 28). If you find it difficult to remove the tacks, and especially if it is a rather precious chair, use pliers and pincers. There are no springs in this seat, so the webbing goes on top of the rails. You know all about webbing up (pages 29–31), but as this chair has a fairly wide seat I would advise putting four pieces of webbing each way. Fasten tarpaulin hessian over the webbing.

Stuffing and Covering

Now we come to the first stuffing. No doubt, you will have removed the old first stuffing with the stitched edges still intact, and, you say, 'Couldn't we just put this back?'. Edges which have remained in good shape can be saved and put on again, provided they are well vacuum cleaned, then covered with hessian and stitched again. But I would rather you made up a new edge for your chair. Seeing a job right through is the only way to learn.

Put in the stuffing ties about 25 mm (1 in) from the edge of the frame all the way round (**fig. 66**). Then tuck and shape the horsehair under these ties to make a wall of stuffing on all four sides. I would advise you to make this wall about 10 mm ($\frac{3}{8}$ in) higher than you intend the edge to finish, and to extend it out so that it overhangs the rails by about 20 mm ($\frac{3}{4}$ in); however, this is a matter for your own interpretation. Fill up the centre of the seat with hair to form a domed shape (pages 44 and 55).

To cover this first stuffing you can use scrim or 280 g (10 oz) hessian. I like to use scrim as it is stronger and more manageable. Measure and cut off a piece, allowing 25 mm (1 in) all round for turnings. Mark the centres of the front and back of the scrim and also the centres of the front and back rails of the chair. Lay the scrim over the stuffing and

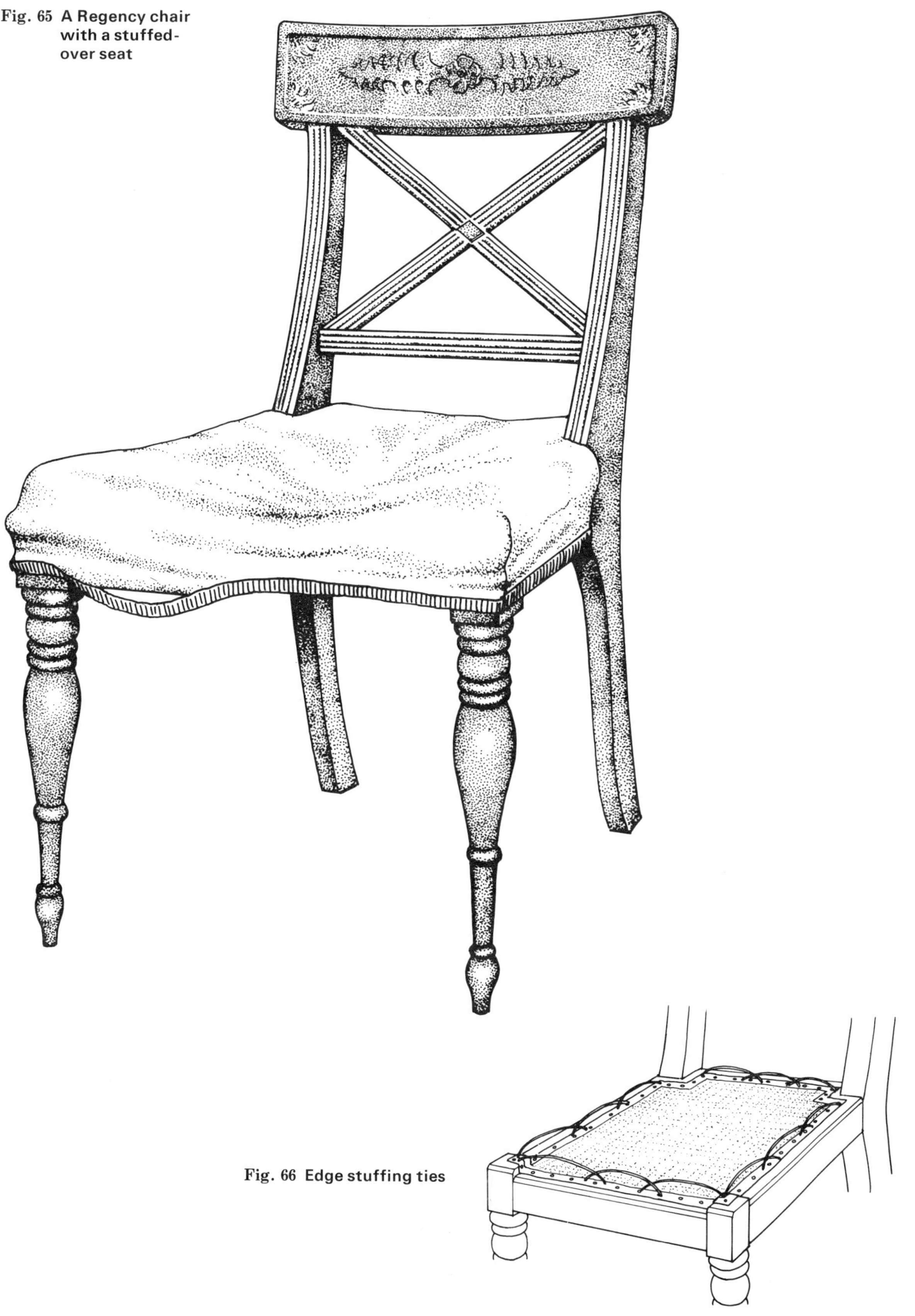

Fig. 65 A Regency chair with a stuffed-over seat

Fig. 66 Edge stuffing ties

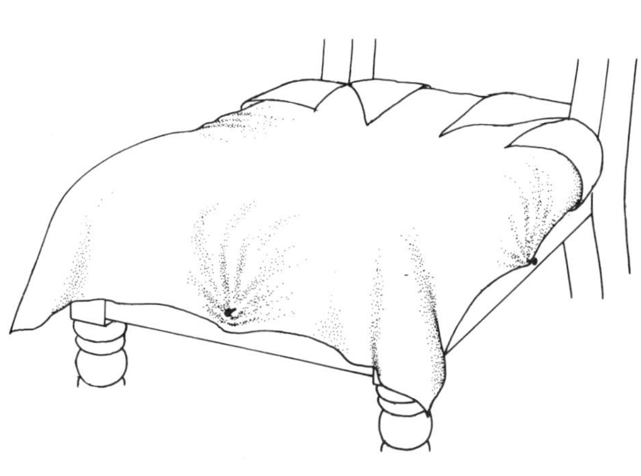

Fig. 67 The hessian cut away from the back upright ▼

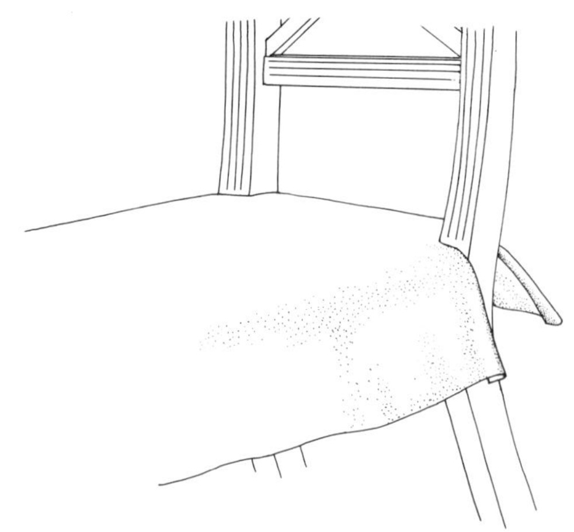

Fig. 68 The surplus to be cut off at the corners ▼

Fig. 69 Through stuffing ties placed ▶

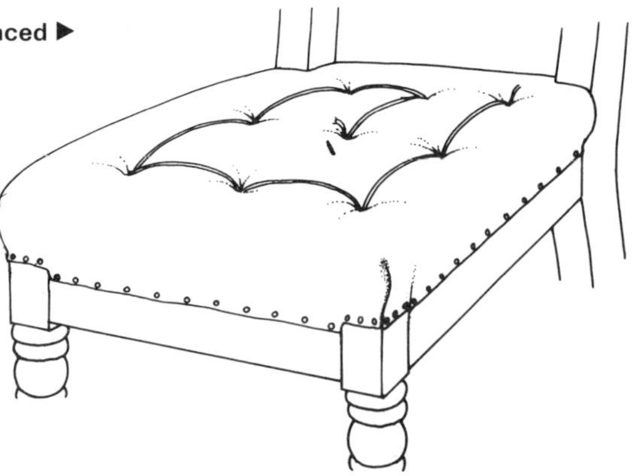

position it at the front and back marks with temporary tacks.

After making sure that the threads of the scrim are straight, lay back the two back corners as shown in **fig. 67** and cut from the corner of the scrim to within 10 mm ($\frac{3}{8}$ in) of the back upright. Turn over the scrim, cut off the surplus and, using the regulator, tuck in the remainder (**fig. 68**). Put in temporary tacks all the way round the seat, adjusting until you are satisfied with the shape. Then turn in the scrim and fasten it permanently along the tacking chamfer on the edge of the frame, placing the tacks no more than 20 mm ($\frac{3}{4}$ in) apart. Work to the weave when fixing the back and front so as to keep the edges uniform in height and the back and the front of the seat parallel. Because of the domed shape of the seat top you will have to take up a thread or two near the back uprights and also at the front corners.

Put in through stuffing ties to pull down the centre of the seat and hold the filling in place (**fig. 69**). Now stitch the edge, following the procedure laid down in Chapter 3 (pages 47–49). Two blind rows are needed on the two sides and the front; one blind row of stitches is usually sufficient at the back. When you come to put in the through stitches to form the roll edge, begin with the front edge—and do not forget the single stitch at the right-hand corner. After you have stitched the front, continue on the right side as far as the back upright, then stitch the left side, doing the back last.

Next, put in lines of stuffing ties for the top

Fig. 70 Placing the top stuffing ▼

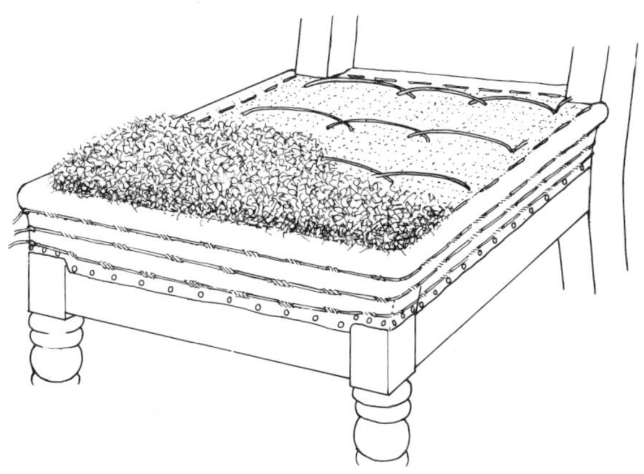

Fig. 71 Cardboard stiffener fitted at a corner ▼

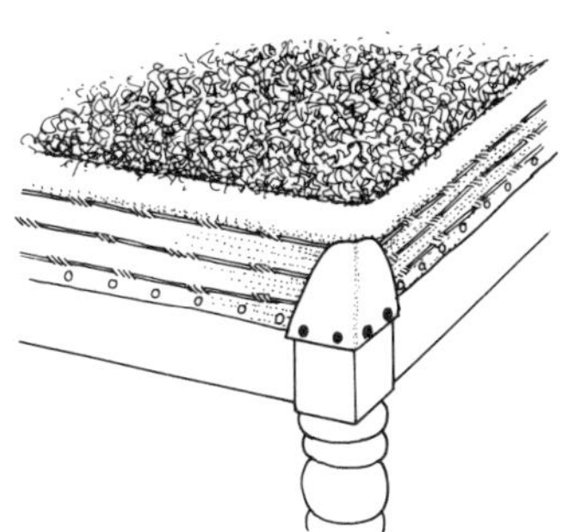

▼ Fig. 72 An undercovering of calico

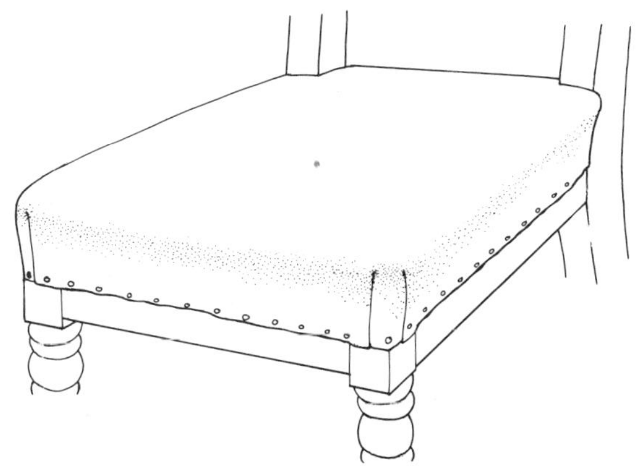

▼ Fig. 73 Surplus fabric to be cut away from the back upright

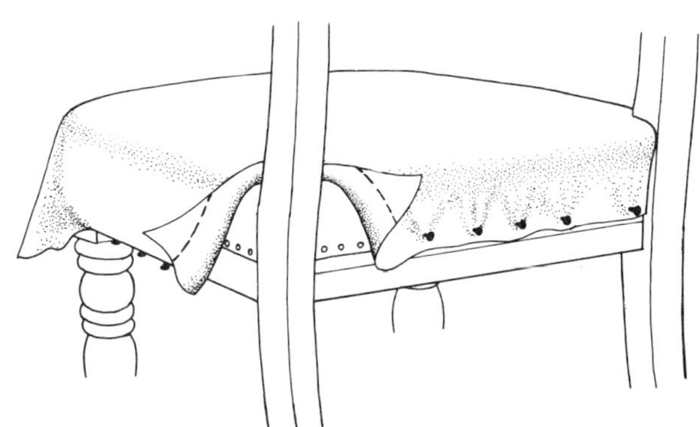

stuffing and pack stuffing under them. In **fig. 70** notice how the filling 'feathers' off at the roll of the edge. It is very important that no hair is left hanging over the rolled edge.

To keep the front corners in good shape and to give support to the covering material and in particular to the corner pleats, it is as well to cut and fit some stiffeners (from medium thickness cardboard) and tack them around the corners as shown in **fig. 71**.

The next step is to fasten on an undercovering of calico, to pull down and contain the top stuffing, bringing the seat to its finished shape (pages 55–57). The calico should be fixed to the sides of the rails, with no turnings (**fig. 72**). Put one or two layers of cotton wadding over the top of the undercovering, to prevent the hair penetrating and also to insulate the two covers and give a little extra richness to the feel of the seat.

Now, there are one or two points to note when you come to put on the top cover. Firstly, when you have marked the centres of the back and front of the cloth, positioned it and temporarily fastened it with three or four tacks on each side, cut the two corners into the back uprights as you did with the scrim covering, up to within 6 mm ($\frac{1}{4}$ in) of the wood (**fig. 73**). Take care when you are cutting off surplus material, lay the material in to see just how much you can cut away, then tuck and turn it in to the back uprights. Stretch these turnings down and temporarily tack them.

The second point relates to the front corners. In my opinion these always look best

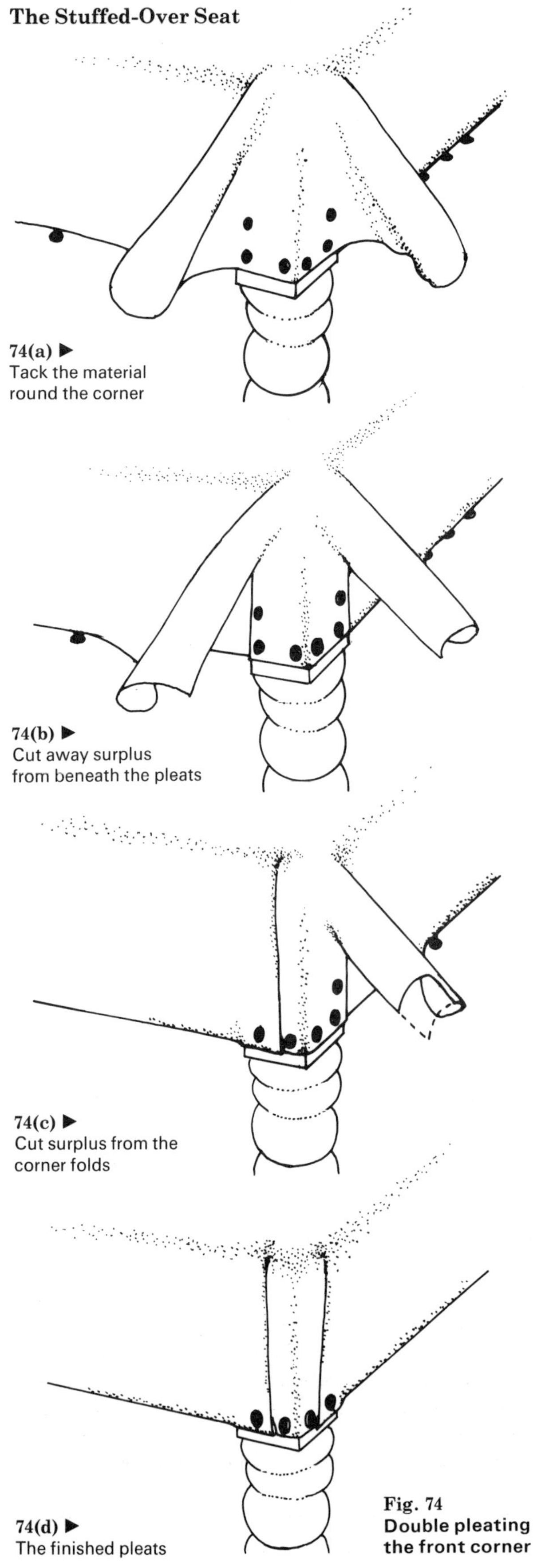

74(a) ▶ Tack the material round the corner

74(b) ▶ Cut away surplus from beneath the pleats

74(c) ▶ Cut surplus from the corner folds

74(d) ▶ The finished pleats

Fig. 74 **Double pleating the front corner**

when they are double pleated (except where the corner has been made sharp and square). The drawings in **fig. 74** show you how this is done. Stretch and tack the corner of the material in the centre of the seat corner, positioning the covering so that there is equal fullness on each side of the centre of the corner. Tighten and tack the material round the corner, but making sure the tacks are far enough away from the corner to be obscured by the pleats (**a**). Cut away surplus material up to these tacks to eliminate bulk beneath the pleats (**b**).

Fold in the pleats and, holding each one down with the point of your regulator, note where the double fold comes at the bottom; cut off any remaining surplus material there is here, so as to keep the material as close and flat as possible—you do not want any lumpiness that would ruin the evenness of the line of the trimming (**c**).

Finally, fasten down the fold of each pleat with tacks, then tuck and press the folds with the flat end of your regulator (**d**). For a very sharp, square corner, however, a single-fold pleat is best. The pictures in **fig. 75** show you how to make a single pleat.

Put one temporary tack to the side of the corner, making sure that the threads of the weave of the material are vertical. Cut the material at the angle shown in (**a**) so that it can be taken under the seat rail and neatly folded at the junction of the side rail and the front leg. Temporarily tack the fabric here. Cut off the surplus material (**b**).

Fold the fabric under, bring it round the leg corner and fasten it with two tacks on the front of the leg top, placing the tacks at least 20 mm ($\frac{3}{4}$ in) in from the corner so that they will be obscured by the pleat (**c**). Cut off surplus material, as shown in (**d**).

Fold in the pleat so that its edge comes right up to the corner. Hold this down with the point of your regulator and cut off the surplus material from the double thickness at the bottom of the pleat, and also cut up to the junction of the front rail and the leg (**e**).

Lastly, fasten the pleat with two tacks, as shown in (**f**). For extra neatness, these single pleats may be sewn up with very small ladder stitches. Begin sewing from the top of the pleat, making sure that you hide the starting knot inside the fold.

Fig. 75 **A single-fold pleat for a sharp, square corner**

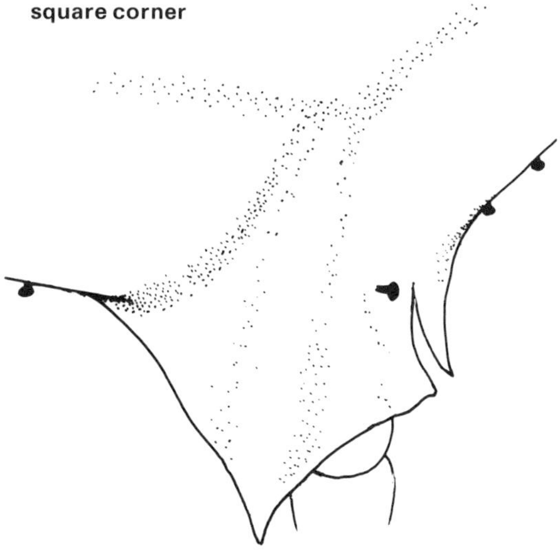

▲ **75(a)** Cut the material at the angle shown

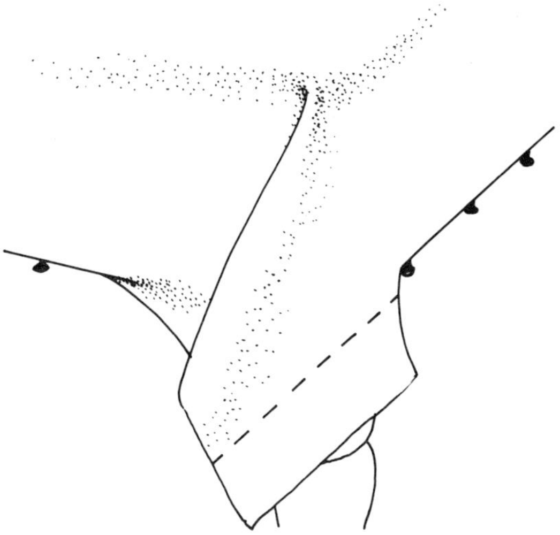

▲ **75(b)** Cut off the surplus material

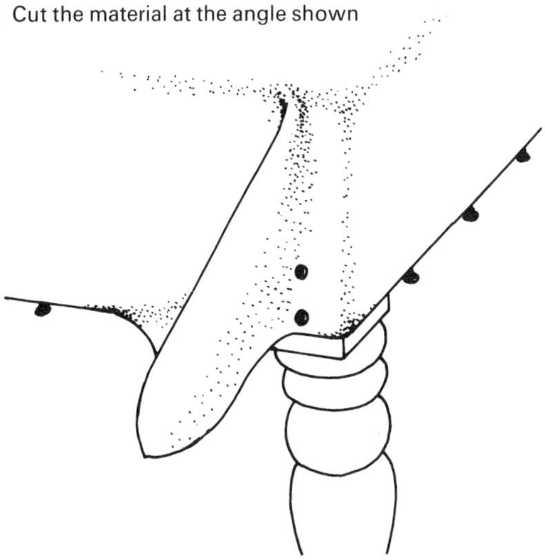

▲ **75(c)** Tack beneath the pleat

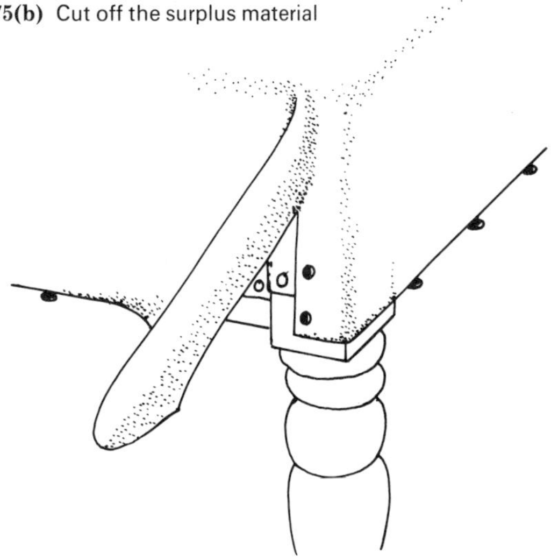

▲ **75(d)** Cut off the surplus

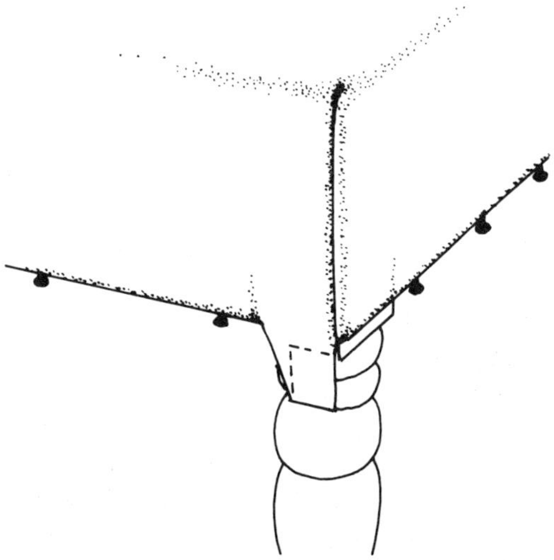

▲ **75(e)** Cut the surplus from under the pleat

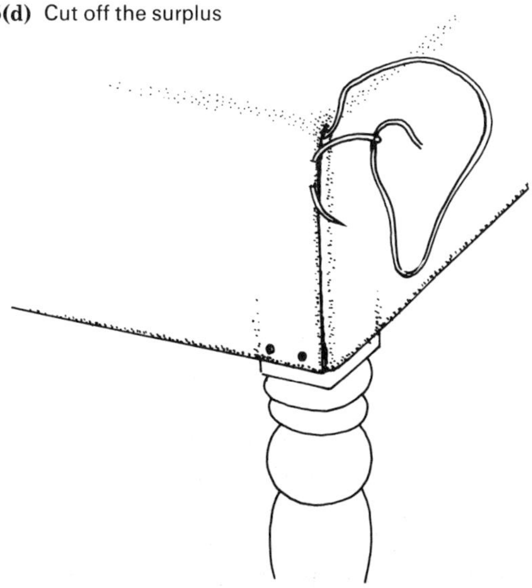

▲ **75(f)** Fasten the pleat with two tacks

Fig. 76 Reupholstering a drawing room chair with a breakfront; note the tie stitches

A SEAT WITH A BREAK FRONT

An attractive drawing room chair with a break front, i.e. the line of the front of the seat is broken near the corner, is shown in **fig. 76**. I would like to point out the difficulties that arise when you come to re-make an edge shaped in this way. A lot of upholsterers will ignore the shape of the frame and upholster the seat as though it just had a D-shaped front, but where possible the roll edge should always follow the line and shape of the frame. Constant regulating at the internal corners when putting in the rows of blind stitches will keep the edges of this break front seat well defined. Then, before starting the through roll stitches, put in a single tie stitch, as shown in **fig. 76**, to pull the angle in sharply. Roll stitch in the usual way.

SINGLE CHAIR SEATS WITH SPRINGS

If you have a single chair with springs I would refer you back to Chapter 3, pages 37–38 for directions but an extra point to note here is that the tarpaulin hessian used to cover the springs should not be pulled any tighter than the spring lacings, or these will just hang loose and serve no purpose. The springs are sewn to the hessian with the usual three stitches per spring and the procedure is the same as for a chair with no springs—with one exception. When you put in the through stuffing ties, these should only go in as far as the spring hessian and not right through the webbing.

A SEAT WITH A SERPENTINE FRONT

The reupholstery of a seat with a serpentine or double-curved front requires particular care. When you are putting on the scrim hessian much adjustment and temporary tacking will be needed to achieve a good shape that follows the line of the frame. Start as usual, tacking from the front centre, and as you proceed outwards from here, take up and almost gather the scrim towards the centre (**fig. 77**). There should be no tension across the protruding centre curve. If you tighten the scrim as you work outwards you will eventually lose this curve, as it will be forced back.

COVERING SHAPED SEATS

When you come to the job of covering seats that have elaborate shapes such as break fronts, serpentine and pronounced D fronts, it is possible to cover them in just one piece of material; when you do so, many temporary adjustments have to be made to eliminate most of the fullness around the fronts and sides. But although you eventually achieve a good appearance, it is later, after the chairs have been in use, that wrinkles and looseness form around the upright borders of the seat, as the upholstery is compressed.

To avoid this problem, cover the seat top separately first, sewing this cover all round just beneath the lip of the roll edge. Then make a separate border by sewing a strip round the seat. The join between the two can be trimmed with chair cord (**fig. 78**). If the border is padded out just a little this makes a really first class job and everything will be smooth, there will be no fullness or gathering and, of course, no corner pleating to bother about.

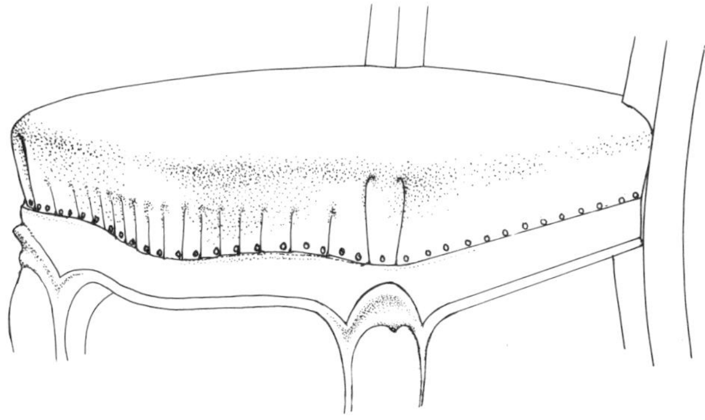

◀ Fig. 77 A seat with a serpentine front, showing gathers made in the scrim in the front

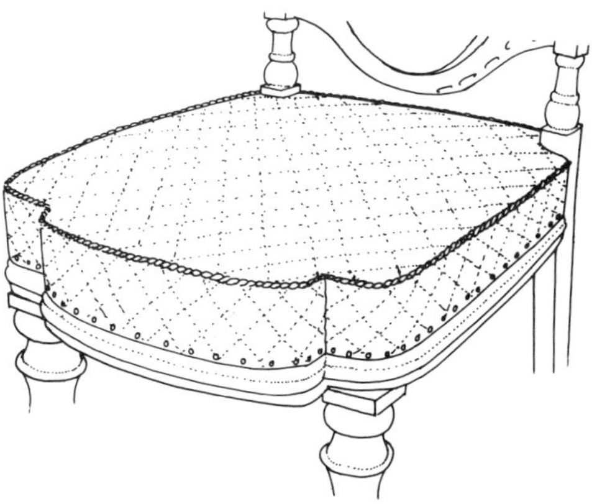

Fig. 78 A shaped seat bordered and trimmed with chair cord ▶

6 A Modern Wing Fireside Chair

To show the techniques of modern upholstery I have chosen to reupholster a wing fireside chair. So that I can cover most of the methods that have been used in the trade in recent years I have included design points from many leading makes (fig. 79), so please do not take this model and expect to find that the chair you are working on has exactly the same construction and innovations. When measuring up this chair use the chart, fig. 25 in Chapter 3, showing each cut. This is a project of medium difficulty.

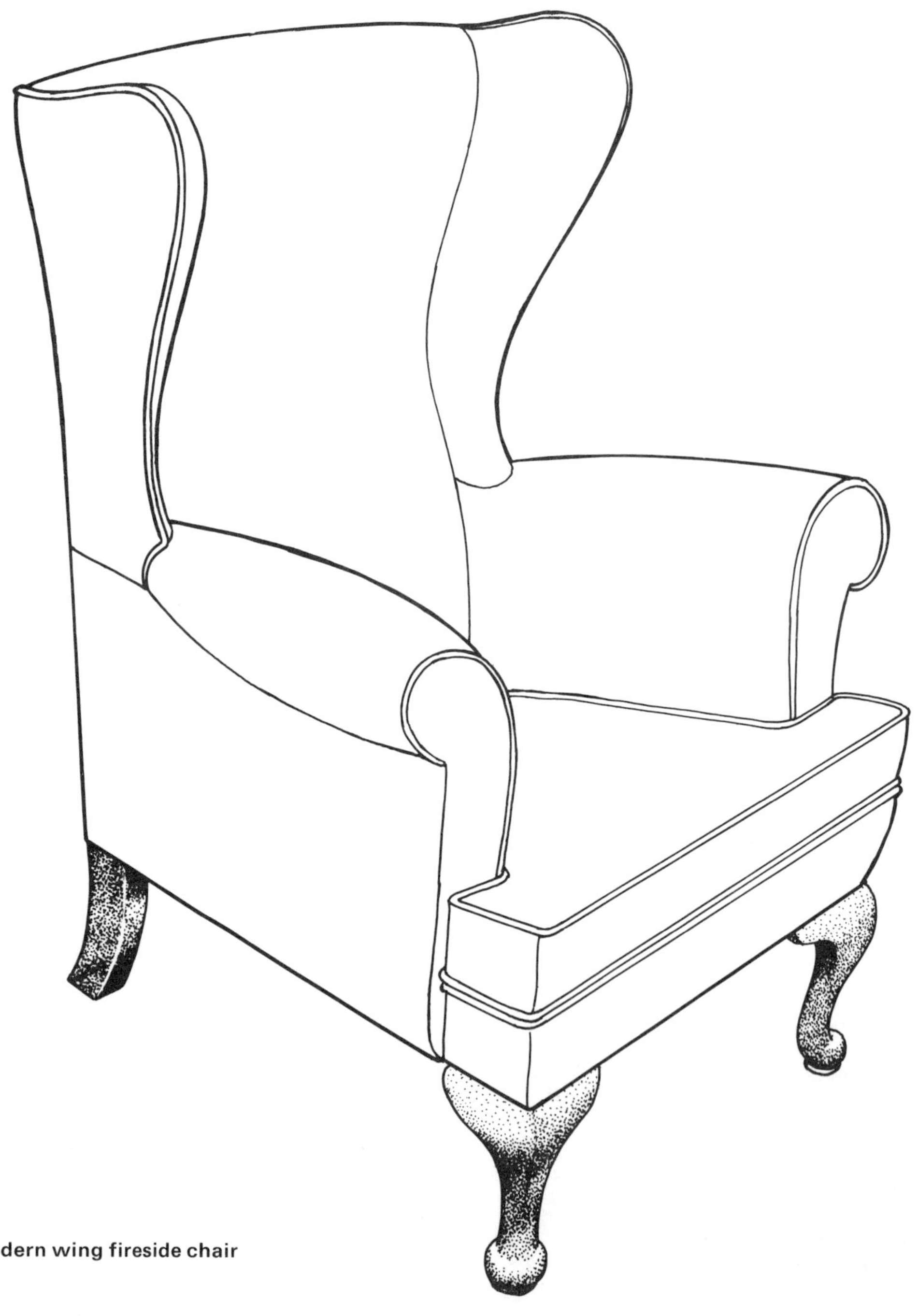

Fig. 79 A modern wing fireside chair

Removing Staples

Staples used with staple guns are a very quick and efficient way of fastening modern upholstery, but they take a lot longer to remove than tacks. You can try using a ripping chisel, but unless the wood is very soft all you will do is cut off the tops of the staples, leaving sharp little needles of steel which are difficult to extract. I find that the best way is to prise the staples up a little by pushing a regulator point underneath. This makes them sufficiently proud for your pincers or adapted side-cutting pliers to be used.

Stripping the Chair

Turn the chair upside down and unfasten the material round the bottom of the frame. Then you can remove all the outside coverings. You will see that the wings, which are made of solid wood, are screwed with three or four screws to the back upright. Unscrew and remove the wings. The bottom of the wing boards are usually held by one or two dry

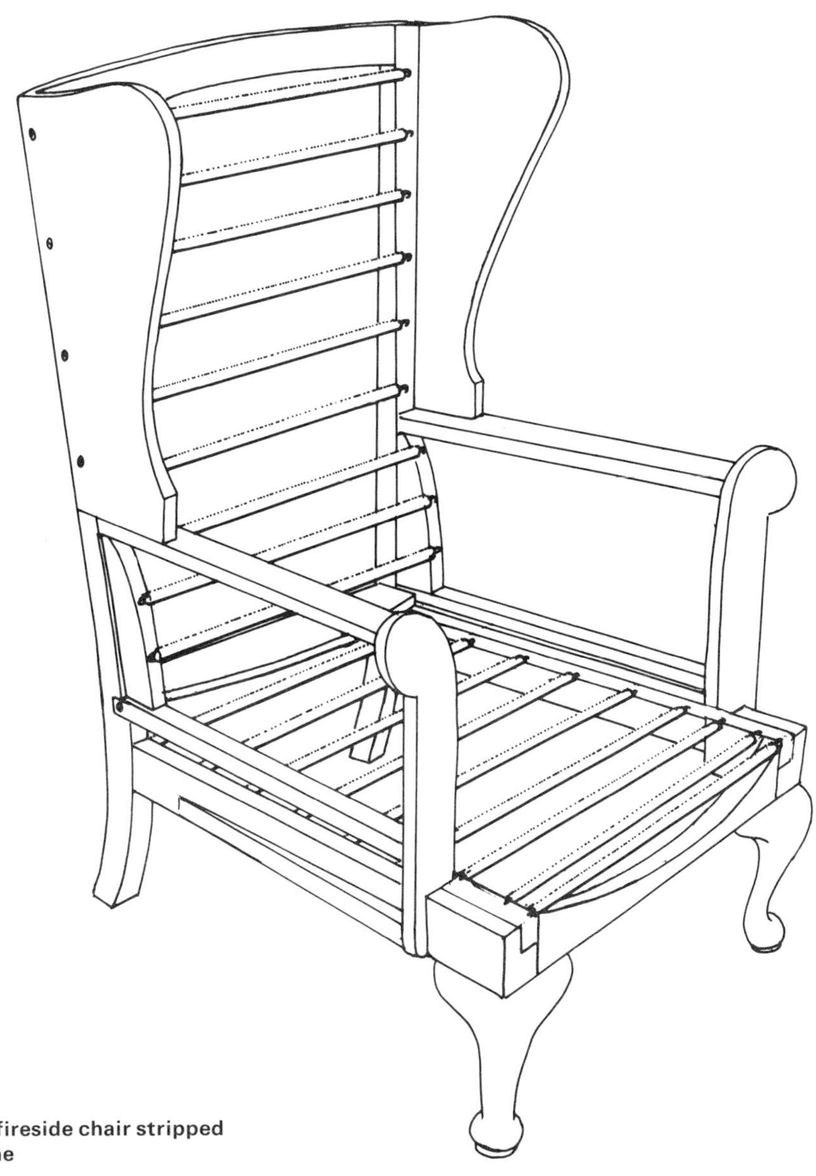

Fig. 80 The wing fireside chair stripped to its frame

dowels, so lift the wings upwards to remove them. Take note of the upholstery and the way in which it has been done as you strip the chair, especially if the covering is the original. Remove all the cotton felt filling from the wings and discard this, it has become too hard and consolidated, and soiled where heads have rested for many years. The same applies to the cotton felt stuffing on the arms, but I think that you can leave the rubberized horsehair pads that are underneath; having been kept from the light, these are as good as new.

The inside back upholstery is of kapok and this has deteriorated into lumps and fine particles of dust, so take it off—it is made up in a separate closed case—and discard it. The cushion interior has perished, so throw this away too.

Remove the springs from the seat and place them carefully to one side. Now the frame is bare (**fig. 80**), look at the joints, dismantling and re-glueing any that are loose. You can then attend to the legs and make them look like new again by stripping them and repolishing with French polish or polyurethane.

Tension Springs

The best quality fireside chairs still have coil tension springs under the cushions. Less expensive chairs have the tension springs fastened to the rails with clips, eyelets or hardened steel nails and on better chairs webs with eyelets are fastened to the side rails with glue and nails and the springs are then hooked into the eyelets. The most important seat springs should be examined. Any that have stretched and have coils pulled apart must be discarded and replaced by new ones. The tension springs that you find under the back upholstery are thinner and softer and are usually fastened with screw eyes or staples put into the back uprights; check these springs also for wear or looseness and replace them if in doubt. Getting springs of the right length is important; they need to be about 25 mm (1 in) shorter than the distance between fixings; no more or the spring will be over-stretched. The better quality springs are fabric covered, the cheaper ones encased in plastic.

When the side fixing webs need replacing, write to the manufacturers quoting the name and number of your chair and they will usually send a renewal pack complete with instructions. However, certain chairs with side webs will present a puzzle for you because the webs seem to be fastened so that the fixing nails are obscured by the bottom tacking rail of the arm. How on earth do we get these webs off, let alone fix the new ones? Well, if you look at the outside of the arm you will see that the tacking rail is fastened to the back upright with one screw. Remove this screw and you will be able to take the rail out, because the front end is only held by a dry dowel. Now you can get at the webbing.

If there are other methods of holding the springs, these fastenings should be examined carefully for signs of wear and put right if they are unsatisfactory. It is best to leave the tension springs out of the seat for the moment.

New Upholstery for the Back

The first job in reupholstering this chair is to make up a replacement stuffing for the back. Measure the size of the back from the extremities of the sides and from the top to the bottom and, using a good strong calico, cut out and sew up a case that is 50 mm (2 in) wider and 25 mm (1 in) longer than these measurements. I think we can improve on the original kapok filling by making a stuffing of foam and acrylic wool. Cut a piece of 12 mm ($\frac{1}{2}$ in) flame-resistant polyether foam to 25 mm (1 in) less in width and length than the inside back; wrap several layers of acrylic wool sheeting round this core. Put the stuffing inside the calico case, and if necessary add more layers to improve the shape. Sew the case up. Tack this stuffing unit to the frame with a roll-over at the top, as shown in **fig. 81**. Put in through stuffing ties (page 46) to hold the filling in place. Alternatively, you can make a good filling from several layers of cotton felt, or kapok as in the original chair. Kapok has to be gently packed in a little at a time. Whichever filling you use, it is as well, before covering it with your furnishing fabric, to overlay it with one or two layers of cotton wadding.

Covering the Inside Back Remove the two wing boards from the chair. Measure the back of the chair over your new upholstery and cut a piece of your covering fabric to fit.

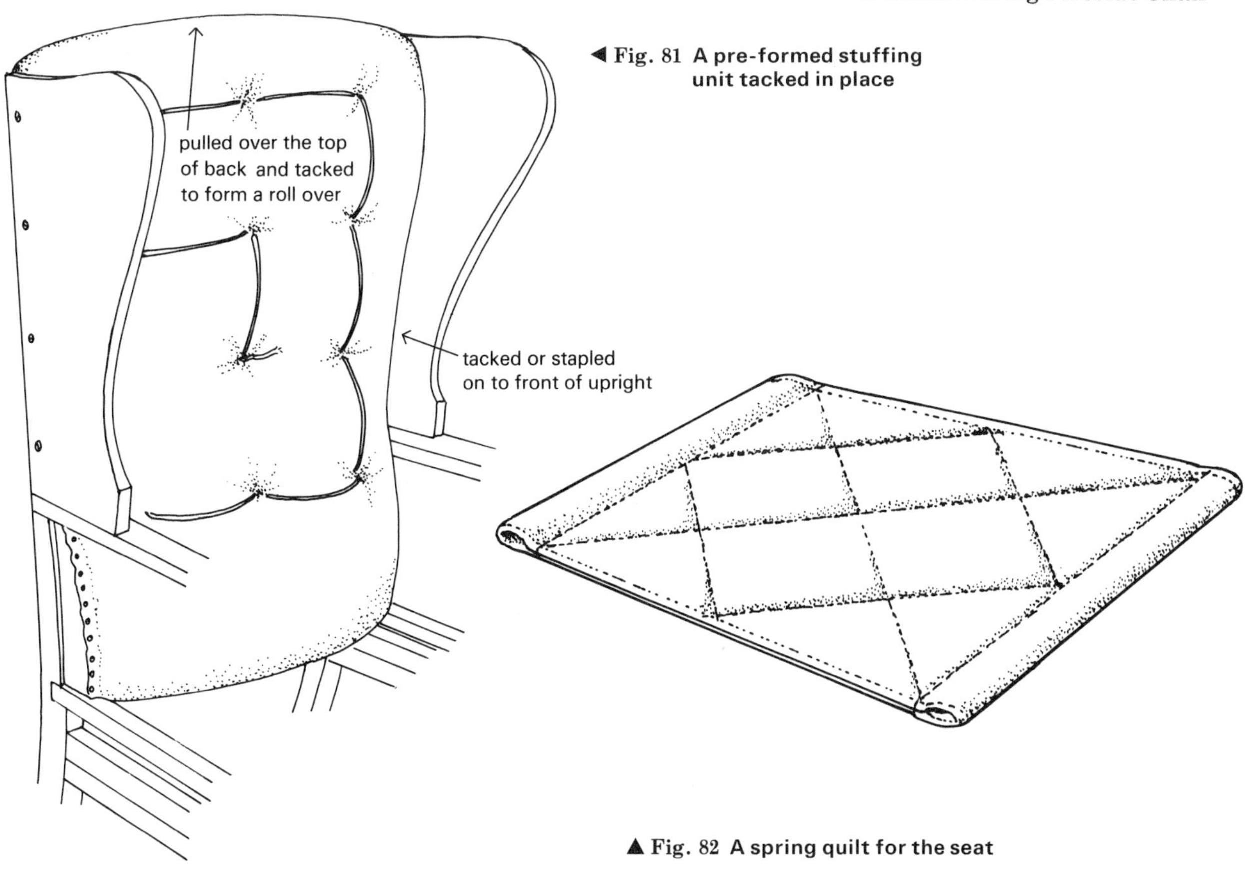

◀ Fig. 81 A pre-formed stuffing unit tacked in place

▲ Fig. 82 A spring quilt for the seat

The tension of the fabric on this type of chair back is critical. It must not be stretched too tightly or you will just be pushing the soft tension springs in; and it must not be loose, or after some use the covering will develop wrinkles or fullness. Take particular care with the diagonal corner tension, so that when you stretch the fabric to the corners you get rid of all the edge fullness and no pleats or gathers are necessary anywhere. I have seen some of these chairs upholstered by people with perhaps only a little experience, who have put pleats in or gathered up the material when, if only they had spent another ten minutes or so in further temporary tacking and adjusting, they would have found that every part could be smooth and shapely. Take this as a rule for every part of this chair; no unsightly fullness anywhere in the covering.

Making a Spring Quilt for the Seat

If the seat springs are left exposed, the cushion cover tends to suffer and when you turn the cushion over you find that the springs have left their impression in the form of indented lines which take a long time to disappear. A spring quilt (**fig. 82**) laid over the springs will prevent this sort of damage.

Put back the tension springs so that you can take a couple of measurements. It is a good idea to start by making a drawing of the shape of the seat. Then measure and note the width across the seat at the front spring between the spring fixing webs and the width at the position of the back spring.

Now, measure the length from the back to the front springs and mark it on the drawing. Transfer these measurements to a piece of fairly stout black platform cloth or lining or even a good quality calico, adding 12 mm ($\frac{1}{2}$ in) to each side for seaming and 75 mm (3 in) to the front and the back for the pockets for the springs. Cut two pieces to this size and shape. Cut a piece of 12 mm ($\frac{1}{2}$ in) flame-resistant polyether foam to the exact size of your drawing. Put the two pieces of platform cloth together and seam down each side on your sewing machine. The lines of stitches should be 10 mm ($\frac{3}{8}$ in) in from the edges. Turn this open-ended bag the right side out, and lay the piece of foam inside, equidistant

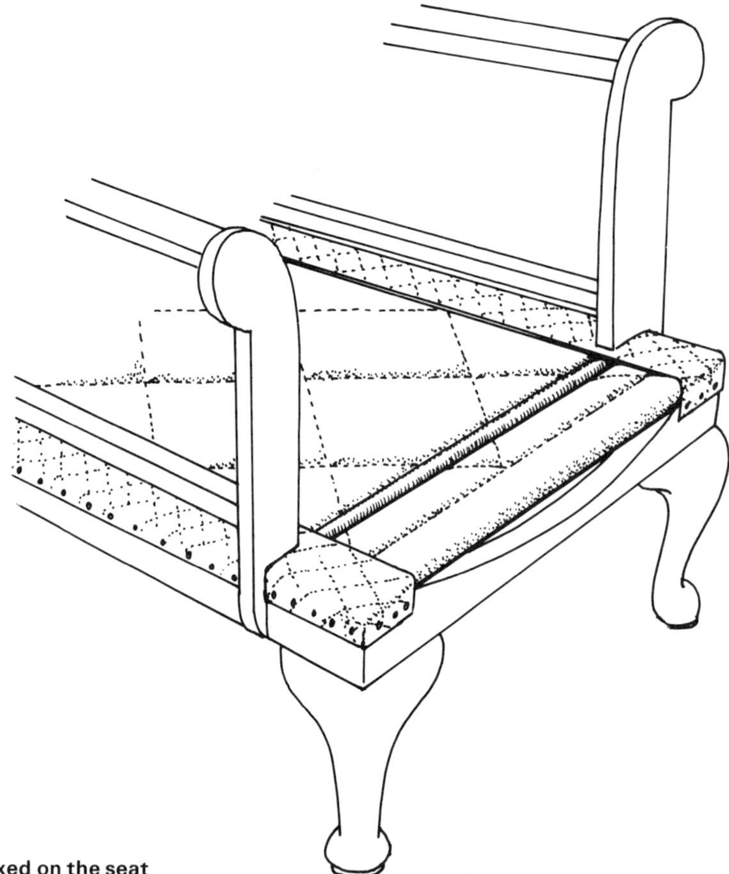

Fig. 83 Side flanges fixed on the seat

from the ends. Sew a row of stitches 20 mm ($\frac{3}{4}$ in) in from each side to hold the foam in place, then lay the quilt over the springs. To gauge the exact length which is to be hemmed, mark on the cloth where the back and front springs come. Fold over a wide hem at the back and the front, allowing at least 30 mm ($1\frac{1}{4}$ in) from the edge to the stitches to make a pocket large enough for the spring to go through. Stitch along these hems, finishing off neatly with returned stitches. Now draw some very light diagonal pencil lines across the quilt to form a series of diamond shapes. Follow these lines with stitches and there you have a very professional-looking quilt. Remove the back and front springs and thread them through the hem pockets of the quilt, then hook the springs back on again. The spring that lies exactly between the two arm front uprights has to be left above the quilt because this will hold the back of the small seat platform.

Making Side Flanges for the Seat

Also to protect the cushion from wear from the springs, make two side flanges that will overlap the quilt (**fig. 83**). These can be made and fastened as you see in the illustration. Each piece is hemmed on three sides then fixed on the top of the seat rail and on the front rail. Notice how the flanges dip under the tension spring reserved for the platform and border fastening.

The Front Seat Border and Seat Platform

Next, cut out and stitch up a covering for the small seat platform and front border (**fig. 84**). There are two ways of making a covering. If the material is plain, you can cut out the covering in one piece, (**a**) so that it extends from behind the tension spring that is above the spring quilt to 50 mm (2 in) under the front seat rail. Lay the piece of material over this area to be covered and pin the corners to form a box shape. Remove the piece of material and stitch the two pinned-up corners on the sewing machine and then cut away the surplus cloth leaving flanges of about 13 mm ($\frac{1}{2}$ in). A patterned cloth may look better if it is made up in two pieces with a top panel and a border; you can pipe the seam between the two (**b**).

Whichever method you use, sew a flap or fly piece such as lining, hessian or thick calico to the back of the cover. The free long edge of this flap is then taken underneath the tension spring that is on the top of the quilt, brought forward and tacked on to the front seat rail as you can see in (**c**). This flap now forms a floor for the platform and border padding which can be made from foam or two layers of cotton felt. Draw the cover down over the padding and temporarily fasten it beneath the front rail, cutting the cloth in at the legs. The final fastening can be left until all the covering has been done.

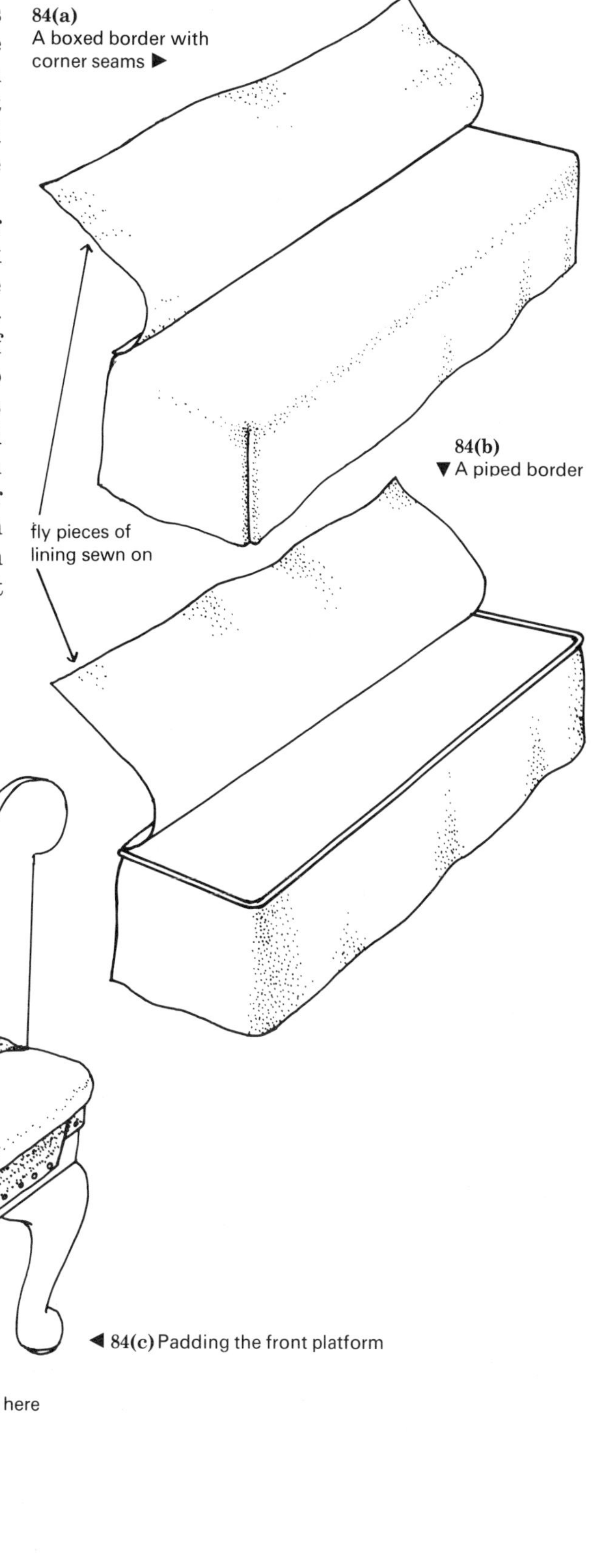

84(a) A boxed border with corner seams ▶

84(b) ▼ A piped border

◀ **84(c)** Padding the front platform

Fig. 84 **The front seat border and seat platform**

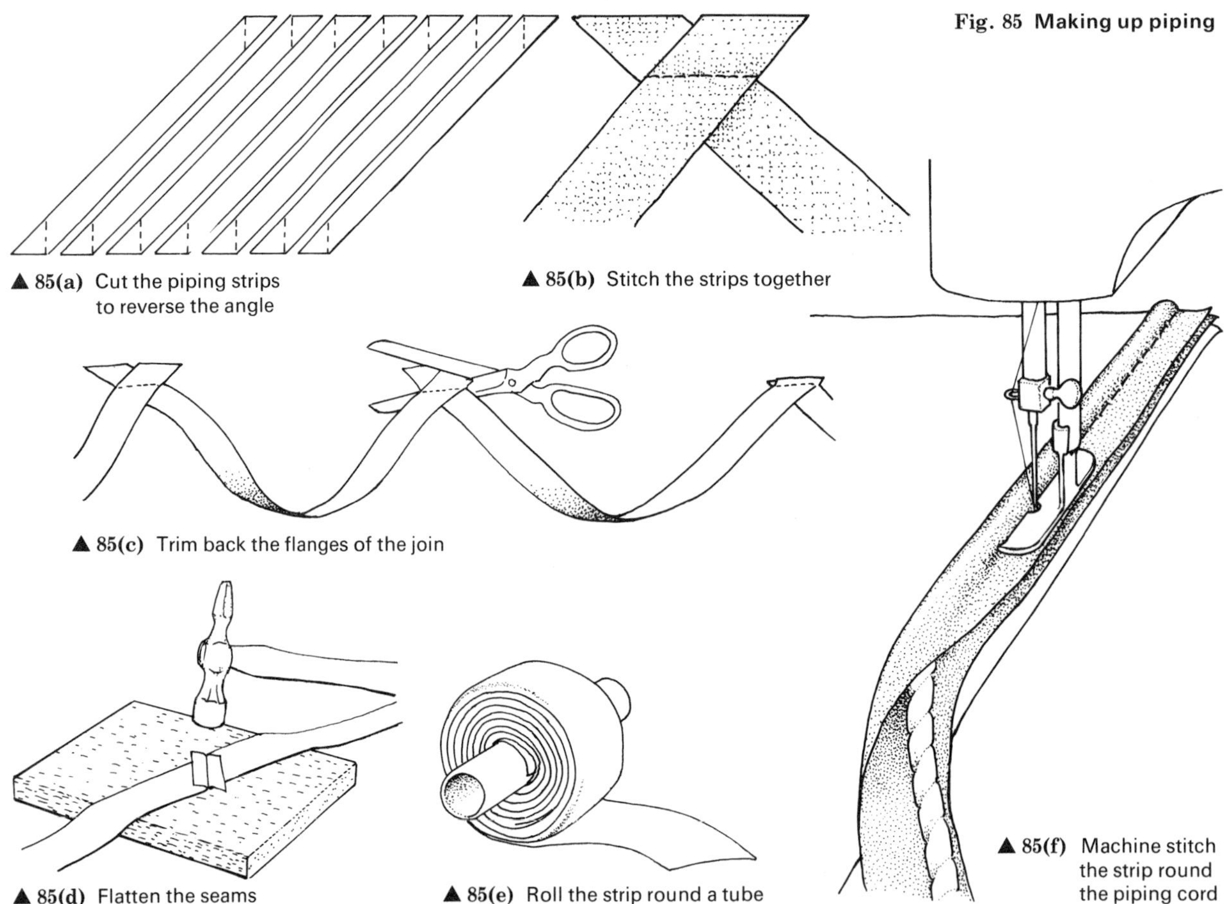

Fig. 85 Making up piping

▲ 85(a) Cut the piping strips to reverse the angle

▲ 85(b) Stitch the strips together

▲ 85(c) Trim back the flanges of the join

▲ 85(d) Flatten the seams

▲ 85(e) Roll the strip round a tube

▲ 85(f) Machine stitch the strip round the piping cord

Making up Piping

I mentioned piping above, and I think this would be the moment to make up sufficient for the whole chair—for the border (if piped), the scroll fronts to the arms, round the outside of the back and wings, and, of course, the cushion (**fig. 85**). So measure round everything to see how much you need.

Take your furnishing fabric and, using tailor's chalk, mark out the strips for the piping diagonally, at an angle of roughly 45° to the weave. Piping strips should always be cut on the bias, from the bottom left to the top right of the fabric, to give a good even shape to the piping when it is stitched. This is because in most fabrics the more robust threads run across the width, and these put up more resistance against the drag under the foot of the sewing machine. The strips should be at least 60 cm (2 ft) long. For **No. 1** piping cord they need to be 38 mm ($1\frac{1}{2}$ in) wide. Thicker or thinner cords need correspondingly wider or narrower strips to give the required flange to the piping.

When you have cut the required number of strips, join them to make one long length. The joins must show as little as possible, so this is what you do. The end of each strip is at an oblique angle; cut each of these to reverse the angle (**a**), because most cloths join better along the lengthwise threads than across the width. Pile up the strips of cloth one on top of the other, keeping them in order of cutting and all facing the same way. Now stitch them together on the sewing machine (**b**). There is no need to cut the cottons, just carry on from one join to the next, and when they are all sewn up snip through the cotton between each join (**c**). Trim the flanges of each join to about half their width. To flatten the seams, place each piece of piping on a clean hardwood block or a piece of flat iron and tap it with a broad-faced hammer (**d**). Or alternatively, press the joins with a hot iron and damp cloth. Roll the strip round a tube to keep it tidy and manageable (**e**) and from this it can be fed beneath your piping foot and folded evenly so that the edges are together (**f**).

Reupholstering the Chair Arms

This chair has scroll arm fronts (**fig. 86**); I have purposely used this sort as it is the most challenging. Other types of arms require less work.

First of all, temporarily replace the wing boards (**a**). Most modern wing chairs have rubberized hair pads on the arms. These must be re-padded. Firstly, lay on cotton felt. Place about three layers on the arm tops, but avoid too much bulk down the sides, as this would restrict the width of the seat (**b**).

Cut two pieces of 12 mm ($\frac{1}{2}$ in) polyether foam to the shape of the arms and two more pieces to the shape of the scroll fronts. Make these up like arm sleeves, joining the scroll-shaped ends into the ends of the larger pieces of foam with soft bond impact adhesive (**c**).

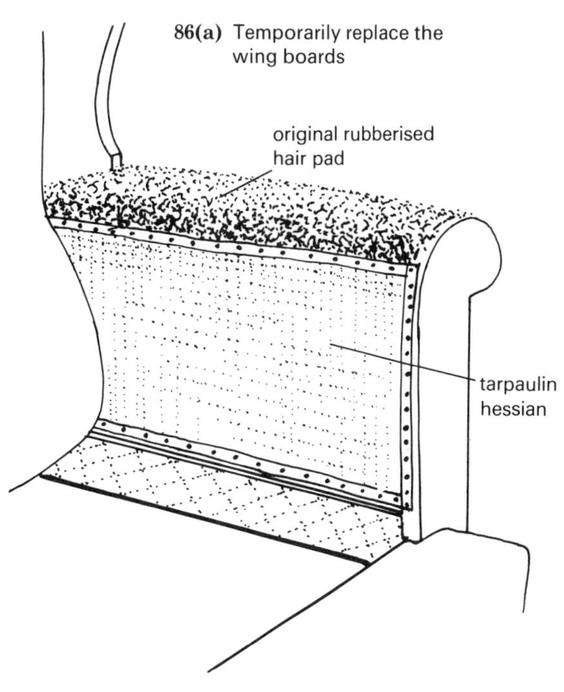

86(a) Temporarily replace the wing boards

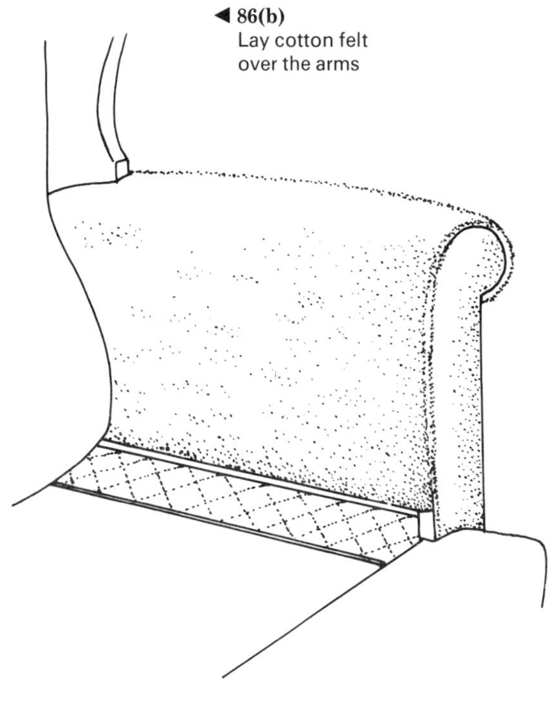

◀ **86(b)** Lay cotton felt over the arms

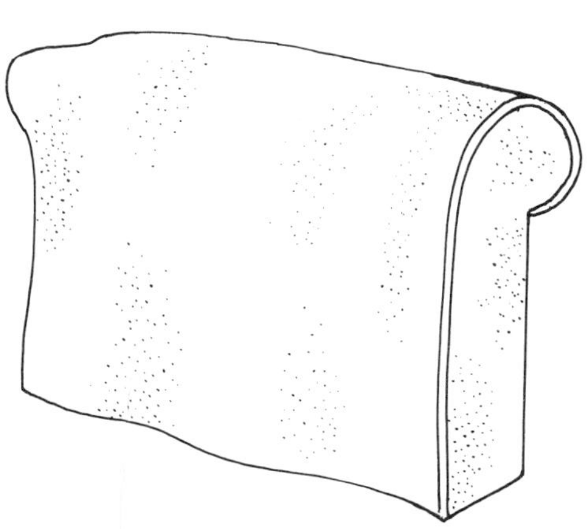

▼ **86(c)** Make up arm sleeves in foam

Fig. 86 Re-upholstering the arms

▼ 86(d) Tighten the covering fabric round the periphery of the scroll

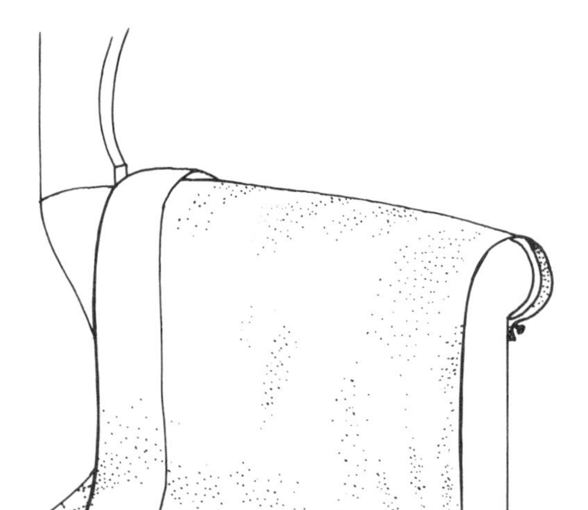

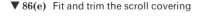

▼ 86(e) Fit and trim the scroll covering

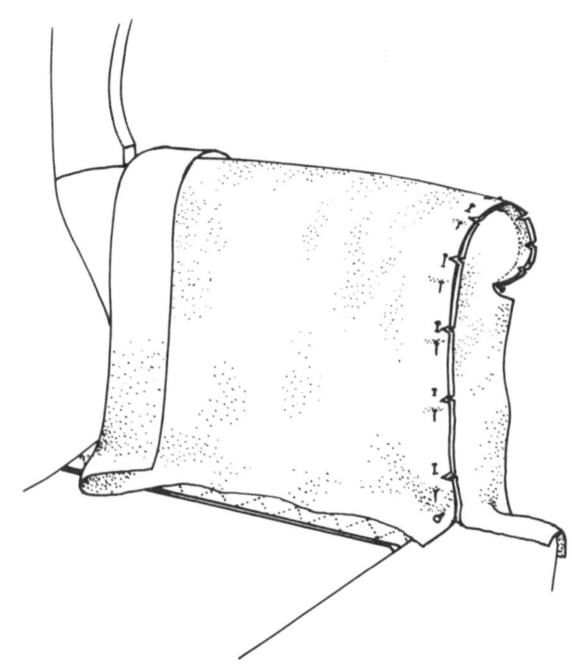

This makes a complete foam arm cover which can be fastened tightly with staples. If the two arm shapes are cut out together it will help to get the arms to the same shape.

Measure and cut off a piece of material to cover the main body of each arm and a piece to cover each front scroll. Position one of the arm covers over an arm, allowing 12 mm ($\frac{1}{2}$ in) to extend forward of the front scroll. Tighten the material round the periphery of the scroll, temporarily fastening it with tacks (**d**). Use small pins to pin a scroll cover to the arm cover that you have already positioned. Trim off the surplus material, then, to mark the position of the two pieces of fabric, nick or snip the seam flanges at intervals through the two thicknesses (**e**). Mark the first snip with a pen or chalk.

Remove this cover from the arm, take out the pins and lay the already trimmed pieces on top of the pieces for the other arm, right sides together. Trim the second set of covers to match, and also transfer the positioning snips. 'Make' the piping on to the two front shapes, allowing plenty of length at each end of the scroll.

Pin together the arm coverings and front shapes, matching the positioning snips—now you see why it is necessary to mark the first snip. The pins should be on the front. Machine stitch the two pieces together, with the front scroll piece uppermost. Stitch just inside the row of piping stitches, so that these joining stitches do not show when the cover is turned the right side out.

Cover the whole of the arm foam surfaces with a thin layer of wadding.

You are now ready to put your made-up covering on, so remove those wing boards once again. It is quite simple to put on the covering—just turn it inside out and get the scroll positioned against the front of the upholstery (**f**), lay the piping flanges outwards then roll back the covering and tension towards the back, cutting in and tucking through as shown in (**g**). Fasten the cover to the back upright. Then fasten it at the bottom along the outside rail, and at the top beneath the roll over of the arm. I have shown the cutting in that is necessary before the final permanent tacking is done and you can see that the material is placed with wooden dowels protruding through holes made with a regulator.

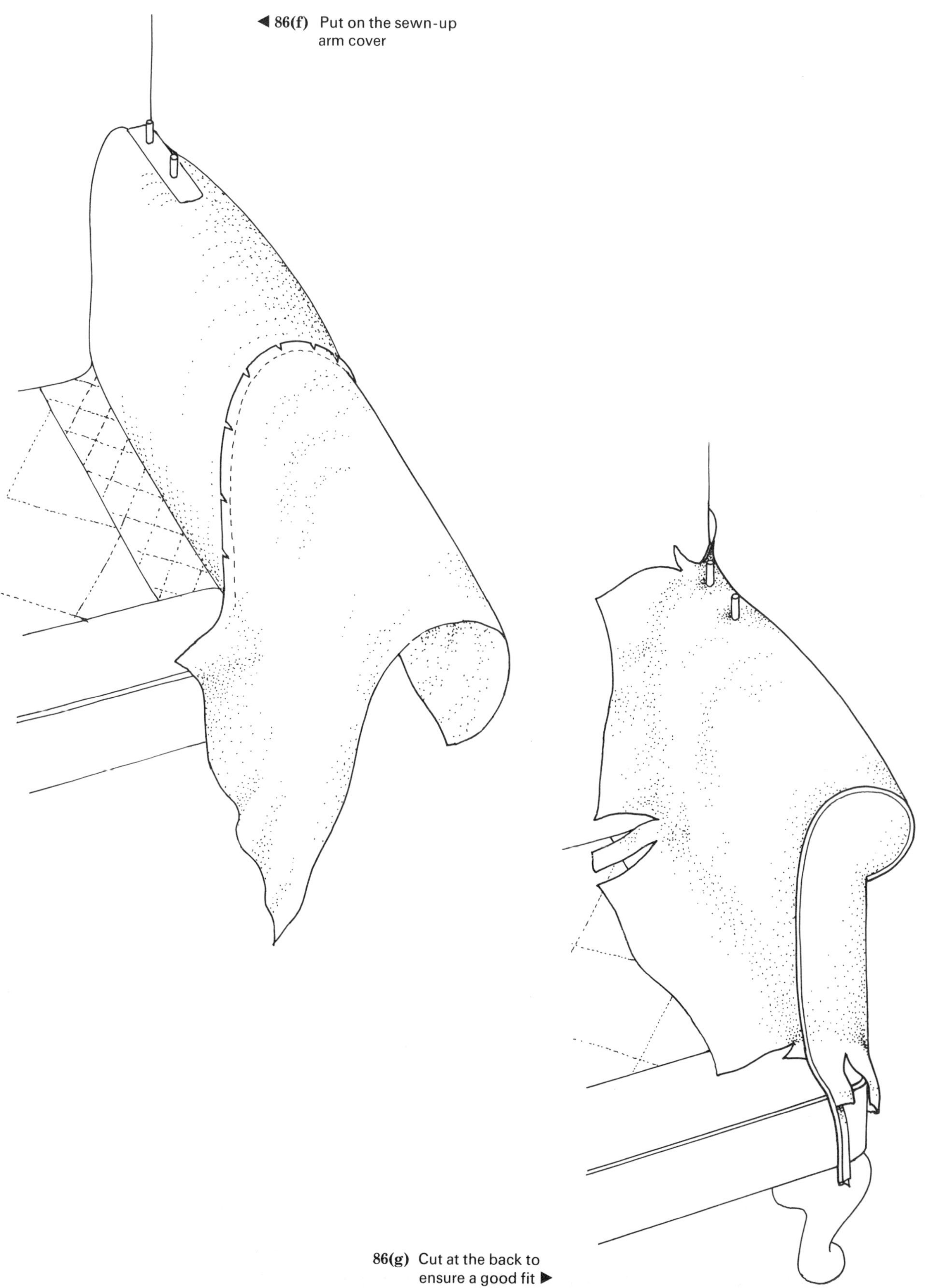

◀ **86(f)** Put on the sewn-up arm cover

86(g) Cut at the back to ensure a good fit ▶

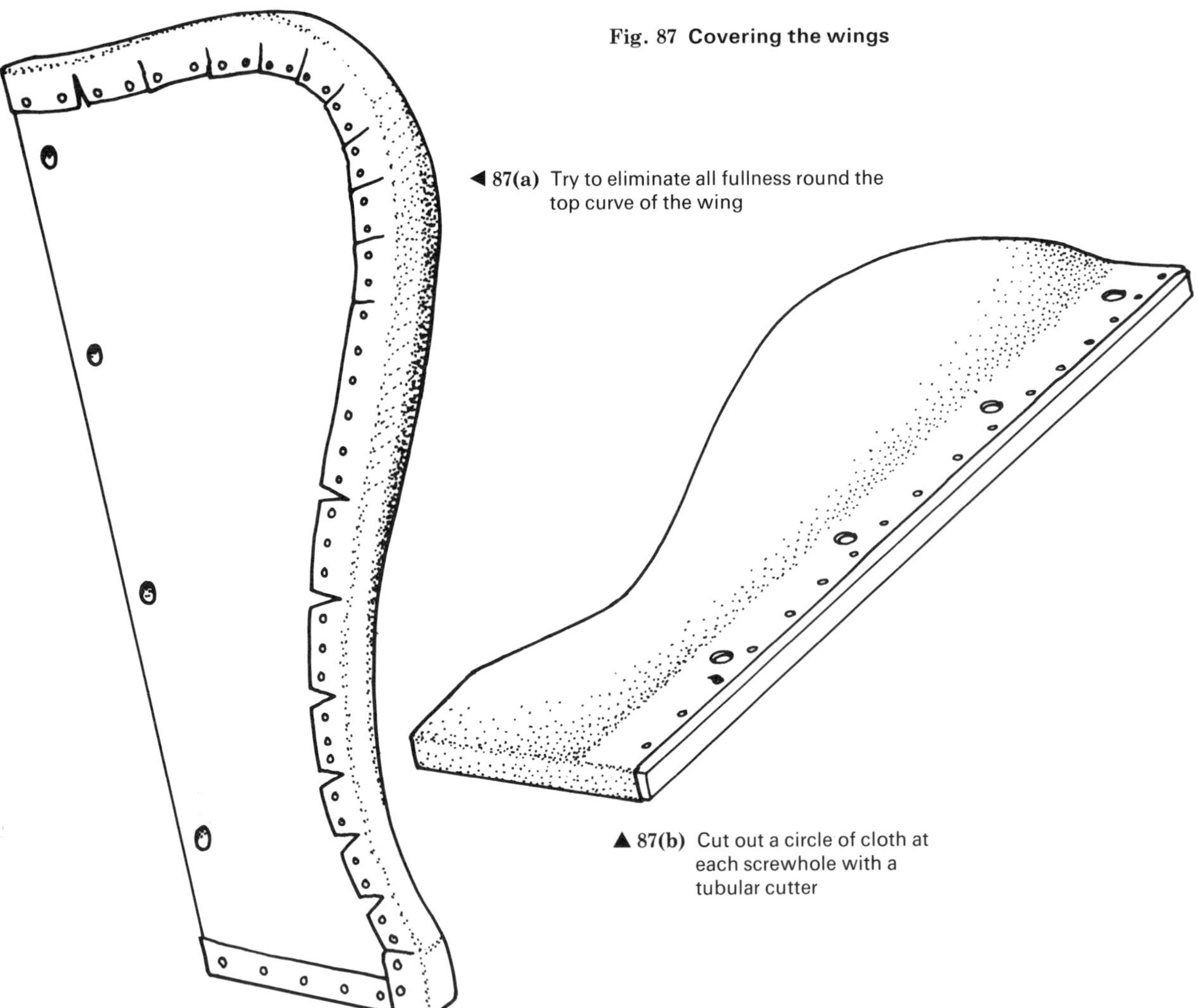

Fig. 87 Covering the wings

◀ **87(a)** Try to eliminate all fullness round the top curve of the wing

▲ **87(b)** Cut out a circle of cloth at each screwhole with a tubular cutter

Reupholstering the wings

Try the wing boards on the chair and note the space where each board touches the back upright. No padding is needed here. Also, while the boards are temporarily in position, mark a vertical line on the outside of each—this will give you a guide to help you get the covering on perfectly straight. Lay the boards flat and pad the inner surfaces with several layers of cotton felt. The shape of this upholstery is a matter for your personal choice; I like to see the wings well rounded but soft, with the filling feathering off on the top and front edges to define the curve of the wing (**fig. 87**).

Measure and cut off the pieces of fabric to cover the inner surfaces of the wings. Temporarily tack the cover to the inside of one wing board. Adjust the fabric until you have eliminated all fullness round the top curve and the gathers are neatly made on the outside (**a**). Make sure that the weave of the cloth is straight, then permanently tack the cover down. Cover the inner surface of the second wing board in the same way.

With a small tubular cutter or small scissors, cut out circles of cloth at each screw hole (**b**)—otherwise when the screws are put in they could catch and pull a thread in your material, making a nasty mark. Screw the wings in position.

Pin piping round the edge of the wings (**c**). Then pad the outer surfaces of the wing boards with a single layer of cotton wadding.

Cut the wing coverings roughly to shape and pin them in position close up to the piping (**d**). Tack the back edge down the rear facing side of the back upright and the bottom edge under the rail at the bottom of the wing. Sew round the curve of the top and front edges as described on page 43 in the section on incorporating piping into a seam.

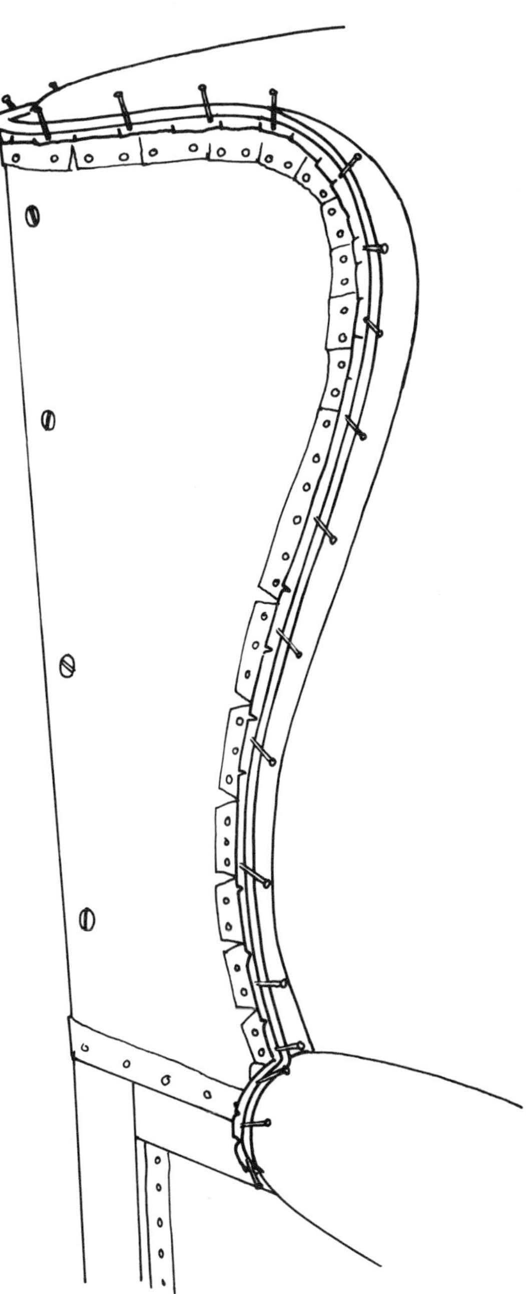

▲ 87(c) Pin piping round the edge of the wings

▼ 87(d) Pin the outside covering in position

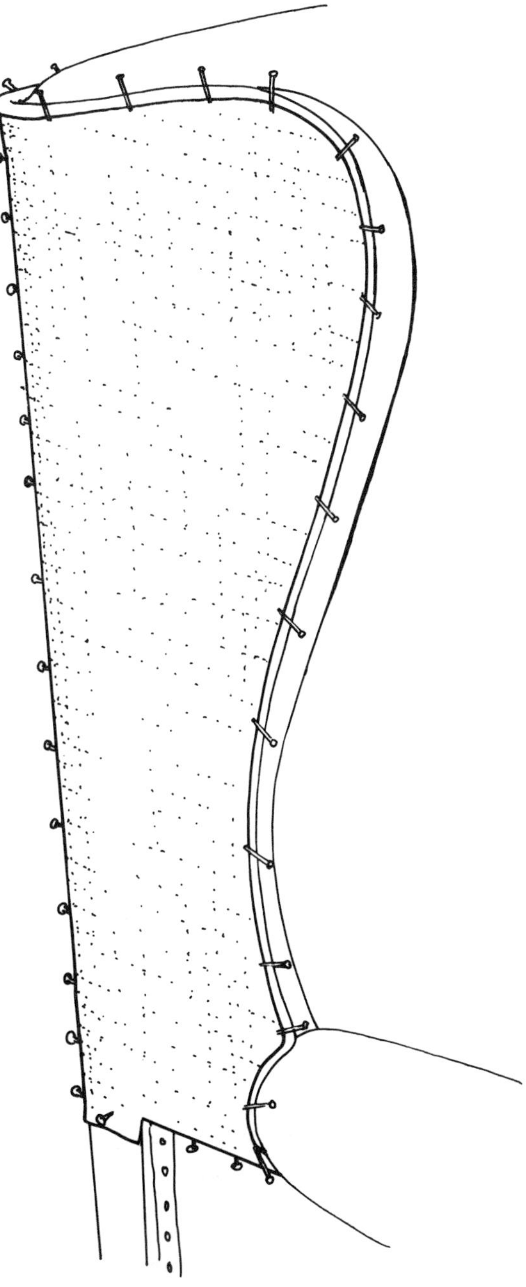

Fig. 88 Covering the outside arm panels

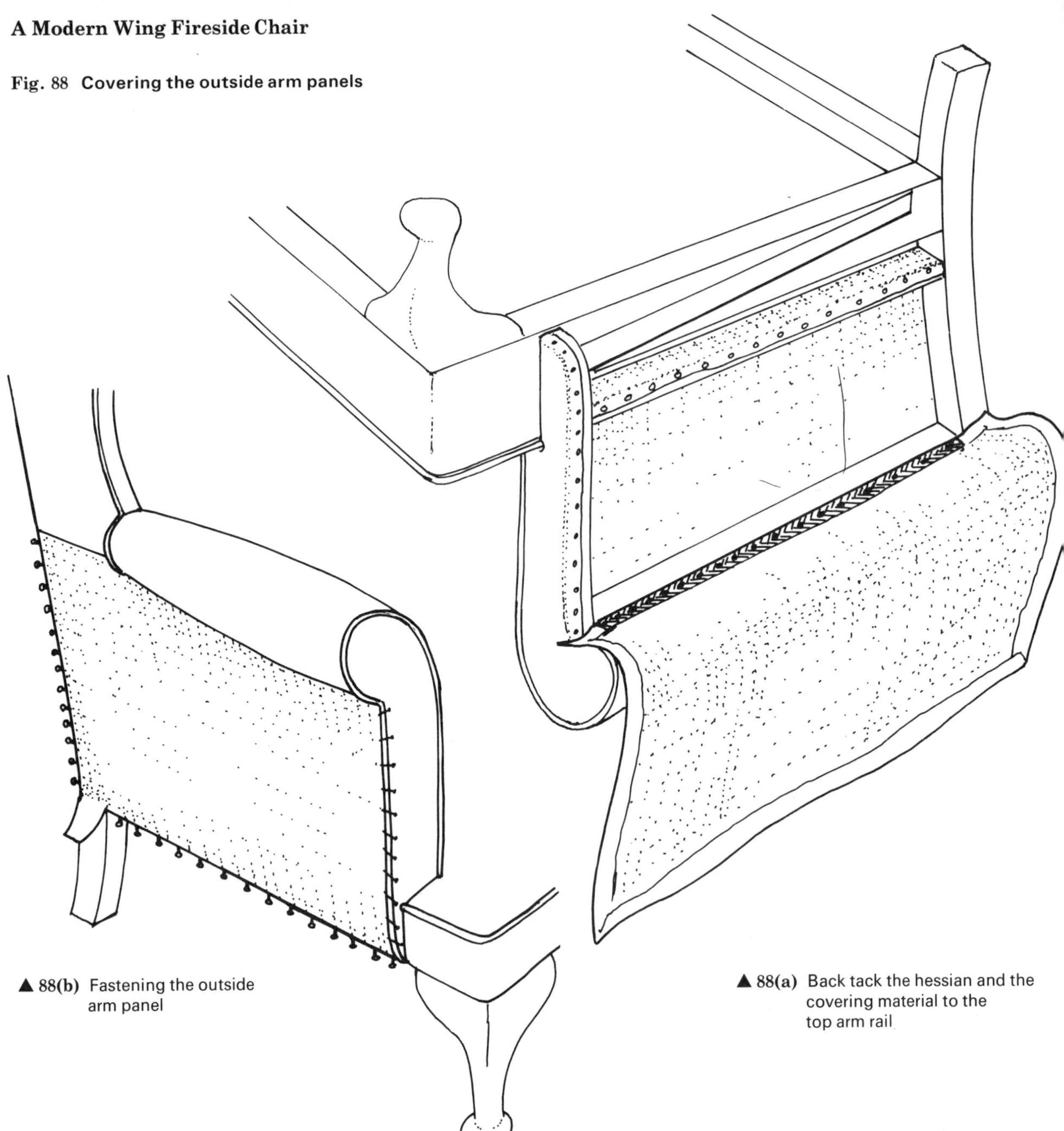

▲ 88(b) Fastening the outside arm panel

▲ 88(a) Back tack the hessian and the covering material to the top arm rail

Covering the Outside Arm Panels

Half a width of material will probably be enough to cover each outside arm panel (**fig. 88**). Measure and cut off the lengths required. Turn the chair upside down (**a**). Here you can see the covering material and a piece of 280 g (10 oz) support hessian fastened on to the arm rail using a 50 mm (2 in) wide strip of webbing folded in half down its length, stretched tightly along the length of the rail so that it sandwiches the edges of both the covering and the hessian. This webbing is fastened with 13 mm ($\frac{1}{2}$ in) Improved tacks at 25 mm (1 in) intervals. Care must be taken to keep the 'back tacking' straight and the webbing taut in order to keep the join close. Be careful—on some chairs the arm rails are not parallel with the seat rails below. Stretch the support hessian very tightly and fasten it round the outside of the chair frame. Tighten and temporarily fix the covering material under the bottom seat rail and down the rear of the back upright. Pin together the front seam (**b**), then ladder stitch it.

Covering the Outside Back

If a wing chair has a substantial top rail, you can back-tack the top of the outside back covering on to this rail. However, I prefer to see the top seam and the sides sewn, it takes a bit longer to do, but it makes a proper job of the upholstery. So pin the outside back panel to the side, arm and front covers and temporarily tack it on beneath the bottom rail (**fig. 89**). Ladder stitch (pages 40–41) the two upright seams and sew the top seam in the same way as you did on the wings.

Finishing the Chair

Turn your chair upside down again now and turn in, neaten off and permanently tack the material onto the bottom of the seat rails. Make nice straight lines of your turnings and space the tacks evenly so that it looks like a really professional job.

The final task is making the seat cushion. For directions, see Chapter 10 (pages 153–157).

Fig. 89 **Covering the outside back**

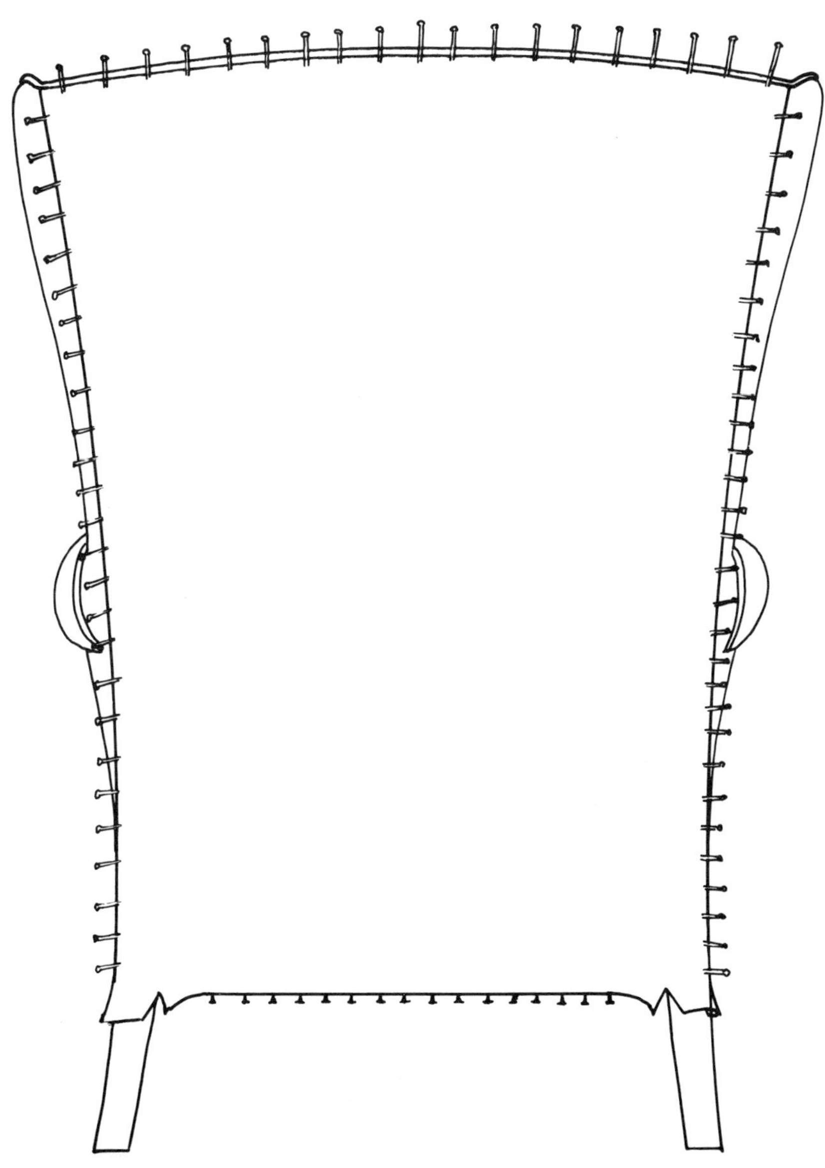

7 A Large Easy Chair

I should like you to look back to the beginning of Chapter 3 where I describe an easy chair of the 1900s (page 27). In my workshop I have a chair of this description (fig. 90). It stands in my bottom storeroom, looking very bedraggled, dirty and sad, but underneath all that worn, torn and ragged upholstery I know that there is a very good, well made frame.

It differs in one detail from the chair in Chapter 3—it has a buttoned back. I would like to take you in words and pictures through the job of reupholstering this chair, because this will help you with most chairs of this type and period. This is a fairly difficult work project.

Fig. 90 An old chair from my storeroom, looking very bedraggled, dirty and sad

Measuring for a Buttoned Back

You will remember that the first thing to do before any of the old upholstery is disturbed is to measure up for the new covering material; you know how to do this, but what about the buttoned back to this chair? Obviously it is going to take more material than the plain back.

First of all, study the layout of the old buttonwork to see if you can improve on it. Perhaps there could be another row of buttons and more in each row so that they are closer together.

Take a measurement from the top to the bottom, allowing for plenty under the top roll-over, and pushing the end of your steel tape down in between the seat and the back until you feel it touching the tacking rail. Read off this measurement and add 38 mm ($1\frac{1}{2}$ in) for every button that is in a straight line, from the top to the bottom. Measure across the widest part of the inside back and allow 20 mm ($\frac{3}{4}$ in) for the turnings on each side. Count the buttons in a straight line across and add the same allowance, 38 mm ($1\frac{1}{2}$ in) for each button; this will give you the rough width measurement. For this chair you will have to allow a full width of material; the narrow off-cut may do for facings or piping.

Now you can go ahead and rip off until the frame is clean, bare and completely tack-free (**fig. 91**).

It is very seldom that I strip a frame and find that it is completely sound—there is usually a joint or two that needs re-glueing, a leg loose or a trace of woodworm. So examine your bare frame very thoroughly and put things to rights. And even if no woodworm holes can be seen, it is a good plan to soak the frame in a woodworm killer. Leave the frame for a few days until the liquid has penetrated and dried. Then you are ready to start refurbishing.

Webbing up the Back and the Arms

When reupholstering a frame like this, especially when working on the back upholstery, try to visualize the approximate height that the seat will be when it is finished. A well shaped chair back will bulge out near the bottom into what we term a 'lumbar swell', which, as the name implies, should be made to fit the small of the back of a seated person.

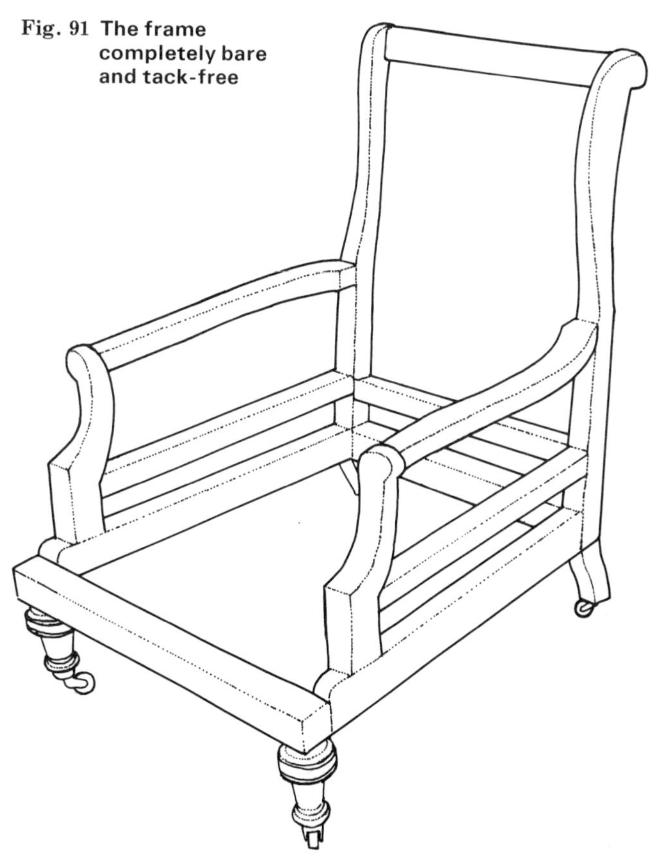

Fig. 91 The frame completely bare and tack-free

Fig. 92 The webbing of the back ▶

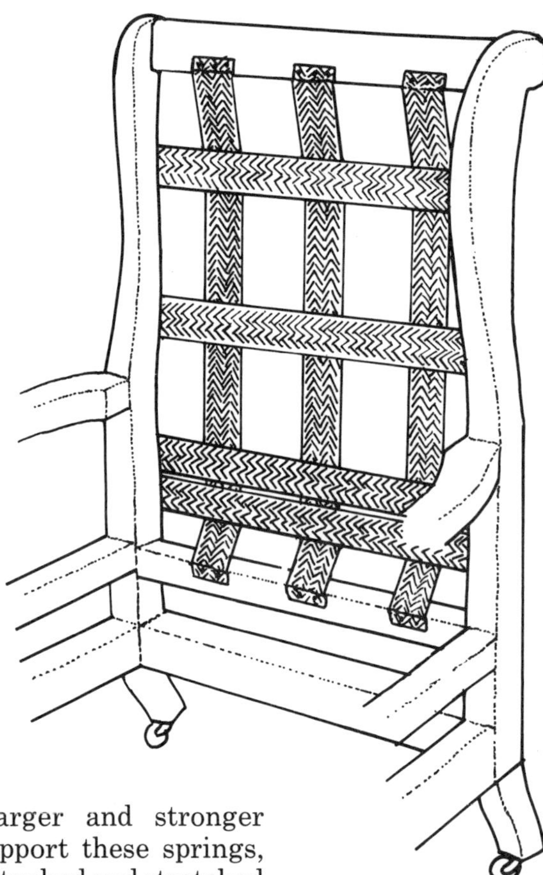

To form this swell, larger and stronger springs are used. To support these springs, two strips of webbing are tacked and stretched close together across the back frame, just above the tacking rail as in **fig. 92**. To work out the height of the seat and the position of the back swell, sit in another chair and note whether the height of the seat and the shape of the back are comfortable and, if not, where improvements could be made. Transfer your findings to the chair frame you are working on.

First, put all the lateral webbing on the outside back, then fix the lengthwise pieces from the top to the bottom. Note in **fig. 92** how these are tacked top and bottom to the front side of the frame. They are not woven in and out of the cross pieces but all run behind so that when tightened they bring the cross pieces forward slightly. This prevents the webbing becoming loose after some use, bulging out at the back and distorting the outside back covering.

Now, stretch a piece of webbing from the tacking rail to the top rail of each arm at a distance of about 25 mm (1 in) from the back upright, and another piece up the centre of the arm space (**fig. 93**).

Fig. 93 Two strips of webbing on an arm ▼

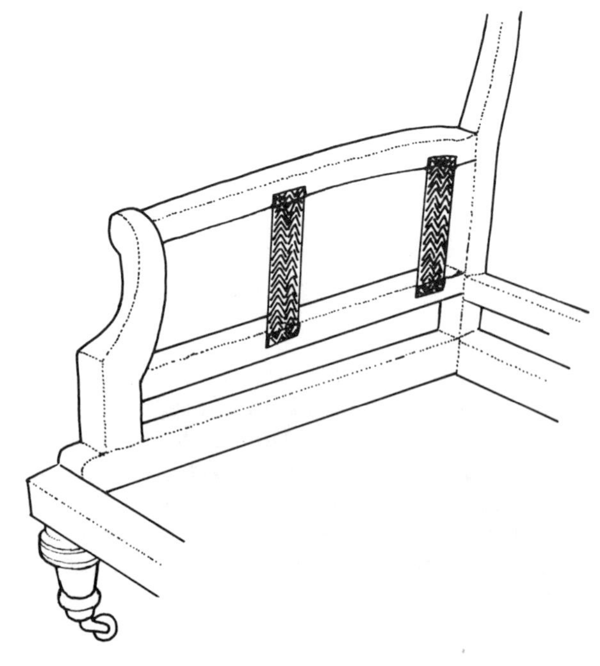

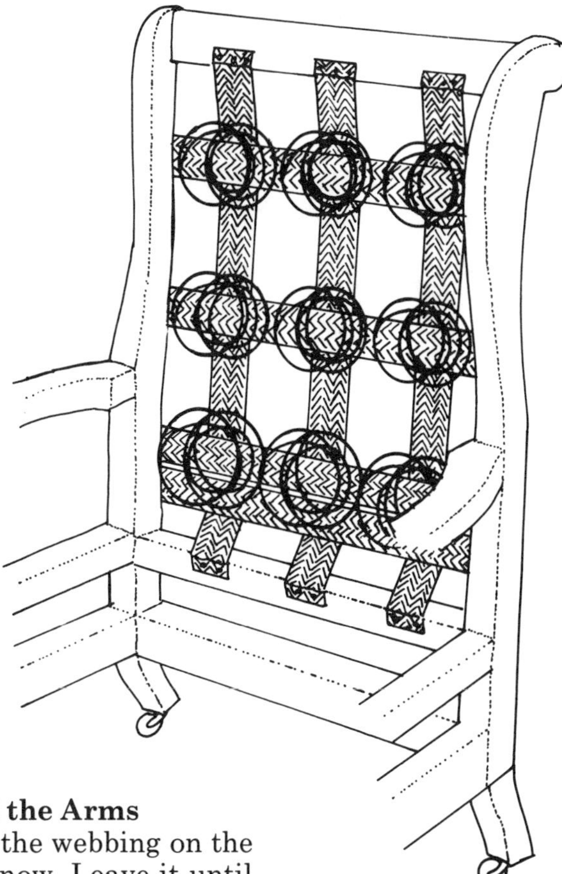

Fig. 94 The position of the back springs

Springing the Back and the Arms

Do not be tempted to put the webbing on the bottom of the seat frame now. Leave it until later, because keeping the space open will give you good access when you are upholstering and covering the back and the arms. With easy chairs the seat is the last upholstered part to be built in.

You can re-use the back springs if they are in good condition. They do not get the punishment that seat springs receive. But if you have to use new springs, try to get soft ones, 12 gauge or thinner, if possible. Remember that you have to build a buttoned back, so you must not bring it too far forward or there will not be enough depth for the buttonwork. The three springs for the lumbar swell will be deeper of course.

The back springs should be positioned as shown in **fig. 94**. It is not necessary to lace these springs. Just fix them with twine as described on page 37, then stretch over the heavy hessian. Temporarily tack the hessian down and, through the spaces between the webbing on the outside back, adjust the springs until you are happy with their position. One way to test whether the shape is good is to place a small stool inside the frame

▼ **Fig. 95** A length of webbing holding down the arm springs

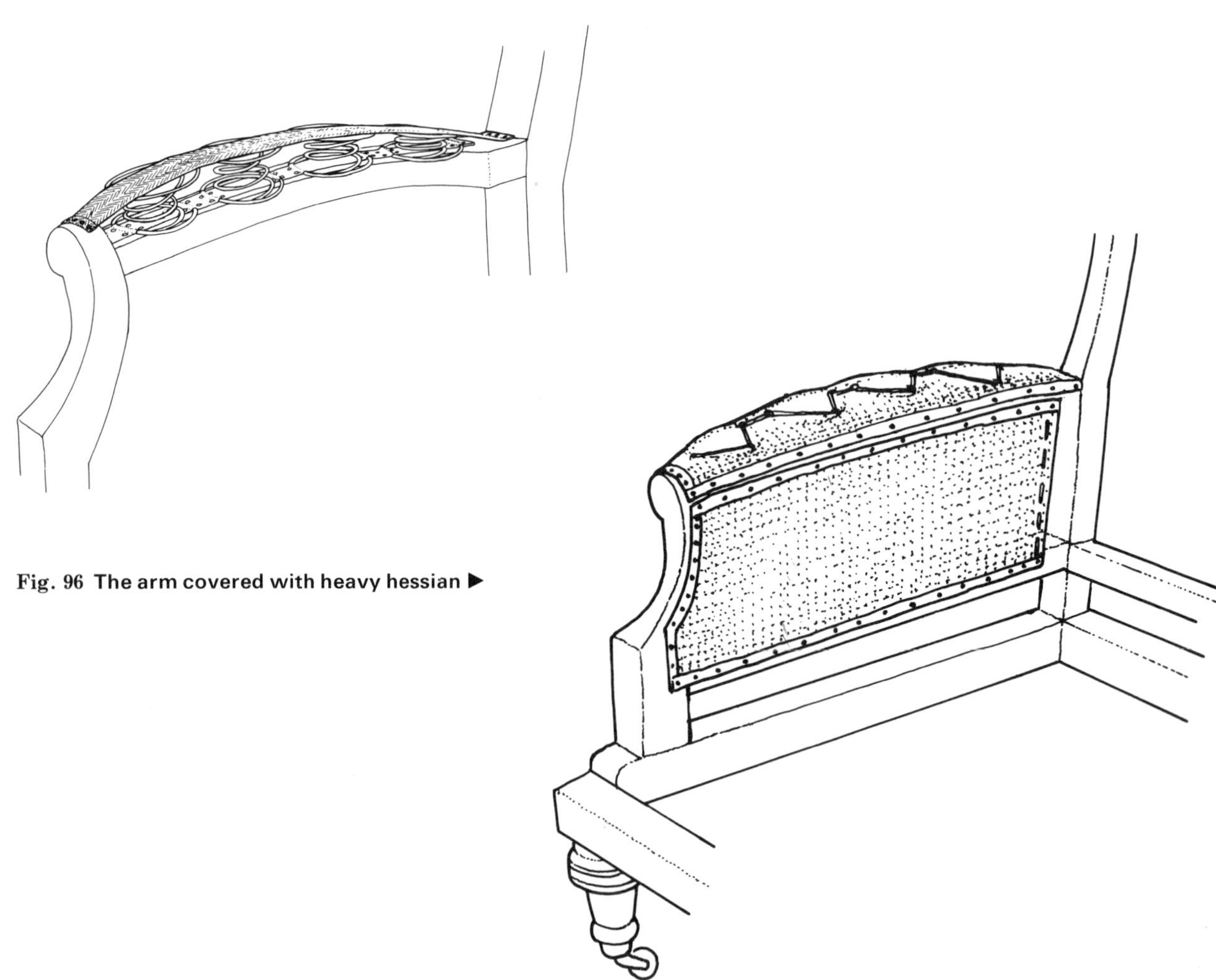

Fig. 96 The arm covered with heavy hessian ▶

at roughly the seat height. Pack it up if necessary. Sit on this and lean back to see if the contours of the springs fit your back.

If you need new springs for the arms, again, get soft ones—about 100 to 125 mm (4 to 5 in) high and 12 to 14 gauge. Harder springs defeat the object, which is to give buoyant support to the modest weight of one's arm. Position the springs as shown in **fig. 95**. Here, they are fixed to the arm spring platform with a strip of webbing run down the length of the platform and tacked over the base of each spring. If you prefer, you can fasten the springs to the platform with 20 mm ($\frac{3}{4}$ in) wire staples, three or four to a spring. To pull the springs down to their correct height either lace them with laid cord from back to front, as described on page 38, or, as shown above. Here I have stretched a length of webbing over the springs from the back to the front and fastened the springs to the webbing with twine, with four stitches per spring top. In **fig. 96** you can see how the whole arm is covered with hessian so that the springs are completely boxed in. The hessian extends (sometimes as a separate piece) over the open space of the frame below the spring platform and, again, the springs are fixed with stitches through the hessian. The lower part of this support hessian is sewn with large running stitches to the piece of webbing next to the back upright.

The First Stuffing

The most difficult first stuffing to do is on the arms, so let us begin with that.

Put in some stuffing ties in lines from back to front, one line on each side of the spring 'box', another along the top of this, then one line near the centre of the area below the springs and another near the bottom tacking rail. From now on carry out each stage on both arms so that eventually you get them to the same size.

Put some short loose loops as stuffing ties all round the wooden scroll fronts, about 20 mm ($\frac{3}{4}$ in) in from the front (**fig. 97**). This is where you begin your stuffing. Now, take a good look at the chair frame and try to get a mental picture of the shape that you want the arms to be when they are finished. The wooden arm fronts give a rough guide to the finished shape. If you reckon on building out the stitched edges to about 25 to 38 mm (1 to $1\frac{1}{2}$ in) larger than this timber shape you won't be far out—although keeping rigidly to this distance will give a rather uninteresting curve to the scroll. You can improve the line by tightening in the top and bottom of the scroll line (**fig. 98**).

Tuck some horsehair under the stuffing ties round the wooden arm fronts to make a dense, tight wall, about 6 mm ($\frac{1}{4}$ in) larger than your visualized finished size for the scroll. Spend some time at this stage in getting both arm fronts to the same shape. Place horsehair under all the other stuffing ties so that you have lines of hair along the arms, decreasing in thickness towards the back. Fill up the empty spaces in between with more hair, making sure that all is even and the two arms are padded to the same shape and density.

Now cover the arms with scrim hessian, or the 280 g (10 oz) hessian if you prefer. To get the arms the same size, with the same curve to the scroll, cut off the two pieces of hessian to exactly the same size. Then, when you put them on, note the exact amount taken up for turnings top and bottom and tack the hessian to exactly the same place on the frame of each arm. But, of course, the character of the scrolls can still differ within these confines, so in the end you will have to rely on your eye, plus a few measurements taken across the scroll at various places, to get the two looking the same.

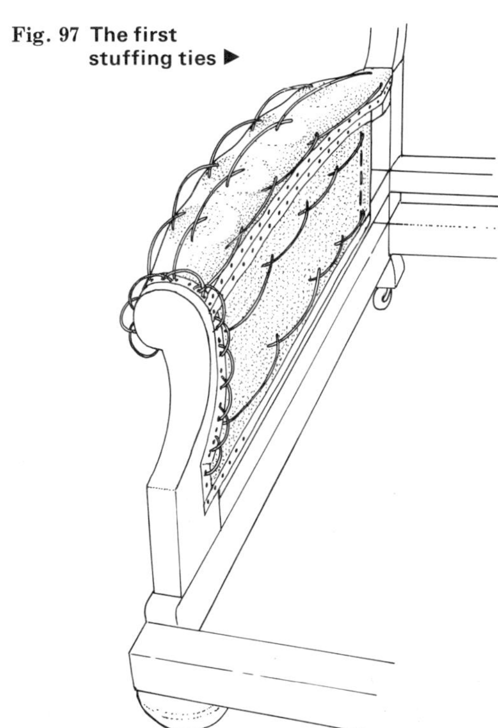
Fig. 97 The first stuffing ties ▶

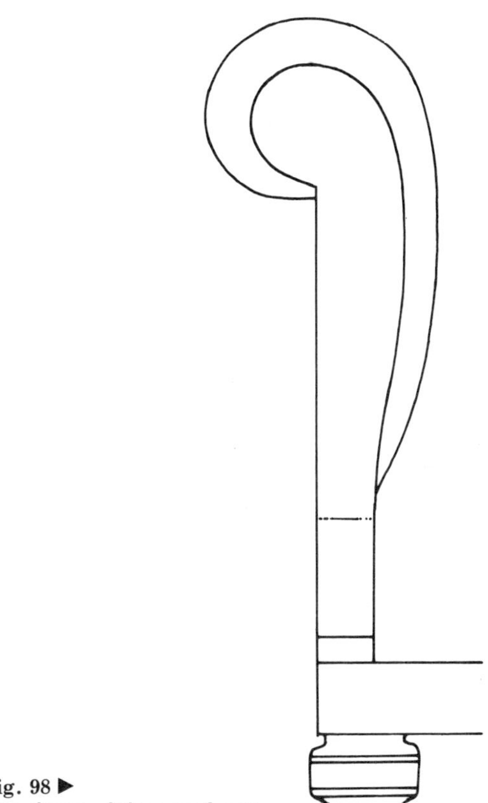
Fig. 98 ▶ The shape of the arm front

Fig. 99 **Fixing the hessian over the first stuffing for the arms**

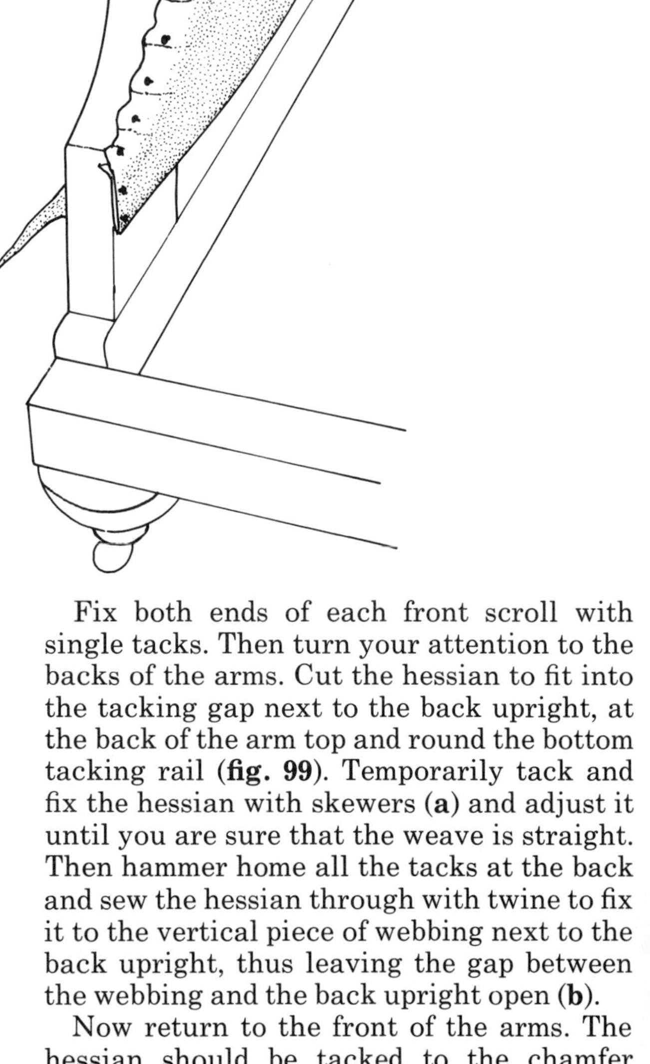

99(a) Cut the hessian in at the back of the arm ▶

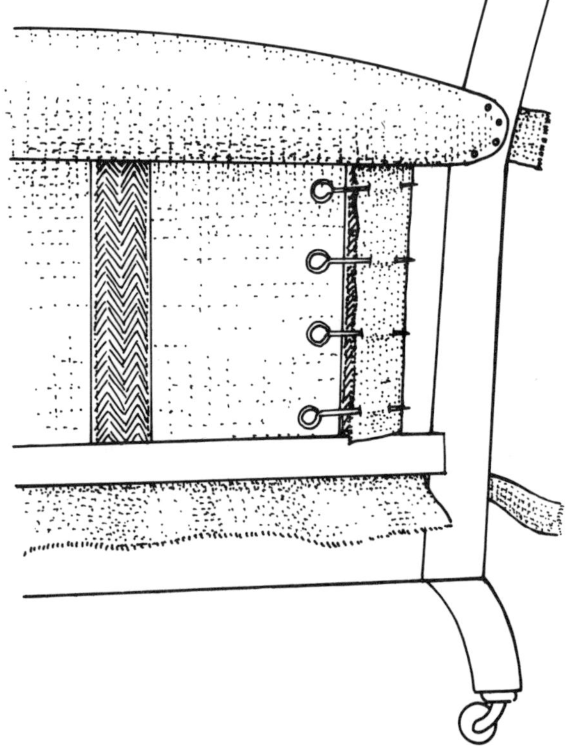

99(b) Temporarily fasten the hessian at the back of the arm ▼

Fix both ends of each front scroll with single tacks. Then turn your attention to the backs of the arms. Cut the hessian to fit into the tacking gap next to the back upright, at the back of the arm top and round the bottom tacking rail (**fig. 99**). Temporarily tack and fix the hessian with skewers (**a**) and adjust it until you are sure that the weave is straight. Then hammer home all the tacks at the back and sew the hessian through with twine to fix it to the vertical piece of webbing next to the back upright, thus leaving the gap between the webbing and the back upright open (**b**).

Now return to the front of the arms. The hessian should be tacked to the chamfer round the woodwork. Mark with a pronounced dot the centre of radius of the top circle of the scroll, and begin pleating and

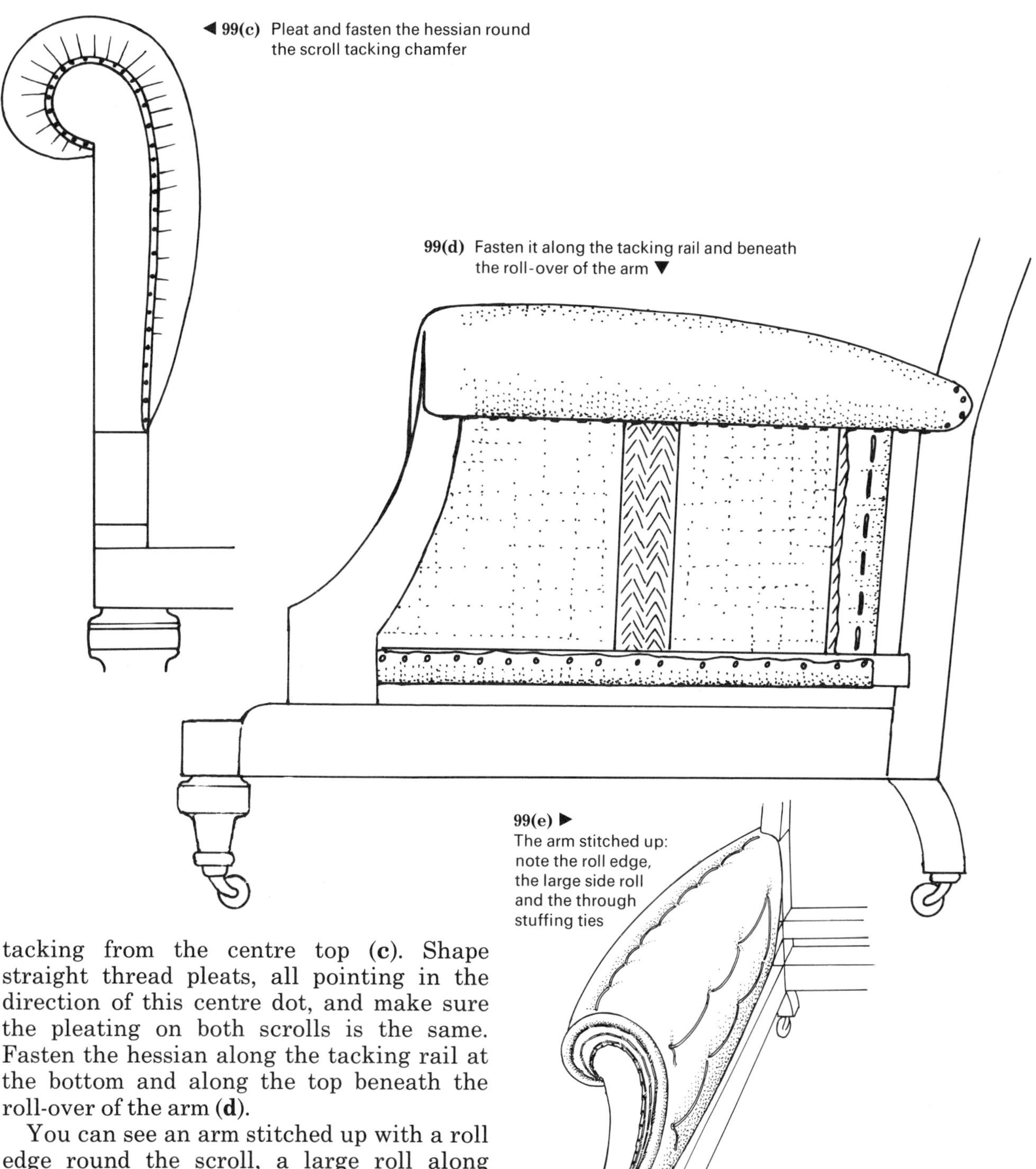

◀ **99(c)** Pleat and fasten the hessian round the scroll tacking chamfer

99(d) Fasten it along the tacking rail and beneath the roll-over of the arm ▼

99(e) ▶ The arm stitched up: note the roll edge, the large side roll and the through stuffing ties

tacking from the centre top (**c**). Shape straight thread pleats, all pointing in the direction of this centre dot, and make sure the pleating on both scrolls is the same. Fasten the hessian along the tacking rail at the bottom and along the top beneath the roll-over of the arm (**d**).

You can see an arm stitched up with a roll edge round the scroll, a large roll along the outside and through stuffing ties on the inside. The large side roll is made with the same large through stitches that you use for the edge rolls; it will keep the stuffing from moving down to the bottom of the arm roll-over and also form a line of foundation to give support and shape to the length of the arm (**e**).

A first stuffing on the inside back is the

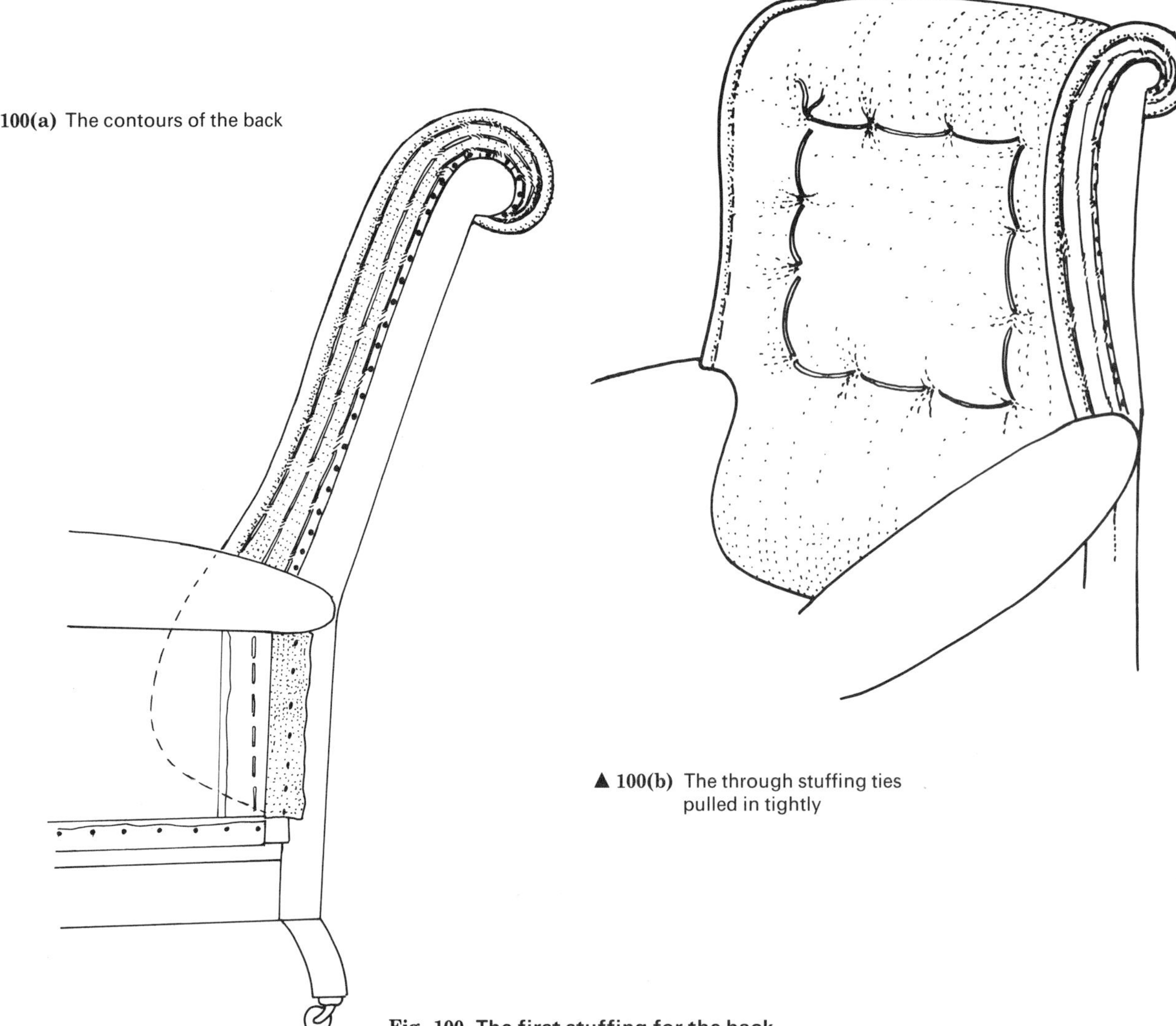

100(a) The contours of the back

▲ 100(b) The through stuffing ties pulled in tightly

Fig. 100 The first stuffing for the back

next task, so put lines of stuffing tie loops across the spring hessian. On each side of the back you will be making scrolls similar to the arm front scrolls, but smaller; put in stuffing ties about 20 mm ($\frac{3}{4}$ in) in from the edge of the wood so that you can build up stitched roll edges here. This back will also need a roll along the top and, since the roll will oversail the outside back, the ties here should be put in as close to the edge as possible. I suggest that you lay the chair on its back to put on this first stuffing. Remember to put plenty of hair over the area that will form the lumbar swell, graduating it down in thickness as you proceed to the top of the back. Keep the stuffing thin over the centre to allow depth for your buttons. The hessian covering for this stuffing must not be stretched vertically but should be tightened from side to side to form contours something like those seen at **fig. 100a**. You can now see the purpose of the gaps left at the back of the arms, for it is through these gaps that all the fixings for the lower back are made. Form the scroll edges at each side of the upper back in the same way as the arm front scrolls, with plenty of temporary tacking before finally pleating and fastening. In (**a**) you can also see the finished scroll after stitching. Next, put in through stuffing ties (**b**) and pull them down very tightly so that a recess is formed to take a thick top stuffing to give the buttonwork the depth that is necessary. Stitch up the side scrolls with one or two blind rows and one through row to form the roll (pages 47–49). Stitch the large roll across the back top in

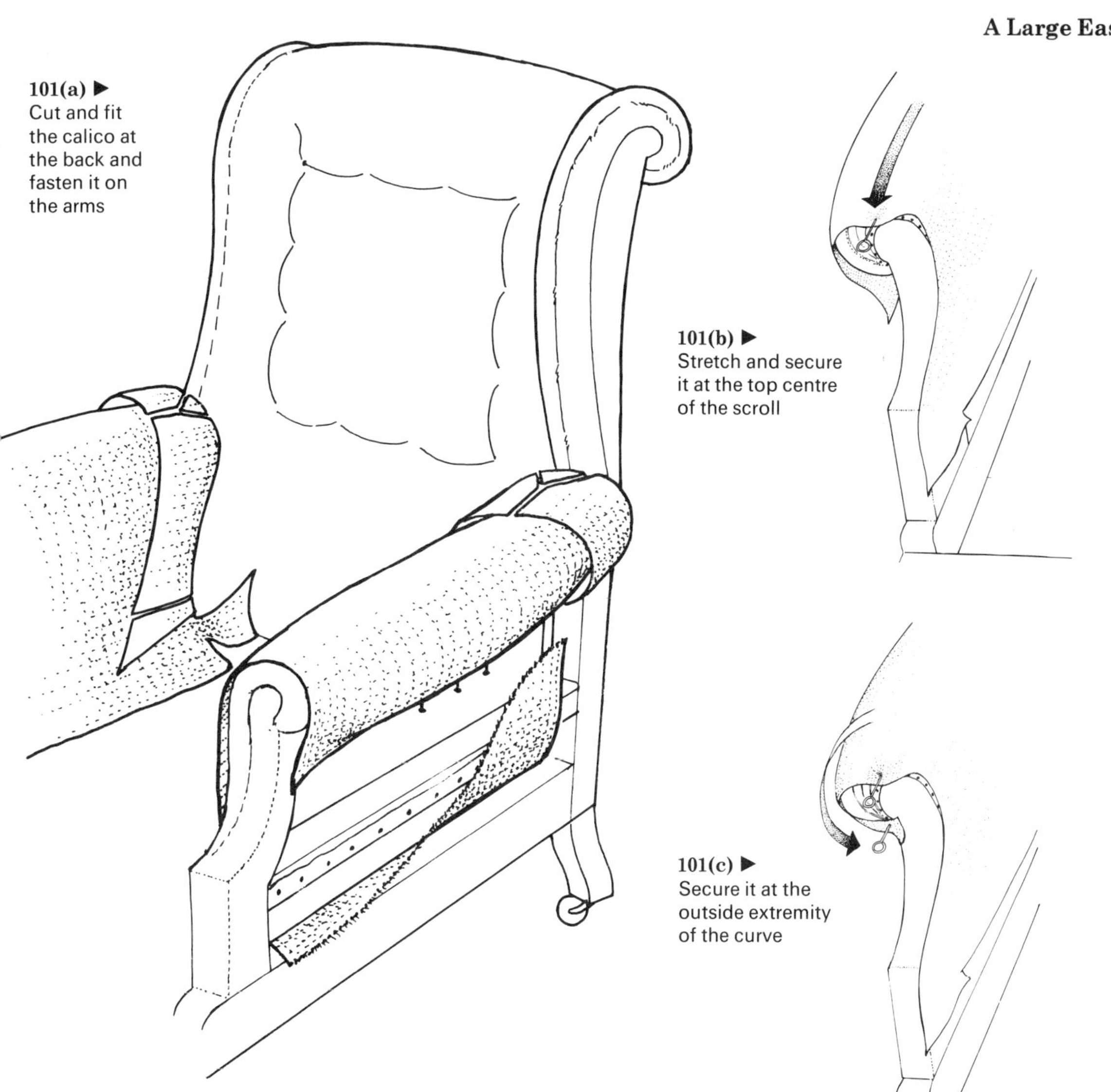

101(a) ▶
Cut and fit the calico at the back and fasten it on the arms
101(b) ▶
Stretch and secure it at the top centre of the scroll
101(c) ▶
Secure it at the outside extremity of the curve

Fig. 101 An undercovering of calico

the same way as you do the side rolls on the arms.

Now it is time to put the top stuffing on the arms. Use good quality long-stranded horsehair to give that soft and springy feel to the upholstery. Again, make stuffing ties in lines about 100 mm (4 in) apart along the length of the arm and apply the hair in lines, filling in afterwards. Do not use too much stuffing for these are quite elegant arms and you do not want them to take on an inflated, bulbous look. Weigh the horsehair first to make sure you use exactly the same amount on each arm. You can use kitchen scales for this, but place the hair in a plastic bag first.

The Undercovering

The next step is to cover the chair with an undercovering of strong calico (**fig. 101**). When covering arms, whether with calico or the top covering, the rule is: secure at the back and stretch to the front before doing any stretching top to bottom. This will ensure a nice, even shape. So first secure your calico at the back, having cut it in to the back upright and around the tacking rail. As these arms are slightly curving I would recommend that you then fasten the calico with a few temporary tacks just under the roll-over and on the lower tacking rail, to keep the curved shape of the arm (**a**).

Now stretch the calico towards the front and fix it with skewers just under the lip of the scroll edge. Stretch and secure it at the top centre of the scroll (**b**), then at the outside extremity of the curve (**c**), stretching the

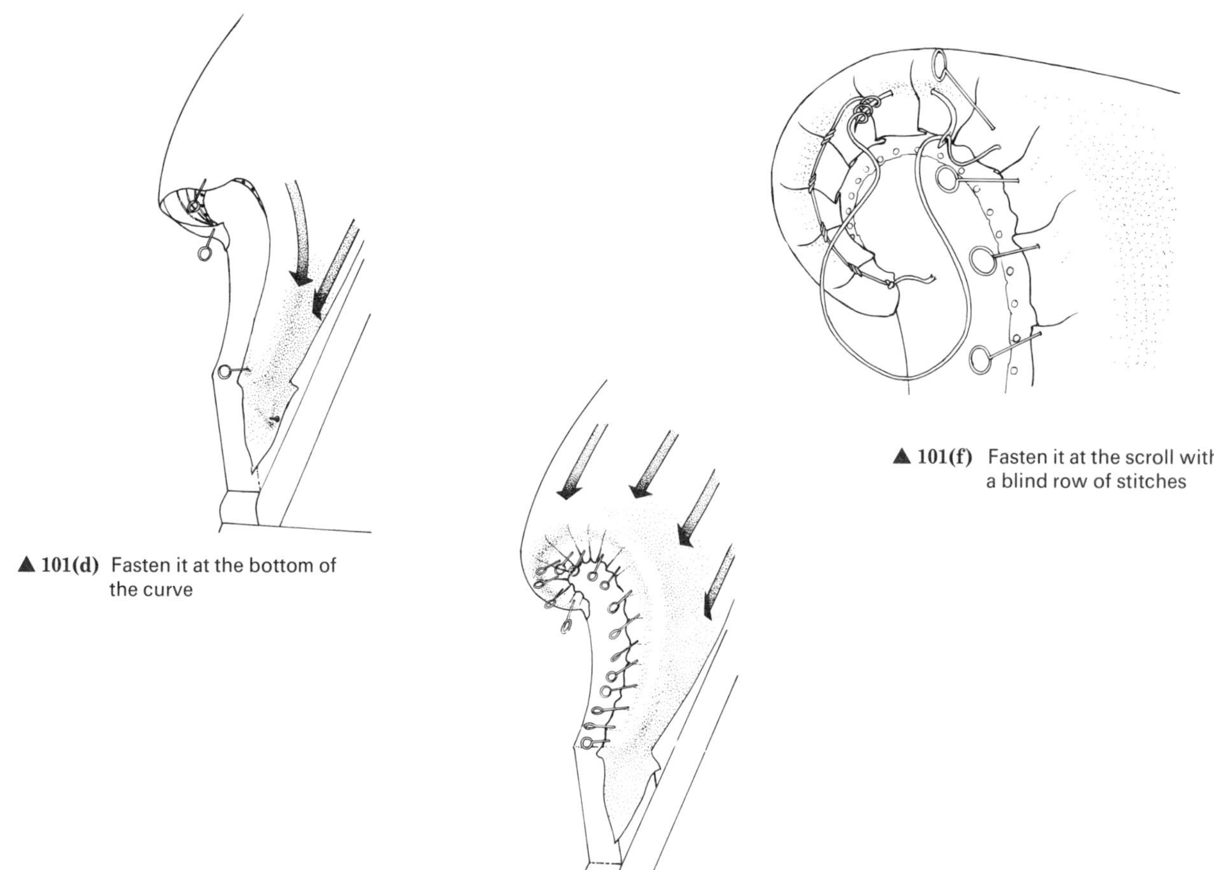

▲ **101(d)** Fasten it at the bottom of the curve

101(e) Stretch it forward and fix it ▶

▲ **101(f)** Fasten it at the scroll with a blind row of stitches

calico tightly round the perimeter of the scroll as well as pulling forward. Stretch and fasten the calico at the bottom of the curve of the scroll (**d**), then all round the remainder of the scroll shape (**e**). Only when you have done this on both arms should you tighten the calico over from the bottom to the top. The material passes right under the arm tacking rail and is fastened on the outside of this rail. Start at the front of this rail and tack towards the back. Work the same way fastening the calico under the top roll-over of the arm. Stretch the fabric as described on page 57, stroking with one hand while the other hand takes up the slack. Just tugging at the cloth will only cause unevenness. Much of tight cover work relies upon touch, and as your hand moves over the surface you will be able to feel when it is correctly tensioned. So coax and caress those arms into a really good shape.

At the scrolls the calico is sewn in with a blind row of twine stitches under the lip of the roll edge (**f**), to lend support to the edge. You can use a straight double-pointed needle for this but I would prefer you to try stitching with a semi-circular curved needle—your 75 mm (3 in) one will do. The same rules apply for this as for the straight needle (page 39). By inserting the curved needle so that the point emerges back along the row, you simulate the action of a straight needle being returned through the edge. The rule of three turns of the twine leading from the previous stitch around the needle is observed. There are two reasons for sewing the calico to the underside of the roll edge: first, it lends support to the edge, and, secondly, if the calico is fixed in this position, it will not be in the way when the facing is eventually sewn into the scroll front.

Now lay one or two layers of cotton wadding over the arms, bringing the wadding well over the front edge. Then cover the arms with your furnishing fabric, in just the same way as you put on the calico.

The Buttoned Back

Now for the buttoned back (**fig. 102**). First sew in stuffing tie loops across the first stuffing of the inside back. Make four or five horizontal rows across, from edge to edge. Why should you use stuffing ties if all the stuffing is to be held in with buttons? Well, buttonwork must be fairly firm and carded horsehair packed in at the right density would be an unmanageable bulge without the restraint of ties.

After the ties have been placed in lines fairly close together, pack the hair beneath them quite tightly, keeping the lumbar swell well defined (**a**). A layer of cotton wadding goes on next to help to keep the hair from working through. Stretch a layer of 71 g ($2\frac{1}{2}$oz) bonded polyester wadding over this.

Tack the polyester at the bottom tacking rail and then temporarily fasten it with skewers around the side scrolls, cutting and tucking in at the arm junctions and keeping the tension across the back to define the curved shape. Fasten the polyester with tacks under the roll-over at the top (**b**). When stretching the polyester over the stitched roll edges at the sides, tuck back the excess hair so that none is left on the outside and you keep the edges sharp.

Some upholsterers say that using polyester is cheating when you are working on period upholstery. But, personally, when I can see a way of improving traditional work with the aid of modern materials, I am all for it, as long as the foundations are made to the period specification. There are three advantages in using polyester in this instance. Firstly, it helps to hold the second stuffing in place, compressing it nearer to the finished thickness. Secondly, it makes setting out the places for the buttons much easier. And, thirdly, it gives an even, richer appearance to the surface of the covering fabric. I can remember what a difficult job buttoning was before the advent of bonded polyester wadding, when there was nothing but cotton wadding to keep the hair in place while you were putting in the buttons.

Fig. 102 The buttoned back

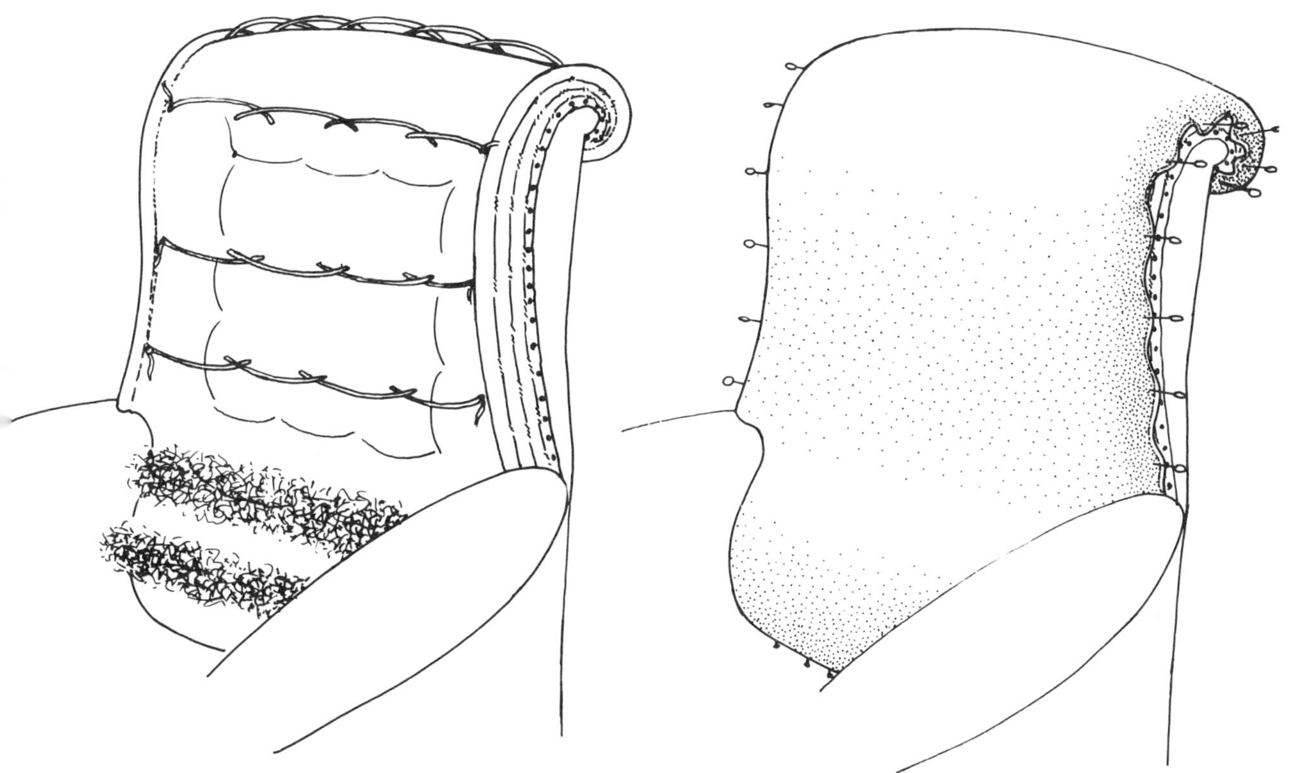

▲ **102(a)** Put in stuffing ties and tuck lines of hair under them

▲ **102(b)** Cover the back with thin bonded polyester wadding

Setting out the Buttonwork

Take a very soft pencil, your steel measuring tape and a ruler or straight edge. With the aid of your straight edge, draw a vertical line down the centre of the back, taking the line over the top roll-over. A soft pencil will make a clearly visible, if faint, mark—I am a little nervous about using anything like a felt tip or a ball point pen on material immediately behind a covering. Should the cover ever get wet, the pen colour might come right through.

Beginning at this centre line, set out the place where you want the buttons to be, using skewers pushed into the wadding (**fig. 103a**). When setting out for buttonwork, there are several points to remember. The spaces between the buttons should form diamond shapes, with the length always greater than the width. Where possible, the distances from the buttons to the edges of the sides should be no more than the width between the buttons, and no less than half this measurement. The buttons should be spaced equally and in straight lines. To allow for a good lumbar swell, the bottom row of buttons should be placed just below the height of the arms. And the buttons in the top row should not be placed too high. When you are initially setting out, just roughly place your skewers and try to judge how many rows and how many buttons in each row would look best, then, when you are satisfied with the result, measure and place your skewers more accurately. Remove the skewers one by one and make a dot in each place with a felt tip pen. I use a 25 mm (1 in) tubular cutter (page 12) to cut holes through the wadding at each dot, but if you do not have a cutter, make a star cut through each mark with a sharp-pointed knife. Deepen each hole right through the stuffing to the spring hessian with a couple of fingers or a large regulator. To mark the spring hessian on the outside of the back, push a long felt tip pen through the spaces between the webbing and put crosses which correspond exactly with the button positions on the front.

Make a drawing, showing all the button positions (**b**). Take a measurement by inserting the end of your steel tape into a top button hole and bending the tape over the roll-over to the far edge of the top rail, read this off and enter it on your diagram. On the sides, take a measurement over the lip of the roll edge and add 25 mm (1 in). Enter this figure also. At the bottom, measure from inside a hole in the bottom row to well under the swell, nearly as far as the tacking rail. To each between-button measurement on the back of your chair you must add extra to allow for the depth of the button. The between-button allowance can vary from 25 mm (1 in) to 50 mm (2 in), depending on how deep you wish the work to be. In this instance I would recommend 38 mm ($1\frac{1}{2}$ in) for fairly deep buttoning. Look at (**b**) once more and you will see the measurements written in, and at the side a couple of sums added up to give the total length and width of the piece of cloth that you require.

Cut off your piece of cloth and lay it out on the table, right side down. Mark the top with a 'T'; this may sound a bit obvious, but it would be rather sad if you did your setting out on the back of the cloth only to find when you turned it over that you had done it top to bottom! Using a piece of tailor's chalk, lightly mark lines across for the lines of buttons to the measurements and position noted on your diagram. These lines should follow the weave of the cloth accurately across the piece. Now mark the position of the buttons on these lines. Double-check that all your marks are according to your diagram, then, with a regulator, pierce the fabric at each mark so that the hole can be seen on the face side. Finally, on the back of the material along the bottom and top edges make small, clear marks corresponding with the position of the button marks in the rows nearest these edges.

COVERING AND BUTTONING

Everything is now ready to begin covering and buttoning. You will need a double-pointed 250 mm (10 in) needle, some nylon tufting twine, some small pieces of webbing to roll up for toggles, scissors, your two button-fold sticks (page 12) or two regulators and, of course, the buttons—which you will probably have got your local friendly upholsterer to make up for you. Have your chair on low trestles so that you can work comfortably.

Before recent legislation, polyether foam was used and this had to be insulated from direct contact with the covering fabric—especially if the cover was of velvet—or the

Fig. 103 Setting out the buttonwork

103(a) Set out the button positions ▶

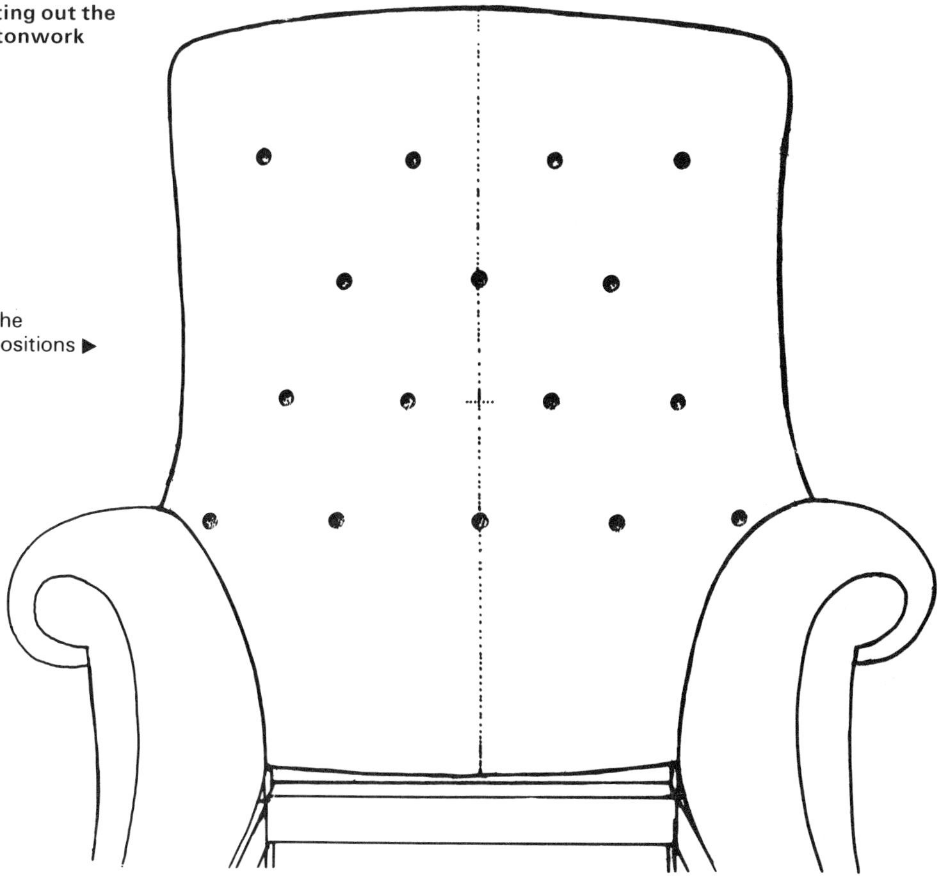

▼ **103(b)** Diagram for setting out buttons. (Figs. in brackets include extra allowance for depth of buttons.)

Add:	18
	14
	14
	14
	18
Total width	**78cm**

Add:	30
	22
	11
	35
Total length	**98cm**

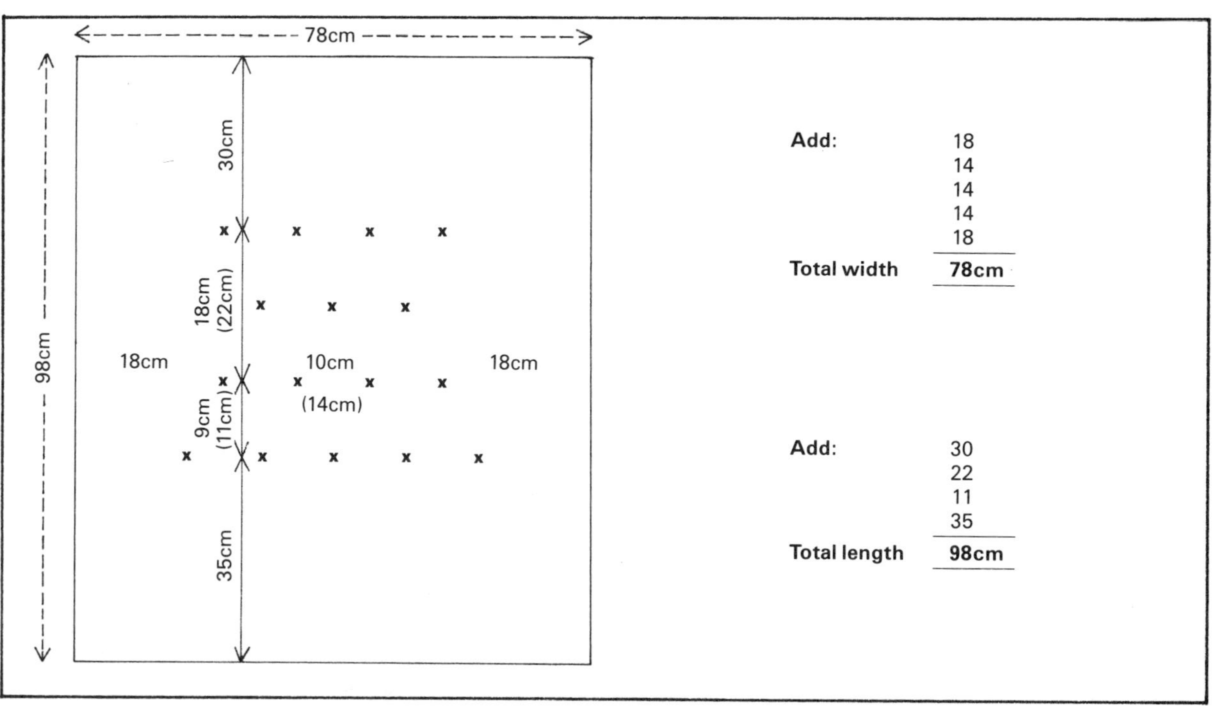

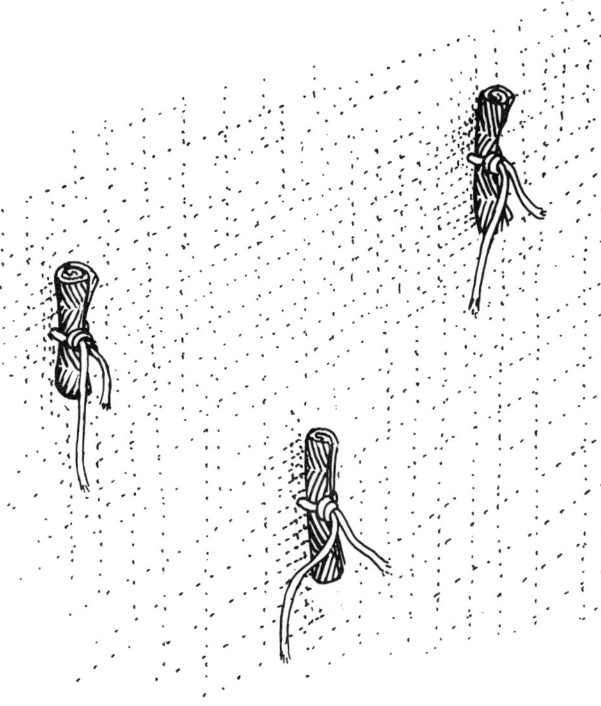

Fig. 104 Rolled-up pieces of webbing form toggles behind the knots

friction between the foam and the fabric would shorten the life of the fabric considerably. A layer of cotton wadding would also prevent cling, and made it easier to pull the buttons into their appointed places.

Throw the cover over the inside back, with all back buttonwork you should begin at the centre of the bottom row, because this makes it easier to manipulate the loose material. Then fold the material over on itself lengthwise, and position together the bottom centre mark and the button hole. As you have springs in the back of this chair it may prove rather difficult to knot the button cords at the back, but if you leave your cord ends long, and if you are blessed with long fingers or small hands, you will probably manage. If tying at the back proves too difficult, have a look at Chapter 9 (page 144) where I describe how to tie from the front.

Thread your needle with tufting twine and insert it a little to one side of the bottom centre mark on the back of the spring hessian. Bring the needle through the centre hole in your covering, thread on a button, return the needle through the same hole in the material and back into the hole through the stuffing to emerge a little to the other side of the mark on the back of the hessian. Hold the two cords and, with your other hand, hold out the button to make sure there are no twists in the cord. Still holding the button so that it cannot twist round, draw it into the hole, taking in the covering but not too deeply. Now, from the back, draw the cord through until you have a length of about 150 mm (6 in) left, then tie an upholsterer's slip knot (page 34). Draw the button in a little more but do not lock the slip knot, just cut off the cord so that the draw cord is longer than the other one (so that you will know which one to pull later). Roll up a piece of your webbing into a toggle and place this behind the knot to stop the cord cutting through the hessian (**fig. 104**).

Following this procedure, fix all the buttons in the two bottom rows.

At this point, lay the chair on its back. To make the diagonal pleats or folds between the rows, use two button-fold sticks or the flattened ends of two regulators. Hold one stick or regulator under the cloth and tuck the other in the fold on the front of the cover (**fig. 105a**). By this method a very neat fold

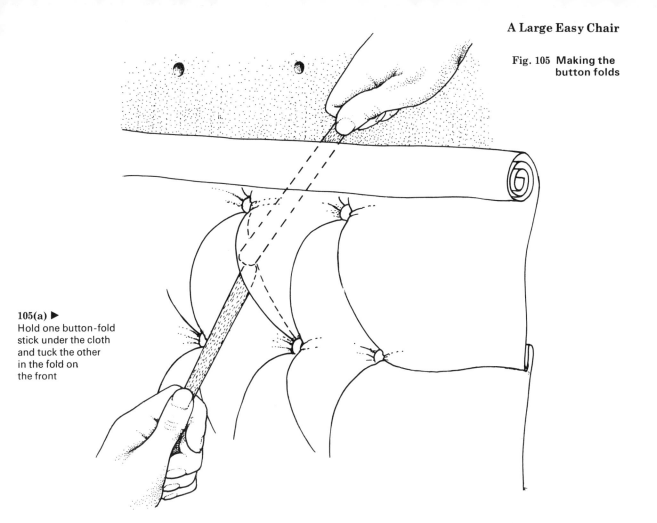

Fig. 105 Making the button folds

105(a) ▶ Hold one button-fold stick under the cloth and tuck the other in the fold on the front

can be made between buttons and any bunching of material can be smoothed out. Note that all the tucks or pleats in buttonwork are folded downwards. Not only do the folds look better like this, but dust is less likely to accumulate in downwards folds.

Carry on up the back, row by row, until you have all the buttons placed and every fold satisfactorily made. Then make and temporarily fix the folds from the outside buttons to the edges of the sides and to the top roll-over and those over the swell.

Turn up the cover from the bottom, exposing the swell upholstery; with a very sharp-pointed knife, cut the wadding from the button holes of the bottom row downwards to just under the swell (**b**), then, with a button-fold stick or the rounded end of your regulator, part the wadding and hair beneath back to the scrim hessian. Cut some small strips of wadding and line the slits to prevent hair coming through when the covering is tucked in.

105(b) Cut the wadding from the button holes downwards ▼

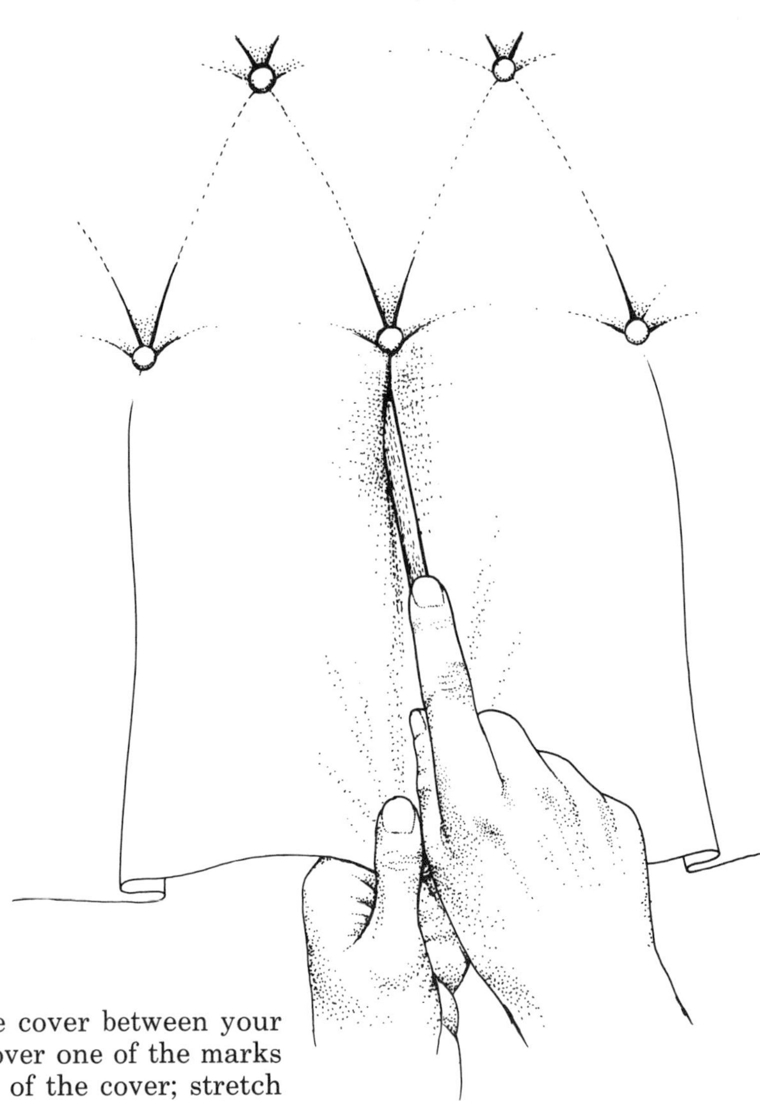

105(c) Ease the material into the crevice ▶

Hold the edge of the cover between your thumb and forefinger over one of the marks along the bottom edge of the cover; stretch tightly and, using a button-fold stick or a regulator, ease the material into the crevice from the button downwards (**c**). Fold the material at this mark, taking up the between-button allowance in the fold. Take the fold under the swell and fasten it temporarily with a skewer pushed up into the underside of the swell as shown at (**d**).

Make a fold at each of the edge marks and the marks at the top of the material, and pin them as shown (**e**). With one hand, take each fold at the top and pull the material in a straight pleat round into the button. Several attempts will have to be made with each fold in turn before you get it exactly right. Secure each one with a temporary tack under the roll-over. You will find the folds leading out to the scroll edges much easier; these can be fastened with skewers.

Cut your covering in as shown in (**f**), to enable you to make a good join at the junction

105(d) Fasten the folds temporarily with skewers ▼

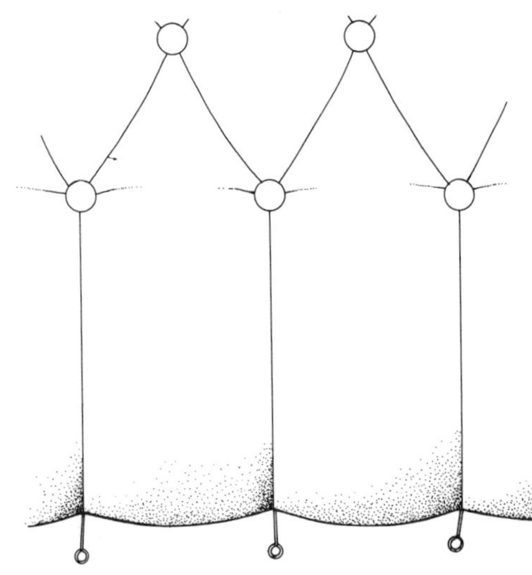

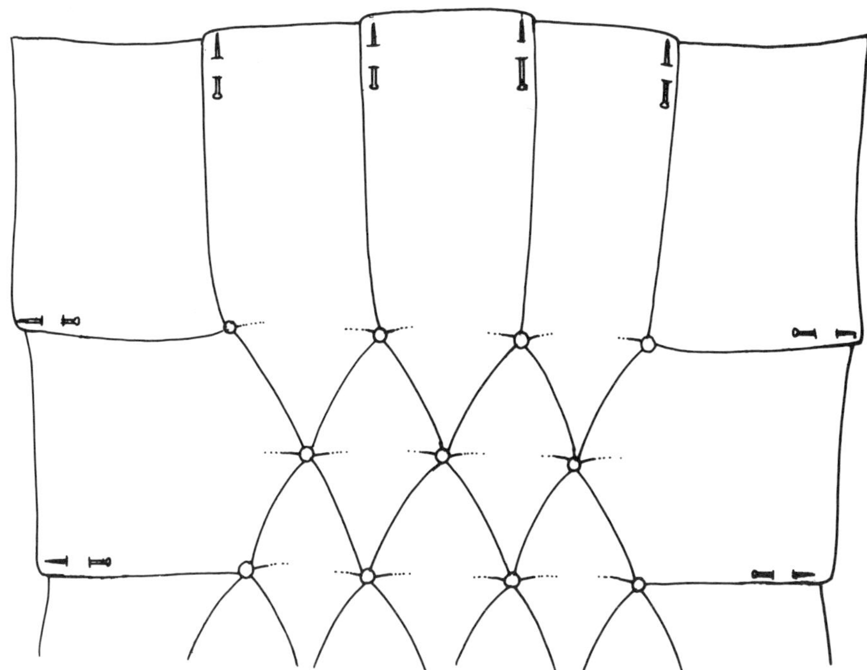

105(e) Make a fold at each edge mark and pin it ▲

of the arm and so that you can tuck that lower flap of material through the gap at the back of the arm beneath the arm tacking rail. Take a lot of time and thought over this—you can make some very nasty mistakes just here.

It is now time to pull all the buttons in as far as they will go. Begin at the top and work down—and go easy with the bottom row for it may not be necessary to pull these in so far. Take them in little by little until any fullness between these and the buttons forming the top of the diamond shapes is taken up. They will then be sufficiently tight. Lock each button slip knot with three half hitches.

Give the top folds a last stretch and tug, and permanently fasten them over the roll-over. Make final adjustments round the side scrolls and then fasten the covering with a blind row of stitches put in with a curved needle, as you did with the arm scrolls. Just a final stroke and tuck with your button-fold stick at each of the folds between the buttons and you can leave the back and turn to the seat upholstery.

105(f) Cut the fabric in at the junction with the arm and permanently fasten all the folds ▼

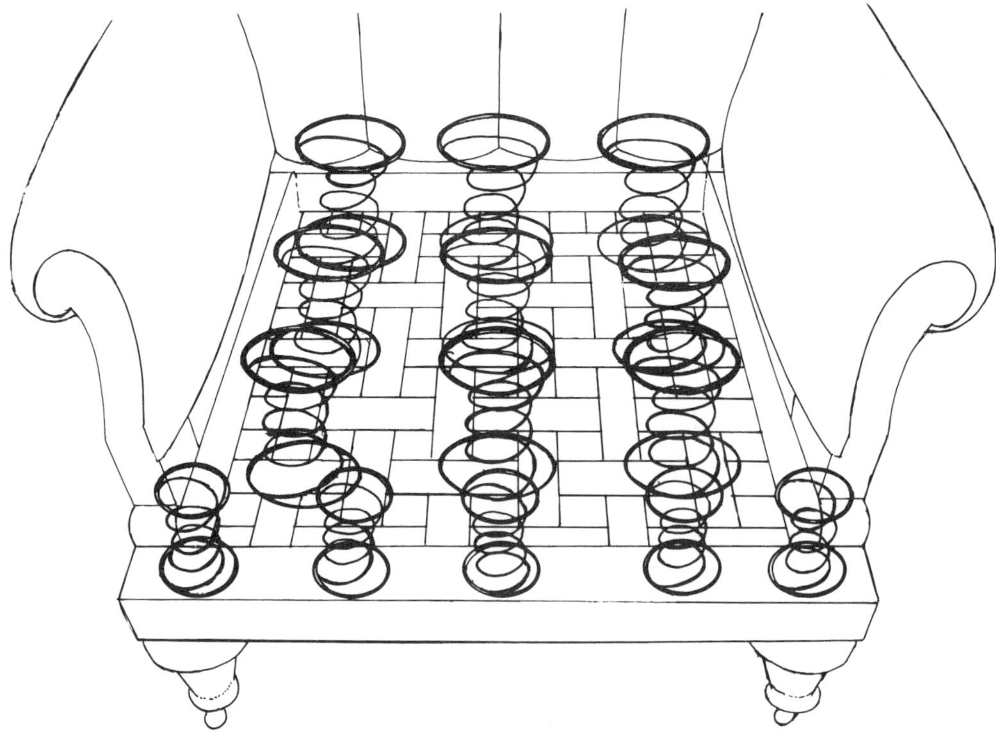

▲ 106(a) The positioning of the seat springs

Fig. 106 Building a spring-edged seat

106(b) Tie down the edge springs to the correct height ▼

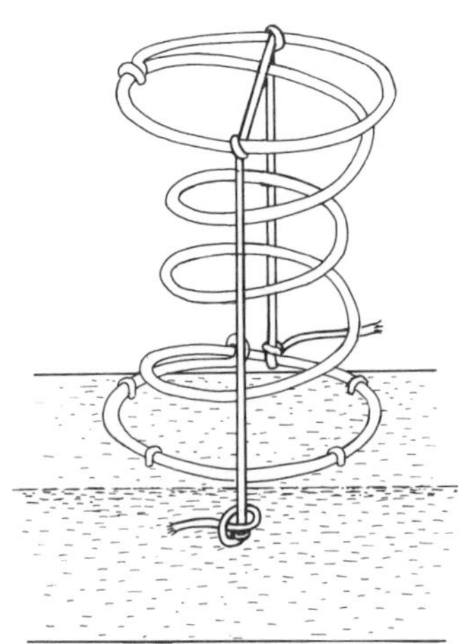

Building a Spring-Edged Seat

When buying new springs for the seat you can of course use the old springs as a guide, but do check that they are the correct size, for the previous upholsterer may have made a mistake. As a rough guide, the springs should be about 38 to 50 mm ($1\frac{1}{2}$ to 2 in) higher than the tacking rails at the bottom of the arms, so that they just squeeze under the swell upholstery with a little compression. Use **No. 10** gauge springs for a seat of medium softness, **No. 9** gauge if you want a very firm seat. The four edge springs should be **No. 9** gauge and, of course, these need to be shorter, so that they stand at near the same height as the main seat springs.

Spread some softening (old cushions, foam or an old blanket) on the floor and with great care turn up your chair on this. Put a trestle or stool under the front rail to keep the chair frame level. Then fasten the webbing across the underside of the seat (pages 29–30). A fairly large seat like this needs a strong support for the springs, so stretch six pieces of webbing from the back to the front and six from side to side. Next, fix the springs. For easy working move your chair to medium-height trestles. The diagram in **fig. 106a** shows the placing of the seat springs. Fix the four edge springs in position first. These

106(c) Lace the edge springs

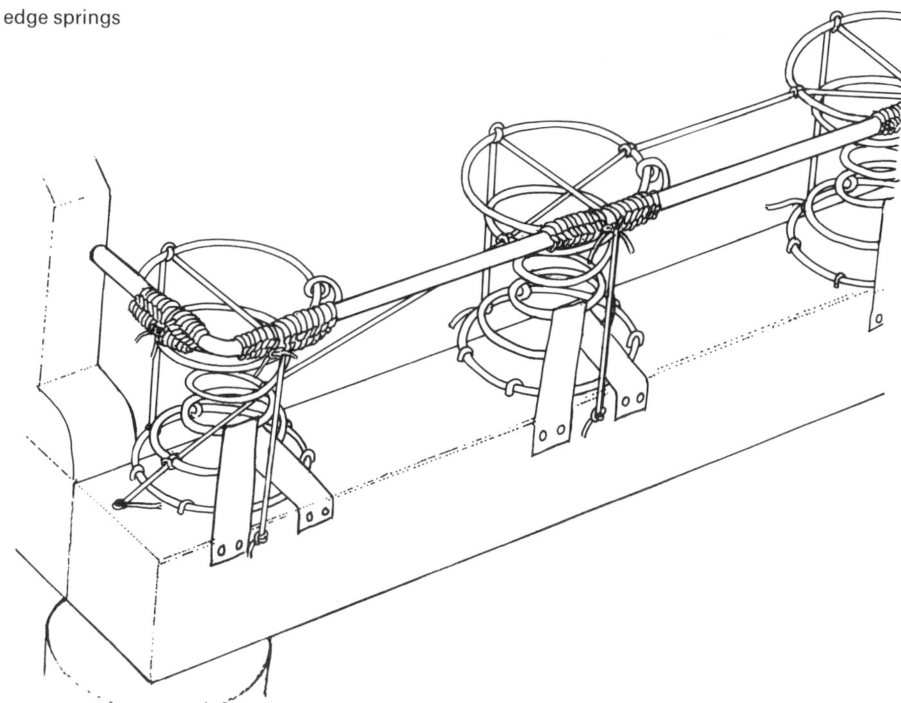

springs sit on the wide front rail of the chair, with the knuckle of the bottom coil towards the back, and they need to be independent of the rest—you will see why later on. They may be secured with wire staples (four per spring) or held in place by a strip of webbing tacked over the bottom coil of each spring.

The larger main springs are positioned in three rows of three. The front row leans forward to give that fanning-out effect; so do not place them too close to the edge springs. Once the springs are in their proper place they should be laced and tied down. Begin with the edge springs.

Cut off a couple of metres of laid cord and, starting with the spring on the right-hand side, tie a slip knot on the back of the bottom coil where it overlaps the seat rail. Bring the cord up to the top of the spring, pull the spring down to the required height (in this instance, about level with the lower arm tacking rail) and tie the cord with a single half hitch. Now bring the cord to the front of the spring top and tie it again with a half hitch (**b**). Hammer a 20 mm ($\frac{3}{4}$ in) wire staple halfway home into the front of the seat rail at dead centre of the spring and below it. Thread the cord through the staple and pull it down until the spring top is level, then drive the staple home and tie a half hitch round the taut cord to make it fast. Do the same with the spring on the left-hand side, fixing its height at the exact height of the first spring. Do the same with the two centre springs.

Seats of this period often have a piece of cane bent at the ends, fastened along the front of the spring tops. If this is in good condition it can be used again. But if it is split or worn or is brittle, use an edge wire instead. This can be made from an ordinary coil spring, straightened—just hold one end of the spring in a vice and unwind it. In this case we will assume that the cane is all right, so lay it along the spring tops, then fix it to the springs by whipping it with twine (page 37). Make sure that the ends are also securely fastened to the springs.

To bring the springs forward a trifle and to help to keep them there, thread a small strap of webbing folded in half lengthwise over the second or third coil up from the bottom of each spring. Pull the straps down and fasten them in inverted Vs with 12 mm ($\frac{1}{2}$ in) improved tacks. Then, to brace the springs sideways, make a lacing with laid cord from side to side. Begin near the bottom of the left-hand spring, rise to near the top of the centre springs, and then move down to near the base of the spring on the right (**c**).

106(d) Lace the main springs ▼

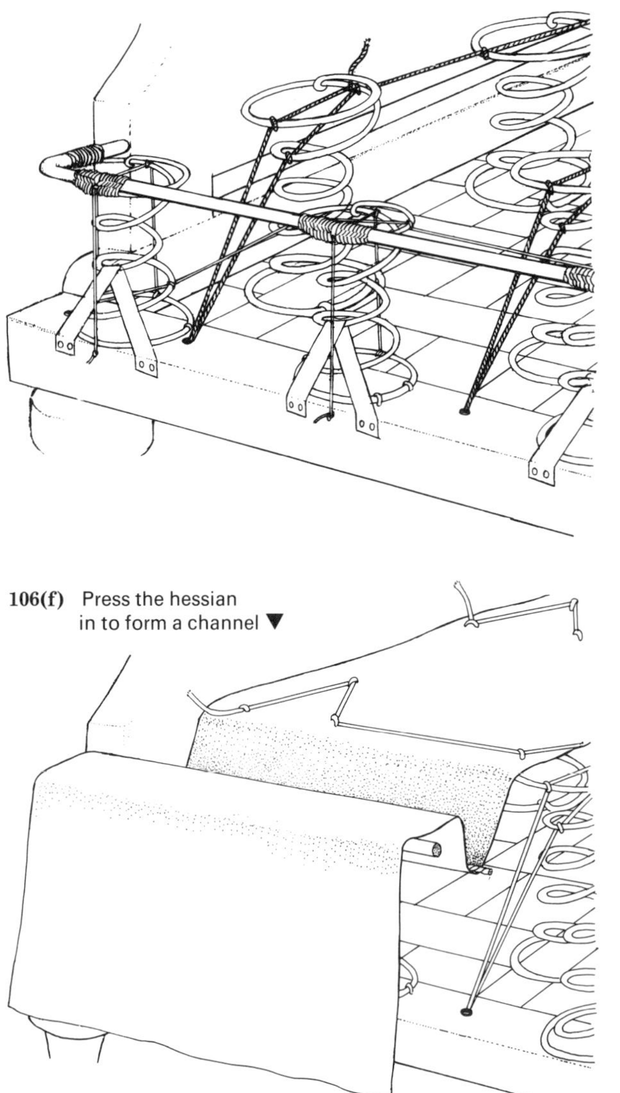

106(f) Press the hessian in to form a channel ▼

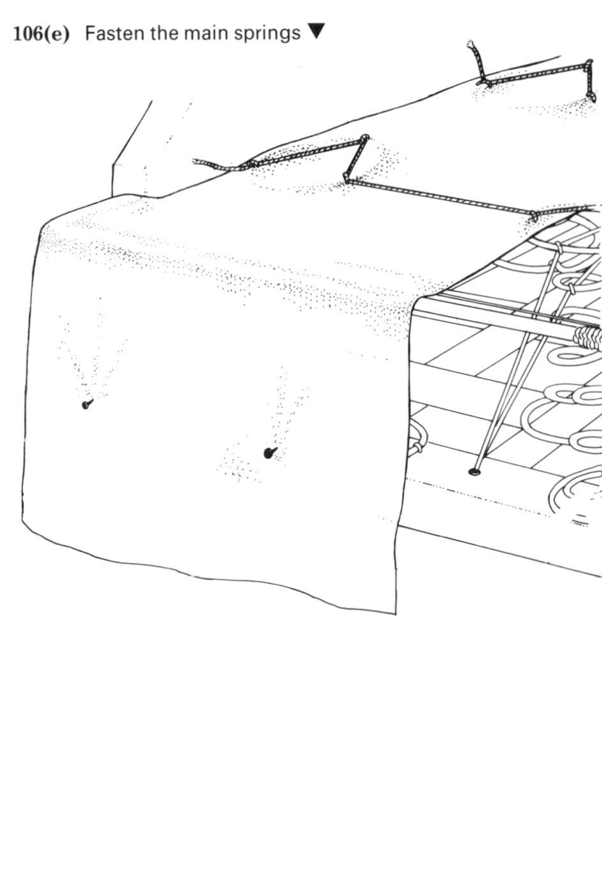

106(e) Fasten the main springs ▼

Lace up the main springs, giving them the necessary fanning out (**d**). Fasten the cords at the front on the top of the front rail between the edge springs. The life of the seat depends upon the proper placing of the main springs, so take great care to get this right.

To calculate the amount of tarpaulin hessian needed to cover the springs, place your steel tape over the springs and extend it beyond the back rail by 25 mm (1 in). Push the tape down between the main springs and the front edge springs to a depth of about 38 mm ($1\frac{1}{2}$ in) to allow enough length to form a well. (I will tell you about this in a minute). Keep the loop of tape in and continue to take it over the edge springs to the bottom of the front rail; read off this measurement. Measure the width 25 mm (1 in) beyond the outside of the seat rails. Cut off the hessian and lay it over the springs, then fasten it at the back on top of the seat rail, making the usual 25 mm (1 in) turnover to tack through. Cut diagonally into the back corners, then come round to the front of the chair and pull the hessian over and down to the front rail. Temporarily tack it there, in about four places. Next, fasten the sides also along the top of the rails, about 10 mm ($\frac{3}{8}$ in) in from the outside edges.

Fasten only the main springs at this stage, with the usual three stitches per spring (**e**). Then release the temporary tacks at the front.

106(g) Fasten the well cord at each end ▼

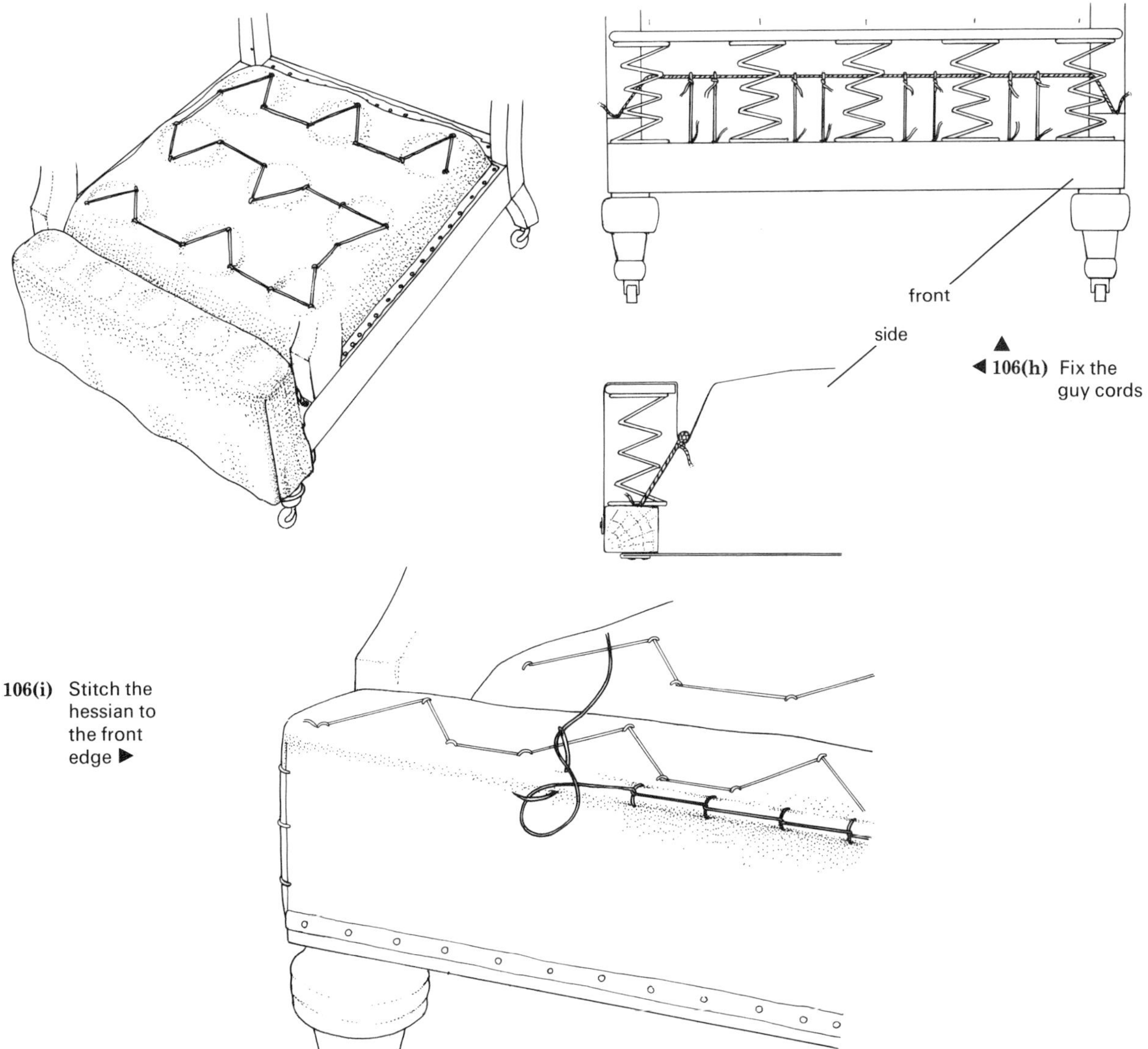

◀ **106(h)** Fix the guy cords

106(i) Stitch the hessian to the front edge ▶

Press the hessian in to form a 38 mm ($1\frac{1}{2}$ in) well or channel at the back of the edge springs (**f**). Take a length of laid cord and lay it along the bottom of this channel.

Stretch the cord across and fasten it at each end with two 15 mm ($\frac{5}{8}$ in) improved tacks (**g**). Lift the loose hessian up from the front and throw it back over the main springs. Cut six pieces of laid cord about 38 cm (15 in) long to make guys. Fix two of these lengths of cord between each pair of front springs, as in (**h**). Thread each length through the hessian round the well cord, tie it with a slip knot and cut it off at least 77 mm (3 in) away from the front seat rail, leaving plenty to pull on. When all these guy cords are in place, pull them tight and fasten them with staples or 15 mm ($\frac{5}{8}$ in) improved tacks to the top of the front rail between the edge springs. The guy cords assume the position and role of hessian, in a seat without a spring edge which would continue to the front rail. The well and guy cords also restrain the edge springs, keeping them from being pushed back into the seat.

Bring the hessian forward again over the edge springs and tack it at the front as shown in (**i**). Sew the hessian to the cane or wire edge and close up the side pleats with a lock stitch (page 39). The usual three stitches of stout twine to hold the hessian to the spring tops are put in to make doubly sure that the springs remain in position.

Fig. 107 The first stuffing for the seat

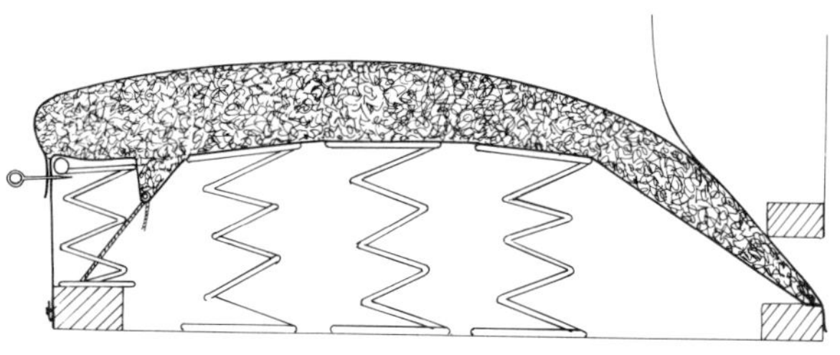

▲ **107(a)** Section through the seat showing the first stuffing temporarily fixed

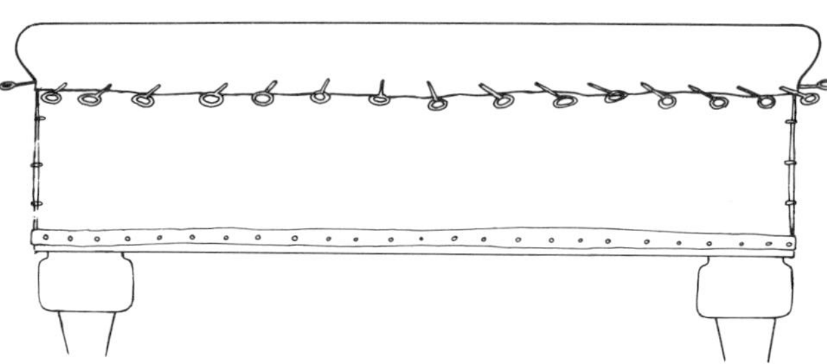

▲ **107(b)** The first stuffing with the hessian cover held at the front with skewers

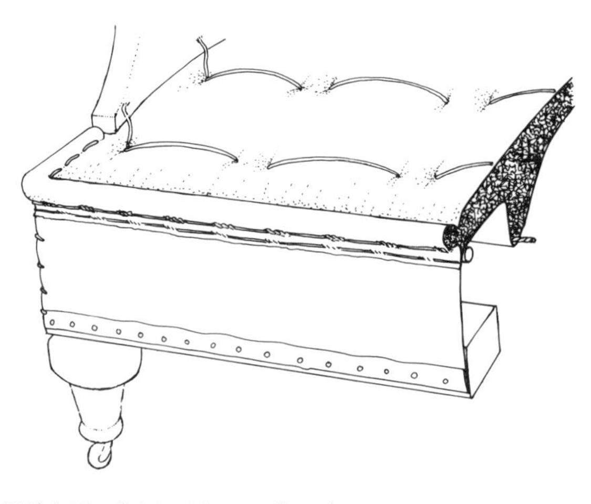

107(c) The finished first stuffing ▲

The First Stuffing on the Seat

Horsehair is the best material for the first stuffing of this type of seat, but coir fibre or Algerian fibre would also be suitable. Put in the stuffing ties in the usual way (page 44) but about 38 mm ($1\frac{1}{2}$ in) from the edge, and build a roll of stuffing along the front, to a thickness of not more than 45 mm ($1\frac{3}{4}$ in) above the cane edge. Fill up the well in the hessian, packing the stuffing in fairly tightly.

Working from the inside and the outside, push stuffing into the cavities between the arms and seat and the back and the seat. Do not be too heavy-handed here or the action of the springs will be hampered and the seat may become too hard.

Measure, cut off and lay a piece of scrim hessian over this first stuffing as a cover, tucking it in and pulling the edges through to the outside on the sides and back. Securely tack it on the top sides of the seat rails, level with the edges. At the front, where the roll is to be formed, pull the hessian over and temporarily fix it immediately below the edge cane with skewers (**fig. 107a**). Stitch up the rolled edge first, so that the scrim hessian is pulled tightly from the back to the front.

Adjust, stretch and finally fix the hessian along the sides and back. Adjust the scrim held by the skewers at the front, folding the scrim hessian under and re-skewering it leaving about 10 mm ($\frac{3}{8}$ in) of folded hessian below the line of skewers (**b**). To fix the scrim permanently, sew a row of fairly close blind edge stitches just below the skewers so that the scrim is fastened beneath the edge cane. Sew another row of blind stitches along the top of the edge cane, to bring the horsehair firmly to the front. Regulate the stuffing, then stitch a roll of about 30 to 45 mm ($1\frac{1}{4}$ to $1\frac{3}{4}$ in) diameter (pages 48–49). These roll stitches should be only a thread or so above the last row of blind stitches so that the roll is made no higher than necessary.

Now put in the through stuffing ties (**c**). Your longest double-pointed needle will be needed to negotiate the thickness of the seat, but these ties must only go through to the heavy hessian covering the springs. It is difficult to see through the gaps in the webbing

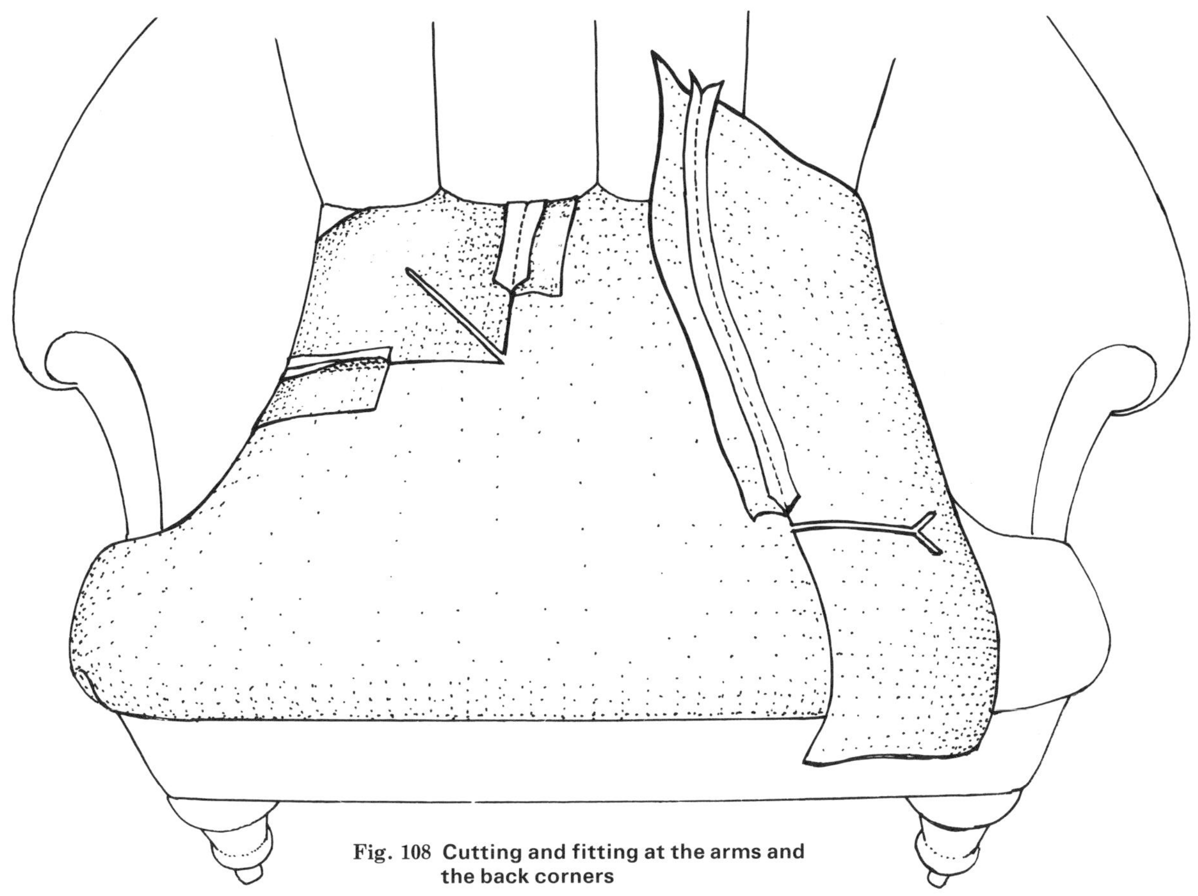

Fig. 108 Cutting and fitting at the arms and the back corners

underneath, but do make sure when you are returning the needle to the top surface that the twine has not ensnared any of the spring coils.

The Top Stuffing for the Seat

The top stuffing needs to be of the best quality. Sheep's wool or long-stranded curled horsehair are ideal. Put in the stuffing ties and pack in the lines of hair beneath the ties, as always taking great pains to get the lines to an even depth and density. Dome up the centre to a depth of at least 75 mm (3 in). An undercovering of calico will help give the seat a good shape. Tension the undercover across the seat front and into each back corner. After adjustments and temporary tacking, permanently fasten the undercover down, sewing the front beneath the seat edge roll with blind edge stitches. Place a layer or two of cotton wadding over the calico.

Covering the Seat

Measure the seat for the length of the covering from about 76 mm (3 in) underneath the swell of the back to underneath the lip of the front edge, allowing 25 mm (1 in) below this lip. To ascertain the width of the material measure across the front of the seat to 25 mm (1 in) below the lip on each side. Cut off the piece of material and sew on fly pieces of hessian or calico to the back and sides—by making up the seat covering in this way you save yourself quite a lot of expensive cloth. Fasten the top cover in exactly the same way as you did the undercover. You had a bit of practice in covering the seat when you put on the calico, but nevertheless, do take care when cutting in, especially at the arm front uprights. With this kind of seat, where the arms are short of the seat front by three or four inches, do all your stretching from the back to the front and then the cloth will be in the right position for you to cut into the arms (**fig. 108**). When fastening the cover at the front, pleat or gather the corners and put in neatly blind holding stitches in a straight line close under the roll edge. For these stitches use thin twine or stout thread and a 75 mm (3 in) curved needle.

Fig. 109 The front border

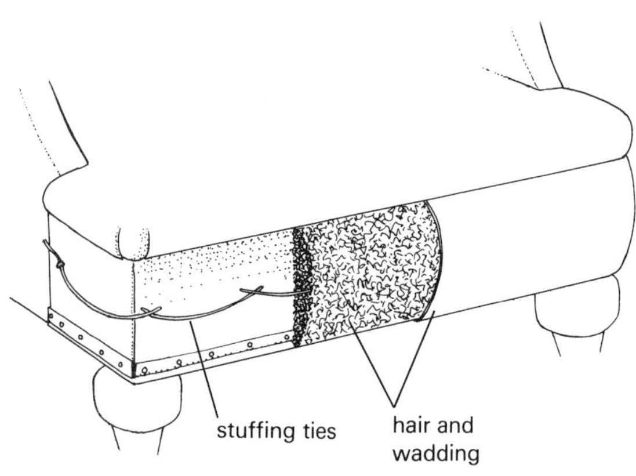

▲ 109(a) Stuffing the border

109(b) Covering the border ▼

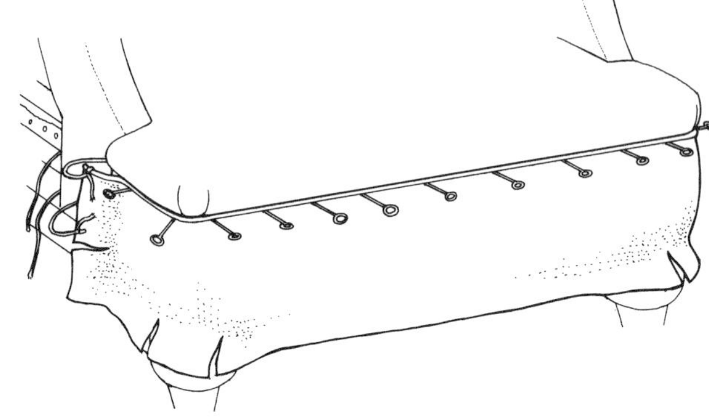

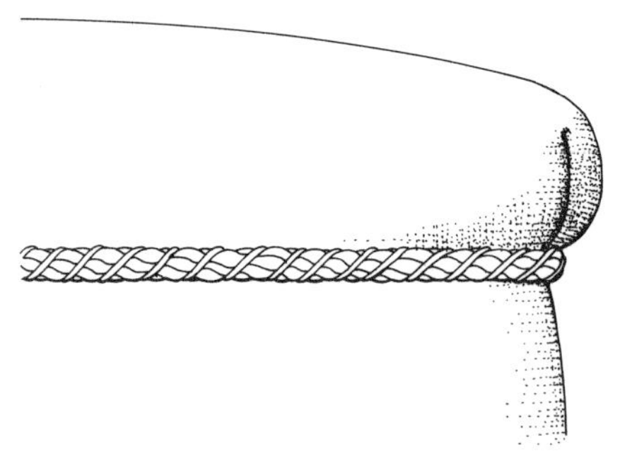

◀ 109(c) A trimming of chair cord

Covering the Front Border

The drawings in **fig. 109** show the sequence for upholstering and covering the border.

Place stuffing ties in a single line midway on the hessian. Add a layer of hair, then a layer of wadding (**a**). Make up the border cover and pipe the top edge. Stretch this cover across the front of the chair and skewer it. Knot twine ties to the ends of the cover and pull them through to the sides by using a large curved needle (or spring needle), or simply by tucking the twine down in between the seat and arm upholstery and bringing it through to the outside and pulling tightly. Fix the border cloth under the rails, cutting in round the legs (**b**). Fasten the border to the underside of the seat lip with ladder stitches (pages 40–41), sewn as close as possible to the row of machined stitches holding the piping.

As an alternative to piping, you can, if you like, trim the border cloth with decorative chair cord, as shown in (**c**).

Covering the Scrolls

Now you can turn your attention to the scroll fronts of the arms and the sides of the back. First fasten the piping round the inside of the scroll lip with pins or skewers, then put on the stuffing—usually of cotton felt or hair with a wadding overlay. Pin the scroll covering in place, using the pins or skewers already holding the piping. Ladder stitch the cover and the piping together as described in Chapter 3 (page 43).

If you are trimming with chair cord instead of piping, then, of course, you can simply ladder stitch the scroll cover and sew on the cord afterwards (page 42).

Covering the Outside Arms and Back

Before you start to put on the outside panels, try to eliminate all sharp or rough corners on the framework. Cover the outside arms first. Lay something soft, such as underfelt, old carpet or a sheet of plastic foam, on the floor and turn the chair on one side. It is easier to fasten the panel in this position.

Back-tack a half-width strip of webbing, a reinforcing undercover of 280 g (10 oz) hessian and the covering material together under the roll of the arm (page 88). Stretch the hessian over the side frame as tightly as possible. Place a thin layer of cotton wadding over it. Pull and stretch the covering material down. Fix it under the bottom rail first, cutting diagonally into the back leg and the front leg. Turn the front edge under and pin it in a straight line near the edge. Stretch and tack the back edge to the back face of the back upright (**fig. 110**). Ladder stitch (pages 40–41) the front seam with very small stitches and then follow the same procedure with the outside back covering, ladder stitching both sides.

Finally, turn the chair upside down, supporting the arms on a well padded trestle. Cut, fit and tack a piece of hessian or black lining over the bottom.

Fig. 110 Fastening the outside arm cover

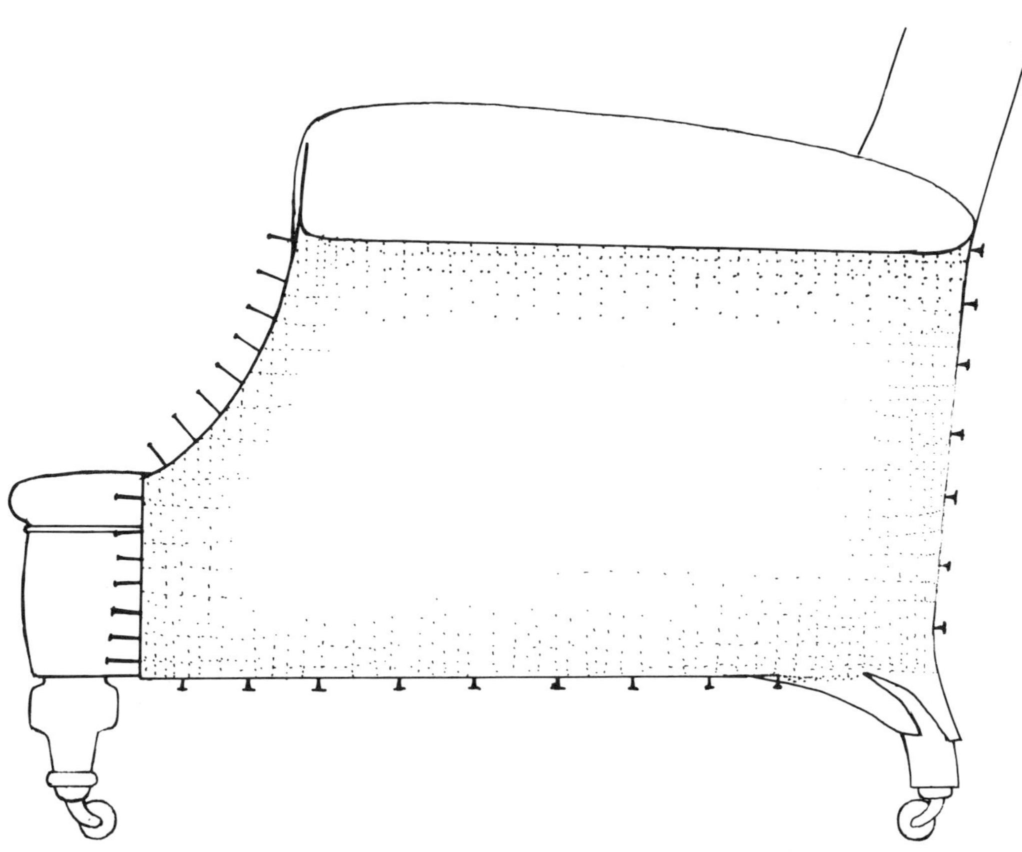

8 A Crinoline Chair and Other Iron-Framed Chairs

Crinoline easy chairs (fig. 111) are Victorian in origin, made from about the 1860s to the 1890s. For a brief discussion of the possible origin of the name, and a description of the structure, see page 19. Crinoline chairs are fairly difficult to upholster.

Fig. 111 A crinoline chair

Repairing and Strengthening the Seat Frame

We will assume that you have already stripped the frame of all old upholstery (**fig. 112**). When you examine these chairs you will usually find that the framework needs a fair bit of repair. The most important part, the seat frame, may have loose joints and legs and these must be seen to. The ironwork, usually fastened to the seat frame with large-headed nails, often has to be fixed—you are likely to discover that some of the nails are missing and others are loose. Sometimes I find that the iron superstructure was never very accurately placed on the woodwork. If this is the case with your chair, you can now put it right. Finally, the ironwork itself is likely to be rusty; if the rust is left it will eat through the hessian of the upholstery, so give the frame a good clean with a wire brush and then paint it with red oxide or any other rust-resistant paint.

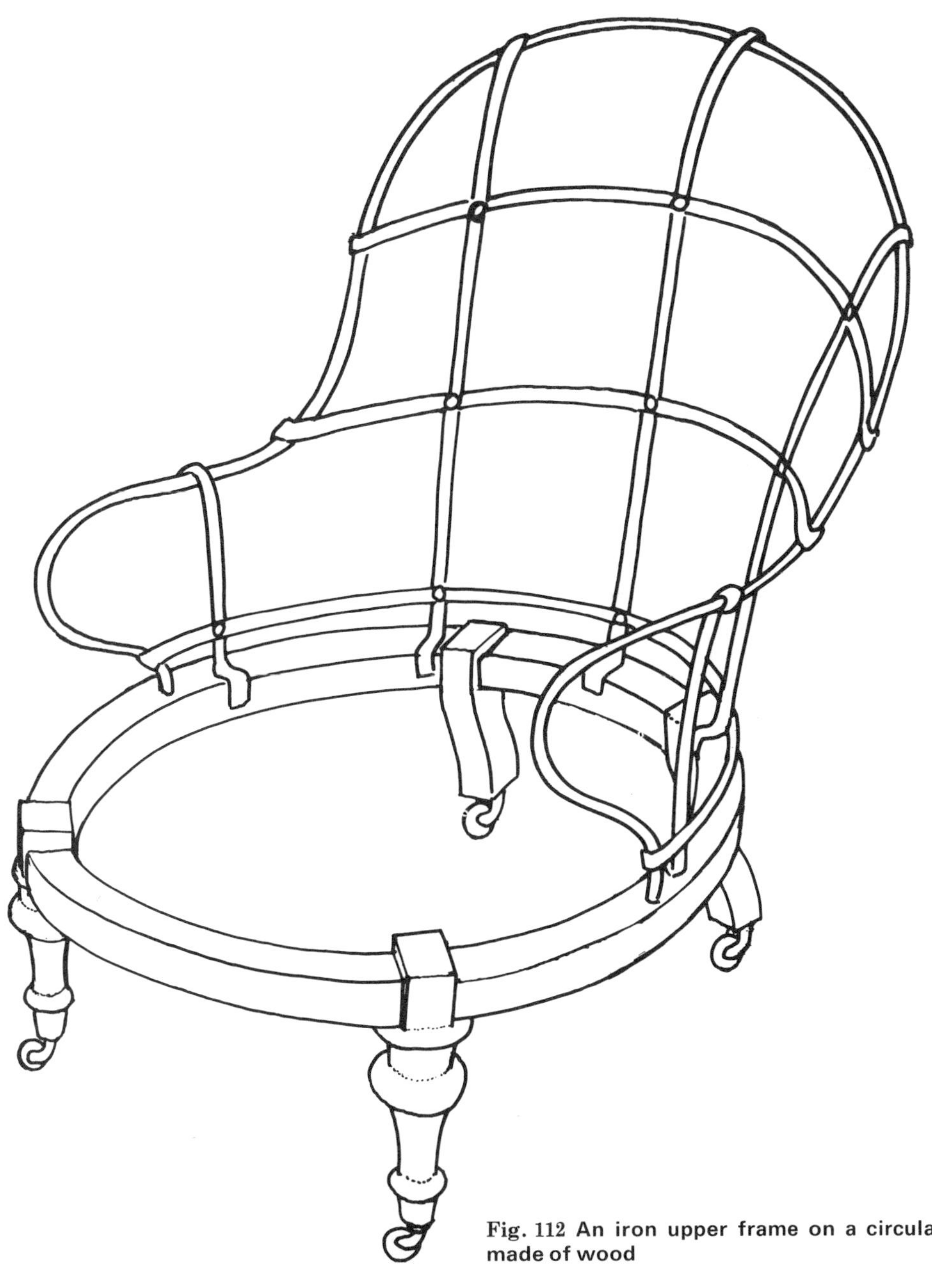

Fig. 112 An iron upper frame on a circular seat frame made of wood

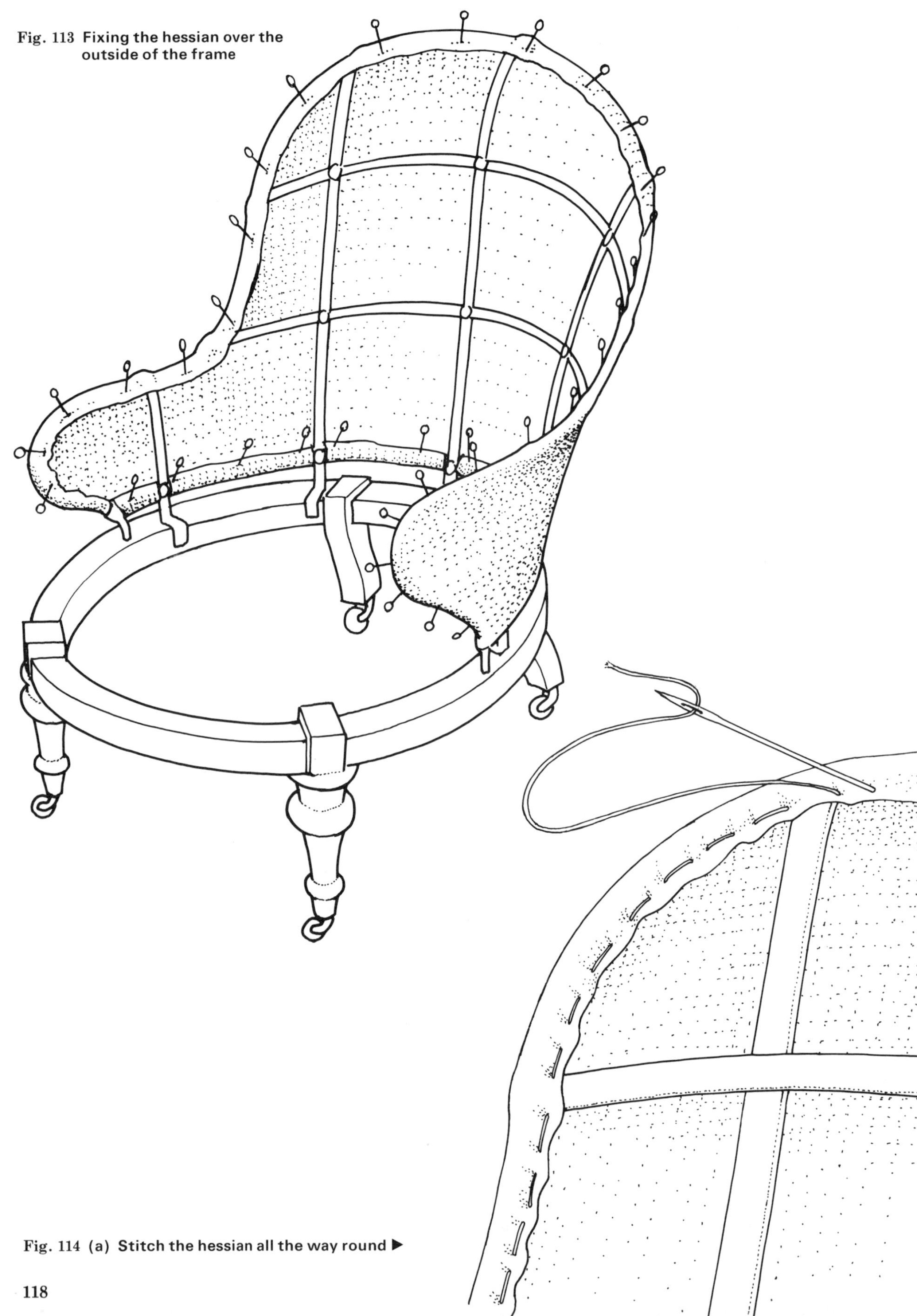

Fig. 113 Fixing the hessian over the outside of the frame

Fig. 114 (a) Stitch the hessian all the way round ▶

The Basic Support for the Upholstery on the Upper Framework

As a basic support for the upholstery on the back and arms of these chairs, use stout tarpaulin hessian. Because of the hoop construction, no webbing is required. Contrary to what you would expect, the tarpaulin hessian is stretched over the outside of the framework (**fig. 113**). It may be all in one piece, or, for the arms, small pieces can be stitched on to each side of the piece for the back. The hessian is stretched as tightly as possible from bottom to top of the chair, temporarily fixed with skewers and then stitched all the way round with fine twine, as shown in **fig. 114a**. The hessian is also fastened with large stitches—about 25 mm (1 in) apart—to all the iron hoops and upright members, as in (**b**).

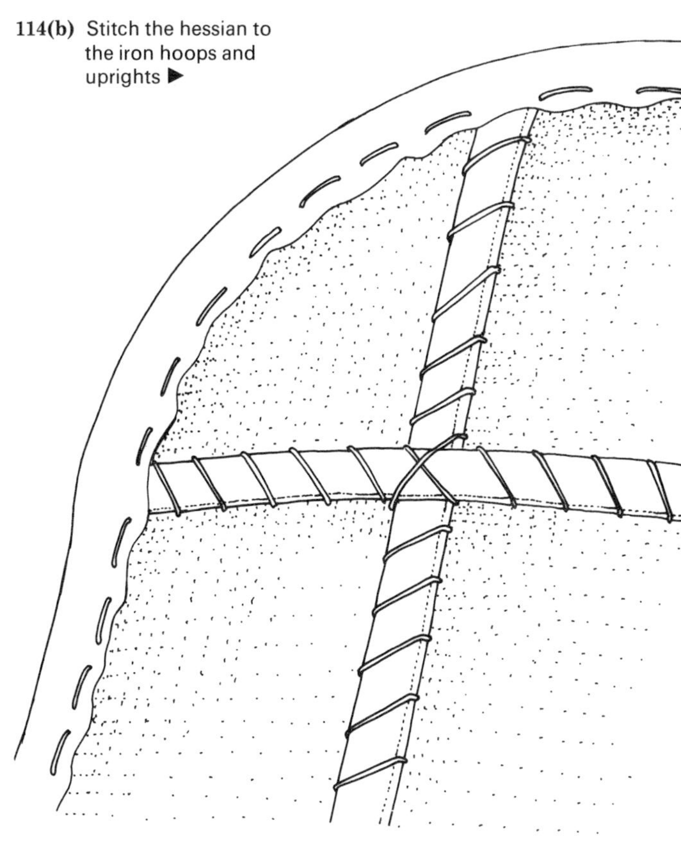

114(b) Stitch the hessian to the iron hoops and uprights ▶

Setting out for Edge Foundations for the Back and Arms

The setting out for building the edges on the back and arms is fairly exacting work, for the more accurately this is done, the more uniform the finished upholstery will be.

The original upholsterer of this chair was paid a piece rate and probably worked in a sweat shop. He had no time for such niceties as measurements. This is where you can put some of yourself into the work, adding your own interpretation to the finished shape and comfort of the piece.

As aids to setting out, make up some small measuring sticks; several pieces of ordinary wood of about 5 to 10 mm ($\frac{3}{16}$ to $\frac{3}{8}$ in) square in section and cut off marked clearly to exact sizes will do fine. Different types of chairs require different lengths of stick, so the chair type should also be marked on the sticks. You need two sizes of measuring stick for this chair, one 90 mm ($3\frac{1}{2}$ in) long and the other 250 mm (10 in). Take the shorter stick and scribe a line from the outside edge all round the back, as shown in **fig. 115**. Then find the exact centre of the back at the top and the bottom and draw a vertical line, again shown in **fig. 115**, on the back and front of the hessian. You can also see that a horizontal line has been marked across the back; this marks the top of the lumbar swell (page 122). This line varies in position according to the chair size, but usually it should be just below

Fig. 115 Marking the back inside and outside ▼

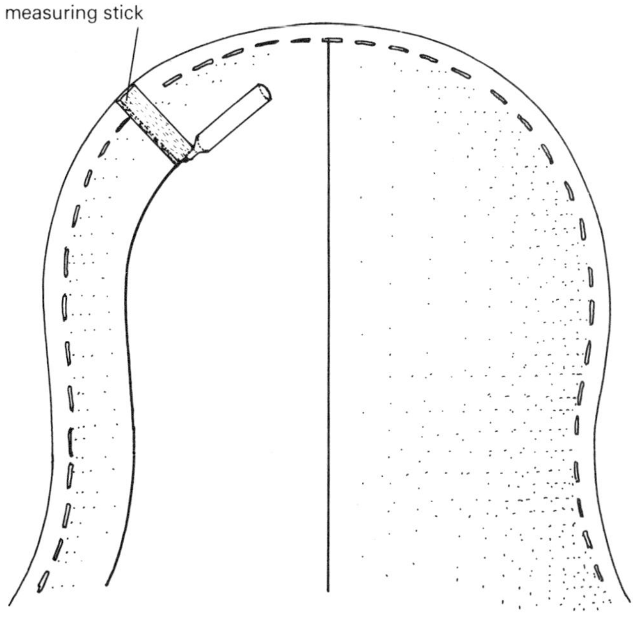

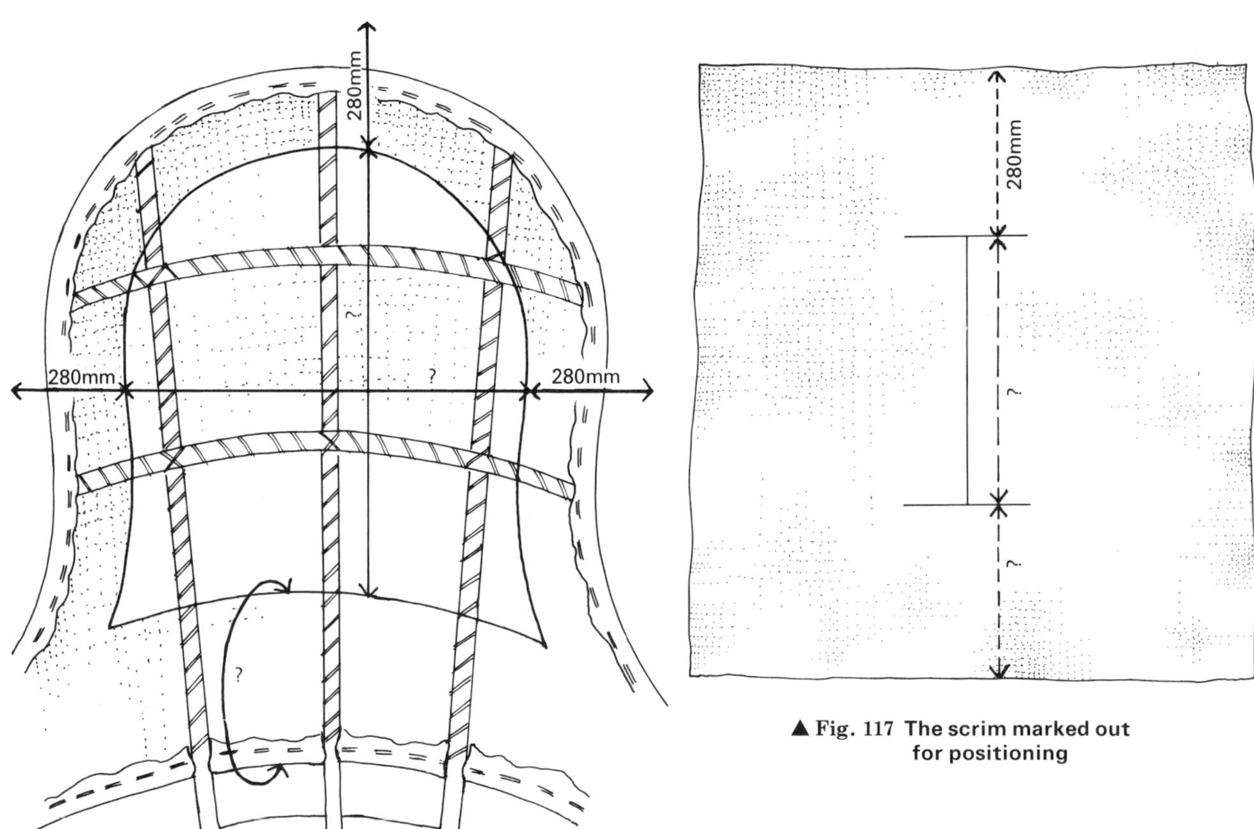

▲ **Fig. 117** The scrim marked out for positioning

◀ **Fig. 116** Measuring for the scrim covering. Some of these measurements are unknown and indicated with ? as they relate to the size of the chair.

the level of the arm frame height and about 150 to 175 mm (6 to 7 in) above the iron hoop forming the bottom of the back framework.

You now need some scrim hessian to form the covering of the edge rolls and lumbar swell and the first stuffing on the arms. In **fig. 116** you will see the measurements to be taken to determine the size of this piece of scrim. For the width, measure across the space in the centre of the back, formed by your lines, at the widest point. Ignore the arms for the present as they will need separate pieces of scrim for covering; add 280 mm (11 in) to each side of this measurement. For the length, measure the length of the centre space and add 280 mm (11 in) to the top. To determine the size of the lumbar swell, use your steel tape measure, holding it out in a bow about 100 to 125 mm (4 or 5 in) from the tarpaulin hessian, measuring from the bottom line to about 50 mm (2 in) below the bottom hoop. Add on this measurement and you have the total length.

Cut off the piece of scrim and lay it flat. Mark it as in **fig. 117** with a vertical centre line and two short horizontal lines that correspond to the top and bottom of the area marked out on the tarpaulin hessian on the back of the chair. Lay this scrim over the front of the chair back and position it so that the marks correspond with the marks on the tarpaulin. Fasten all round with skewers. Now sew the scrim hessian on with fine twine, following the marks.

Take the 250 mm (10 in) measuring stick and place one end on the line of stitches. Mark off the length in dots all round the scrim. Join the dots up to form a guide line for fastening the scrim round the outside edge (**fig. 118**). Trim the scrim to 25 mm (1 in) outside this line.

There is one more guide line to draw: for this use your upholstery gauge (page 11), gauging a line from the edge of the back all round on the outside back and outside arms about 25 mm (1 in) in (**fig. 119**).

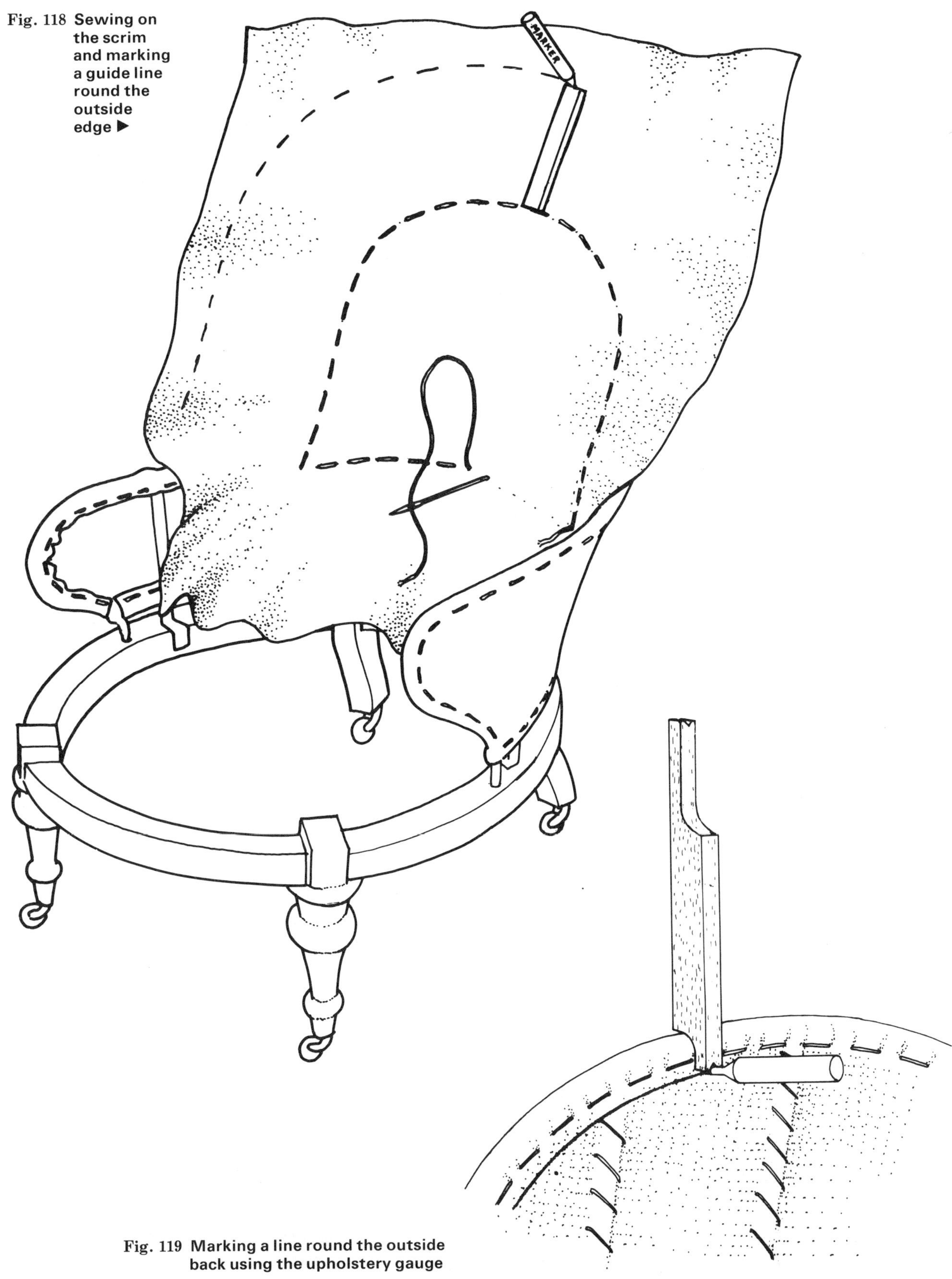

Fig. 118 Sewing on the scrim and marking a guide line round the outside edge ▶

Fig. 119 Marking a line round the outside back using the upholstery gauge

Fig. 120 The first stuffing for the edges

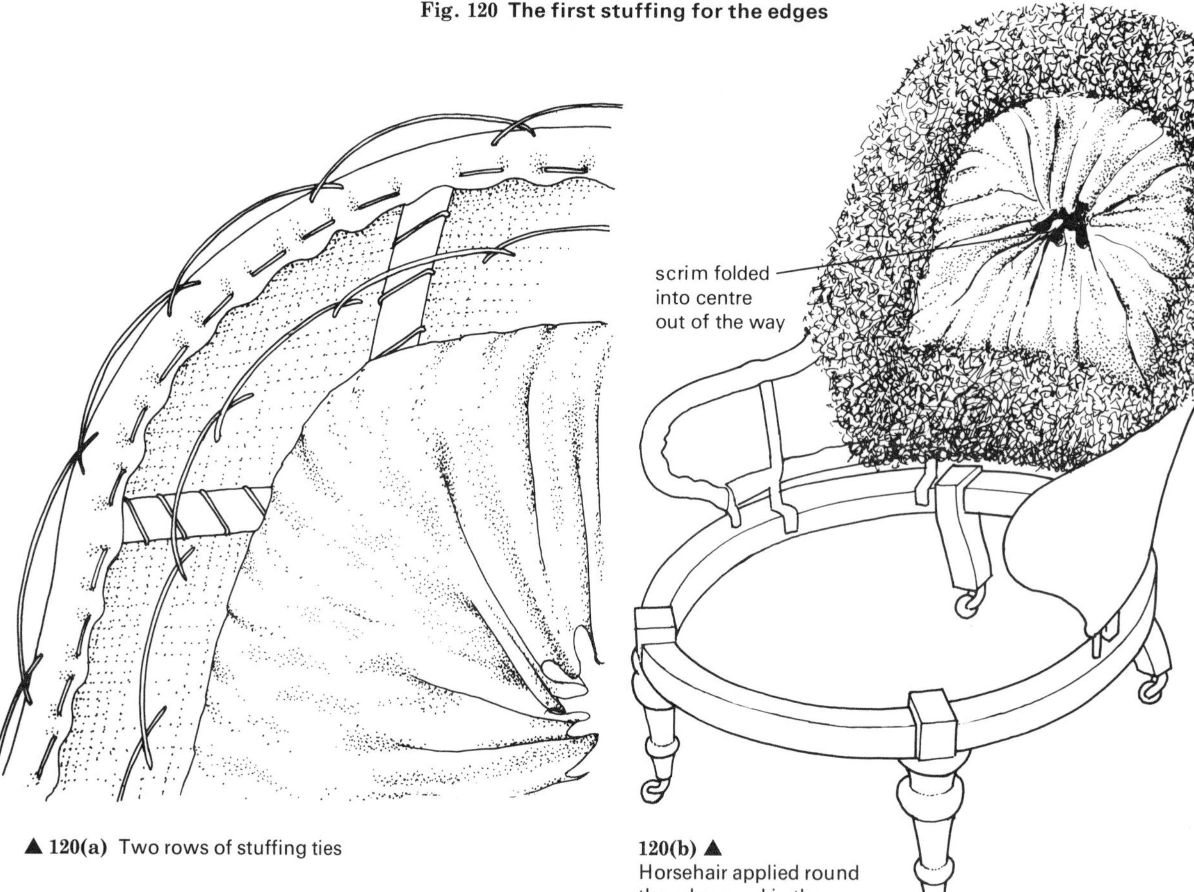

▲ **120(a)** Two rows of stuffing ties

120(b) ▲
Horsehair applied round the edges and in the lumbar swell space

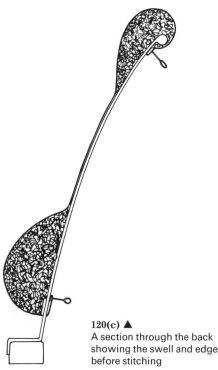

120(c) ▲
A section through the back showing the swell and edge before stitching

Put in two rows of stuffing ties (page 44) all round the back and on the arms (**fig. 120**). Tuck horsehair fairly firmly under the ties, starting at the top centre and working round to the left and right down to and including the arms. When a small portion of the edge has been formed, try the scrim over it, holding guide line to guide line: if you have applied enough hair this should feel very firm. Carry on applying hair in this manner round the entire edge and then fill up the lumbar swell space (**b**).

Working out from the top centre once more, begin to pull over the scrim, tuck in the surplus (beyond the guide line) and, with skewers, fasten guide line to guide line. As the bends sharpen as the back descends, you will need to gather the material. Stretch the scrim over the lumbar swell and fasten it at the back of the bottom hoop. In (**c**) I show a section through the back of the chair, to give an idea of the size of the swell and the edge rolls before stitching.

Fig. 121 The arm first stuffing

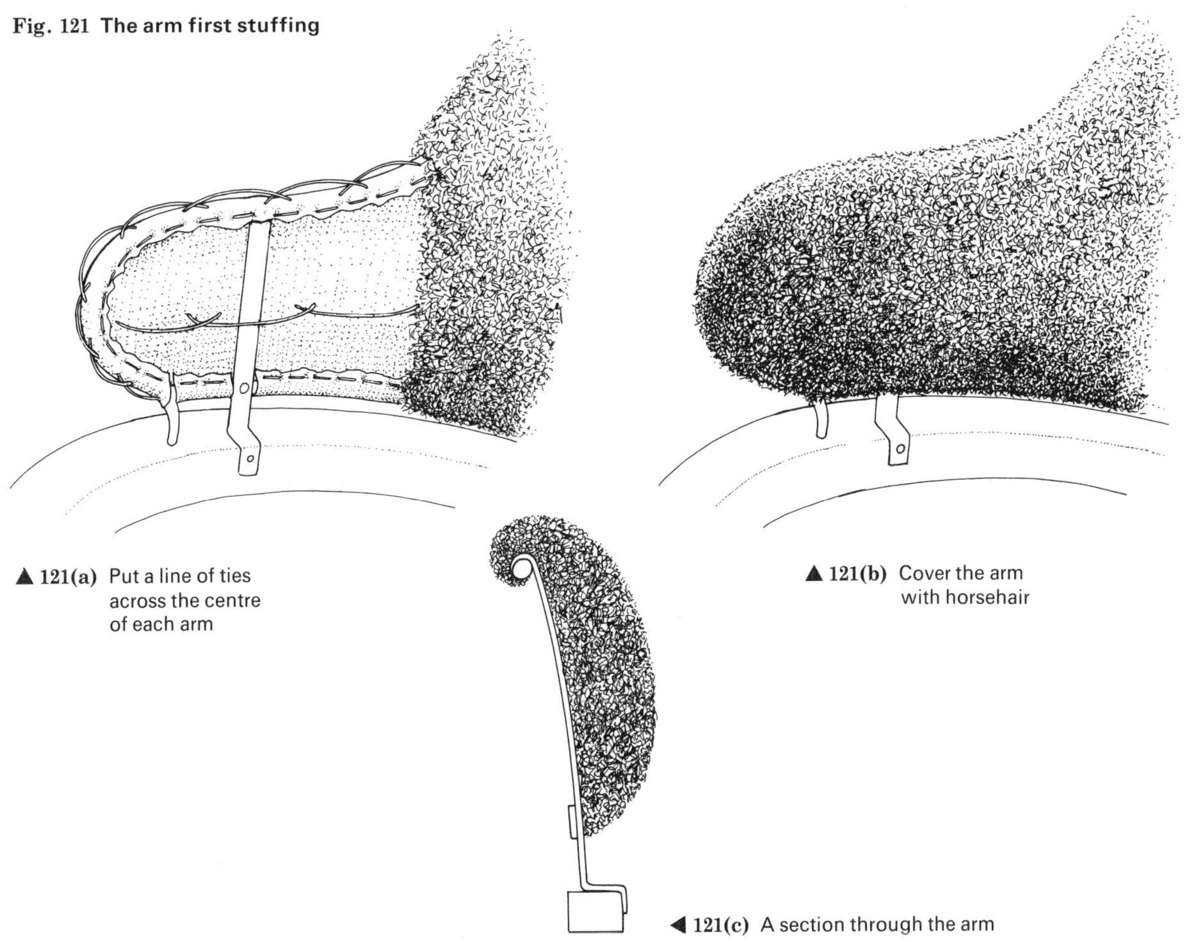

▲ 121(a) Put a line of ties across the centre of each arm

▲ 121(b) Cover the arm with horsehair

◀ 121(c) A section through the arm

The First Stuffing for the Arms

You can now turn your attention to the arms; the chair illustrated is of the most common design but I have come across earlier types with scroll fronts to the arms, and other much larger versions with frames down to the floor and wide buttoned borders running round the edge of the back and arms. However, let us stay with this simpler version for a start.

Put a line of stuffing ties across the centre (inside) of each arm, as in **fig. 121 (a)**, and cover the arm with horsehair (**b**). In (**c**) is a section through the arm showing the stuffing. Measure over the stuffing from 25 mm (1 in) beyond the guide line on the outside to 50 mm (2 in) below the bottom hoop. Now measure from the side of the lumbar swell over the most forward part of the rounding arm to 25 mm (1 in) past your outside guide line. Cut off two pieces of scrim to exactly this size and position them over the arm stuffing. Adjust and fasten with skewers many times until you are satisfied that the arms look alike. You can ensure by measuring that the height and the width of the two arms are identical; but for the definition of the curves you will have for the most part to rely upon your eye.

This is the point at which you get sewing again. The first task is to fasten the arm scrim to the lumbar swell scrim hessian where they meet; use either ladder stitches or locked slip stitches here (pages 39–40). Then, using a 250 mm (10 in) double-pointed needle, or a 100 mm (4 in) or 130 mm (5 in) curved needle, fasten the scrim round the outside of the arms and back with blind stitches.

With your regulator, even out any bumps and dents in the stuffed edge and try to get the density equal in every part. Put in another row of blind stitches above and close to the iron frame, go over the stuffing again with your regulator, then mark out and through stitch to form the roll edge (pages 47–49).

Fig. 122 The corner buttons

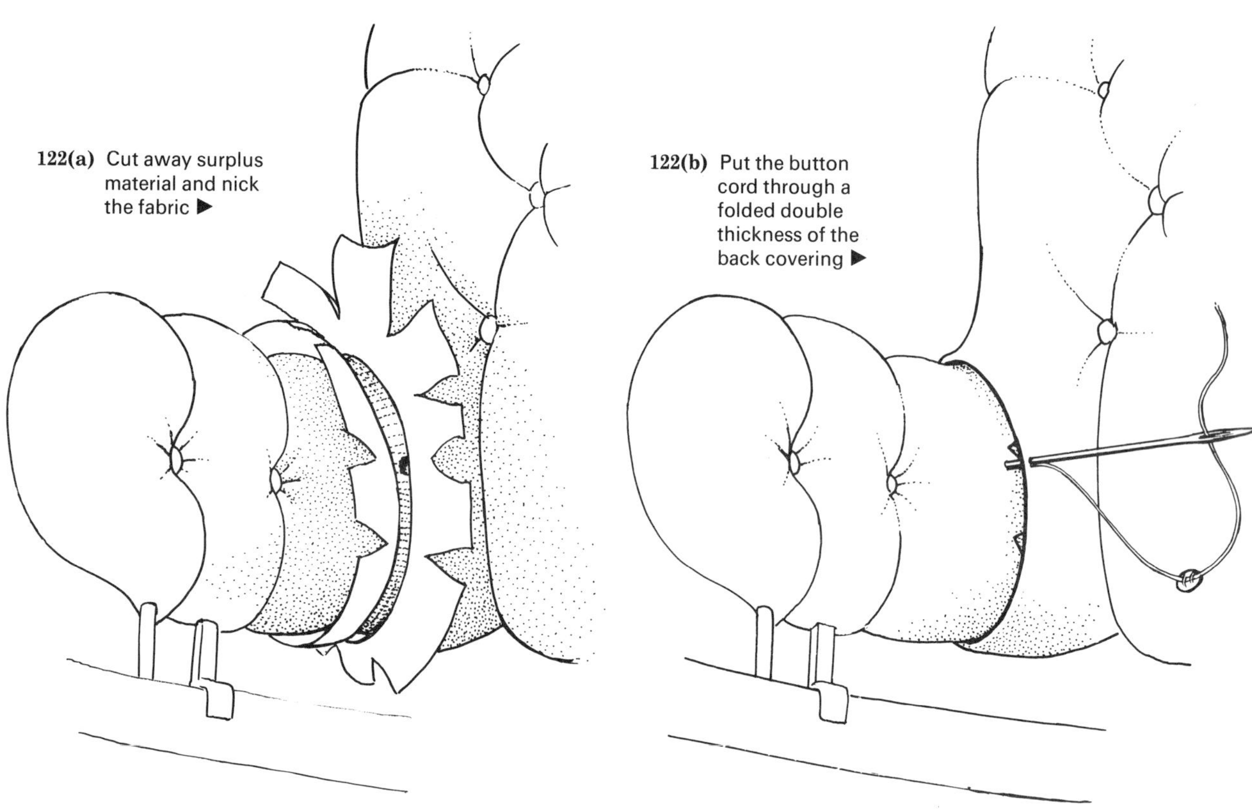

122(a) Cut away surplus material and nick the fabric ▶
122(b) Put the button cord through a folded double thickness of the back covering ▶

The Top Stuffing for the Back and Arms

Put in lines of stuffing ties across the back and the arms in the same way as on the back of the large easy chair (page 101). Place a thin layer of cotton wadding (half the thickness of the sheet, which easily splits in two) over the hair and cover the whole of the back and arms tightly with 71 g ($2\frac{1}{2}$ oz) thin bonded polyester wadding.

Setting Out the Buttonwork

Setting out the buttonwork on this chair is very similar to the setting out on the large easy chair described in Chapter 7 so I will refer you to that section (pages 102–104), just noting for you the small differences caused by the curved shape of the crinoline chair.

Because the back of the chair curves, the distances between the lateral button settings on the outside back have to be slightly greater than those on the front; to gauge this difference, push a needle through from the front button mark, note the angle that looks correct and then mark the back hessian in the usual way.

Draw a diagram of the button positions and make an allowance of 32 mm ($1\frac{1}{4}$ in) extra to the between-button measurements. When you transfer this setting out to the covering cloth do not perforate the two button marks at each end of the lowest row because these buttons will be on the joins between the back and the arms and may need to be adjusted. Make a separate diagram for the arm covering, allowing 25 mm (1 in) of cloth to be left beyond the button that will be on the junction of arm and back.

When you come to covering do the arms first. Finish them except for the buttons but just put a tie of twine through the button marks where the arms join the back. Then, later, buttons can be put in to hold both back and arm coverings. If you look at the picture of the completed chair at the very beginning of this chapter (**fig. 111**), you will see how the fold from the buttons run vertically and the

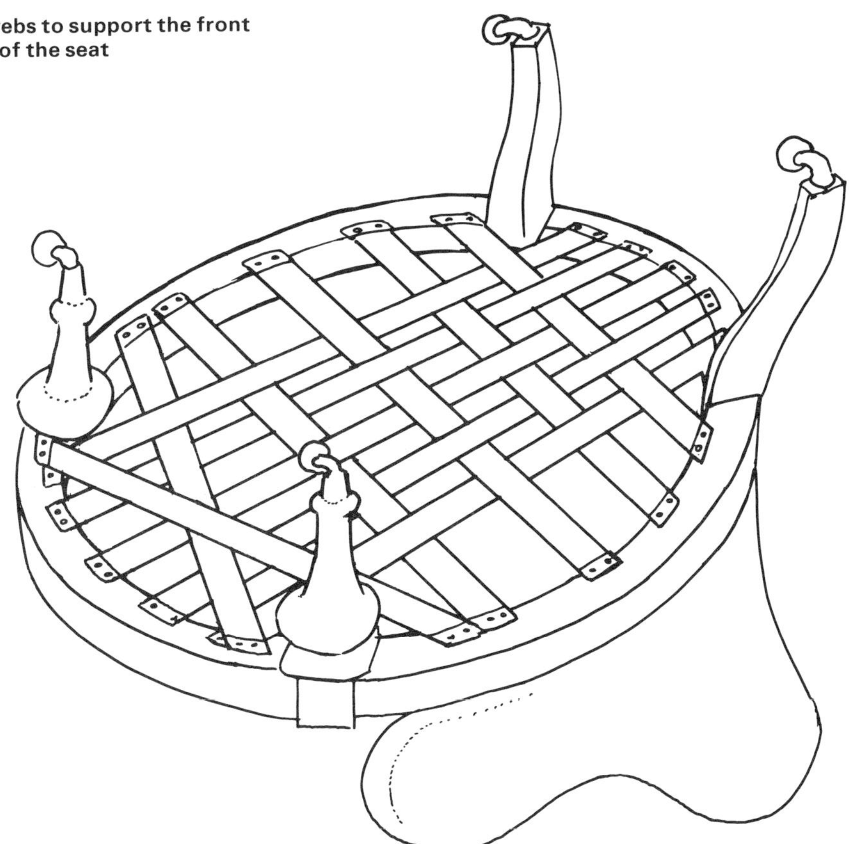

Fig. 123 Cross webs to support the front springs of the seat

material is gathered on the round of the arms.

When you have completed the back buttoning, turn your attention to those corner buttons. Cut away surplus material from the arm covering and make a few nicks so that the covering will lie flat (**fig. 122a**). Then put in each button, the cord going through the folded double thickness of the back covering, as shown in (**b**). The join between the arm and the back should be ladder stitched to prevent it gaping at some future time. If you turn back the fold a little and ladder stitch a little way in then it will still resemble a fold and look the same as the others.

When you fasten the covering at the bottom you will probably have to make snips a couple of centimetres long between the button-fold marks to release tensions.

The covering has to be stitched all round the outside and it is important that the line of stitches should be put in at exactly the same distance from the edge all the way round. If you follow the iron frame beneath, this will make a good guide line when you come to sew on the outside cover. Fasten with a blind row of twine stitches put in with a curved needle.

THE SEAT UPHOLSTERY

The seat upholstery is fairly straightforward and with your previous experience all you will need here are a few reminders and notes on special points peculiar to these chair seats.

Webbing

A trestle with a pad of foam to a height to support the arms and a thick foam cushion on the floor under the head of the back will keep your upturned chair level and fairly firm while you attach the webbing.

The seat is round or, on some chairs, round at the back with a front rail that is straight or slightly bowed. The webbing is put on in the same way as on a square-framed chair (pages 29–30), except that on the round frame it may be necessary to add two cross pieces of webbing to support the front springs (**fig. 123**).

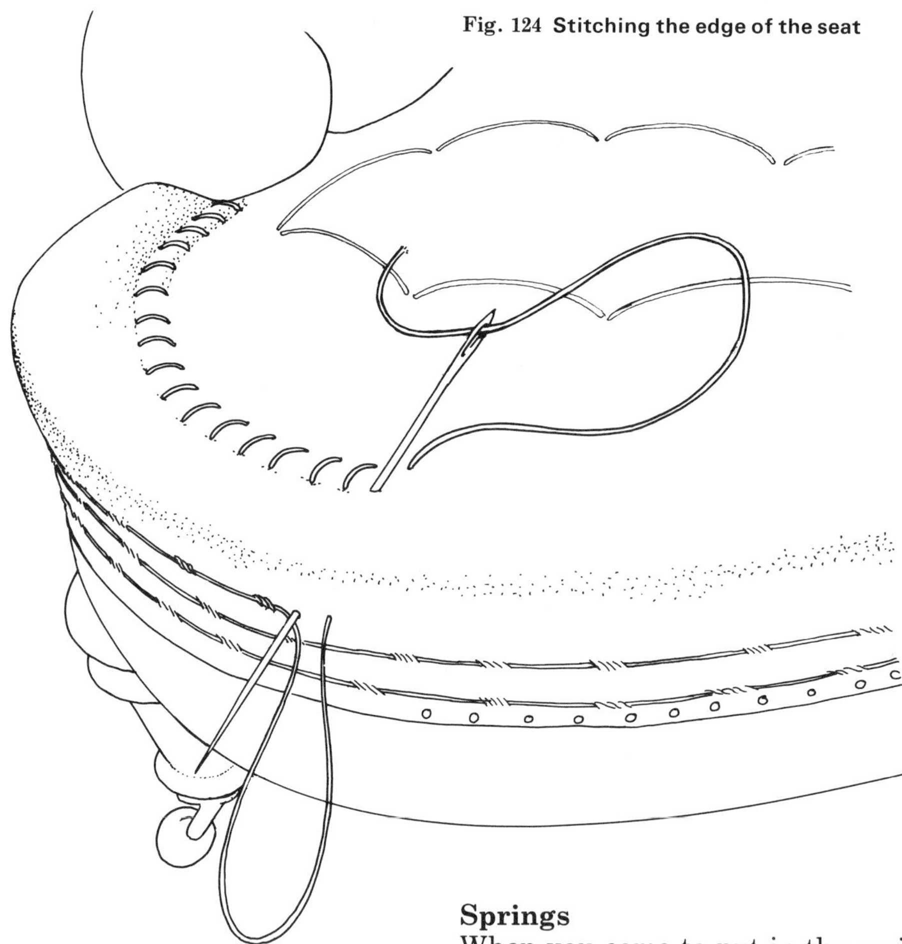

Fig. 124 Stitching the edge of the seat

▲ 124(a) Put in through stitches to dish the top

Springs

When you come to put in the springs, again, ignore the round shape of the frame and arrange the nine springs in three straightforward rows of three. For a fairly firm seat use 10 gauge springs; a very firm seat (for a heavy person) needs 9 gauge, or for a very soft seat 12 gauge can be used. The length of spring required varies with the size of the chair and the depth of the seat; 150 or 175 mm (6 or 7 in) is the usual size, but a larger chair may need 200 mm (8 in).

For spring lacing, the hessian covering and the first stuffing refer back to Chapter 3 (pages 37–38, 44–45) and Chapter 7 (pages 108–112).

A Special Stitched Edge for a Round Seat

When forming the front stitched edge of a rounded seat, it is important to build a *very firm* wall of horsehair for the core of the edge. If this is a good shape before it is covered with scrim hessian the covering scrim will fall over the shape in a natural way and will require little adjustment and

▲ **124(b)** Stitch the roll edge

less exasperating undoing and retacking.

The edge will probably have to be built up to 75 to 100 mm (3 to 4 in), so four or five rows of stitches are needed in all. The bottom two or three are blind rows (pages 48–49). The stitches in the row next to the top (roll stitches) are put in in a special manner and are through stitches to dish the top surface of the seat and make a more robust, durable edge. If you study **fig. 124a** you can see how this is done. One line is drawn with the aid of the upholstery gauge (using your finger as the gauge fence) about 63 mm ($2\frac{1}{2}$ in) in from the edge and another line 83 mm ($3\frac{1}{2}$ in) in. The two lines are then about 20 mm ($\frac{3}{4}$ in) apart. Through stitches are made by taking your needle through and out at the farthest line, then returning it through the front line directly in front of the place where the twine emerges on the farthest line. Each stitch is locked with the usual three turns around the needle before it is pulled clear. These stitches are pulled in very tightly to recess the top. After this row is finished the usual roll edge made (**b**).

The Second Stuffing

Make the usual rows of stuffing tie loops and tuck in the second stuffing of good long curled hair, building the stuffing up to a domed loft of about 125 mm (5 in) at the centre. Stretch over the undercovering and fasten it at the front just under the lip of the roll edge, as with the seat of the large easy chair (page 113).

Lay a layer of wadding over the undercover. Put on the top covering, fastening it under the lip of the front roll edge—this chair always looks best with a separate front border. As with the large easy chair, to save costly cloth a fly piece can be sewn on to the back of the seat cover.

Now fasten all the temporarily skewered bottom edges of the arm and inside back covering permanently with tacks to the outside of the seat rails. Pipe the border and sew it in place, stretching and fastening at the lower part of the outside arms (**fig. 125**). For details of the procedure see Chapter 7 (page 114). As in that case, you can use decorative chair cord instead of piping.

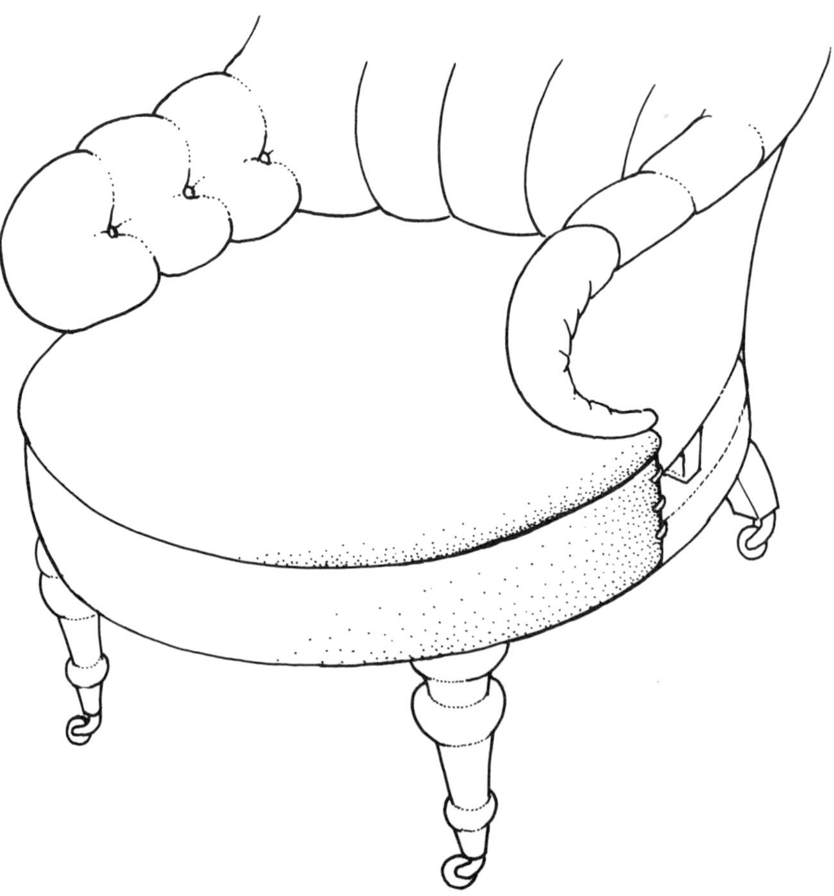

Fig. 125 The border fastened at the side of the arm

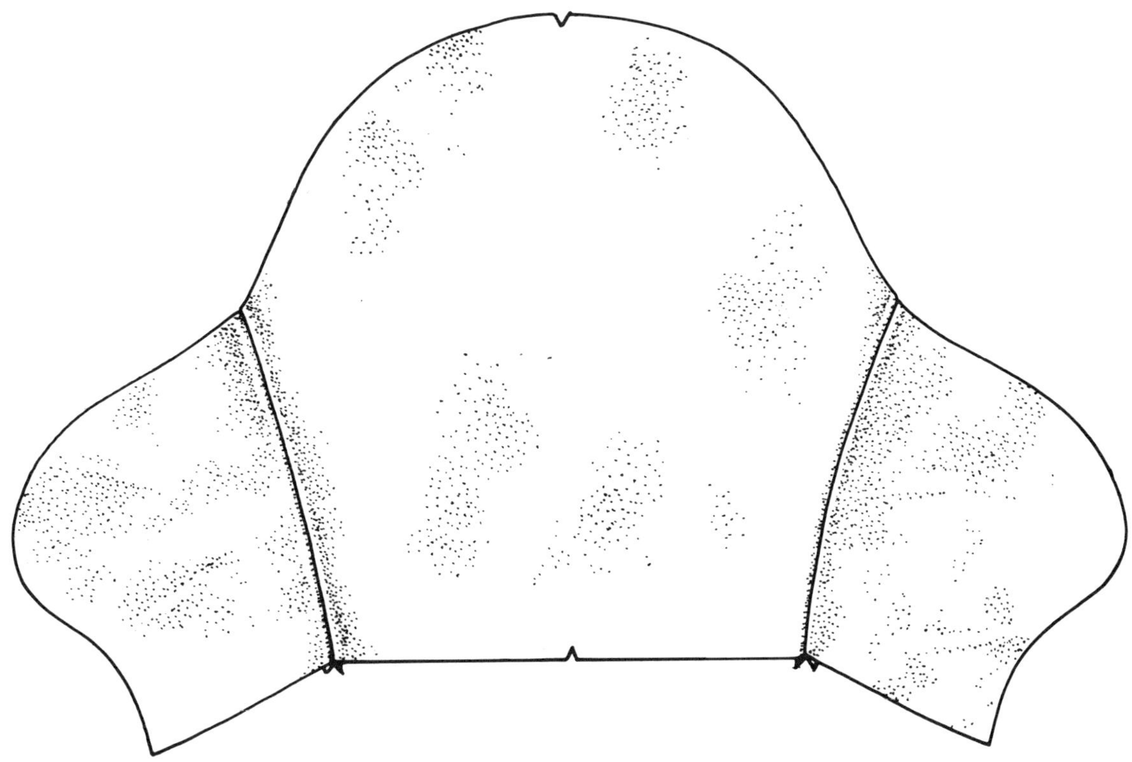

Fig. 126 The outside covering made in three panels

Covering the Outside Arms and Outside Back

At this point I would make up a length of piping for the outside covering seam. I remember a builder friend of mine saying, 'If you've got to make a join make it apparent.' In other words, make a feature of it. Some upholsterers just ladder stitch the outside panels on; this is quite all right if it is painstakingly done with very small stitches, but I always think a seam looks much nicer enhanced with a line of piping. Or, here again, chair cord can be used.

Some softening will be needed to pad out the back a little and for this you can use wadding in, perhaps, two layers, or some cotton felt. This padding will even out and cover the lumps and bumps caused by knots, toggles, protruding ironwork and the unevenness of the fabric tacked round the outside of the seat frame; it will also enhance the roundness of the outside of the chair.

The outside back and arm covering is made up in three panels (**fig. 126**). So far as possible, the tops of the seams should correspond to the folds of the joins of the inside arms and inside back coverings where these extend

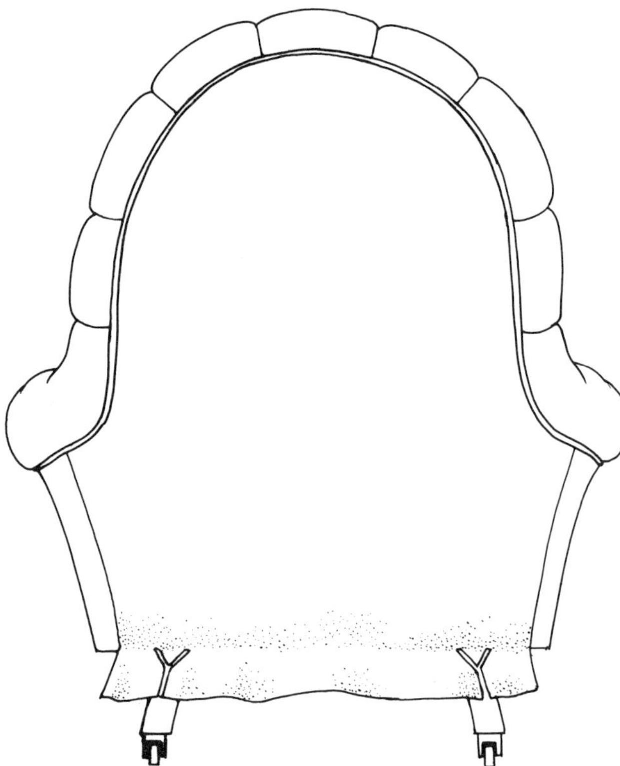

▲ Fig. 127 The covering cut in at the back legs

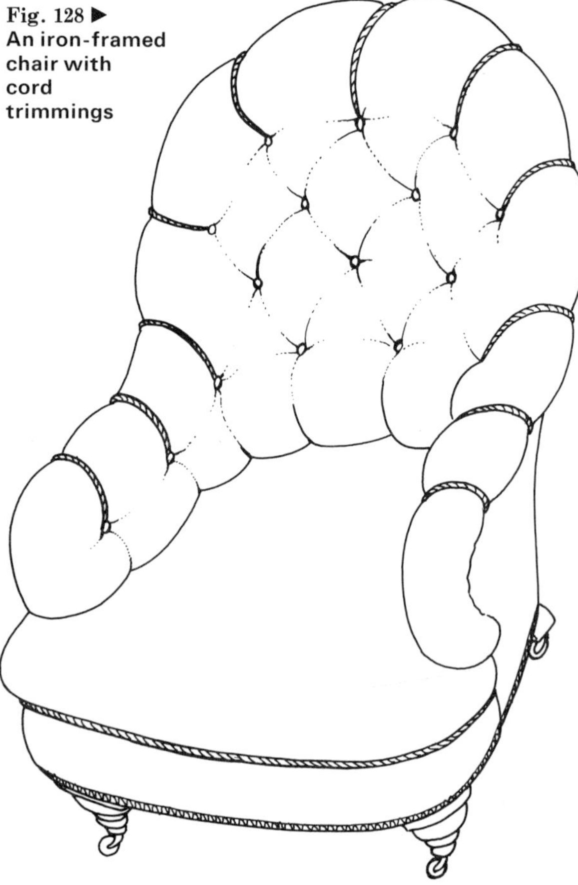

Fig. 128 ▶ An iron-framed chair with cord trimmings

over to the outside of the chair. Measure and cut off the centre back panel first. Mark the centre of the top and bottom edges, pin the panel into position, then measure and cut off pieces for the side panels. Pin one outside arm panel in position on the chair and pin the back edge to the side of the back panel. Trim off the surplus cloth to leave 12 mm ($\frac{1}{2}$ in) flanges, then roughly trim the cloth round to the shape of the chair. Remove both panels, snip the seam flanges at intervals as a guide for repositioning, and unpin the seam. Cut out the opposite outside arm panel to the shape of the one you have fitted—transfer the snips in the flanges as well. Take the outside back panel and fold it in half lengthwise so that you can cut it to make both sides alike, again transferring the snips. Now pin all three panels together, positioning snip to snip, and stitch the seams on your sewing machine.

Using 38 mm ($1\frac{1}{2}$ in) upholsterer's pins, fasten the piping just above your line of twine or thread stitches, finishing at the bottom of each arm with a tack under the seat frame.

Position the outside covering with just a few pins here and there and with a few temporary tacks under the seat frame, then trim back the edges all the way round to about 20 mm ($\frac{3}{4}$ in) outside the line of piping. Then, starting at the top centre, take out a pin at a time, turn in the covering and pin again through both the covering and the piping, thus holding these in the exact position for sewing. When all is pinned, stretch tightly downwards and fasten with temporary tacks beneath the seat rails. Cut the fabric round the two back legs (**fig. 127**). Ladder stitch the seams, incorporating the piping (page 43). Finally, cut, fit and tack on some hessian or black lining to cover the bottom.

Extra Trimmings

Sometimes it is nice to add a few small refinements, such as a band of braid all round the bottom or, if the chair has a deep frame, a fringe round the base. **Fig. 128** shows an iron-framed chair with cord trimmings; you will notice that, as well as cord round the outside edges and the front border, cord has been stretched from the outermost buttons over to the back. The folds from the buttons are ladder stitched up and each cord is put in

Fig. 129 A small Victorian sewing chair with an iron back frame

with a separate draw twine attached to one end and pulled through the button hole before the buttons are finally placed.

OTHER IRON-FRAMED CHAIRS

I would like to add a word or two about the special problems which arise with some variations on the iron-framed chair. The small sewing chair pictured in **fig. 129** presents a few problems. To suit the shape of the back, the buttons must be positioned rather differently in straight lines and the number and position should balance within the rectangular shape. The foundation work for the scrolls at the sides of the back requires care to get the scrolls exactly the same size.

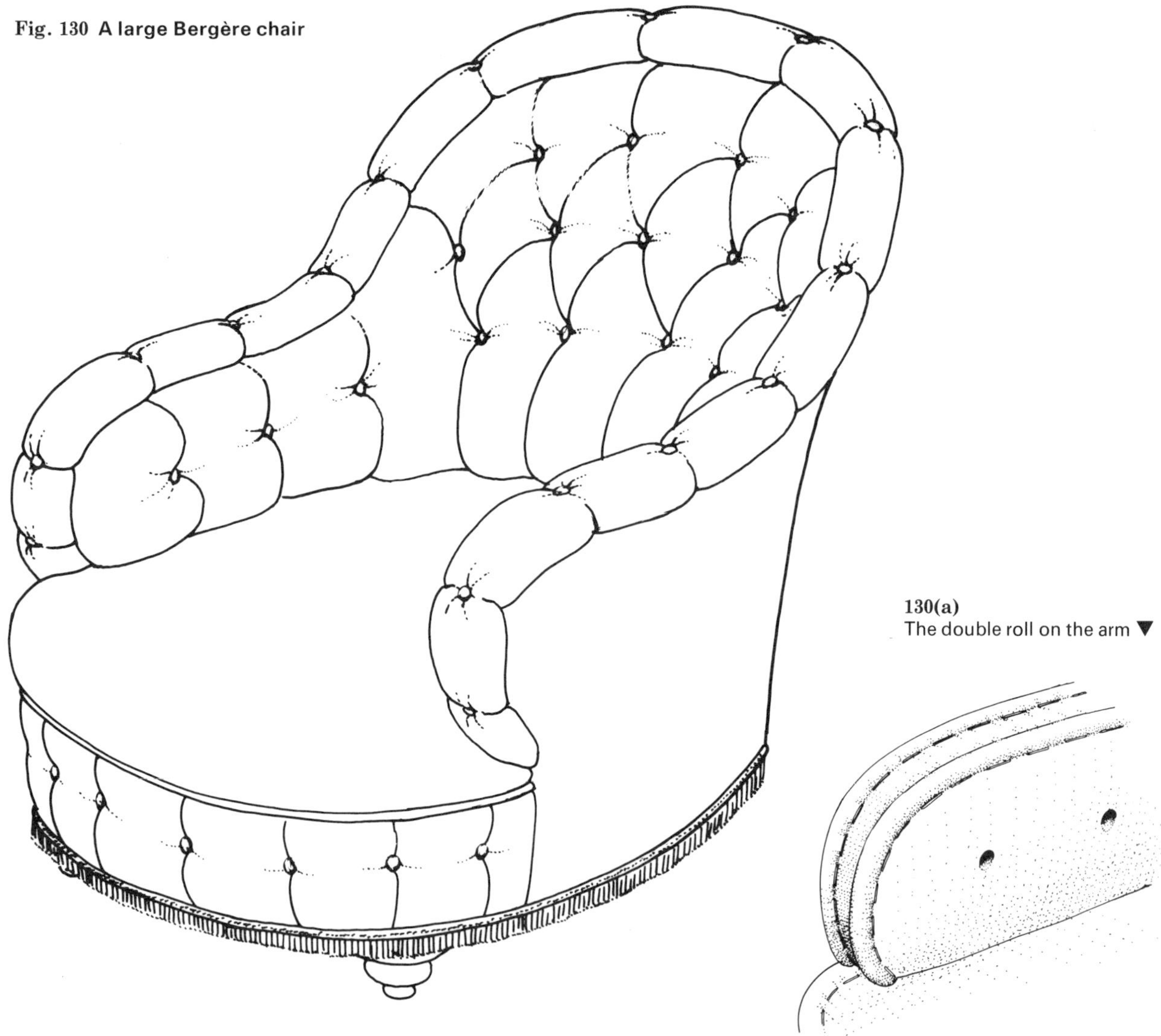
Fig. 130 A large Bergère chair

130(a)
The double roll on the arm ▼

Reupholstering a large Bergère chair such as the one shown in **fig. 130** entails a lot of meticulous work; the buttoned bordered top to the arms and back needs a special double roll foundation (**a**). This arm and back edge is built up very flat and regulated until it is firm and even, then two edge rolls are stitched on the inside and outside of this border. Sometimes springs are incorporated into the backs of these chairs. They are usually very soft shallow springs which are sewn to the heavy hessian support, then covered and retained by a lighter hessian. The deep front seat border with a single row of buttons is another feature; this is made in exactly the same way as the border on the chesterfield settee described on pages 148–149.

The Victorians also made iron-framed rocking chairs (**fig. 131a**) and similar chairs made to stand firm by the addition of small ball feet at the front and a modification to the bottom of the frame at the back (**b**).

Now, here is something unusual in the way of upholstery, for all the ironwork of the scrolled sides has to be covered with material. On both of these chairs the cross rails between the two scrolled sides are bolted on and the two holding the seat can be removed and put back when the seat and back assembly is ready. On the fireside chair shown here the arm panels are completely filled in and upholstered—the foundation for these is shown in (**c**). The rocking chair has small arm pads which are made of wood bolted to the iron frame and upholstered in the same manner as the arm pads described on page

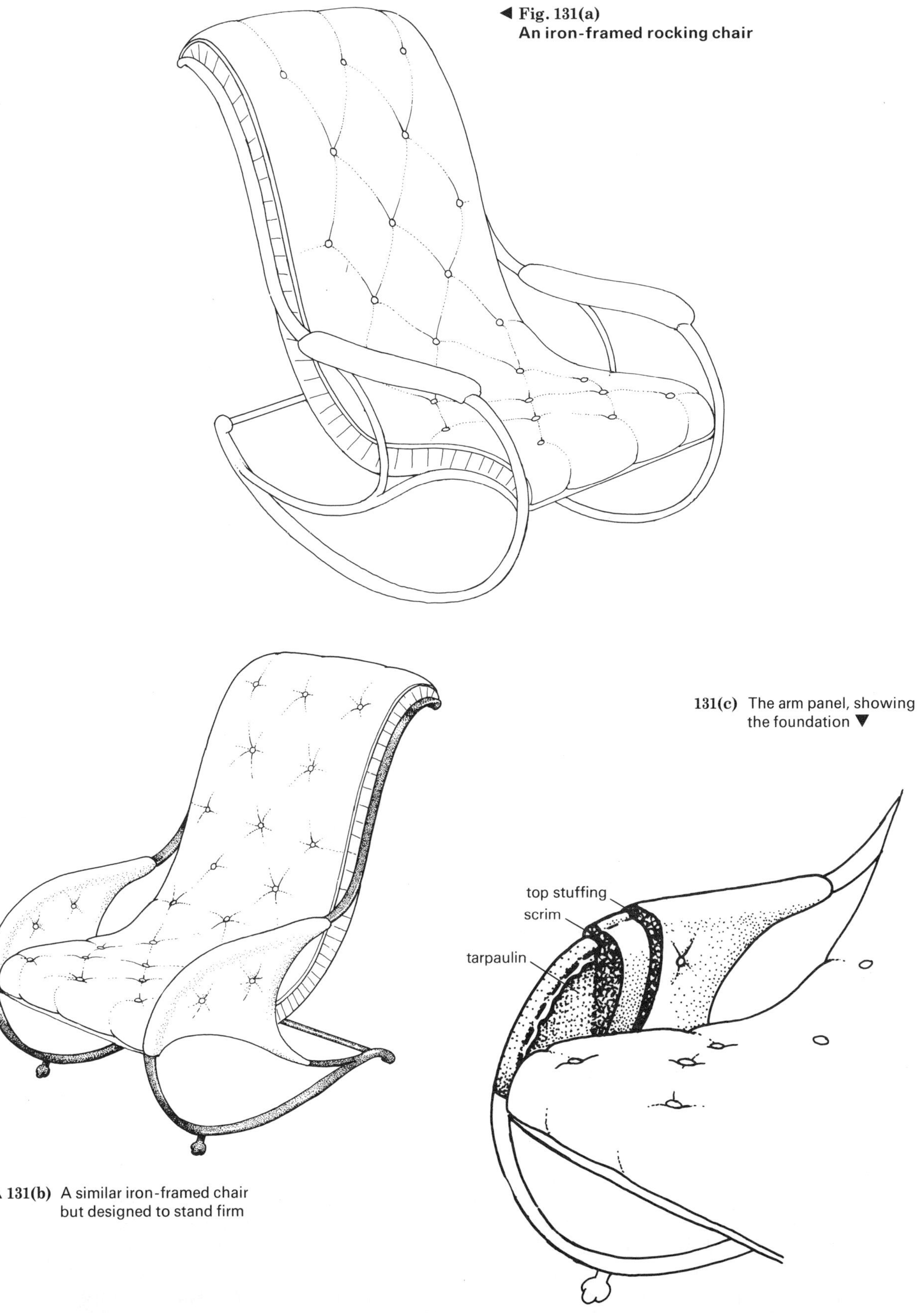

◀ **Fig. 131(a)** An iron-framed rocking chair

131(c) The arm panel, showing the foundation ▼

▲ **131(b)** A similar iron-framed chair but designed to stand firm

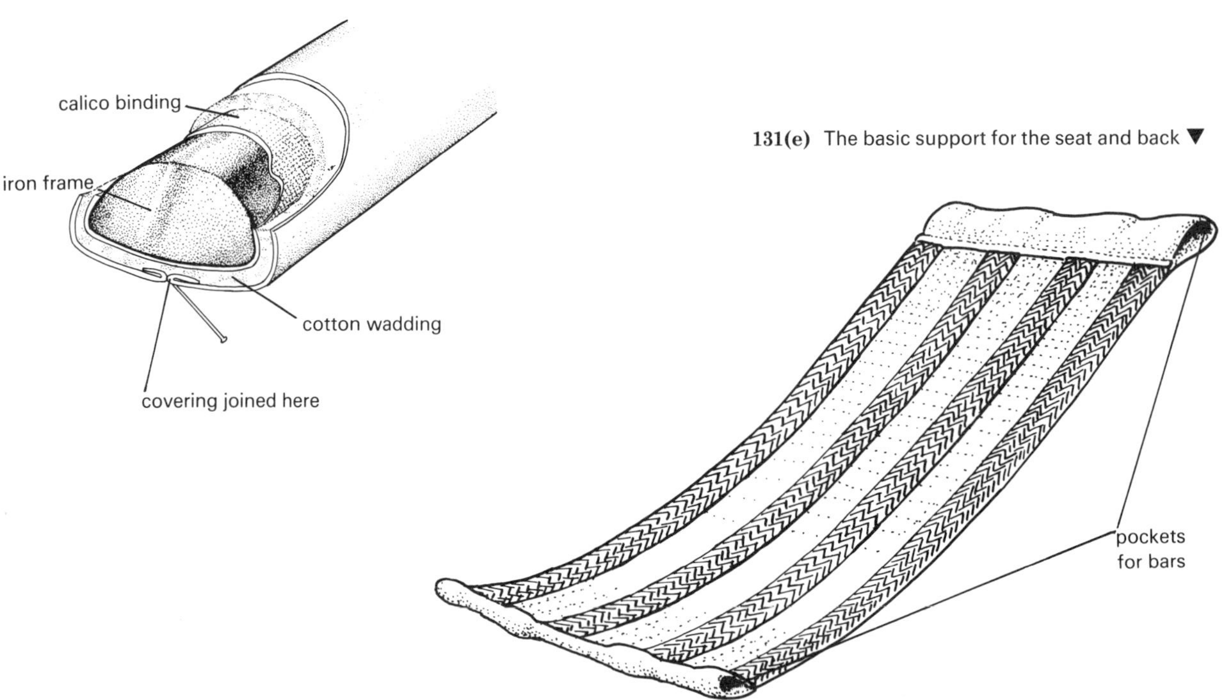

131(d) A section through part of the frame ▼

131(e) The basic support for the seat and back ▼

167. The rest of the ironwork on both types of chair has to be covered in the following manner. First, after treating the iron with a rust-proofing paint, bind it with cotton tape or strips of calico 25 mm (1 in) wide. Tear off 50 mm (2 in) wide strips of cotton wadding (this tears lengthwise) and wrap them evenly round the ironwork to be covered.

The method of covering depends on the sort of covering cloth that you have chosen; if you are using a velvet or piled cloth, strips wide enough to cover the iron with allowances for turning can be cut straight with the weave of the cloth, but be careful to keep the pile running as much as possible all the same way. With less flexible fabrics, such as tapestry, strips may have to be cut on the bias if the fabric is to lie well on the more acute bends. If possible, pin the material with the seam on the underside of the frame, as in (**d**), then ladder stitch it with small stitches. However, if the cloth is very unmanageable the seams can be made on the tops of the frame members and braid sewn over the joins.

Now we come to the most difficult part—the seat and back, which is made up as a squab and slung, deck-chair fashion, between the top and bottom rails.

The first step is to make up a support of tarpaulin hessian with four pieces of strong webbing machine stitched lengthwise (**e**). Pockets are sewn at each end through which the seat and top bars will be threaded when the squab is completed. Making this support to the right length is critical, because if it is made too short the chair's seat will have an uncomfortable forward slope; if it is too long the seat will dip lower than the front bar and also be rather uncomfortable. So before you sew up the pockets skewer the support in place and observe the curve of the seat and back, and, if you can skewer it fairly securely, gently sit in the chair to see if it feels right, allowing in your mind for the fact that it will be approximately 50 mm (2 in) thicker.

The squab's interior case is made of calico (**f**), stuffed and edge stitched in the way detailed on pages 162–165. The outer cover is

131(f) The squab interior ▼

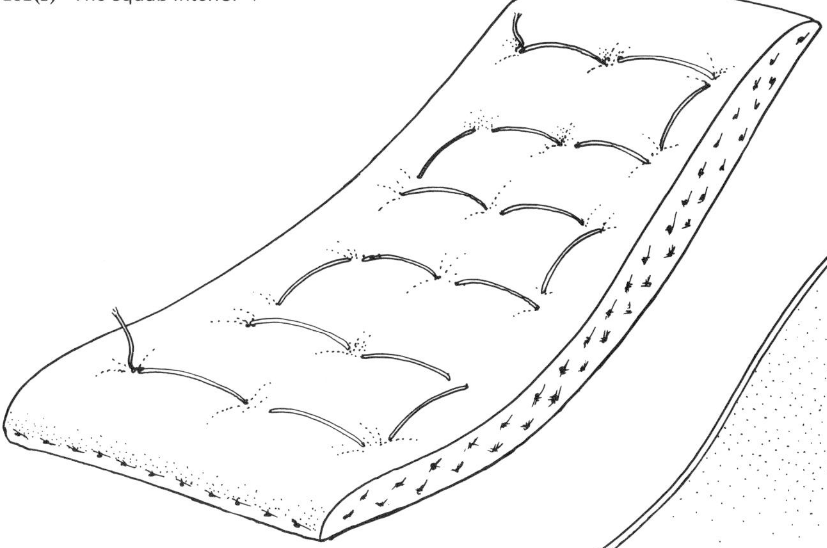

holes left for bars

131(g) The cover made up ▶

black lining underneath the seat portion

open end

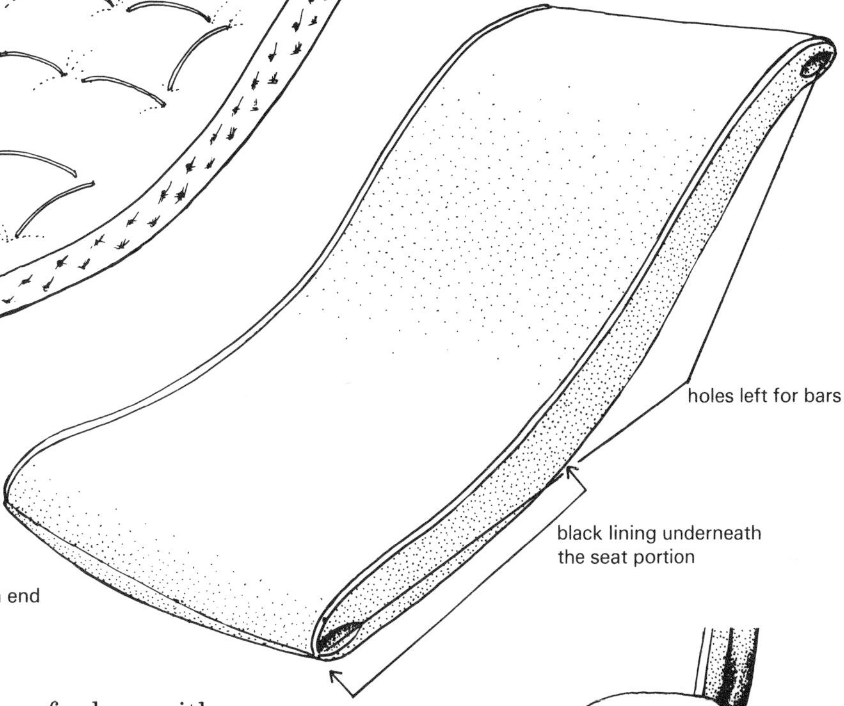

made up complete in the form of a bag, with black lining used under the seat portion. One end is left open and holes are left at the corners of the other end, for the bar to be slotted through (**g**). The top surface of the squab's inner case is then covered with two layers of cotton wadding, the outer cover is pulled on and the open end is sewn up, again leaving spaces for threading the bar through. Measure and set out for the buttons, which are to be tied in very tightly, a button being used on both back and front. Be sure to leave the button cords nice and long so that they can be threaded back into the stuffing.

Now all that remains is to push the seat and back bars through the pockets and bolt the squab on to the frame. The covering material where the bars extrude is stitched to the side frame fabric (**h**) and the chair is completed.

You will come across many variations of these iron-framed chairs but I am sure you will be able to adapt the procedures accordingly.

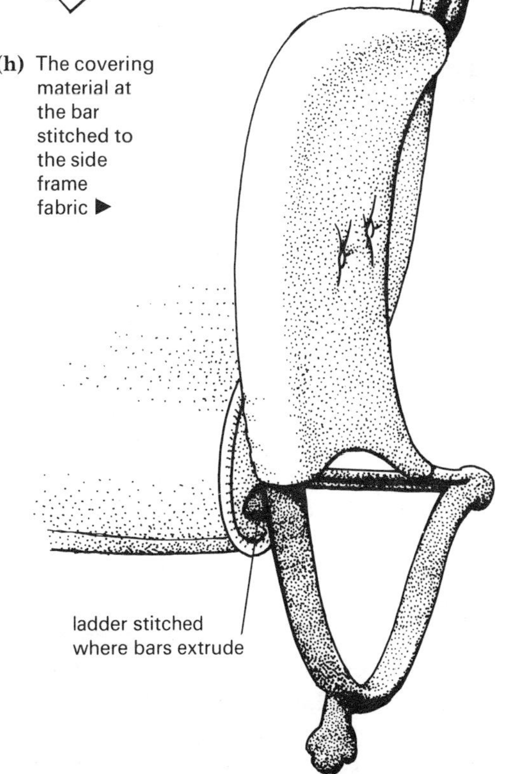

131(h) The covering material at the bar stitched to the side frame fabric ▶

9 A Chesterfield Settee

And so we come to the job that is not necessarily the most difficult, although it is fairly complex, but certainly the one that will take the longest time.

The chesterfield settee is to be found in many sizes, from about 1.2 m (4 ft) to about 2 m (7 ft) in length. The earliest, dating from about the mid-nineteenth century, have beautifully made frames of prepared beech or birch wood very accurately machined. The legs are well designed and turned in walnut, mahogany or oak and fitted with good brass castors, the front castors usually being of the cup variety. Later in the century there appeared chesterfields with drop ends operated by steel ratchet mechanisms. Most of them had a single drop end but on some both arms were made to drop.

During the 1920s and 1930s, the quality of the construction of chesterfields—apart from a few made by reputable makers—diminished markedly. Frames tended to be made of poor timber which was skimpy in size and badly jointed; the drop ends, operated by wooden ratchets, were sometimes very weak and soon gave way. Chesterfields are made today, indeed last year I myself made one to the earlier traditional design and construction for a customer who required one of a certain size for a specific room. But most of the chesterfield settees that you now see in furniture stores are poor semblances of their nineteenth-century equivalents. You have only to lift one end of many chesterfields to realize that there is nothing inside but vestigial springs and plastic foam. There is nothing traditional about the interiors of these pieces, although they command high prices. The methods of upholstery of chesterfields fall into three categories. There are those that are plainly upholstered and tightly covered, perhaps in a patterned cloth that needs no further embellishment; those that are covered in a strong union, calico or cotton as an undercovering for a fitted loose cover; and those that are upholstered with deep buttoning on the back, arms and seat (fig. 132). It is the reupholstering of the last type that I would like to give instruction on. This is a job that will really test an upholsterer's skill.

Stripping Off

To begin at the very beginning with the stripping off of the old upholstery, prepare yourself for a dusty time for there is nothing more full of dust and dirt than an old chesterfield whose inside has not seen the light of day since perhaps the end of the last century. So, masks on and if the weather is fine do the job out in the open air.

Before you start, make a drawing of the settee noting the measurements—the height, width of the back upholstery, seat height, number of buttons, distance between buttons, and so on; also noting how the general shape can be improved. You will then keep a picture of the finished article before you when you are building up from the skeleton frame. If you have a camera take a photograph, it will be interesting to show your friends the 'before and after' of this piece of furniture. May I remind you once more to examine the old upholstery carefully as you strip, noting the methods used, whether good or bad, and learning what you can.

There are materials that you can use again. As well as the usual horsehair and fibre fillings, save all those lovely little soft springs from under the back and arm upholstery, except those that have obviously buckled. I hear you say, but you told us to discard old springs because they will be suffering from metal fatigue after all these years. Yes, I know, but here is an exception to the rule, for only those springs along the top of the back and arms will have had a lot of use—people tend to sit on the backs and arms of chesterfields—the rest have just served to support the upholstery and will have had but gentle

▲ Fig. 132 A typical late Victorian high quality chesterfield settee

Fig. 133 The bare frame of a chesterfield

use from back pressure of sitters. Also, comparable new springs are difficult if not impossible to come by, the modern equivalent size is now made in a thicker gauge wire and therefore is much less resilient.

When the frame is bare (**fig. 133**) you must, of course, as always, check the frame joints, treat the wood with woodworm killer, see to the castors and polish the legs.

Fig. 134 Webbing and springs for the back and arms

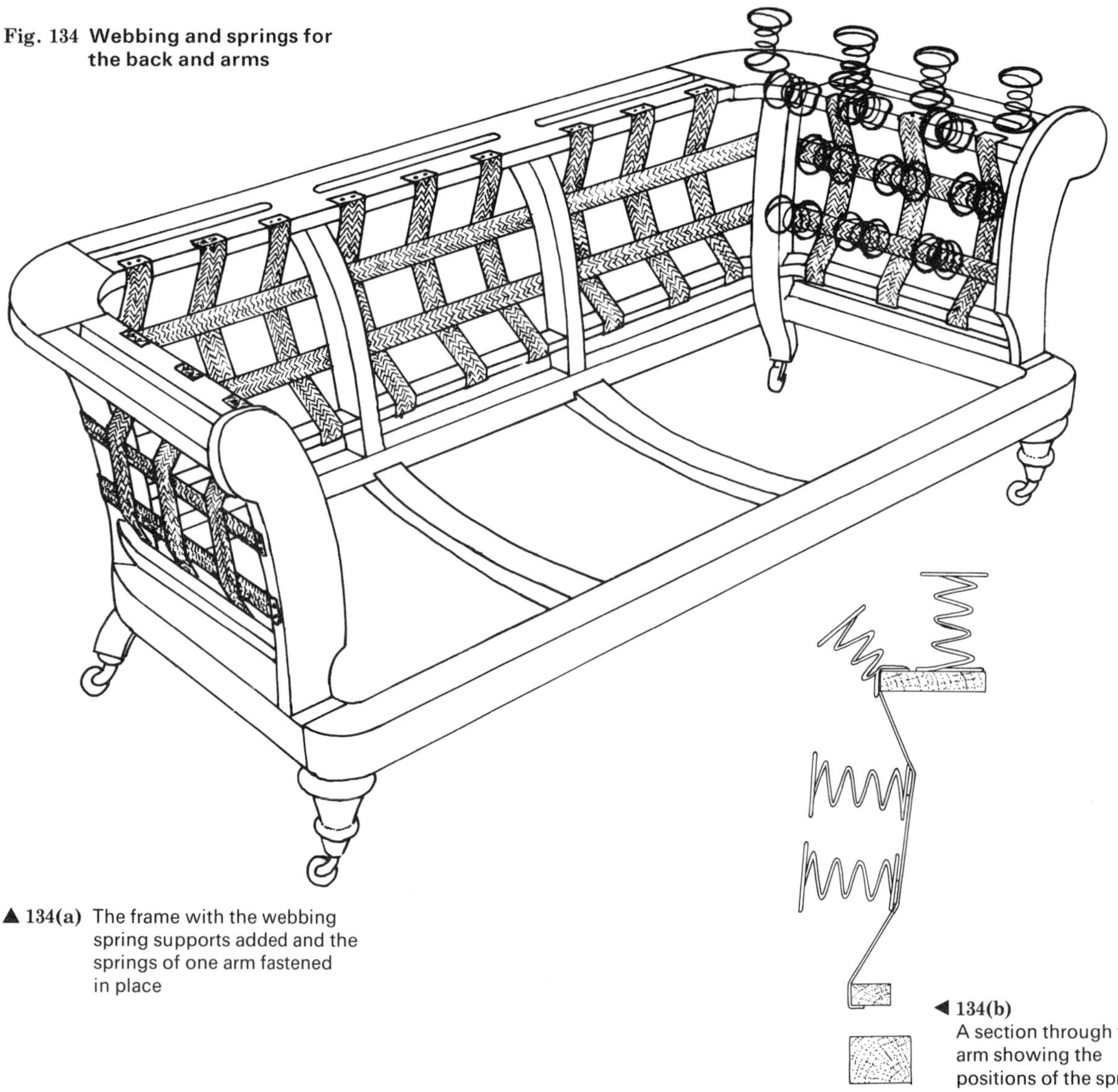

▲ **134(a)** The frame with the webbing spring supports added and the springs of one arm fastened in place

◀ **134(b)** A section through the arm showing the positions of the springs

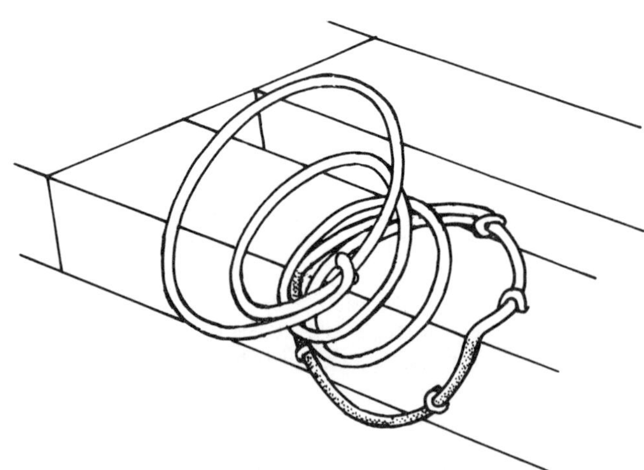

134(c) The base of a spring bent over the edge of the spring platform

Webbing and Springs for the Back and Arms

The webbing spring supports for the back and arms are added to the chesterfield frame (**fig. 134a**) and you can see the springs of one arm fastened in place; close-ups of fastenings appear in (**b**) and (**c**). The number of vertical webs corresponds to the number of springs in the horizontal rows. Since, as I have mentioned, chesterfields come in all sizes, it is impossible to specify an exact number of webs and springs, but the springs should be 125 to 175 mm (5 to 7 in) from centre to centre. For instructions on fixing springs, see pages 37–38. These springs need to be pulled in and laced so that their only movement is in and out. A lacing method is shown in **fig. 135**.

Begin with the top row, along the spring platform. Here each spring is tied down to an exact height; be as accurate as possible with the depth measurements, making sure that all the springs are of the same height along the top line. I must emphasize again the importance of exactness when building the foundations, as this makes for the perfectly symmetrical finished job.

Lateral ties are now placed along the top row; here, make sure that all the springs are perfectly upright. Retaining ties similar to those of seat edge spring fastenings (page 109) are applied to prevent the top springs from falling forward (**a**).

A loose zigzag interlacing will keep the other springs in a soft and independent tension (**b**). Laid cord of the usual thickness is used for this. A thinner laid cord can be used for lacing the springs. Secure the lacings with the knots specified in Chapter 3 (pages 35–38). In (**c**) the profile of the arms after lacing is shown.

135(b) Zigzag lacings

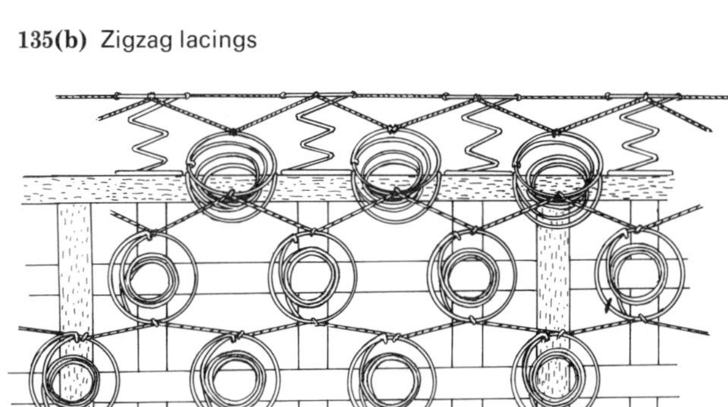

Fig. 135 Lacing the springs

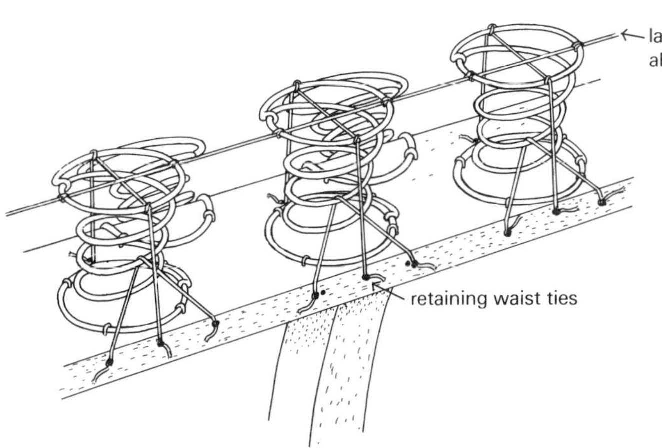

▲ **135(a)** The springs of the top row tied down

135(c) Profile after lacing ▼

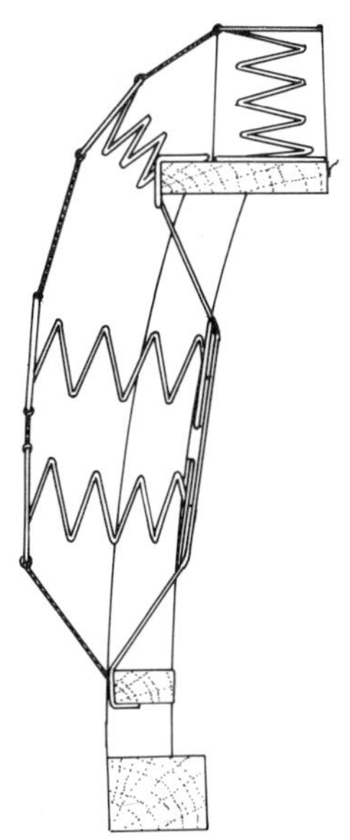

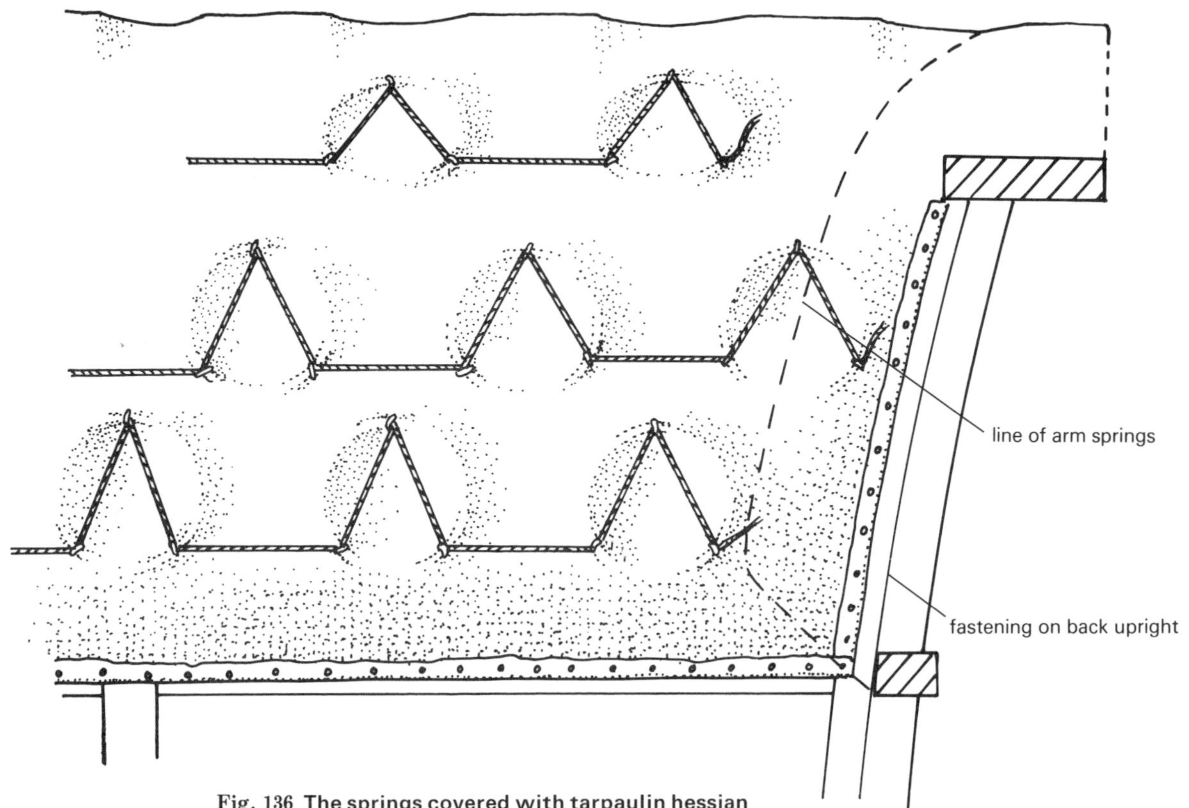

Fig. 136 The springs covered with tarpaulin hessian

All the springs have now to be covered with a good stout hessian—I would use 450 g (16 oz) tarpaulin. Three pieces will be needed; for instructions on measuring up see pages 31–32. When you come to attach the hessian, begin by tacking along the bottom tacking rail, following the line of the hessian weave. Leave 230 mm (9 in) or so untacked at each end—this will need to be taken in more after the ends are fastened. Now, keeping the hessian weave quite straight and at 90° to the tacking rail, fasten the cloth along the back of the spring platform on the backward-facing edge; if you can follow the line of a thread the whole of the back will be kept to an exact size throughout. The ends can now be fastened into the back uprights and some folds and adjustments made at the corners (**fig. 136**).

If the frame permits, the arms should be made to exactly the same profile as the back. Some chesterfields, however, have arm frames smaller in thickness than the back frames.

The springs are fastened through the hessian with the usual three stitches per spring top (page 32). Then you are ready to begin thinking about the first stuffing.

The First Stuffing for the Back and Arms

To accommodate the depth of the button-work, the first stuffings on the back and arms need to be thin over the centres, but heights of firm filling have to be built up for the scroll arm fronts, round the outside top edge and along the lower back and lowest part of the arms. So put in appropriate stuffing ties (page 95). A little reminder here about stitched edges; take care to build up the hair to just the required density and shape, especially round the arm front scrolls, then life will be much easier when you come to cover this first stuffing with your scrim hessian. When you have formed the scrolls and put a good roll of hair all round the top outside of the arms and back and a firm cushion of horsehair round the inside base of the back and arms, then fill the remaining areas with a thin layer of hair, to make an even surface over the knobbiness of the springs.

Measure for the scrim hessian to cover this first stuffing. For the arms, measure round the front scroll shape for the length, and from

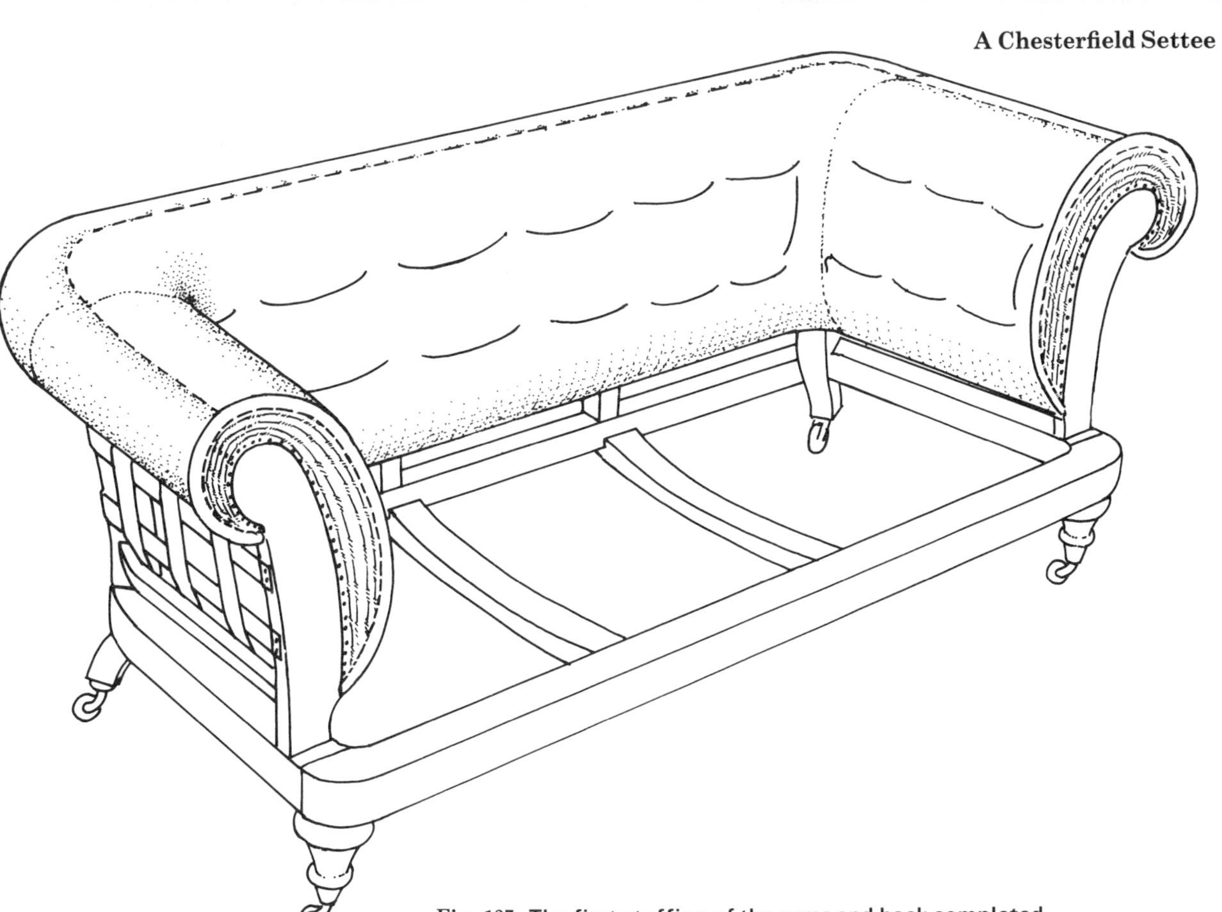

Fig. 137 The first stuffing of the arms and back completed

the wood of the scroll arm front to well over the back roll for the width. For the back, the length (top to bottom) should be the same as for the arms; take the width measurement well over the outside rolls of the arms. Cut off the three pieces and position them over the horsehair. Make sure that the arm pieces are cut exactly to the same length to enable you to get the two arms to the same size.

When you are tacking the scrim covering to this first stuffing (pages 45 & 97), again apply the rule of following a thread in the weave of the scrim. The two back rounded corners of the settee will need much attention and adjustment before they are ready for permanent fixing. I find that it is best to bring the scrim hessian to cover the back over the end of the arm, forming the rounded corner with this piece, and then the arm scrim can be sewn in a straight line up the corner and over the arm roll. If you stretch the scrim fairly tightly round the scroll and fasten it over the arms to an exact measurement at each scroll end, you will again ensure that the scrolls are the same size. Pleat the scrim round the wooden scroll front, so that the threads radiate from the centre of the wooden scroll circle—you can mark this centre with a dot to give you a guide. Using 10 mm ($\frac{3}{8}$ in) tacks, fasten the scrim on the chamfer round the edge of the wood.

Go round all the edges and rolls with your regulator to even out and consolidate the hair stuffing. Then your upholstery is ready for edge stitching (pages 47–49). I like to begin with the arm scroll fronts, putting in four or five rows of blind stitches and then the roll edge stitches to make a nice firm, tight job on this most important part of the upholstery; for these arm fronts are going to take a lot of pushing and shoving from folk who will probably have no inkling of the time and pains you have taken.

To form a large roll round the top of the chesterfield, first mark the position with a felt marker and straight edge and then stitch with wide through stitches, ensuring that each stitch is about 50 mm (2 in) wide and running into each other just like roll edge stitches but larger. Put in the through stuffing ties (page 46) to hold the rest of the first stuffing firmly in place (**fig. 137**).

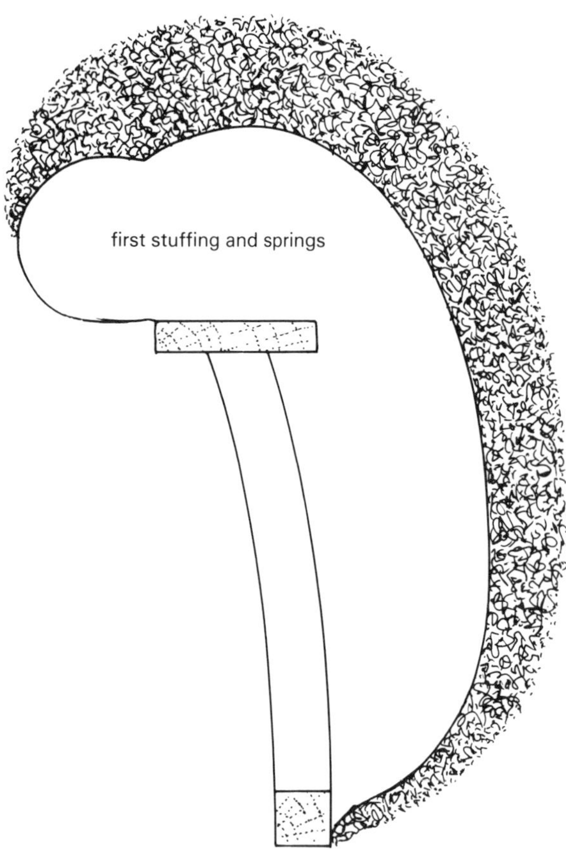

Fig. 138 The second stuffing of horsehair shown in section

The Top Stuffing for the Back and Arms

For the top stuffing you should use a very good quality, long-stranded, curled and well carded horsehair that will have plenty of spring and resilience. If short hair is used it will consolidate into a hard mass and make the buttonwork very ungiving and uncomfortable to rest against.

Although you are going to button the back and arms, and the buttons will hold in the top stuffing, you must put in rows of stuffing ties to enable you to build on the hair evenly and fairly firmly. The loops of the stuffing ties should be 230 mm (9 in) long, the rows 125 mm (5 in) apart and the bottom row about 60 mm ($2\frac{1}{2}$ in) above the intended seat height.

Tuck horsehair under the tie loops to a depth of about 90 mm ($3\frac{1}{2}$ in). When all the lines of hair have been completed, fill in the remaining spaces to give an even, all-over layer (**fig. 138**). The hair should not extend too far over the top roll.

I like to lay a split layer of wadding over the whole of the hair and then cover it with a layer of 71 g ($2\frac{1}{2}$ oz) bonded polyester wadding. Cover your settee in three pieces of polyester and make a mitred join on each of the corner tops—the join will then correspond to a fold in the covering; it would otherwise show as a ridge under the cloth.

So, here we arrive at the most intricate part of the job: the setting out of the upholstery and of the covering material. Shall we start with the upholstery?

Setting Out the Back and Arms for Button Upholstery

In most chesterfield settees there are four horizontal rows of buttons, with the bottom row about 100 to 125 mm (4 to 5 in) above the seat line. The highest row is on the top of the back and arm roll slightly back of centre of the thickness of the roll-over, and, of course, the two remaining rows are positioned at equal distances in between.

The number of vertical lines of buttons depends upon the length of the settee; much measuring and working out is needed here, to ensure that the diamond shapes between the buttons are of the correct number and size to meet and join at the junction of the back and arms. When measuring to determine the number of buttons in the horizontal rows, take into account the fact that the filling on the outside back and arms, and to a lesser degree on the top of the roll-over, is standing out proud. It is best to make a diagram of the profile or section of the shape, which will be slightly larger than the front scroll dimensions; this is best done life-size—use a large piece of brown paper. The width of the back can be determined by measuring between the arm fronts.

Mark the centre of the back and draw a vertical chalk line, making it extend over the back roll-over. Next, measure and mark horizontal chalk lines along the back and arms at the position of the rows of buttons, starting with the bottom line. I like to put a long straight edge across the bottom seat rails of the settee inside the seat area so that I can measure from this up and on to the back and arm upholstery, and get all the lines exactly parallel to the frame. Mark out the vertical positions of the buttons on your profile template and the settee. You can now measure and mark out the button positions, placing skewers along these chalk lines on the settee as your plan indicates. Marking with skewers will enable you to make final adjustments to the between-button measurements until you are satisfied that all will be well. This achieved, mark all the positions with a felt pen dot and remove the skewers. You will need some sort of guide to the button positions at the back and at the outside of the arms. Mark the positions for the two bottom rows on the inside of the hessian covering the springs. On the row along the top of the roll-over the twine fastening the buttons will be pulled through the slotted spring platform, so mark the underside of the platform. The remaining third row can be marked at the inner edge of the spring platform—perhaps in a different colour so that no mistakes are made.

Setting Out the Button Positions on the Covering Material

You will remember from your previous experiences in buttonwork that at this stage you need to draw a diagram to determine the size of the pieces of cloth required and to work out the positions of the buttons (pages 102–103). **Fig. 139** shows the four pieces of material for the back and arms of the chesterfield and how they will fit together. Depending on the size of the back and arms and the depth of the top stuffing, the between-button allowance can vary from 32 mm ($1\frac{1}{4}$ in) to 50 mm (2 in). Just as a rough guide, I would recommend a 38 mm ($1\frac{1}{2}$ in) allowance for a depth of filling of about 63 mm ($2\frac{1}{2}$ in).

The two pieces of covering material for the back can be cut (zigzag, as shown) and stitched after the marking out has been done. Cutting and joining diagonally between the button marks means that the seams will be hidden within the between-button folds. Before stitching these seams it is best to tack them with cotton, or at any rate to pin them together with many pins, especially if the covering material is velvet which will otherwise 'creep' beneath the sewing machine foot.

Transfer your back marks through to the front by sticking your regulator through, but leave the corner marks in case adjustment is needed here. Make marks along the top and bottom edges of your cloth corresponding to the positions of the nearest rows of button marks.

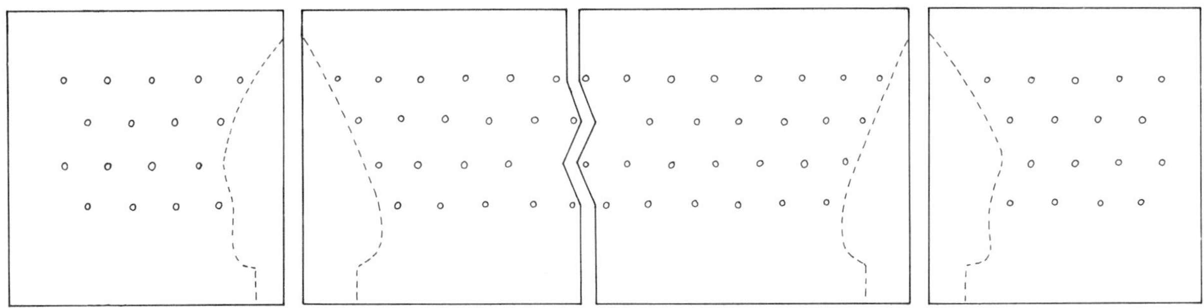

Fig. 139
Setting out the button positions on the covering material. The four pieces of covering material for the back and arms marked out. The dotted lines indicate the probable cuts to be made at the corner joins, but they should not be cut until the material has been fitted.

Covering and Buttoning

To add even more richness to the upholstery, place a layer of cotton wadding over the polyester, teasing the joins to avoid unevenness.

Now, begin buttoning and covering, according to the directions given on pages 102–107. As springs are incorporated in the upholstery it would be very difficult to tie slip knots at the back, so, with the exception of the top row, all your tying will be done at the front. Nevertheless, do place toggles under the loops of twine through the spring hessian, as otherwise the twine will soon cut through. Do not pull the twine too tight at this stage and cut off the twine leaving ends of at least 150 mm (6 in), with the drawing cord a little longer so that you know this is the one to pull.

Upon completing the second row, form the between-button folds with button-fold sticks (page 105) or two regulators. Proceed in this manner until all the buttons have been put in. I can picture you looking aghast at all those ends of twine untidily hanging out. Don't worry, I will tell you later how to make them disappear like magic.

To lay in the folds coming from the bottom rows of buttons turn up the covering exposing the upholstery and with a sharp knife cut through the wadding and the top filling of hair, but not through the first stuffing covering of scrim hessian. Slit from the button hole down to just underneath the swell of the upholstery. Now, by pulling at the mark you made along the bottom edge of the covering you will be able to get the folds to lie in accurately. With a regulator or your button-fold stick, ease each one into the recess that you have cut and temporarily fasten it with a skewer under the swell; when all the folds have been made in this way it is a simple task, working from the back of the settee, to pull the fabric through and put a temporary tack through each fold into the tacking rail.

The folds from the top buttons that extend over the back and arm roll require no cutting of the filling beneath; with these folds begin at the centre of the back and work outwards, making the fold openings face towards the sides. At each edge mark make a pleat, taking up the exact amount of the between-button allowance, and fasten the pleat with a pin. Do this to all the folds and then, from the centre, pull each one tightly over the roll and fasten it beneath the spring platform wood but to the outside of the slots (you need to have the slots exposed when pulling down and fastening the top row of buttons).

Now we turn to the scroll fronts of the arms. The folds here must be taken from the buttons nearest to the front; the pleats should again be made to the amount of the between-button allowance. These folds and, indeed, all the covering here can be fastened temporarily with skewers placed round the inside lip of the scroll edge. Take care to keep the material round the periphery of the scroll, between the folds, as tight as possible so that the pleats and gathers made will not extend over the lip of the edge and spoil the beautifully shaped edge that you have made.

Fastening Off the Buttons

Pull the buttons in to their proper depth. This means just as far as they will go, except for the ones in the corners and the top row, which should be pulled in just until any fullness is taken up. To get the top row of buttons to a uniform depth, use a long straight edge laid along the line of buttons and measure each button down from this. Tie the buttons off with three half hitches or single knots and cut the ends to about 130 mm (5 in).

Now you can make all those nasty ends disappear. Thread both ends through the eye of your largest double-pointed needle and push the eye end in beneath the button. If you push the needle in far enough the twine will disengage from the needle's eye and you can then withdraw the needle. Because of its length, the twine will not become unknotted, nor appear on the face again. In this way you can quickly dispose of the surplus twine. To fasten the top row of buttons and those in the corners, pull each piece of twine through to the other side, wind it round a large-headed tack driven half in, then drive the tack home.

The top and bottom vertical folds and those at the scroll fronts can now be given that final tug and fastened. I would still leave the bottom folds temporarily fastened because after the seat has been built in, a final tightening may be needed. Blind stitch the covering beneath the lip of the scroll front roll edge with a 75 mm (3 in) curved needle.

Making Double Scrolls for the Arm Fronts

Here is a touch of fancy upholstery work for your chesterfield, double front scrolls—that is, two decorative scrolls made one within the other (**fig. 140**).

The outer scroll is made and fitted first. Cut a strip of cloth (lengthways to the run of the fabric as it gathers better this way), to the width of the scroll. Measure this from the lip of the roll edge, allowing for an extra 12 mm ($\frac{1}{2}$ in) for turning, to about 25 mm (1 in) beyond the edge of the wooden scroll front.

To achieve the gathered look that you see in the drawing, the part of the covering that will be on the straight upright part of the scroll has to be gathered and machined before you fasten it. Lay this strip on the scroll to determine at what point the gathering should start, then put in a loose draw cord of thin thread 12 mm ($\frac{1}{2}$ in) from the outside edge. Pull up the cord to gather this portion of the strip, but only temporarily fasten off the end so that when you try it on you can adjust the gathers to correspond with those that you form round the top half-circle of the scroll.

If you intend to use piping, make the piping and stitch it on to the strip at this point. A very thin layer of wadding can be laid on the wooden scroll just to fill out this gathered covering. Now, using upholsterer's pins or skewers, fasten and adjust the fabric on the outside edge, then gather and tack it with 10 mm ($\frac{3}{8}$ in) tacks on to the wooden scroll front, keeping the tacks as close to the material's edge as possible. Place a dot in the centre of the wooden scroll top so that you can make your gathering radiate from this point. Ladder stitch the scroll and then sew on chair cord if you are using it.

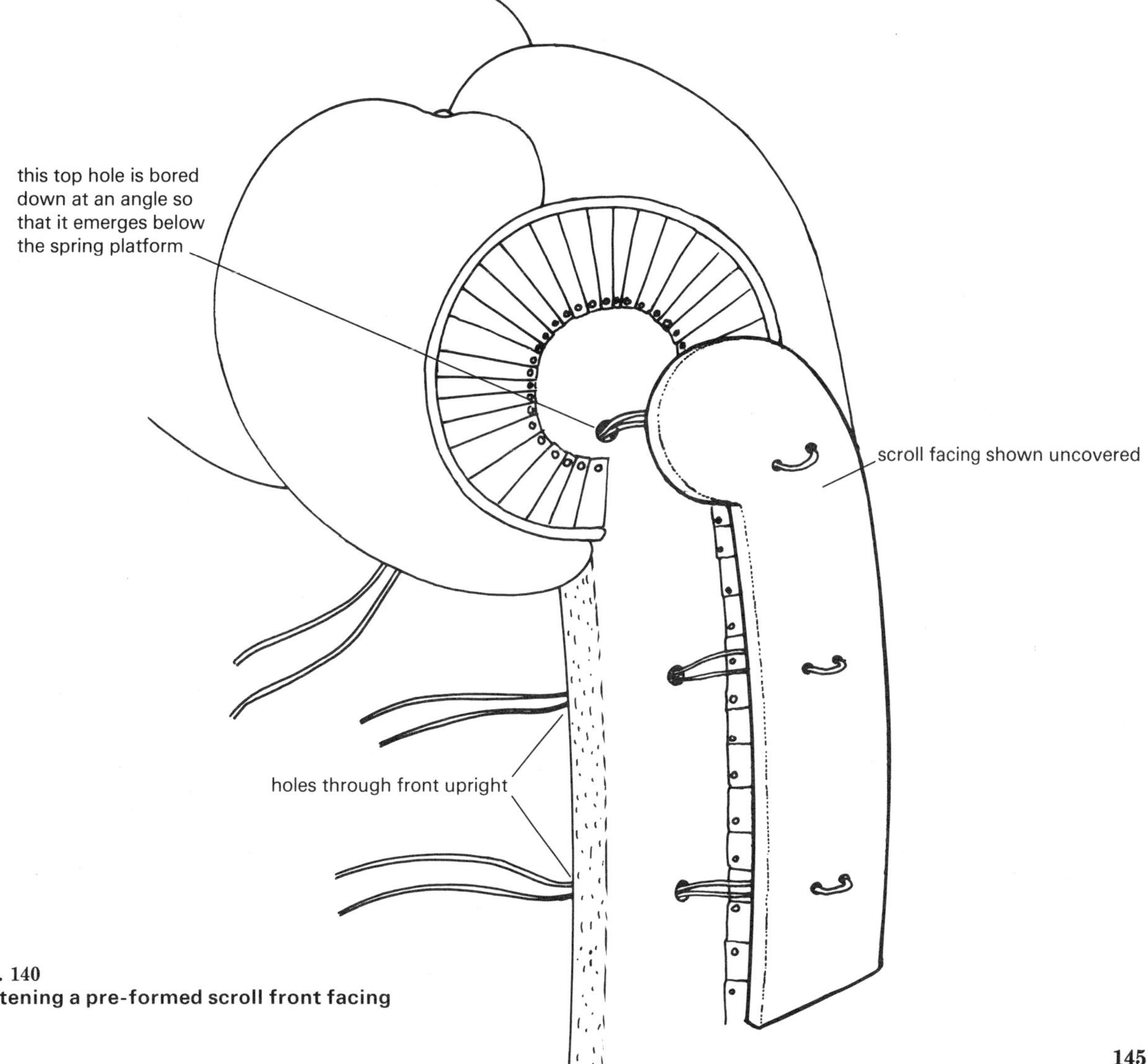

Fig. 140
Fastening a pre-formed scroll front facing

Fig. 141
The waists of deep springs should be laced. This drawing shows the lacings from back to front. The springs should also be laced from side to side.

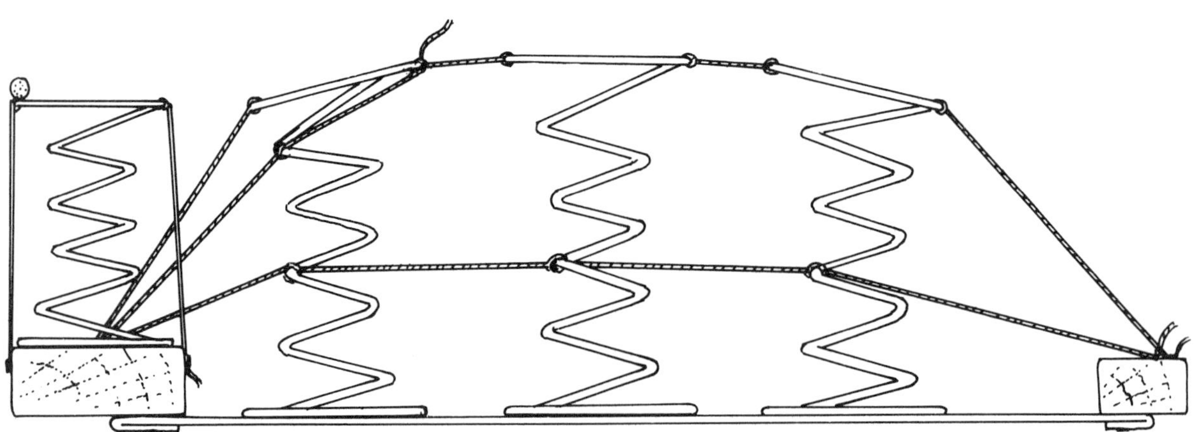

A Pre-Formed Scroll Facing

For the inside scroll I favour using a preformed shape. Cut out the shape you require in 6 mm ($\frac{1}{4}$ in) plywood. In my previous book, *Care and Repair of Furniture*, I have described a method of fixing this type of facing with nails. Another good way to fasten these facings—indeed, a simpler way—is depicted in (**fig. 140**). Drill pairs of holes 10 mm ($\frac{3}{8}$ in) apart in the shaped facing and knot strong nylon tufting twine through, leaving the ends long enough to thread through holes bored in the wooden arm fronts. Three ties should be sufficient. Using this method you can pull the facing well in, fastening the cords with large-headed tacks at the back of the wood of the arm front, and there is no risk of damaging the covering cloth.

Just a word about covering these preshaped scroll facings. Two layers of wadding will provide suitable padding; the covering can be fastened with 6 mm ($\frac{1}{4}$ in) fine tacks or with 6 mm ($\frac{1}{4}$ in) staples. Leave the straight outside edge unfastened until the facing has been put in place, then tack this edge on to the outside of the front upright. Piping, if used, should be tacked or stapled around the facing before it is placed in position. The flange of this piping is fastened evenly behind the facing so that the piping lays evenly around the edge. Decorative cord may be sewn on either before or after fastening the facing.

Upholstering the Chesterfield Seat

I hate turning a settee upside down just when I have made the back and arms look so neat, tidy and new, but it must be done, so sweep the floor well, lay down a clean dust sheet and maybe a sheet of polyether foam, or a few old cushions to act as softening, and turn your chesterfield over on these.

In describing the work on this part of the settee I will only detail the processes that are special to the chesterfield. Otherwise, follow the usual procedure for the spring edge seat (pages 108–113).

The Webbing

Do not be mean with the number of webs that you put on the seat of your chesterfield, for this is where the greatest support strength is needed; the webs should be no more than 50 mm (2 in) apart and may be as close as 38 mm ($1\frac{1}{2}$ in). If there is a centre iron support bar this should be wrapped round with a calico or hessian strip as a protection for the webbing, which has to be placed beneath it, (beneath the bar when the settee is upside down). If there is a centre wooden rail, when the webbing has all been fixed, a length of webbing can be tacked along the length of the rail, the tacks being placed in the spaces between the webs crossing the rail.

The Seat Springs

Trestles of the right height are really essential

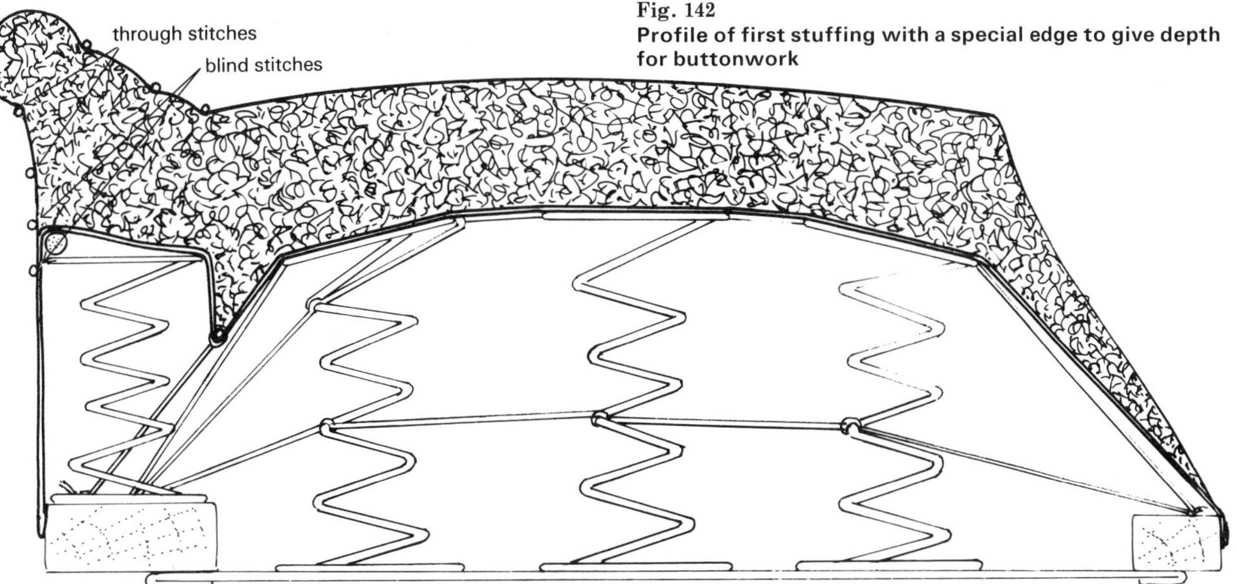

Fig. 142
Profile of first stuffing with a special edge to give depth for buttonwork

for working on the seat of anything large like this settee, especially when fixing the springs, where you will have to be working on the top and underneath the webbing.

Guidance on choosing springs of the correct size and gauge is given on page 108, but for a chesterfield, I would not advise using springs any thinner than 10 gauge.

As to the number of springs, this depends upon the space available; as a rough guide, there are nearly always three rows of main springs running from side to side, and in these rows they should be no more than 75 mm (3 in) apart. Where possible, the edge springs should be placed to correspond with the spaces between the main springs.

Fastening the Springs

Fasten the springs to the webbing and on the front rail in the usual manner (page 37 & 108). When you come to the lacings, if you are using deep springs, put extra lacings to hold the centre waist of each one (**fig. 141**). This gives the springs extra stability and prolongs their life considerably.

Let me remind you how important it is to get all the edge springs to the same height, perfectly upright and securely fastened with whipping to the edge cane or wire.

The Hessian Spring Cover

A spring covering of tarpaulin hessian with a well put in between the edge and main springs is the next step (pages 110–111). When all is fastened and the springs are stitched everywhere, on with the first stuffing.

The First Stuffing for the Seat

You will see from the profile drawing in **fig. 142** that the stitched edge is a different shape in section from the usual edge. The part immediately behind the roll edge is made lower, to give the depth for the buttonwork. To achieve this, when forming the roll of horsehair for the core of the edge, make it a little bit higher than you normally would for the roll of a spring edge seat. The first row of blind stitches— those that fasten the scrim to the spring hessian—and the next row, are made in the usual manner as described on page 112, which brings you to about half-way up the edge. Next comes a row of specialized through stitches, the same as those used to dish the top surface of the crinoline seat (page 126). After a good shape up with your regulator, mark two lines with your upholstery gauge (page 127) on the top of the scrim hessian; the first about 60 mm ($2\frac{1}{2}$ in) from the front, and the second 90 mm ($3\frac{1}{2}$ in) from the front. Make the row of through stitches between the two lines marked and bring the edge up again with your regulator to raise a firm line to be finally stitched as a roll.

The Top Stuffing for the Seat

Work lines of top stuffing ties, about 100 mm

(4 in) apart, across the seat and pack in a reasonable compacted layer of horsehair to a depth of about 75 to 90 mm (3 to $3\frac{1}{2}$ in). Cover the hair with a sheet of wadding and stretch over a layer of 6 mm ($\frac{1}{4}$ in) polyether foam to complete the second stuffing.

Buttoning the Seat

Try to make the button distances the same as those in the back upholstery so that the outside folds correspond to the folds of the bottom back and work out the positions so that the distances from the outside rows of buttons to the sides are between half and the whole of the between-button measurement.

Make a diagram of the seat with all the buttons marked on it. No doubt you will have to make a join somewhere, just as you did for the back, so mark this on your diagram and work out the sizes of the pieces of cloth that you require. Cut off the material from your roll. Remember that you can save on the costly cloth by sewing fly pieces to the back and sides. Set out the button positions and make the edge marks, which are the guides for the outside folds. Begin with the front row of buttons, knotting on the front again, but once more placing toggles behind the loops inside the seat.

When finally tightening the seat buttons, pull them down as far as they will go. Fasten the sides and back with tacks, in particular placing them at each fold, and along the front. After much adjustment and temporary fastening with skewers, using a 75 to 100 mm (3 or 4 in) curved needle, sew a row of blind stitches beneath the roll edge.

Covering and Buttoning the Front Seat Border

Now, here is another tricky little job to test your skill as an upholsterer. We have decided to button the seat border of the chesterfield—this always adds a little more refinement to the job. I find it easier to have the settee down on the floor and tipped over on its back to do this work. Start by putting in two lines of stuffing ties and pack in a softly compacted layer of hair of about 50 mm (2 in) thickness. A double layer of wadding should be added next—if you fold the wadding lengthwise you can stretch it quite tightly from end to end and then set out your button holes through this. There will be just the one line of buttons and these should be placed towards the top of the centre of the border, especially as in this case you are going to trim round the base with fringe. I had better add at this juncture, that the fringe always looks better when placed so that the bottom hangs no more than 6 mm ($\frac{1}{4}$ in) below the bottom edge of the settee; it is then backed by the covering fabric and looks richer. Your buttons should be placed so that they appear centred between the lip of the seat's edge and the top of the fringe.

The button positions in the border should correspond to those of the front row on the seat and when you have made your measurements you will find that you will need two pieces of cloth; the join, therefore, must be hidden beneath one of the folds. Mark out your border material on the back; the between-button allowance needs to be only 25 mm (1 in), as the filling is not very thick. Pin the folds, or tack them with cotton, at the top and the bottom, so that the pleats face outwards from the centre, and run two lines of machine stitches across to hold the pleats permanently. Transfer the button marks to the face of the fabric with your regulator, then fasten the covering along the top edge with skewers, turning in the material to your row of stitches and temporarily tacking beneath the front rail at each fold. Make sure the folds are at right angles to this rail—use a try square if you like.

Put your buttons in with the longest needle you have—I use a 36 cm (14 in) double-pointed one—pushing it through at such an angle that it comes out underneath, through the webbing of the seat. When returning the needle make sure that you have not ensnared an edge spring and also that you have made a big enough stitch to hold the button well. A difficult task, because you will be working in the dark, so to speak. If you look at Chapter 7, **fig. 109b**, you will see how to fasten the sides of the border where they meet the arms. Twine ties are used, three on each end to pull the extra cloth well through between the seat and the bottom part of the front of the arm. Now you can ladder stitch your border and remove the skewers.

I am assuming that you will be trimming with decorative chair cord and this can be put on next; again, use twine tied to each end and pulled through at the sides of the seat. All these twines can be fastened along the sides of the bottom rails with tacks. If you prefer to use piping, stitch it to the top edge of the border cloth before you fix the cloth.

Covering the Outside Back and Outside Arms

Now all that remains is to cover the outside back and arms of the chesterfield. It depends on the size of your settee, but in most cases a half width of material will be enough for the side panels. Unless the settee is very small, the back covering will have to be made wide enough by the inclusion of two extra pieces stitched on the sides. To fasten the outside panels we will back-tack under the spring platform rail. For directions, turn to page 88. Now, to save you a lot of contortion, frustration and general bad humour, might I suggest that you put a clean dust sheet and softening on the floor and turn the settee upside down once more. In this position you will be able to back-tack with ease. Although the outside panels are not large, it is still a good idea to give them some support with a 280 g (10 oz) hessian backing, and this hessian can be back-tacked with the covering all in one go. For your back-tacking strip use a half-width strip of webbing. Fasten the support hessian tightly with tacks, cover this with a layer of wadding, and, with the settee still in the upside down position, stretch the covering and fasten it permanently on the bottom rail. The four joins, two at the back and two at the front uprights, you can ladder stitch together. The bottom covering of black lining or 280 g (10 oz) hessian can be put on before the settee is turned on to its feet.

Sewing on the Fringe

I like to take the fringe, pull it tightly round the settee then pin the ends together, slip it off and machine the join. Then there is no fear of its coming apart or fraying. Fix the fringe on in a perfectly straight line, temporarily fasten it with pins, then sew along both the top and bottom of the fringe flange.

When you can successfully upholster a chesterfield settee and make a proper job of it, then I cannot see why you should be daunted by the prospect of upholstering any piece of furniture whatsoever.

10 Cushion Making

What a lovely word cushion is! When you say 'cushion' you can feel yourself relaxing, tenseness succumbing to the thought of something soft, warm, cosy and comforting. Something that eases us against the hard lumps in life. Now, I hope there won't be any hard lumps in your upholstery, but cushions will add that little extra comfort to backs and arms of upholstered furniture that, for the sake of shape and design, are firm; and, of course, a cushioned seat is always that much softer than the 'all in one' sort.

Fig. 143 Scatter cushions

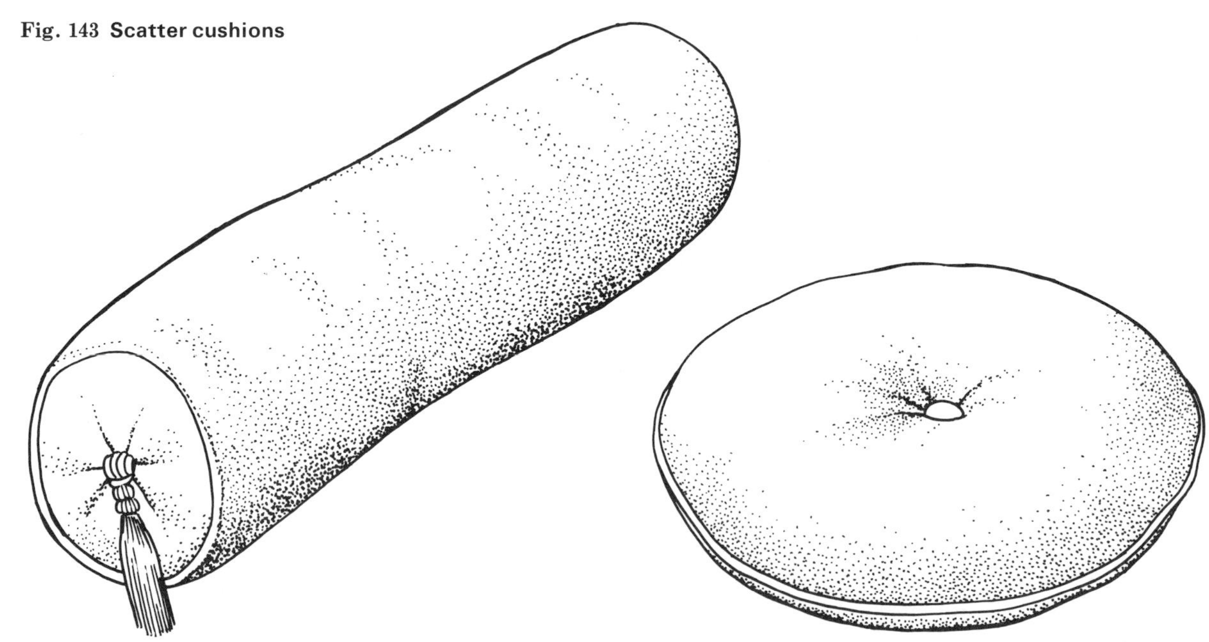

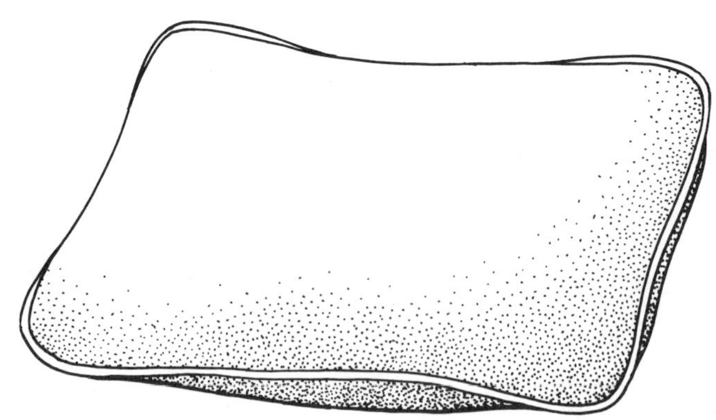

SCATTER CUSHIONS

Scatter cushions (**fig. 143**), the small cushions that can be tucked in the small of the back or behind the neck or head, or under an elbow, are simple to make. The cover is sewn up as a square or rectangular case with or without a trimming of cord, piping or ruching. And the interior can be made from any one of a number of substances—for example, foam, feathers, down, kapok or acrylic wool.

Cushion Interiors

A foam interior can be made of a block of plastic or rubber foam. Plastic polyether flame-resistant foam can be easily cut with a very sharp, long-bladed knife; I have a good old steel carving knife that I keep razor-sharp for this purpose. Rubber block foam or pin

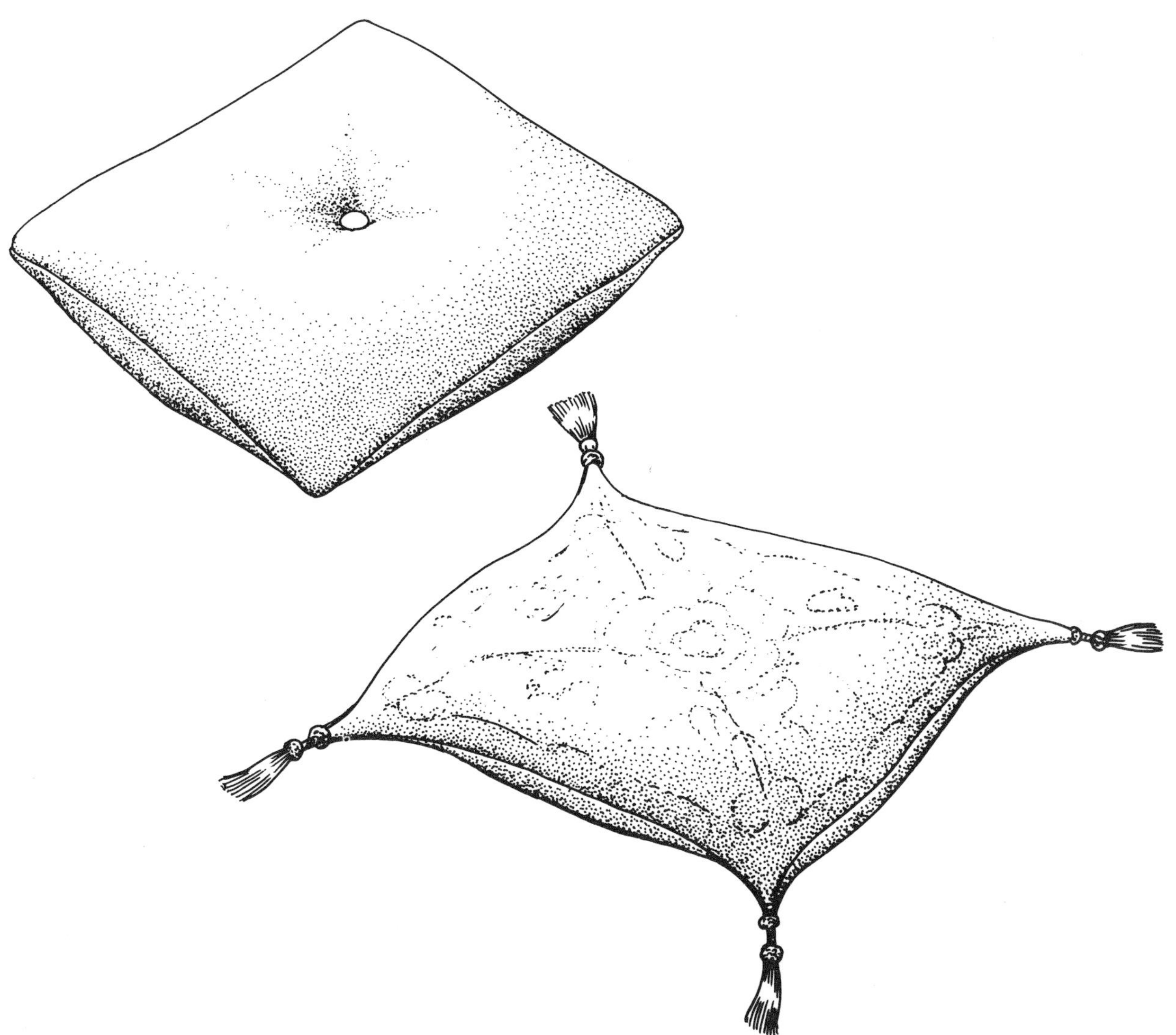

core latex has to be cut with a fine-toothed panel saw. Both types of foam can be finely shaped with the aid of a wire brush with which you round over the edges to make a good cushion shape.

Alternatively, you can make a foam interior from laminated layers of foam finished with a case of 6 mm ($\frac{1}{4}$ in) thick foam to contain them. Use a soft bond impact adhesive to join the layers and the outside foam case.

Sometimes a single large button looks well in the centre of the smaller square cushions and helps to keep the filling in place.

Fillings such as feathers, down or kapok need an inner leakproof case. A cloth known as waxed cambric is most frequently used. This is a closely woven cream-coloured cloth that is impregnated with wax to make it feather-tight. It is much thinner than the feather-proof ticking used for pillows and makes a soft undercover which will not show creases through the outside case. You have to make these cambric cases just a little larger than the outer case so that the outer case is filled out.

Acrylic wool makes super-soft filling for small cushions. It is obtainable in both rolled sheet form and as a mass fill. If it is in sheet form it can be folded up to the size and thickness that you require. In mass form, it can be teased and packed into your cushion case—but do not pack it too densely. Ideally, it is best to have an inner case even with this filling, and then, when you remove your outer case for washing or cleaning, the interior will still be contained as a unit.

Fig. 144 Place cushions

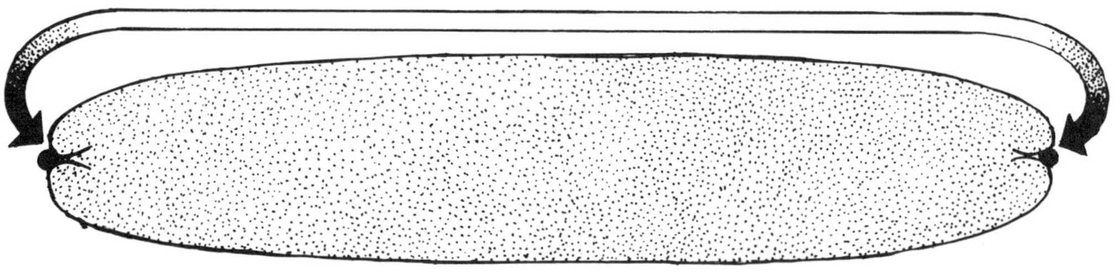

▲ **144(a)** Cut two panels, allowing for the cushion's thickness

144(b) Cut the corners to curve and put in a draw thread round each corner ▼

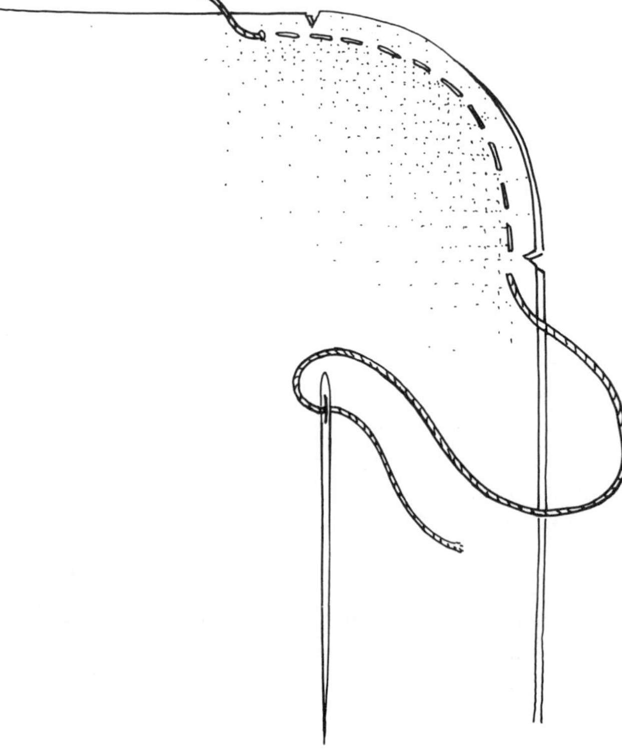

LARGE PLACE CUSHIONS

You may want a cushion that is larger and fuller than can be made by just sewing together two square panels. This can be made in either of two ways. You can border the cushion to give it depth or you can round and gather the corners.

Bordered place cushions are made the same way as seat cushions (pages 156–157), except that for a place cushion the border only needs to be about 38 to 50 mm ($1\frac{1}{2}$ to 2 in) in width.

Now, let me tell you how to give your place cushions an all-over thickness by rounding and gathering the corners. Cut two panels the same size and if you are aiming to make a cushion to a specific size, do not forget to allow for the thickness of the cushion (**fig. 144a**).

At each corner draw an arc of 75 to 100 mm (3 to 4 in) radius. Cut the corners round to your chalk marks, cutting both pieces of cloth together. Snip the cloth to mark the ends of the curves. Using a long darning needle and thin thread, put in a draw thread, through one thickness of cloth, round each corner curve (**b**). As you complete each draw thread pull it up, noting the specific amount of thread withdrawn (it must be the same on each corner) and fasten off with one or two French knots (page 36) to keep the corner gathered up (**c**).

It is a good idea to include piping in the seam between the two parts of this cushion,

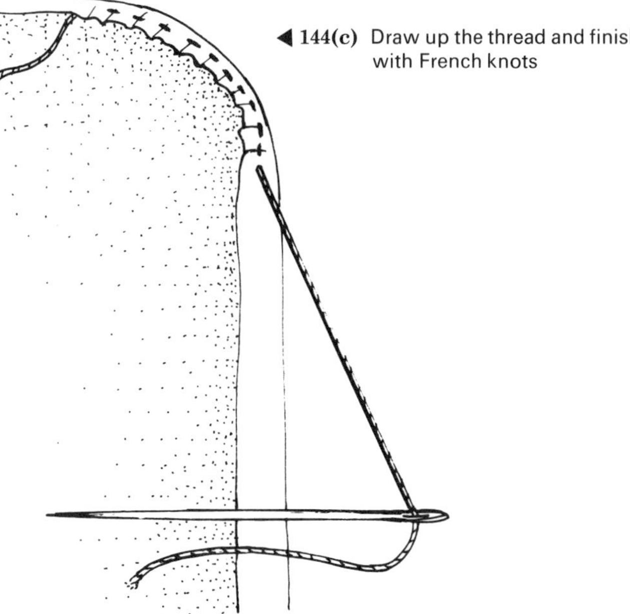

◀ **144(c)** Draw up the thread and finish off with French knots

or you can use ruching. Stitch the piping or ruching to one side first and then pin on the other side piece with the snips positioned together for accuracy and uniformity. Stitch the two halves of the cushion together on your sewing machine (**d**)—but do not forget to leave a 'mouth' open on one side large enough to get your interior inside easily. You will, no doubt, want to occasionally wash or clean your cushion cover, so it is always a good idea to oversew the seam flanges or, if you have a sewing machine with zigzag attachment, stitch all round with this to prevent any fraying. When the interior is in place sew up the mouth, using small ladder stitches.

If you prefer, cushion covers like these can be stitched up with no piping and afterwards trimmed with decorative chair cord—or you can go very Victorian and sew in tassels at the corners.

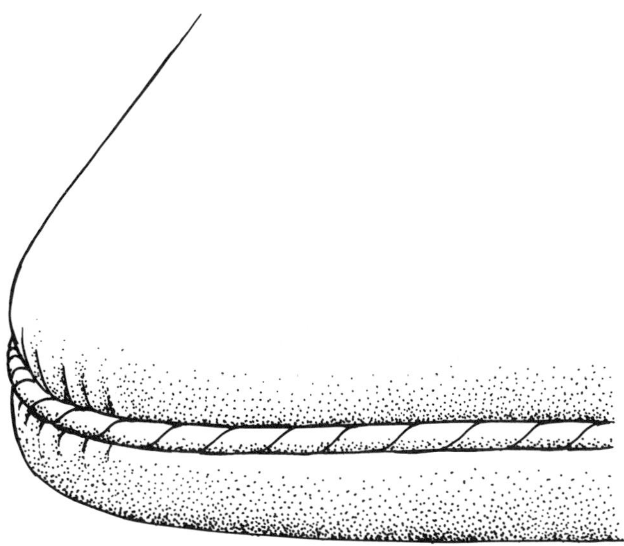

▲ **144(d)** A finished corner

SEAT CUSHIONS MADE TO FIT

I would emphasize at the outset that when you make cushions for the seats of chairs and settees a good fit is most important to the whole appearance of the seat. Nothing looks worse than a cushion that overhangs the seat front or is too short for the seat size. Again, if the cushion is too wide and has to be squeezed between the arms the cover will wrinkle, while if it is not wide enough there will be gaps to be seen at both sides.

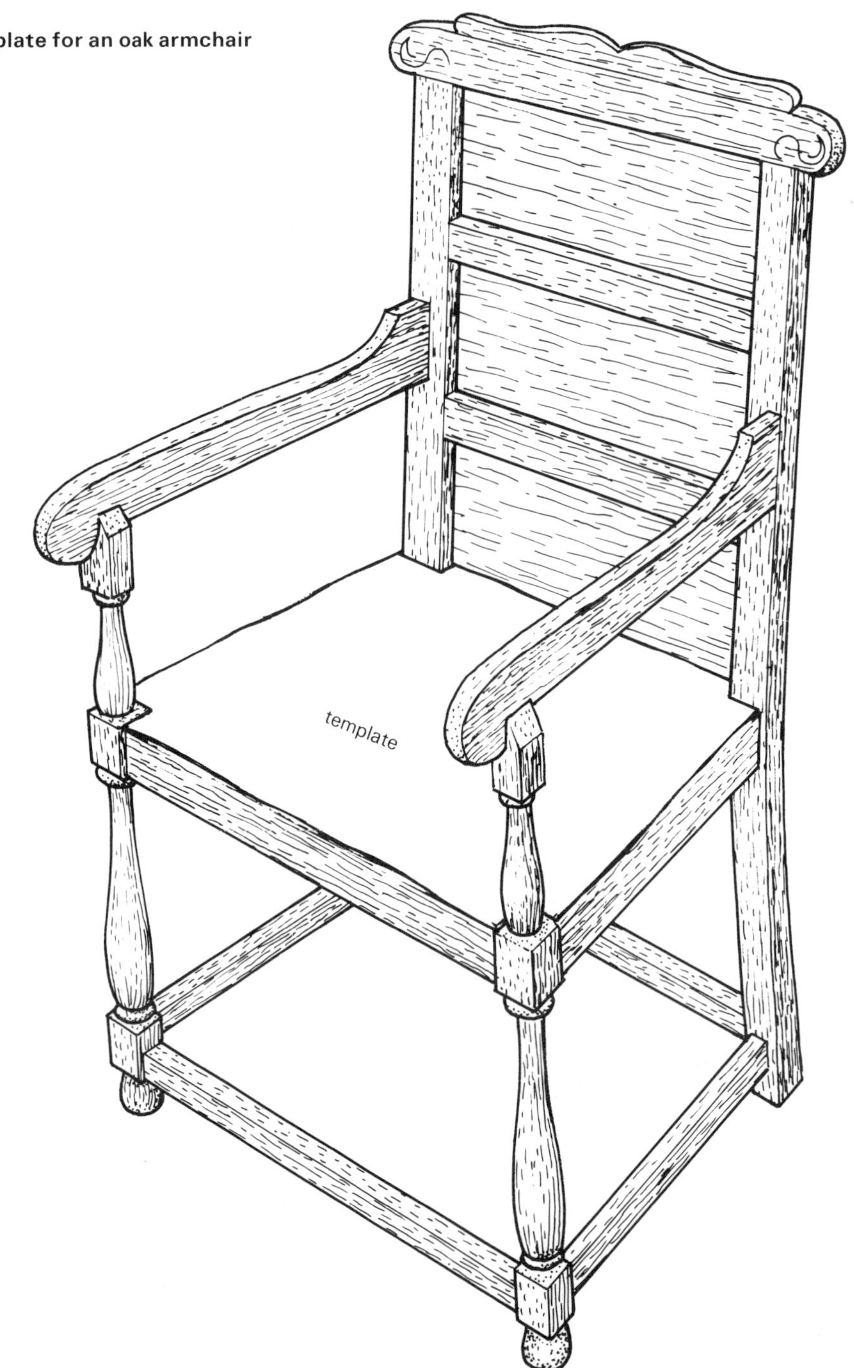

Fig. 145 A template for an oak armchair

Templates

So let us first of all see how to make templates of the seats. The illustration in **fig. 145** shows a template for an old oak armchair. Notice how the template has been cut out at the front uprights: made to this shape, the cushion will be held firmly in place.

To get an accurate template for the seat of an easy chair (**fig. 146**), it is best to make and shape the foam or feather interior first and place this in the seat, then cut the template on top. After cutting the template I like to fold it in half—with the fold running from back to front—and then if any trimming has to be done there are no discrepancies between the two halves and symmetry is assured.

For a settee seat with two or more cushions, cut a single large template of the seat. This can then be divided into the number of cushions required. The two end templates

Fig. 146 A template for an easy chair

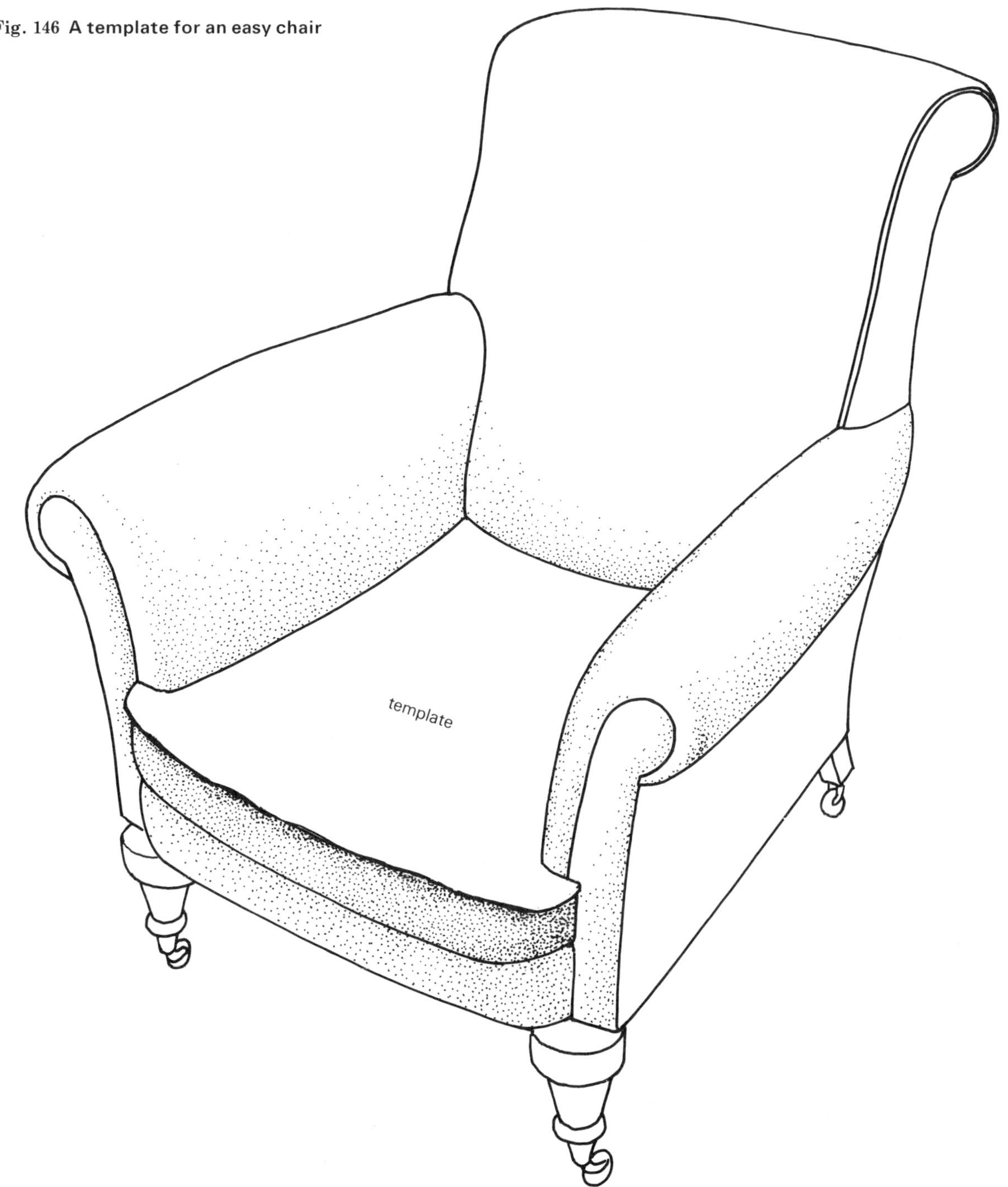

are laid together, their sizes compared and trimmed, and in this way only one template need be used for shaping both cushions.

Remember that the templates you have made are the exact size of the finished cushions, including the piped edges. Also, when you fit the foam interior tightly inside, the fabric will stretch very slightly. Taking these factors into account, I find that 10 mm ($\frac{3}{8}$ in) all round larger than the template is a sufficient allowance for seams.

Lay the template on the cloth, making sure that it is straight with the weave, then mark round the shape—allowing your 10 mm ($\frac{3}{8}$ in) —with tailor's chalk. Only use the template for one panel of all cushions that are identical, then use this first cut panel to mark the others. But keep your template, because you may need it for marking out other foam interiors.

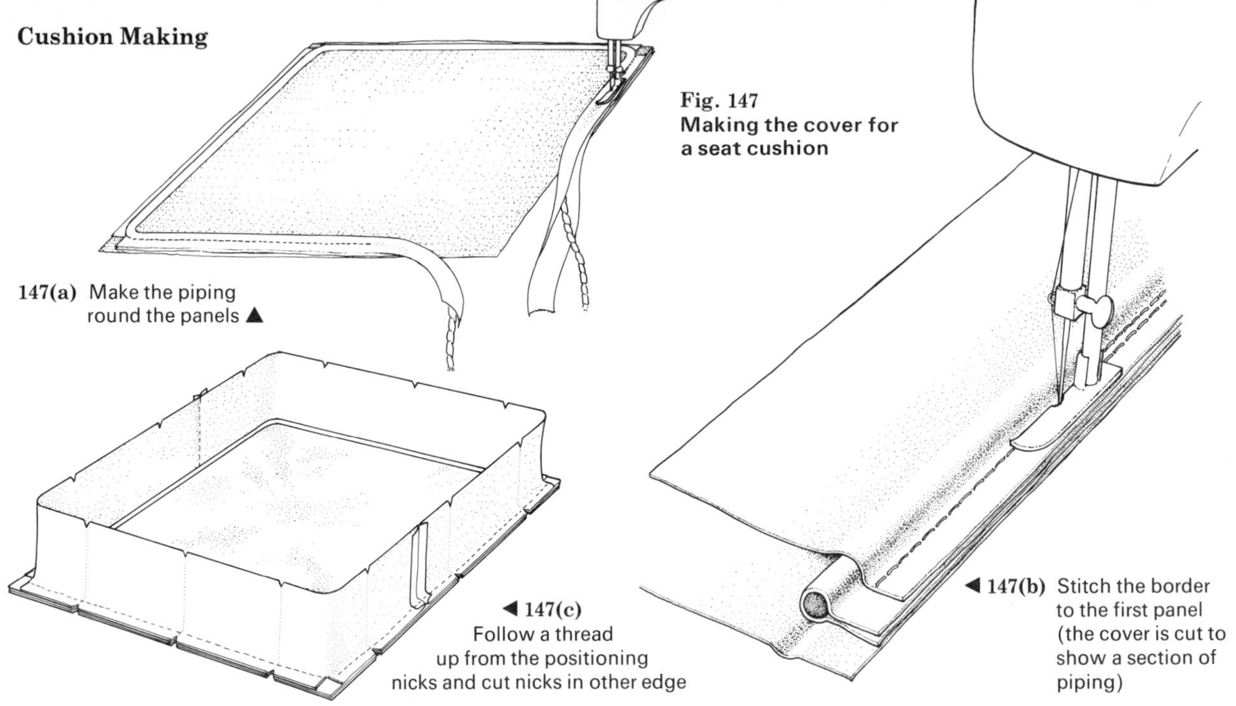

Fig. 147
Making the cover for a seat cushion

147(a) Make the piping round the panels ▲

◀ 147(c) Follow a thread up from the positioning nicks and cut nicks in other edge

◀ 147(b) Stitch the border to the first panel (the cover is cut to show a section of piping)

Making the Cover for a Seat Cushion

Make the piping round the panels that you have cut (see page 82). Begin stitching somewhere on the right hand edge of the panel and then you can make sure that there will be no join in the piping along the front edge, as this is something you must avoid at all costs. When you get to within 50 mm (2 in) of a corner, lay the piping strip and cord along to the corner and make a small nick 10 mm ($\frac{3}{8}$ in) from the approaching edge (**fig. 147a**). This will enable you to make a sharp corner as you turn the work to pipe the next edge.

When you have piped to within 100 mm (4 in) of the place where you started, stop and disengage the work from the machine. Lay the material flat, then cut the piping cord so that the ends butt. Next, cut back the piping strip ends so that they overlap 20 mm ($\frac{3}{4}$ in). The line of cut should be at the same angle as for the other joins. Stitch up the join and treat it as you did the others when you made up your piping strip, making it as flat and inconspicuous as possible. Then stitch down the remaining portion of piping. Pipe all the other panels in the same way.

Now we can think about the cushion borders. Let us assume that your foam interior is 100 mm (4 in) thick. I find that to give the cover a bit of tension it is best to aim for a finished depth of about 90 mm ($3\frac{1}{2}$ in), so if you cut the strips for your borders 110 mm ($4\frac{1}{2}$ in) this should be just right. You will need to join two or three strips together, depending upon the size of the cushion, and if you are using a patterned material you must get a good match at the front of the cushion.

Before going any further I like to put positioning marks on the edges of the panels. If you lay them on top of each other you can cut through them all with a sharp knife or chisel. Now you can start pinning. If your fabric has a design, begin at the centre front and position the design on the border to correspond to that on the panel. Put the pins in on the panel side, heads to the right. When you come to a corner make a small nick in the border edge so that you can make a tight turn round the corner. Make all the joins in the border come either at the sides or the back, where they won't show. When you have finished pinning you can stitch up the last join.

Stitch the border to this first panel in the way shown in (**b**), still using the piping foot and keeping these stitches just inside those that were made to hold the piping.

Put on the other side panel next. Follow a thread up from each nick in the already sewn edge of the first panel and nick the other edge of the border (**c**). Now you will be able to position this other panel accurately as you pin it on. Leave the whole of the back edge, plus 90 mm ($3\frac{1}{2}$ in) at each side unstitched, so that you can insert the interior. When you have finished stitching, turn the case the right side out and examine the piped edges all

Fig. 148 Foam interiors for seat cushions

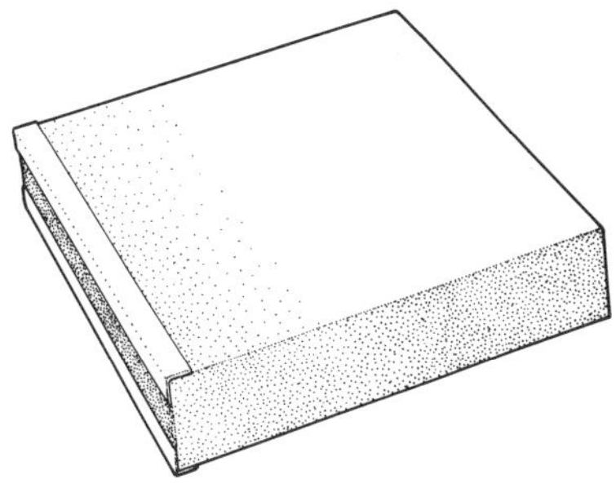

▲ 148(a) Strips of calico glued along the front edges of a foam rubber cushion interior

▼ 148(b) Attaching the interior to the front border of the cushion cover

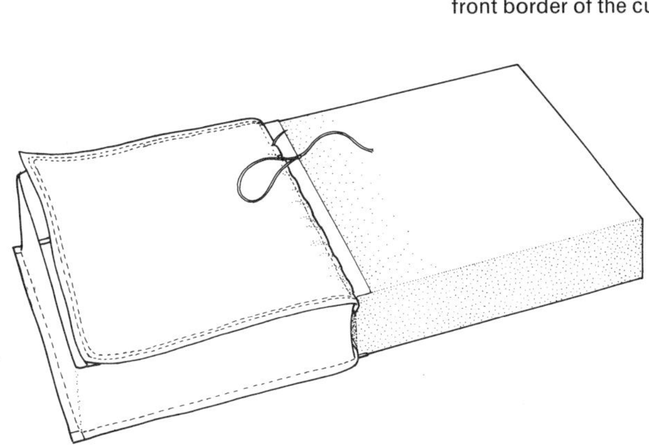

the way round to see that all is correct. Then turn it inside out once again, for something must be done to the seam flanges or they will fray quickly. Here again, if you have a zigzag attachment on your sewing machine, sew along the flanges with a zigzag stitch. If you do not have a zigzag attachment, a line of stitches a fraction from the edge is the next best treatment. Do not forget the back opening when you are securing the seams. If the fabric is loosely woven the border edge should be turned over once and hemmed. An extra line of stitches should also be machined along the piping at the mouth. This will tighten the piping so that it corresponds with the rest.

Foam Interiors

Now, I know that there is a vast difference in the price but I always use rubber block foam for seat cushions—the rubber lasts so much longer and is so much more resilient than plastic foam.

I have already mentioned that rubber block foam should be cut with a fine-toothed panel saw and plastic foam with a very sharp, long-bladed knife. You can use your template for marking and cutting your foam to the size and shape that you need. Mark round the template with a felt tip pen, keeping 10 mm ($\frac{3}{8}$ in) outside to give a bit of tension to the cover.

To enable you to fasten your cover to the interior, glue strips of calico or thin binding along the front edges of the interior (**fig. 148a**). Cut two strips of calico about 60 mm ($2\frac{1}{2}$ in) wide and long enough to go across the front of the foam interior. Coat them with soft bond impact adhesive and also coat the top and bottom edges of the front of the foam to a width of 30 mm ($1\frac{1}{4}$ in) back from the edge and the same distance from the edge down the front. Leave for a minute or so until the adhesive is dry to the touch, then lay the tape over the edges and press firmly. You will then have two angled, taped edges to which your cushion cover can be sewn.

Fig. 148b shows the cushion cover inside out and the front border placed against the cushion interior front. Note how the seam flanges are turned in to lie down the border. Temporarily fix the cover and the interior together with a skewer at each end, then sew them together with large stitches. The stitches go through the calico strip, 3 mm ($\frac{1}{8}$ in) from the edge and the same distance away from the piping stitches in the cover. When the job is complete, pull the cover over the interior as if you were putting on a sock. Adjust all the seam flanges so that they lie behind the border—this will make the piping stand up well. A fair bit of adjusting, with your hand inside the cushion, will have to be done to ensure that the interior is correctly placed. Then close the opening with skewers and ladder stitch it together with small stitches.

Feather and Down Interiors

Feathers are another expensive commodity these days. There are several grades. In the lowest, the feathers are complete with centre quills. In the grade that used to be called 'cut feathers' many of the quills have been removed. The next grade up is feather-and-down mixture, while, of course, the top grade is the real down which is beautifully soft and light, with no lumps or quills at all.

Before you remove the feathers from an old cushion case, place the cushion in the airing cupboard for a few days and you will find that the feathers fluff out. You can then knead and pat them about while they are still in the old case and get rid of most of the lumps caused by feathers binding together.

As I have mentioned before, feathers and down must be contained in a feather-proof case. A simple box-shaped case can be formed by combining a top and bottom panel with a border. I like to cut out and sew up a strip long enough for the complete border all round, then pin the top and bottom panels to this and stitch round, leaving a filling mouth open at the back. This sounds easy enough but there are a few points to note.

First, the panels should be made about 25 mm (1 in) larger in width and length, and the border 10 mm ($\frac{3}{8}$ in) deeper than the size of your top cover, so that the interior will fill out the top cover nicely.

Secondly, the waxed, glazed side of the cambric must be on the inside when the case is finished. Thirdly, when you have sewn all the seams except for the mouth at the back, rub every line of stitches on both sides with beeswax to seal the needle holes and make

Fig. 149 A partitioned case for a feather or down filling

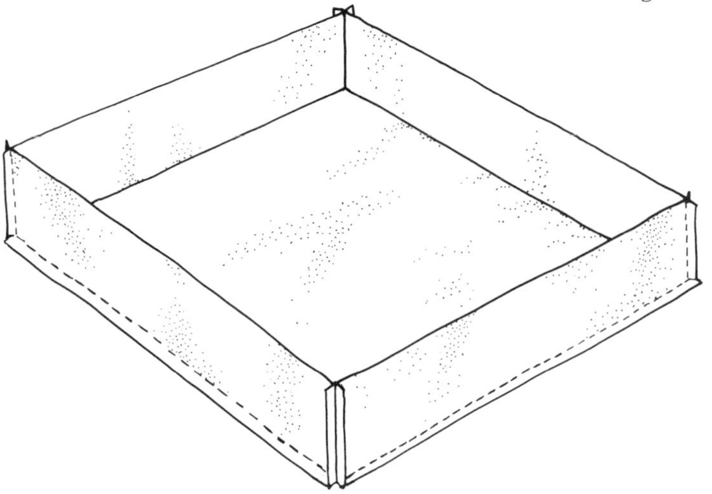

▲ **149(a)** Sew the border to one panel

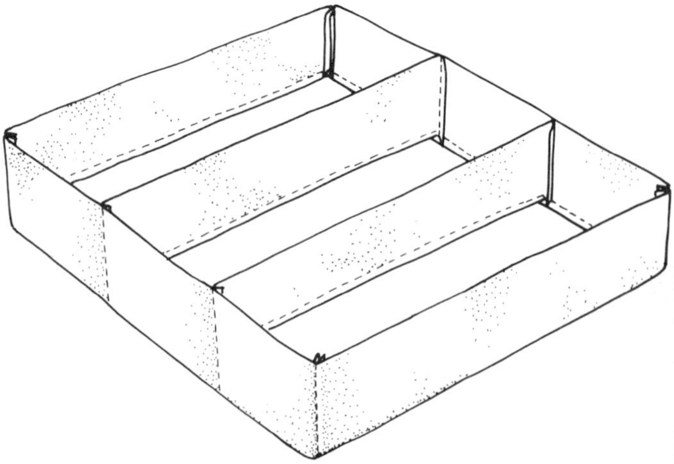

▲ **149(b)** Sew two partition pieces across the inside

the case really feather-proof.

The operation of transferring the feathers from the old to the new case is best done out of doors, for, as you can imagine, feathers can fly about and make a terrible mess. Cut the old case clean across one side, but keep the cut closed until you have placed it in the mouth of the new case. Gradually work the whole of the old case inside the new one, then slowly withdraw the old case leaving the feathers behind. If you are lucky you will spill only a few. Then sew up the mouth on your machine.

If you make your case as described above, the cushion will have to be adjusted and plumped up after being sat on, as the feathers tend to move to the back of the cushion. But you can make a case with three separate sections or compartments for the feathers, so that the feathers are confined and the cushion remains in good shape (**fig. 149**).

Cut out the panels and border strip and machine stitch the border to one panel (**a**). Turn the case the right side out and stitch two partition pieces across the inside (**b**). Stitch the top panel to the two partitions (**c**). Machine stitch the top panel to the border, leaving the ends of each section open at one side for filling (**d**).

Of course you cannot employ the convenient method of filling described above for the one-section interior, so fill the case by hand, putting a handful at a time into each compartment to keep them equal. Do not overfill the compartments—give the feathers a little room to move about. Pin the edges of the filling mouths together and then machine stitch.

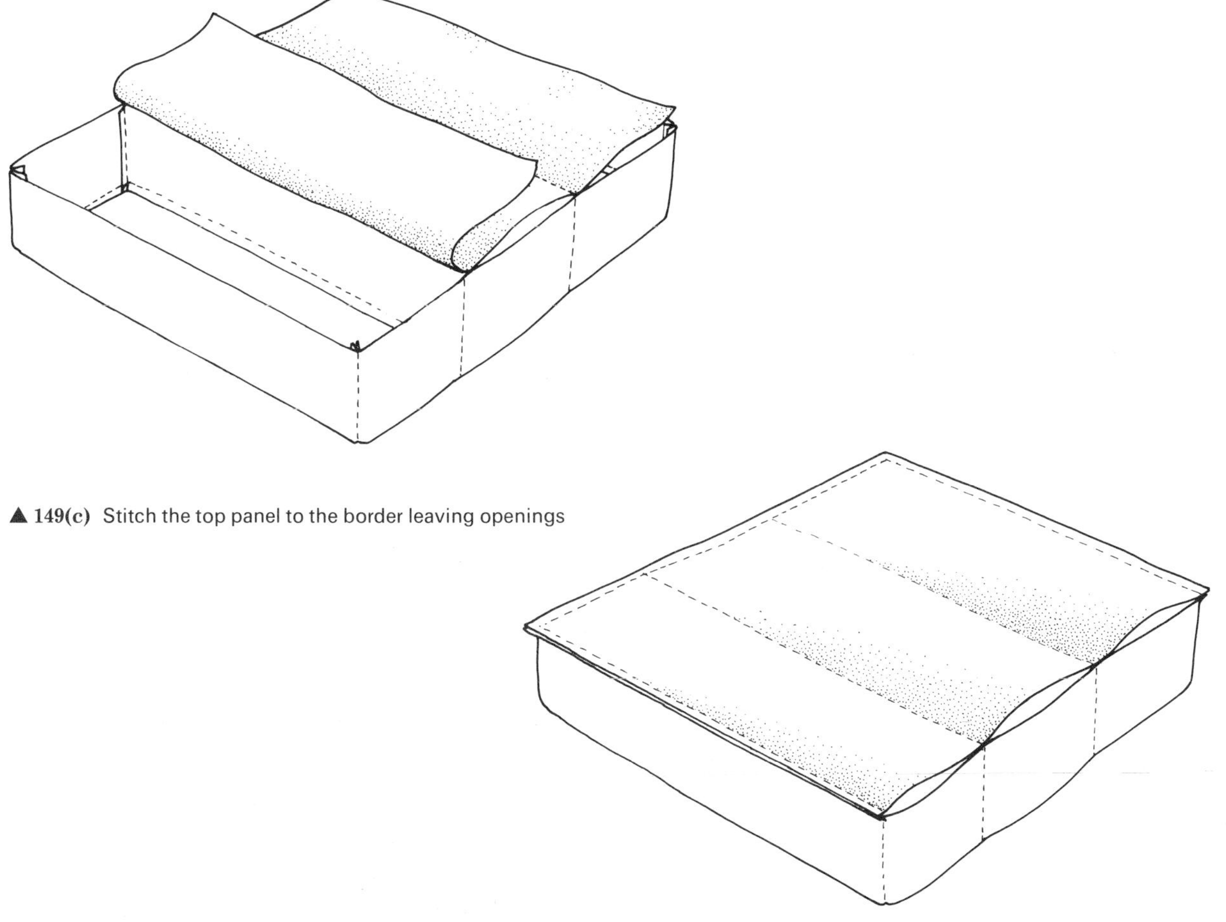

▲ **149(c)** Stitch the top panel to the border leaving openings

▲ **149(d)** Stitch the top and bottom panels together, leaving openings for the filling

Fig. 150 Foam and acrylic wool interiors

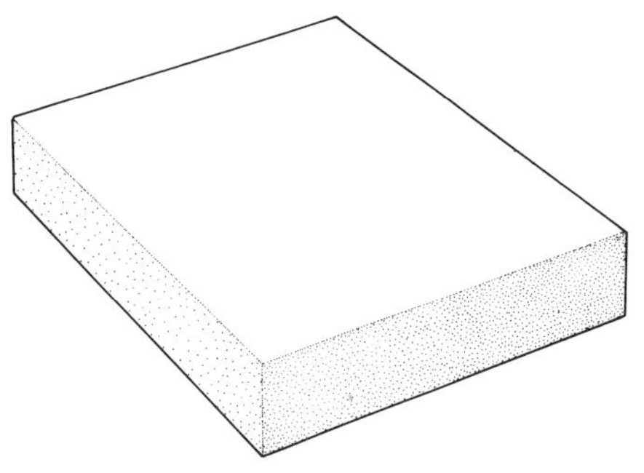

▲ 150(a) Cut a piece of foam to the size of your finished cushion

150(b) Wrap round a layer of batting ▼

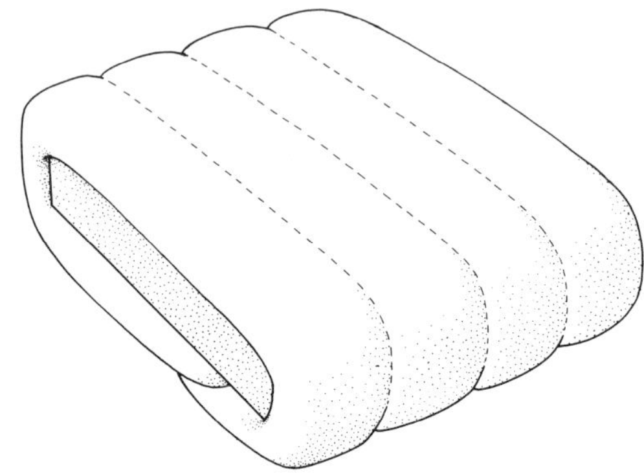

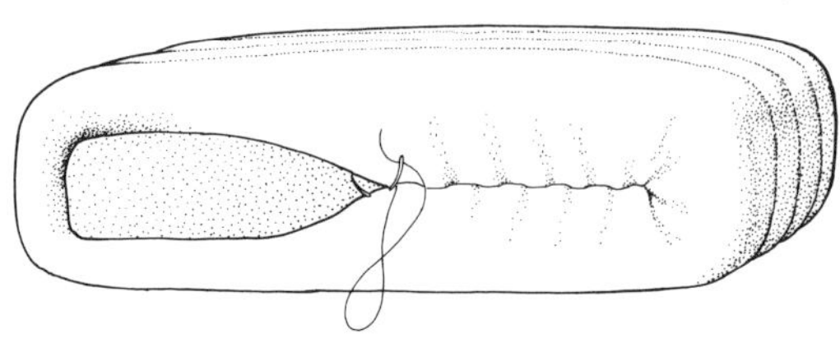

▲ 150(c) Sew round the edges

Foam and Acrylic Wool Interiors

You have seen the large, thick, sumptuous cushions on modern suites and perhaps you have wondered how these are made and what is inside to make them so deep and soft. Well, they are quite simple to make (**fig. 150**).

Select a piece of the softest density polyether foam or latex foam and cut it to the exact size of your finished cushion (**a**).

Take a length of sheet acrylic wool or, to make it even easier, what is known as 'batting'—acrylic fibre ready made up with a quilted cheesecloth cover. If you are using sheet acrylic wool, which is usually about 10 mm ($\frac{3}{8}$ in) thick, wrap about four layers round the core of foam. Or wrap round one layer of batting (**b**). With sheet acrylic wool cover the whole with cheesecloth and sew up by hand. With batting just sew round the edges for neatness (**c**).

Lastly, insert the interior into your cushion cover, again using the inside-out sock method (**d**), and ladder stitch the opening. Or, if you want to be a bit more sophisticated, you can stitch a zip fastener into the cover before you

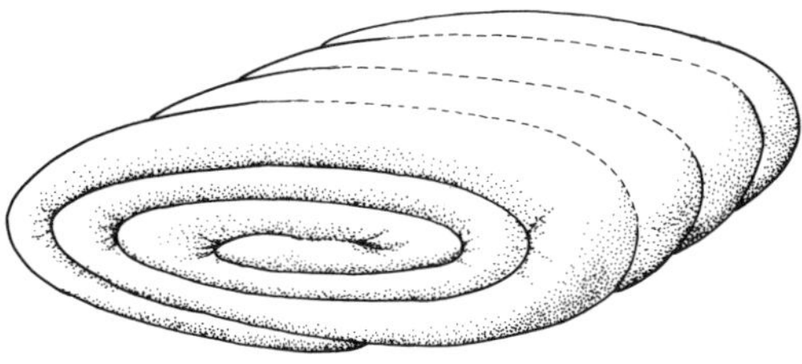

▲ **150(e)** For a dome shape, roll up acrylic wool

▼ **150(d)** Insert the interior into the cushion cover

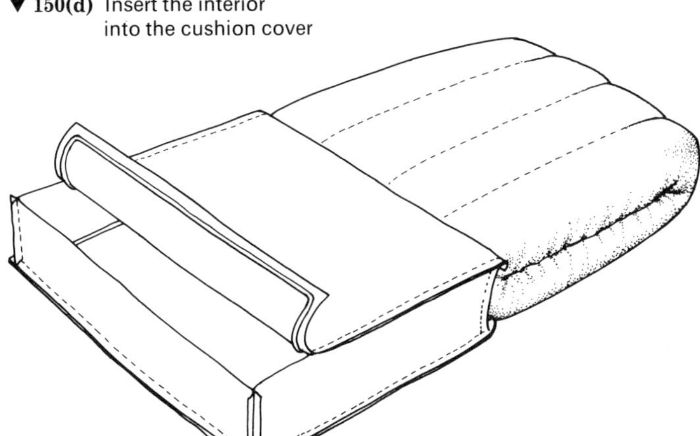

put in the interior. You can also make up cushions with a filling of acrylic wool alone. If you want a dome-shape, roll the fibre **(e)**. To make a squarer, flatter cushion fold it up concertina fashion **(f)**.

SQUAB CUSHIONS

Before the introduction of springs into upholstery in the early nineteenth century, the seats of easy chairs, settees and couches were either stuffed over (built up on the seat frame permanently) or made with separate firmly stuffed removable cushions, called squabs. These rest upon platform bases made with webbing and heavy hessian as supports. The best examples of squab cushions can be found in upholstered furniture of the Regency and William IV periods. What immediately comes to mind are those lovely settees with matching scroll arms, two bolsters that fit the inside curve of the arms, and squab cushion seats. Squabs were also used for window seat cushions and, indeed, are still made and used to this day, although now most people prefer the softness of rubber or plastic foam.

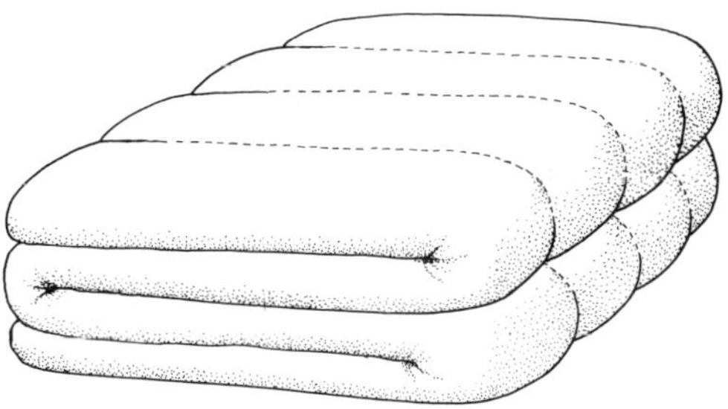

▲ **150(f)** For a flatter cushion, fold the wool

Making Up a Squab Cushion

The case for a squab cushion is generally of heavyweight calico or a good cotton ticking. It is simply made, slightly oversize to the seat measurement, of a top and bottom panel and a 50 mm (2 in) to 60 mm ($2\frac{1}{2}$ in) border with a stuffing mouth left, usually at the back, but in the case of a long seat, at one end (**fig. 151a**). Before the case is filled it is marked out for the tuft ties as you can see in (**b**). These tuft ties secure the filling, which would otherwise move out of position and be displaced when anyone sat on the squab.

To stuff the squab case, first fill it about a quarter full of stuffing and then place it flat on a table. Put one of your arms into the case and gently tease and coax the filling into the corners. Rest your free hand on the top surface of the case to monitor the density of the filling, and to test for hollows where not

Fig. 151 Making up a squab cushion

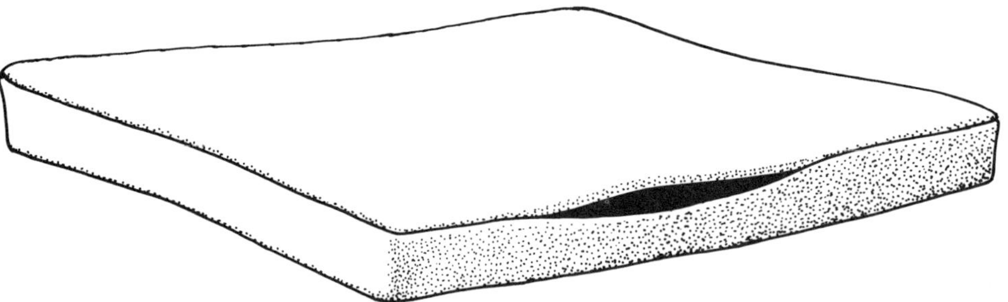

▲ 151(a) Make the case of a top and bottom panel and a border

151(b) Mark the case out for tuft ties ▼

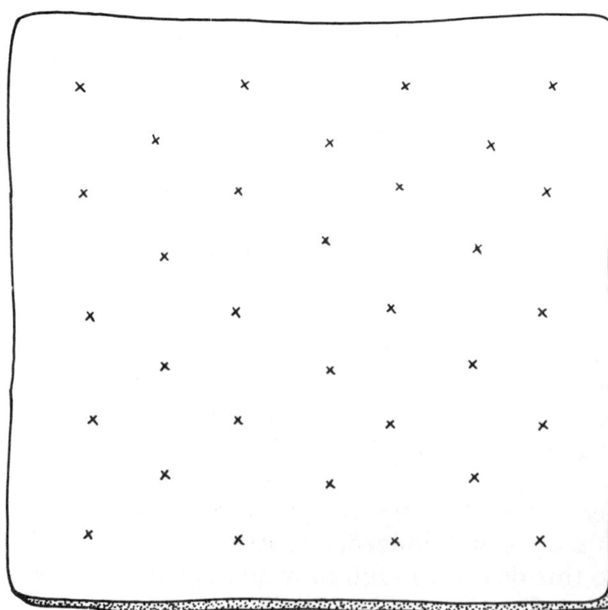

enough filling has been placed. Build up the stuffing across the squab in a wall about 100 mm (4 in) wide and a couple of centimetres deeper than the squab border. When this wall of filling is completed push it firmly forward, consolidating it, then start another wall. Repeat the process, endeavouring to consolidate the filling evenly, until the whole case is filled. It should then feel very firm and appear flat and even. Close the filling mouth with small ladder stitches.

The next stage is to put in the tuft ties with the tufting twine. You can use **No. 1** or nylon twine for this. Insert the twine in a continuous length, going in and out from mark to mark, making stitches about 10 mm ($\frac{3}{8}$ in) long at each mark. You begin the first stitch with the upholsterer's slip knot and tie the last stitch with a bow that can easily be pulled undone.

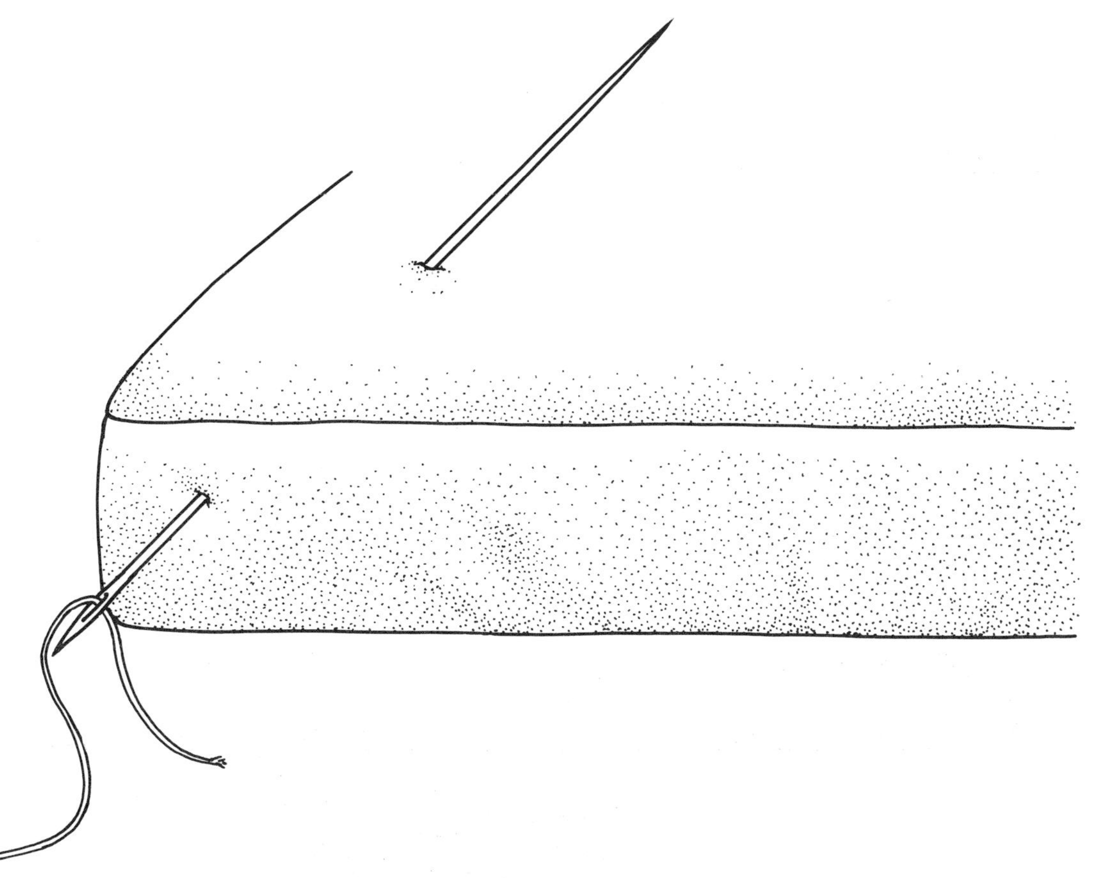

151(c) For the border stitches, put the needle into the side of the case

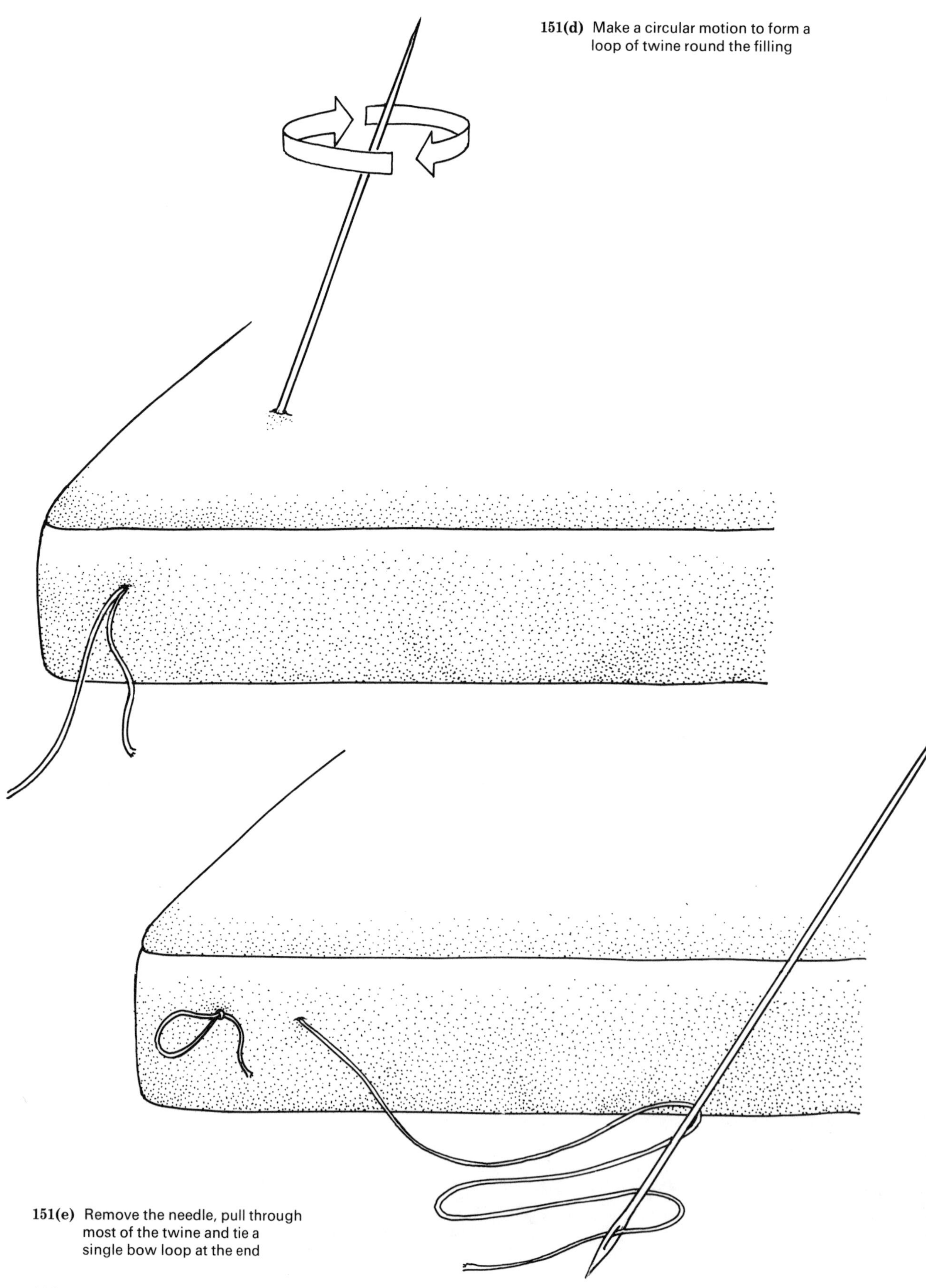

151(d) Make a circular motion to form a loop of twine round the filling

151(e) Remove the needle, pull through most of the twine and tie a single bow loop at the end

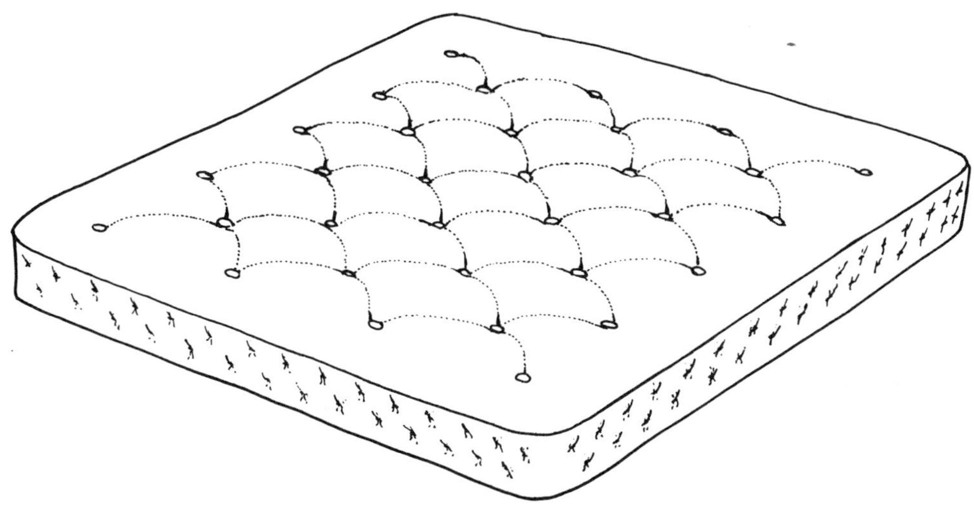

151(f) The finished squab

The border must be edged with neat little stitches, rather like those in an old-style mattress. The purpose of these edge stitches is similar to that of edge stitches in chair upholstery—the interior loops of twine hold the filling up to the edges and borders of the squab. To make the stitches, take a 250 mm (10 in) double-pointed needle and fine, No. 3 twine in about 3 m (10 ft) lengths. Begin at one side of the squab—the left-hand corner if you are right-handed. Put in the needle about 25 mm (1 in) from the corner and approximately 15 mm ($\frac{5}{8}$ in) down from the top edge of the border (**c**). Push the needle through the top of the case, about 100 mm (4 in) in from the edge. Do not take the needle right through, but as in blind stitching on a stitched edge take it just as far as the eye, make a circular motion, as in (**d**), to form a loop of twine round the filling, then return the needle about 30 mm ($1\frac{1}{4}$ in) along to the right of your first entry. Pull through most of the twine and tie a single bow loop at the end, as in (**e**) to stop it pulling through. Leave enough twine to tie off when you have completed the circuit. The size of the stitches should be kept very small, no larger than 3 mm ($\frac{1}{8}$ in). When you come to the end of the row, pull the bow loop that you made at the beginning, tie both ends with a secure reef knot (page 32) and trim the ends.

Turn the squab over and repeat the procedure so that the stitches are staggered to the first row, as you can see in the picture of the finished squab (**f**).

The method of fastening the tuft ties is as follows. Begin in one corner at the slip knot where you started to put in the ties; place a small rolled-up ball of cotton wool beneath the tie stitch underneath and place another under the slip knot, then pull down tightly and lock the knot as described in Chapter 3 (page 34). Repeat this procedure with all the ties, pulling them all down evenly.

The squab forms the interior of the cushion, the outer cover being made of furnishing fabric suitably bordered and piped. Before you place the squab interior inside the cover, wrap it over with a layer or two of cotton wadding to prevent hair leaking and to even out the inevitable undulations of the stuffed squab.

11 A–Z OF UPHOLSTERY SNIPPETS

The previous chapters of this book cover most aspects of traditional upholstery, but occasionally you are sure to come across a chair, a stool or couch that has a peculiar feature of its own. It is these features, which entail deviations from the usual procedures, that I would like to include in this final chapter. So here, in alphabetical order, are some snippets of information on upholstery to help you with individual pieces.

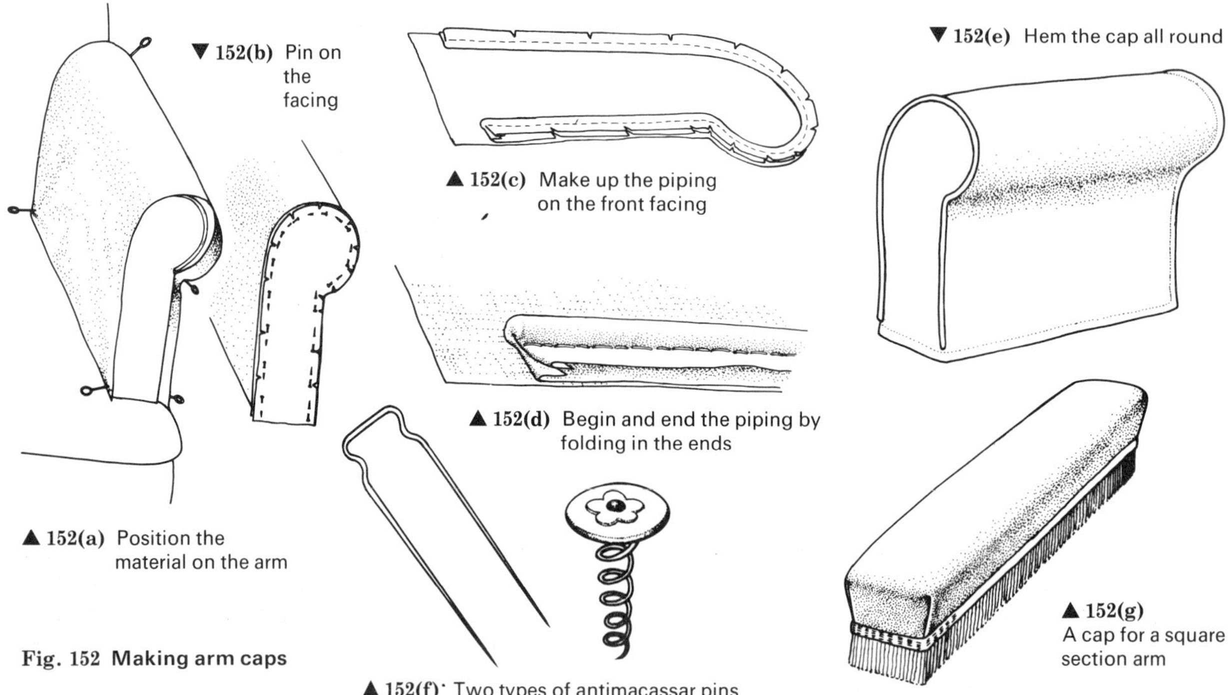

▼ **152(b)** Pin on the facing

▲ **152(c)** Make up the piping on the front facing

▼ **152(e)** Hem the cap all round

▲ **152(d)** Begin and end the piping by folding in the ends

▲ **152(a)** Position the material on the arm

▲ **152(g)** A cap for a square section arm

Fig. 152 Making arm caps

▲ **152(f)** Two types of antimacassar pins

ARM CAPS

Personally, I hate these loose protective covers for arms and I try to put people off when they ask me to make loose arm caps, for, in so many instances, they are never removed from the chair except for cleaning. To my mind they spoil the look of the arm, for even if they are well fitted they move about and require constant adjusting. And this fact of constant movement wears the permanent covering beneath to no little extent. But I am willing to admit that there are circumstances where they do prolong the good looks of a piece of upholstered furniture; mostly where it receives constant use, as in a hotel lounge or in the home of a large family.

Anyway, here are brief directions for making them up (**fig. 152**). If you have enough material, make the caps the full length of the arms and deep enough to tuck into the seat or cushion. If the covering cloth is patterned, it is nice to get the design to match in properly so that when they are on they look as inconspicuous as possible. This requires careful planning and measurement.

Measure and plan your cut so that the design matches that of the arm. Allow enough for hems on the top, back and bottom edges—38 mm ($1\frac{1}{2}$ in) should be enough. Position a piece over one arm. Fasten it with pins or skewers at each end of the scroll edge, the back of the arm roll-over and the bottom back corner (**a**).

Cut the two facings so that the patterns are identical or, if the design demands this, so that one is a mirror image of the other. Pin one on the front of an arm. Trim the edges and cut positioning snips in the flanges through both thicknesses of cloth (**b**). Remove the cap, take out the pins and lay the two pieces of fabric face to face on the second arm cap pieces. Cut the second pieces to the same shape, duplicating the positioning snips (**c**).

Make piping on the edges of the two front facings (pages 82–84), starting and ending 50 mm (2 in) from the bottom (**d**). Fold in the ends of the piping. Pin, or tack with cotton, the fronts on to the main pieces, positioning the snips at the edges. Stitch the two pieces together with the scroll side uppermost. Keep just to the inside of the piping stitches. Zigzag or oversew the flanges of this piped seam.

To finish the arm caps, fold up and stitch a hem round the entire edge (**e**). You will now see why the piping was made to begin and finish 50 mm (2 in) from the ends.

It is no joke trying to sort out and fold over the piping in a hem. Use antimacassar pins (**f**) or small pieces of Velcro, sewn on where they cannot be seen (under the end of the roll-over of the arm and, perhaps, below the cushion line), to secure the arm caps.

These are the simplest form of arm caps; for some chairs more shaping and fitting may well be needed.

In (**g**) I have illustrated an example of a cap for a square section arm. This cap is trimmed with fringe.

ARM PADS

Upholstering an elbow rest or a padded top to an open or show wood arm involves a neat little intricate exercise in edge building (**fig. 153**).

I shall deal first with the arm rests of a Victorian spoon-back chair. To hold the horsehair, first fix a row of stuffing tie loops (page 44) down the centre of each platform with small tacks (**a**). The hair should be put on so that it consolidates to about 35 mm ($1\frac{3}{8}$ in) thick. Have plenty oversailing the edges of the platform, as the finished edges need to mushroom a little.

To ensure that the two pads are made the same size, cut identical pieces of scrim hessian and tack them on with the same amount of turn-under. Follow a thread of the weave with the rows of tacks on the sides.

When you come to stitch round the edges of the arm pads (pages 47–49), just one row of blind stitches above the line of tacks will be enough. Take care to avoid getting this upholstery lopsided. It is wise to put some temporary fixing, such as a row of 30 mm ($1\frac{1}{4}$ in) wire nails, down the centre of each pad before you stitch the roll (**b**). Hammer them in just far enough to hold the hessian while you are stitching the first side, the hessian is not pulled over by the stitches, thus causing the other side to be reduced in height. The nails can be removed when the edges are completed.

Put in more stuffing ties and add a thin layer of horsehair stuffing. Cover the arms with calico and then with two layers of cotton wadding. The arms are now ready for the top covering. Covering the arms pads is a fairly easy job, although it calls for a certain amount of dexterity with the fingers. It is best to stretch the covering over the arm pads lengthwise from back to front. In (**c**) you can see how to cut in to the centre of the arm show wood at the back and at the front: make two small oblique cuts to form a V to a little less than the width of the wood.

The corners of these arm covers are single pleated, in such a way that the open end of the pleats is facing to the front and back (**d**). In (**e**) a longer arm pad is shown and this time it is buttoned. The buttons are set out with the usual between-button allowance (page 102) and placed down the exact centre of the arm, and the material is pleated across the width at each button. Special buttons are made for this sort of arm, with long wire nail shanks instead of the usual wire loop or calico extrusions. The shanks are pushed through the upholstery and hammered into the woodwork beneath. However, it is possible to use ordinary buttons and fasten them with twine. With the aid of a large curved needle you can bring the twine out at each side of the edge and fix it with tacks before the material is pleated and fastened.

Fig. 153 Re-upholstering arm pads

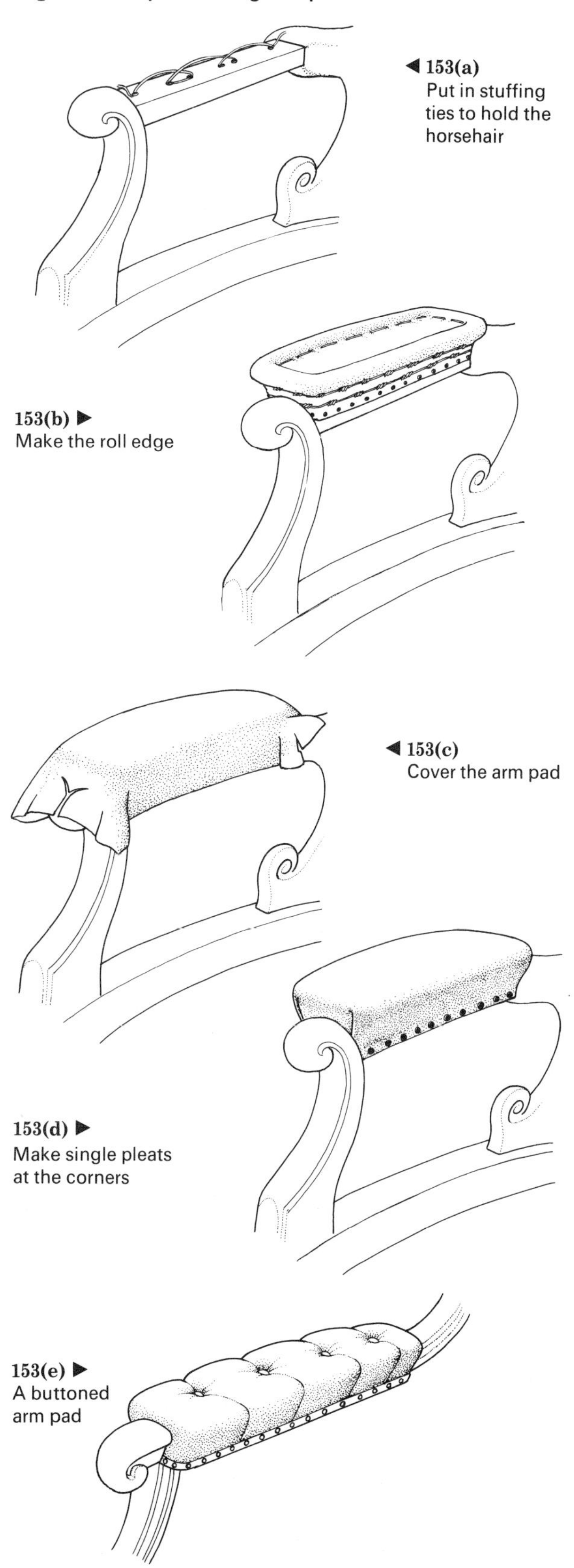

◀ **153(a)** Put in stuffing ties to hold the horsehair

153(b) ▶ Make the roll edge

◀ **153(c)** Cover the arm pad

153(d) ▶ Make single pleats at the corners

153(e) ▶ A buttoned arm pad

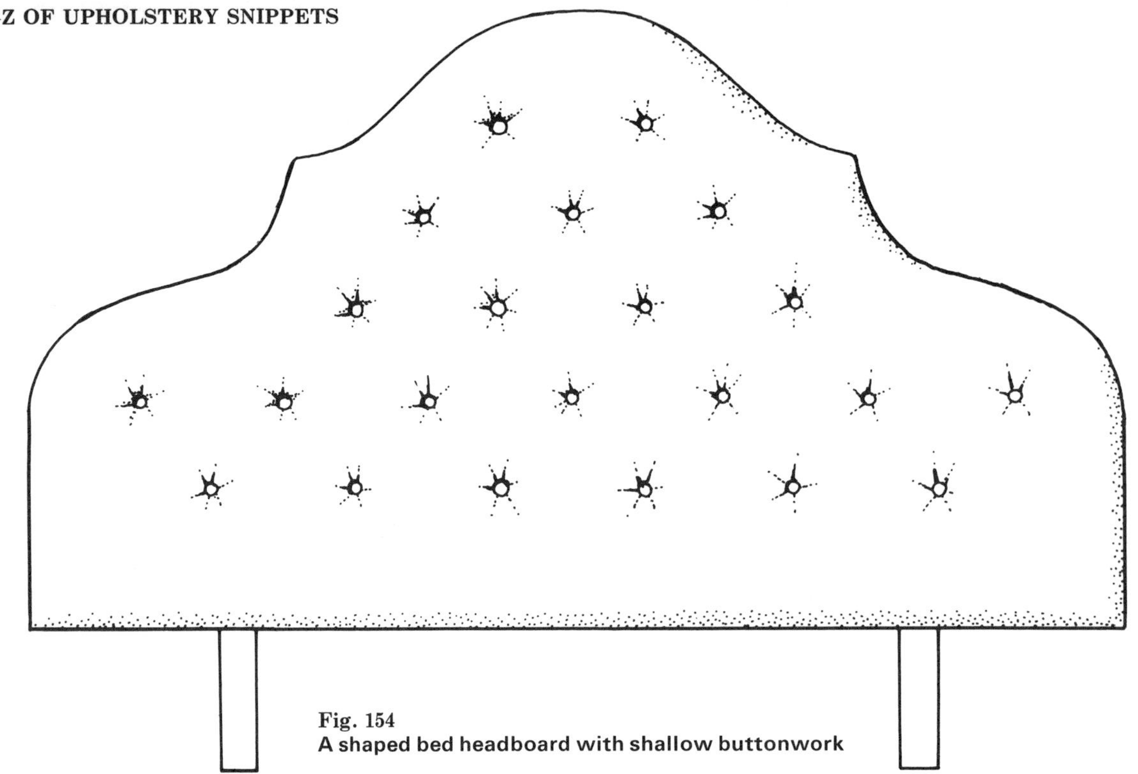

Fig. 154
A shaped bed headboard with shallow buttonwork

BED HEADS

The designs for upholstered bed heads are many and varied. Here are just a few.

Deep-Buttoned Headboards

Deep-buttoning a headboard is a most rewarding job, because on a flat board the buttonwork can be set out and executed to perfection, with the buttons and folds precisely placed. The procedure is basically the same as for any deep buttonwork, so have a look at Chapter 7, (pages 102–107) and Chapter 9, (pages 142–144). However, the back board has none of the give that there is with the hessian support beneath the buttonwork on a chair or settee. Here is a rough guide to the thickness of padding needed for an average depth of buttons.

If you use polyether foam (this must, of course, be flame-resistant), cut a piece of 25 mm (1 in) thickness to the exact shape of the board—place the headboard on top of the foam and cut round it with a very sharp knife. Then cut from 12 mm ($\frac{1}{2}$ in) sheet foam a piece that is larger than the board by 50 mm (2 in) all round and stretch and shape this piece of foam over the 25 mm (1 in) layer. Taking the 12 mm ($\frac{1}{2}$ in) sheet foam over in this way softens the edges. With your tubular cutter, cut holes at each of the button positions, right through the two layers of foam.

If you use acrylic wool, pad the board with a thickness of about 50 mm (2 in), then stretch over a layer of 6 mm ($\frac{1}{4}$ in) foam, cut holes just through the foam then part a way right through the wool with two fingers. A little reminder here: always overlay the foam with some cotton wadding.

These are the quick ways of deep buttoning. If you wish to upholster your bed head in the classic way, using horsehair and making stitched roll edges all round (see pages 47–49), make the head up to a depth of about 50 mm (2 in). When it comes to covering, make the edge borders separately. You can trim with piping, cord or braid.

Period Headboards

A period headboard with a padded panel contained within a polished, painted or gilded show wood frame is usually easy to refurbish, as most panels can be removed for padding and covering. When the panel is replaced the tacks are concealed within the outer frame. The backs of these, and indeed any upholstered headboards, should always be lined with calico or a lining cloth. The padding for a plain headboard can be of cotton felt, cotton wadding, polyether or latex foam, or, for a very rich and soft padding, acrylic wool.

One word of warning: when covering something plain and flat, do beware of making tack marks or tack pulls, especially on thin and delicate fabrics. If cloth is stretched too tightly, the tension at the site of the tack head will make a distinct line over the surface of the work. The solution is to keep tension to the maximum laterally along the edges, and to the minimum across the work. And, again, corner to corner diagonal stretching is important in achieving this. Of course, you must also be careful, when putting tacks in, not to snag a thread in the weave.

Shaped Headboards with Shallow Buttonwork

Headboards of the type shown in **fig. 154** are usually thinly padded. The buttons, which are placed without any prior setting out or folding of the covering, are held by twine pulled through holes bored through the wood. Plain boards like these look good covered in stretchy vinyl leathercloth over a 38 mm ($1\frac{1}{2}$ in) padding of foam. When the buttons are pulled in evenly the effect is very pleasing.

'BIBLE' CHAIR EDGES

A few Victorian easy chairs have shaped seats with fronts in the form of a large roll resembling the rounded spine of a book. These are known as 'bible' edges (**fig. 155a**).

In (**b**) you can see how the bible edge is built. The two sides or ends are stitched up with blind rows of edge stitches and a roll edge is made to define the rounded shape (pages 47–49). Great care must be taken to get the two sides to the same size and shape. After the sides have been finished a loose row of through stitches is put in to hold the filling within the roll (page 97). The top stuffing should be thinly laid so that the book spine shape is retained.

Fig. 155 Reupholstering a 'bible' chair edge

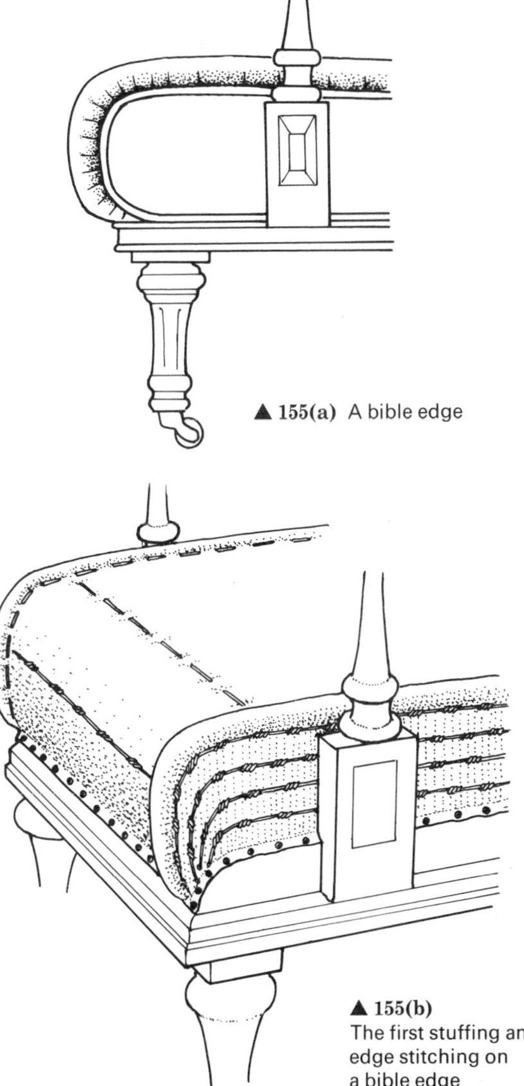

▲ **155(a)** A bible edge

▲ **155(b)** The first stuffing and edge stitching on a bible edge

BOX INTERIORS

Relining a box interior is another task that the upholsterer is expected to be able to do, so I will try to help with a few notes and pictures of the methods used. Most of it, though, is fairly straightforward—really just a matter of common sense.

Relining a Trinket Box

We have decided to line this trinket box in delicate silk (**fig. 156**). You will need some thin cardboard (ticket board) which is fairly stiff—this can be purchased at a stationer's shop—and some slow-setting impact adhesive, preferably the easy to spread thixotropic kind.

Fig. 156 Re-lining a trinket box

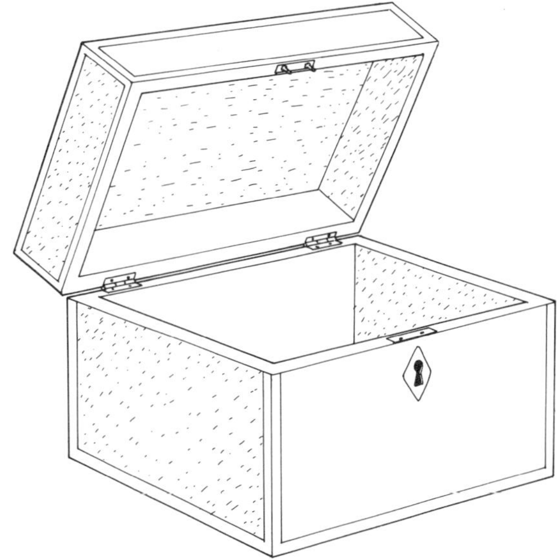

▲ **156(a)** Trinket box ready for re-lining

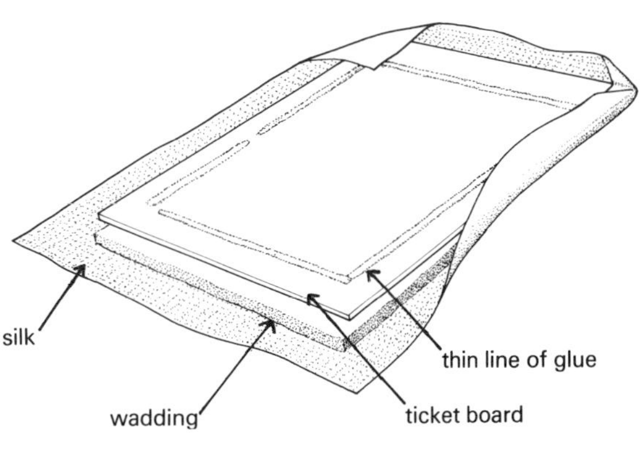

▲ **156(b)** Ticket board, wadding and silk cut ready for gluing of the panel

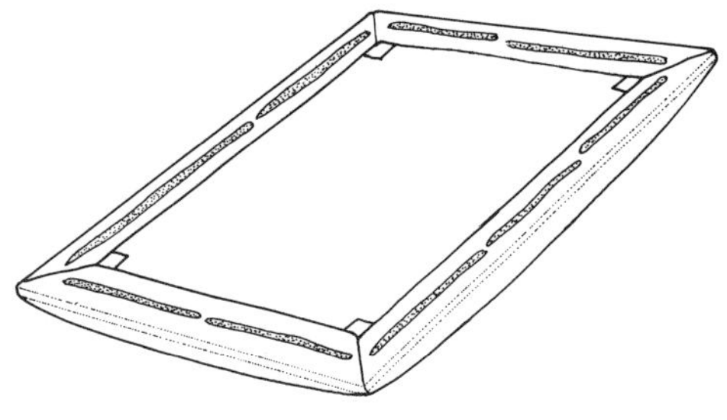

▼ **156(c)** The three layers of the panel carefully glued together for fastening inside the box

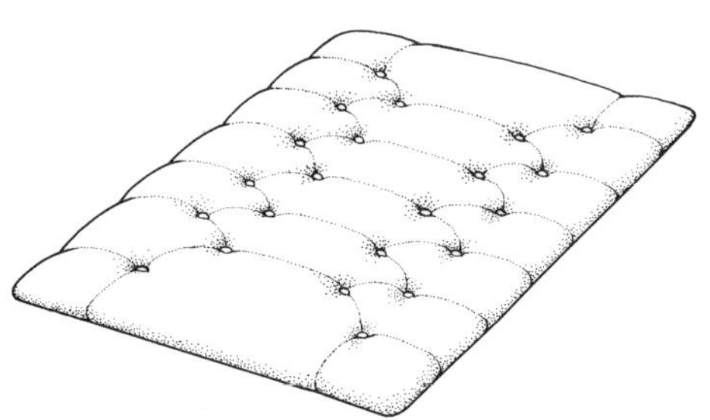

▼ **156(d)** Miniature buttoning

Clean the inside of the box thoroughly, removing all the old lining, glue and dirt. Carefully cut and fit pieces of ticket board as panels for the sides, the top and the floor of the box; these should be a loose fit to allow for the thickness of the lining (**b**). Each panel can be padded with a thin layer of cotton wadding or acrylic wool and covered with your silk. When all the panels have been covered they can be fastened to the inside of the box with just a line of glue near the edges of each panel—but not so near that it will squeeze out and show (**c**).

If you use a panel of slightly thicker card for lining the inside of the lid, you will be able to pad and decorate it in various ways; for instance, you can set out some miniature buttoning using French knots instead of buttons (**d**) (page 36), or random gather the material to give a crumpled appearance.

Covering and Lining a Box Ottoman

Large boxes such as ottoman chests or box ottomans or, larger still, ottoman divans, are, you will probably find, even easier to reline than smaller boxes, as they are less fiddly (**fig. 157**). In this section I will describe how to line a box ottoman. I will ignore the lid/seat upholstery, for this has been dealt with in the chapter on stuffed-over seats (pages 68–73). However, although this section is about linings I must mention the outside covering of the box, as this is closely integrated with the relining.

In many ottomans the base boards are removable, which makes covering and lining much easier. I will assume that you have removed the base board and completely stripped your ottoman (**a**).

If the material you are using has a bit of stretch to it, you can make up the outside covering in panels to the sizes of the sides plus turnings, stitch them together on a machine and pull the whole over the box. With non-stretchy material it is best to cover each side separately. Also, if you want to pad the outside of the box with a layer of wadding you will find it easier to cover the sides separately. Fasten the back and front coverings as you see in (**b**), tacking the covers just inside the top inside rim of the box and round the corners at the sides. Then fit the two side covers and ladder stitch (pages 40–41) the seams at the corners. Leave the bottom unfastened—you have the bottom boards to put back, remember.

Now, using thin strips of cardboard, back-tack the lining over the flange of the outside cover inside the top of the box (**c**). The strips of cardboard are used in the same way as webbing is employed for covering the outside arms of a wing fireside chair (page 88).

Pad each of the inner sides with a layer of wadding and then stretch over the lining and fasten it under the bottom edge of the wood. Line the two longer sides first, stretching the lining sideways, then cover the two shorter sides. Turn in the fabric at the corners and ladder stitch the seams together (**d**).

Pad and line the base and board and fasten it to the box. Stretch the outside covering and fasten it to the underside of the box (**e**). Lastly, put on a bottom covering of lining, hessian or calico.

Fig. 157 Covering and lining a box ottoman

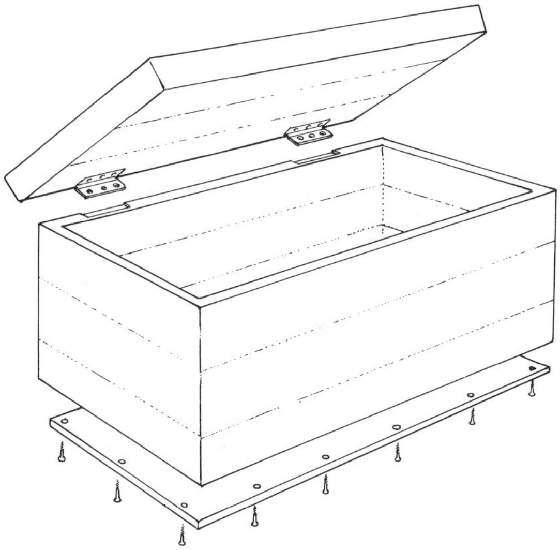

▲ **157(a)** The box stripped

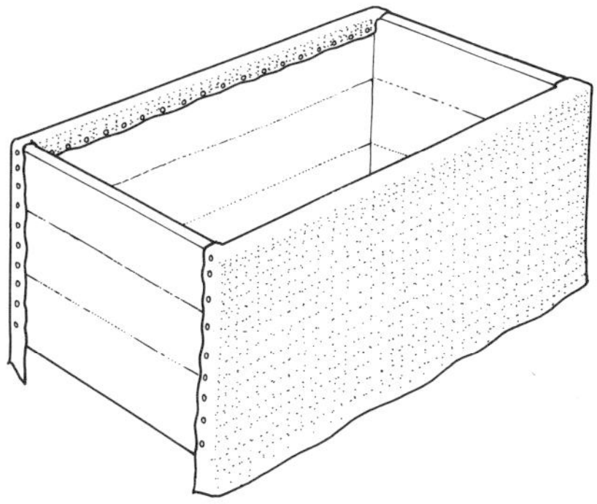

▲ **157(b)** Cover the outside

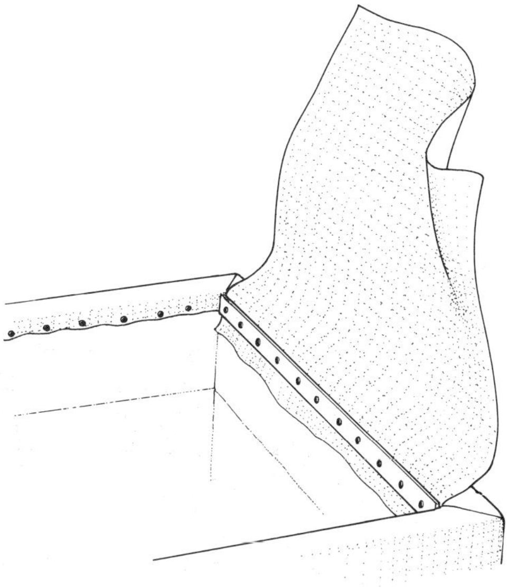

▲ **157(c)** Back-tack the lining to the flange of the cover

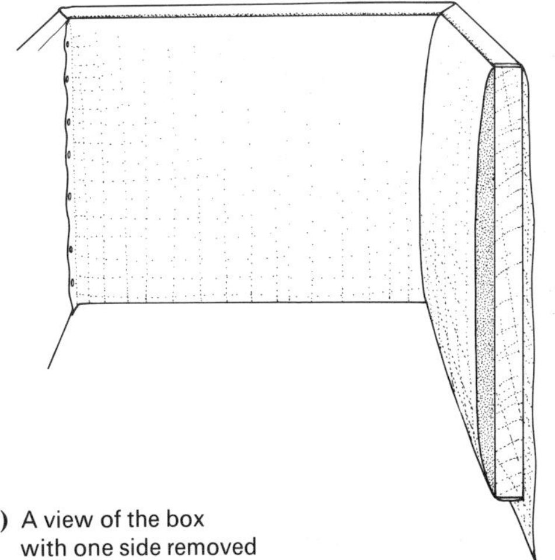

157(d) A view of the box with one side removed

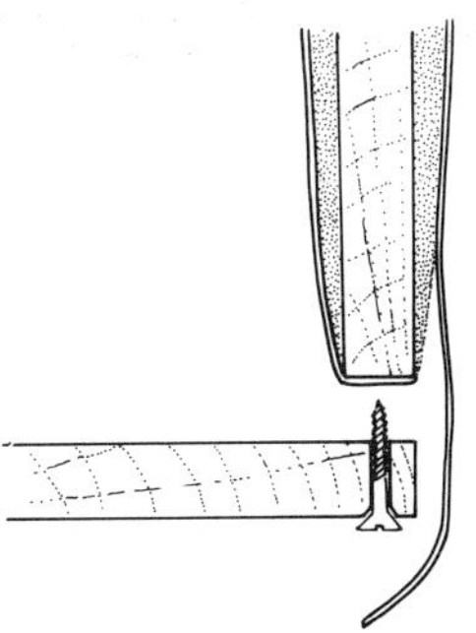

157(e) Re-fix the base board and fasten the cover to the bottom

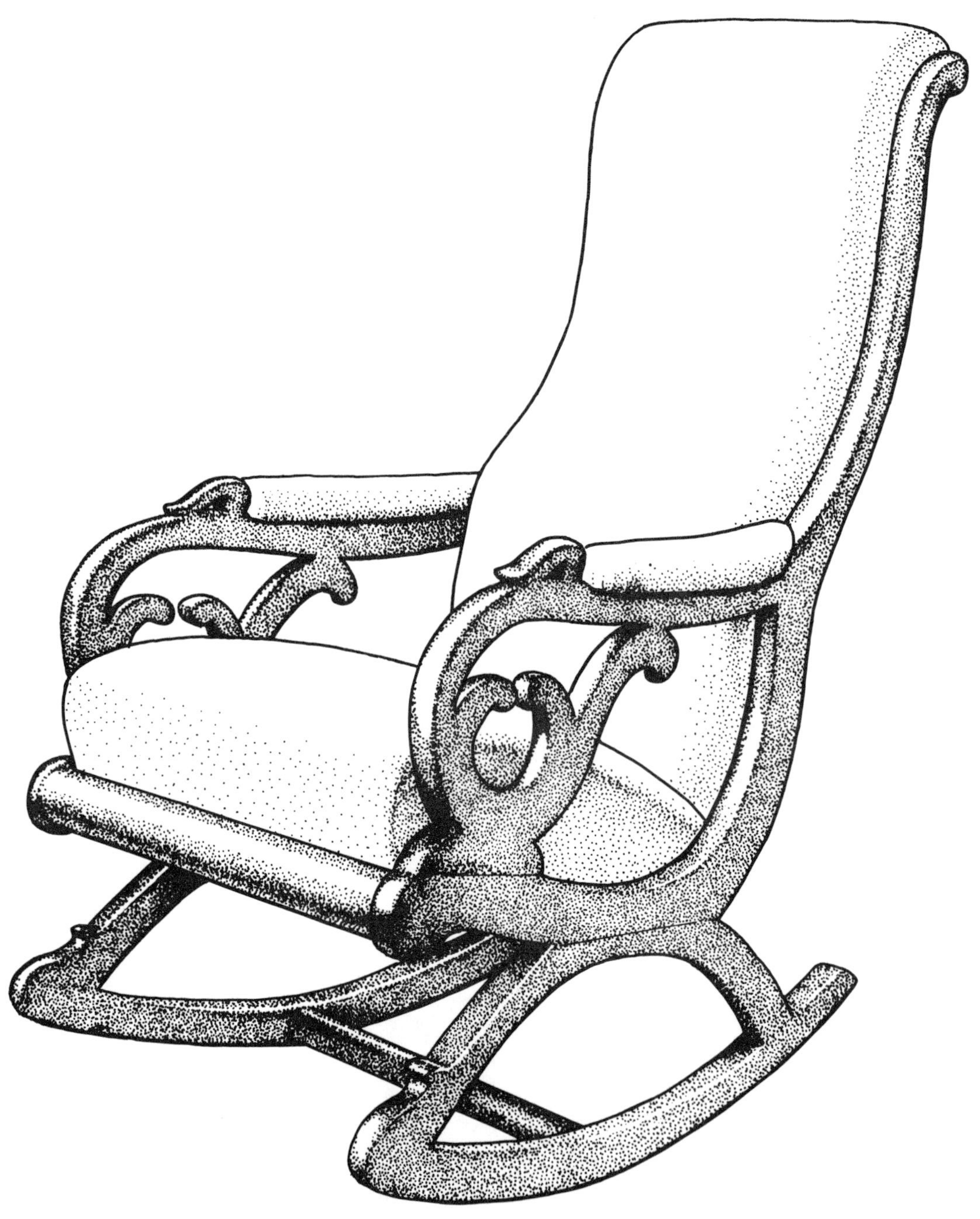

Fig. 158 A Victorian rocking chair with a removable box seat

Fig. 159 An alternative way of setting out buttonwork

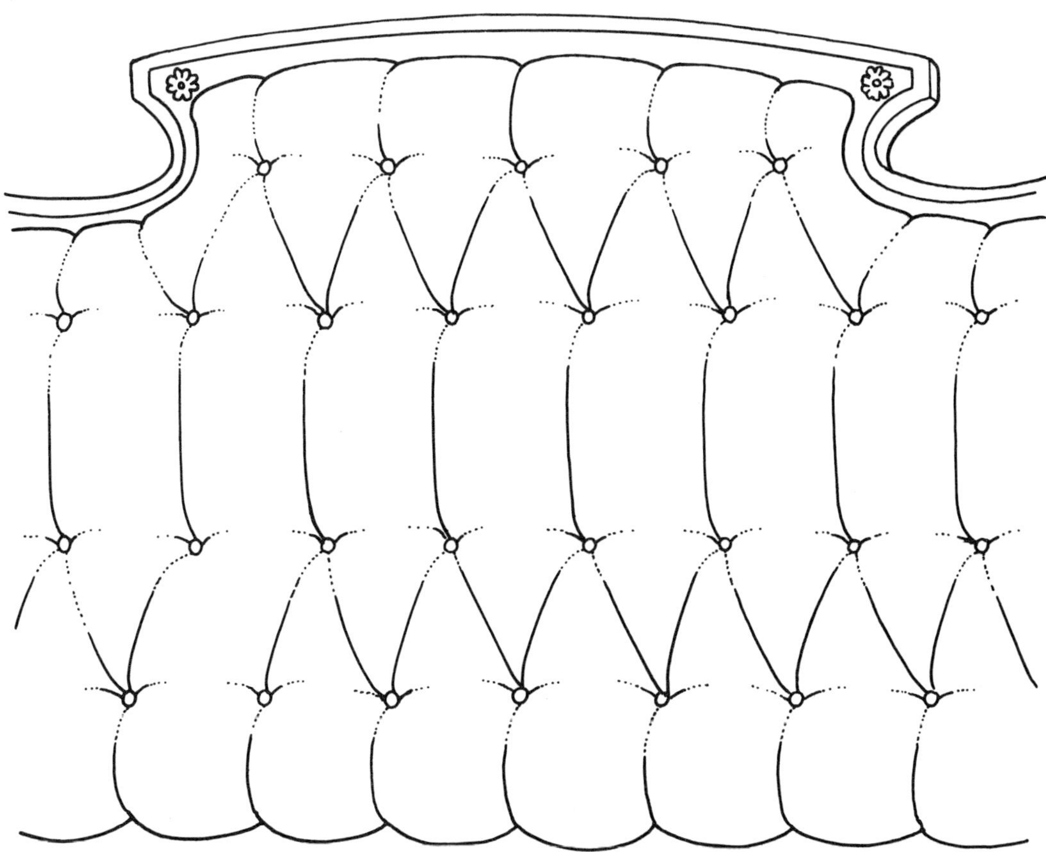

BOX SEATS

Deeply sprung removable 'box' seats are to be found in some Victorian show wood easy chairs, such as the rocking chair illustrated in **fig. 158**. There are two ways of upholstering these box seats. The easier way is to keep the springs to the centre of the seat frame and lace them into a domed shape, then build up the edges to form a high edge with a roll (pages 47–49).

In the second method the springs are kept to the outside edges of the seat frame, edged with spring steel wire and laced into a flat box shape. The springs are then covered with heavy hessian and securely fastened to the springs with twine stitches. A first stuffing is built up, with a roll edge, on to the top of this spring platform.

A box seat can be covered in various different ways. You can make a complete cover and pull it over. Or the top of the seat can be covered first and the covering fastened under the lip of the roll edge with blind stitches. The border is then ladder stitched (pages 40–41) on by hand. Or a stuffed border can be made with piping or chair cord and recessed in just beneath the roll edge. At each stage of the upholstery the seat should be tried in the chair to make sure that it still fits—it is very easy to make the sides too bulky to fit in.

BUTTONWORK

The picture in **fig. 159** of the back of a show wood settee illustrates a variation in buttoning—a style which incorporates straight, vertical pleats between rows of buttons in a diamond formation. This method was often used in carriage and early car upholstery and it can be used on settees, couches and chairs which have rather high backs.

When you set out the measurements between the buttons at the top and the bottom of the vertical pleats (pages 102–107), the distance must be the same on the upholstery as on the back of the cloth. No extra is allowed on the cloth, so that when covering takes place the vertical pleats can be tucked well down into the upholstery and held tightly between the buttons at the top and the bottom.

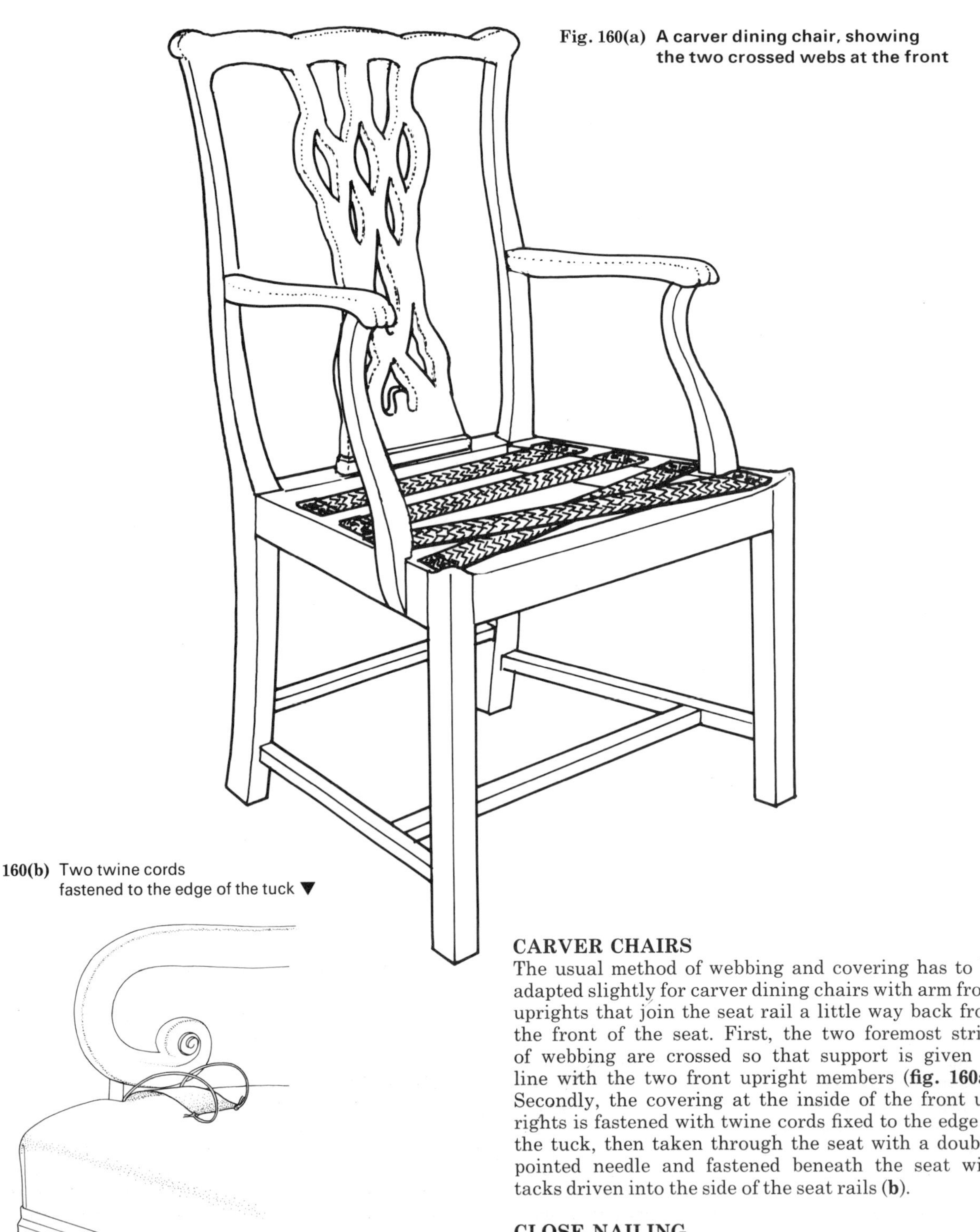

Fig. 160(a) A carver dining chair, showing the two crossed webs at the front

160(b) Two twine cords fastened to the edge of the tuck ▼

CARVER CHAIRS

The usual method of webbing and covering has to be adapted slightly for carver dining chairs with arm front uprights that join the seat rail a little way back from the front of the seat. First, the two foremost strips of webbing are crossed so that support is given in line with the two front upright members (**fig. 160a**). Secondly, the covering at the inside of the front uprights is fastened with twine cords fixed to the edge of the tuck, then taken through the seat with a double-pointed needle and fastened beneath the seat with tacks driven into the side of the seat rails (**b**).

CLOSE-NAILING

Close-nailing is a method of trimming and permanently fastening fabric at the same time (**fig. 161a**). A continuous row of dome-headed chair nails is hammered in so that all the heads are touching. This makes an excellent finish to an edge so long as the line of nails is made perfectly even. It only needs a couple of nails to be slightly out of place to ruin the whole effect. The size of chair nail most used in upholstery has a 12 mm ($\frac{1}{2}$ in) shank, with a 10 mm ($\frac{3}{8}$ in) diameter head, but larger and smaller nails can be obtained.

When buying chair nails, do not get the cheaper sort, which are brass plated on steel. The thin brass plating soon wears off and the nails begin to rust. Better quality nails have solid brass dome heads with steel shanks. You can buy them in three finishes: polished brass, and light and dark antique brass. Where possible, I prefer the light antique finish to the polished brass, which soon becomes dull and lack-lustre. The dark antique nails sometimes have a greyish look like gun-metal. Of course, which of these finishes is most suitable will depend on the colour of your furnishing fabric.

Close-nailing does have a disadvantage in that the close row of shanks tends to perforate the wood along the grain and some woods, such as oak, may then split open along this line.

The trained upholsterer will close-nail very accurately just by eye, judging distance and straightness without measuring aids. But I would recommend for beginners a simply made guide and gauge for positioning chair nails. Teddy, who lives next door to my workshop, is always full of bright ideas, and it was when I suggested that he might trim the dining chair seat that he was reupholstering with domed chair nails instead of braid that he turned his inventive mind to making a guide for spacing the nails accurately. Here is a picture of it (**b**). It is just a bent strip of fairly thick aluminium in which a slot has been cut. The width of the guide is exactly the diameter of the nail head. The slot is filed out so that the shank of the nail is an easy fit and is the length of the radius of the nail head, plus a little extra to allow for the thickness of the shank. If this guide is placed against the edge of the show wood or level with the bottom of the seat rail, a nail can be placed in the slot and hammered home. The guide is then placed close up to this first nail head to give the exact distance for placing the next nail so that the heads just touch. This aid will enable you to achieve a professional look with little skill—but don't rely on it all the time; occasionally try nailing by eye as the real professionals do.

Fig. 161 Close-nailing

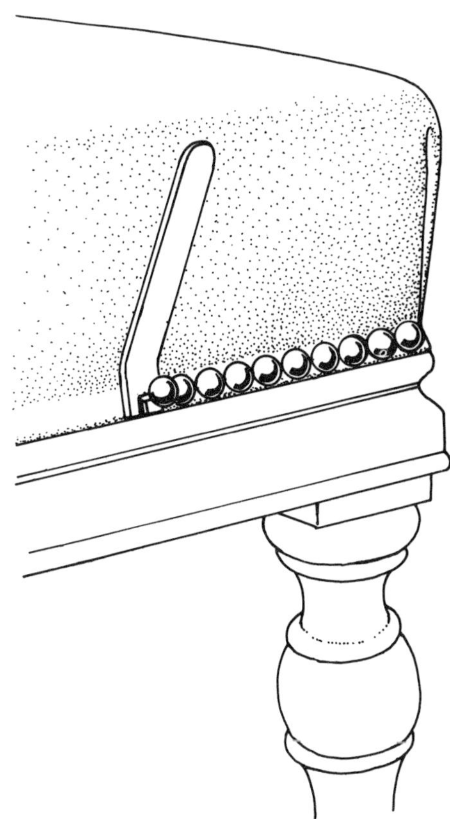

161(b) A simple gauge for close-nailing ▲▼

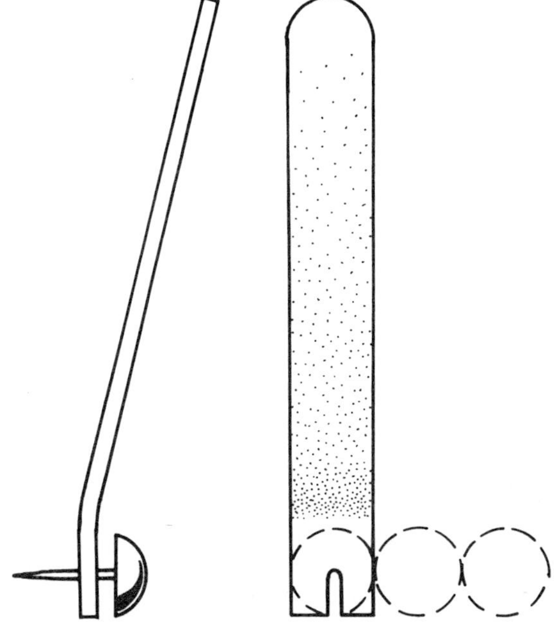

161(a) A close-nailed chair edge

CORNER CHAIRS

These chairs are sometimes termed 'writing chairs', but they are more often used to grace the corner of a room. The seat is diamond-shaped and is usually upholstered with a simple pin cushion seat (**fig. 162a**). A pin cushion seat is normally very easy to upholster but this type, being diamond-shaped, is more difficult, as the covering fabric has to be tacked on the four sides at a diagonal to the threads of the weave—that is, on the bias. However, I will lay down a few guide lines to help you to achieve a satisfactory finish.

I have a complaint to make concerning most chairs with pin cushion seats—that the makers seldom allow enough width in the rails to facilitate the comfortable placing of webbing, hessian and the other upholstery materials necessary for a good seat. Although the covering must run from back to front—from the back corner to the front corner—for the purpose of attaching the webbing you should view the diamond as a square, and place the webbing as in (**b**). You can also see in this illustration that there is a space between the turned-over ends of the webbing and the edge of the tacking rabbet. This must be left clear for the final cover so that a smooth, even turning can be made. The hessian—tarpaulin, of course—can also run in the same direction as the webbing. When the frame is narrow and perhaps the wood is a bit fragile from previous tackings, do use a small amount of P.V.A. glue beneath the webbing and along the edge of the hessian to give strength to the fastening. And be careful to choose tacks which will hold well in the wood but at the same time will not split the rails.

This seat will be 'single stuffed'—there are no edges to stitch up—so put in several rows of stuffing tie loops, add a 100 mm (4 in) domed layer of horsehair and pull the horsehair down with a calico undercover (pages 56–57). The undercover can be tacked down without turnings, then trimmed back all round with a knife or scissors. Place a layer or two of cotton wadding on top and you are ready to cover with furnishing fabric.

Many of these seats are covered in striped damask, which is appropriate to the period of the chairs, but if you use striped fabric you must be meticulous in keeping the stripes straight. The best way to get good results with striped material or patterned cloth is as follows: cut a piece of material roughly to the size of the seat, allowing plenty and remembering that the stripes or pattern will run from the back corner to the front. Ensure that you either have your design or your stripe centred. Lay the fabric over the seat, position it and, without folding in, tack temporarily with one tack in the back corner. Stretch lightly and tack into the front corner so that the pattern or stripe is exactly centred. Now do the same at the side corners, making sure that the pattern remains straight running from back to front and that the threads running across are at right angles to this. Put in one temporary tack to hold the material at the centre of each rail. Cut off the surplus material on each side, leaving about 15 mm ($\frac{5}{8}$ in) for turnings.

Now temporarily tack the material all round, stretching and turning in as you go. Use 10 mm ($\frac{3}{8}$ in) fine tacks or small gimp pins. Or, if you intend to do the permanent fastening with staples, use larger tacks, such as 12 mm ($\frac{1}{2}$ in) fine, which can more easily be pulled out as you fix with the staple gun. In Chapter 1 where I describe the tools and their uses I mention that the regulator is also useful as an extra finger (page 11). This is the sort of job in which this tool will be of considerable assistance. When you turn in the edges of the material on this pin cushion seat, you can give a bit of a stretch and hold the cloth in place with the point of the regulator while you drive in the tack. I find that this way I am able to make a neater and more accurate job than if I tried to hold the cloth with a finger. By the way, if you have a cabriole hammer with a very small head, now is the time to use it, to avoid damaging the polished wood surround.

Start at the back corner and work to the centres of both back rails, placing tacks at 15 mm ($\frac{5}{8}$ in) intervals. Fix alternately, one in the left rail and one in the right rail, taking up any fullness to keep the cross threads of the material straight. Also keep a constant eye on the pattern, to ensure that it is straight from back to front. A material with a uniform design is a great help here. For instance, a tack can be put exactly through a flower, dot or stripe to the right of the centre corner, then the corresponding point can be found and tacked through on the left side—and so on. When you reach the centre of each back rail, stop and begin the same procedure from the front corner to the centre of each front rail. Repeat this process from each side corner.

When all the temporary tacks have been put in and you are satisfied that everything looks right, drive home all the tacks. The seat is now ready for trimming.

COUCHES AND CHAISES-LONGUES

Experience from other upholstery work will carry you through most of the upholstery on a couch or chaise-longue, but there are one or two pieces of advice that I would like to give.

The head, usually an S-curve, requires a strong basic support of webbing which is put on in one direction only, across the frame. And heavy hessian should be stretched very tightly over this, the tension being only across the frame. When building up the upholstery on the head, try to achieve a shape that will be comfortable both for the sitting and the reclining figure.

If the seat has a rounded end it will probably have an extra straight rail a little way in from the rounded end rail. To get springs positioned near to the rounded end you may have to fasten them on to this second straight rail with staples or webbing. They will, of course, have to be shorter so that the tops are level with the springs fastened to the webbing.

The high stitched edge that has to be built round the seat is an exercise in exactness. To ensure that this is straight, even and the same height throughout, you must be very precise in building up the hair stuffing, positioning the scrim hessian and putting in the blind stitches and the rolled edge.

Many couches have a show wood back with a turned balustrade. Where the bottom rail of this is made at the level of the top of the seat you should also stitch up an edge beneath this polished rail, but a finishing roll may not be necessary.

Fig. 162 Reupholstering a corner chair

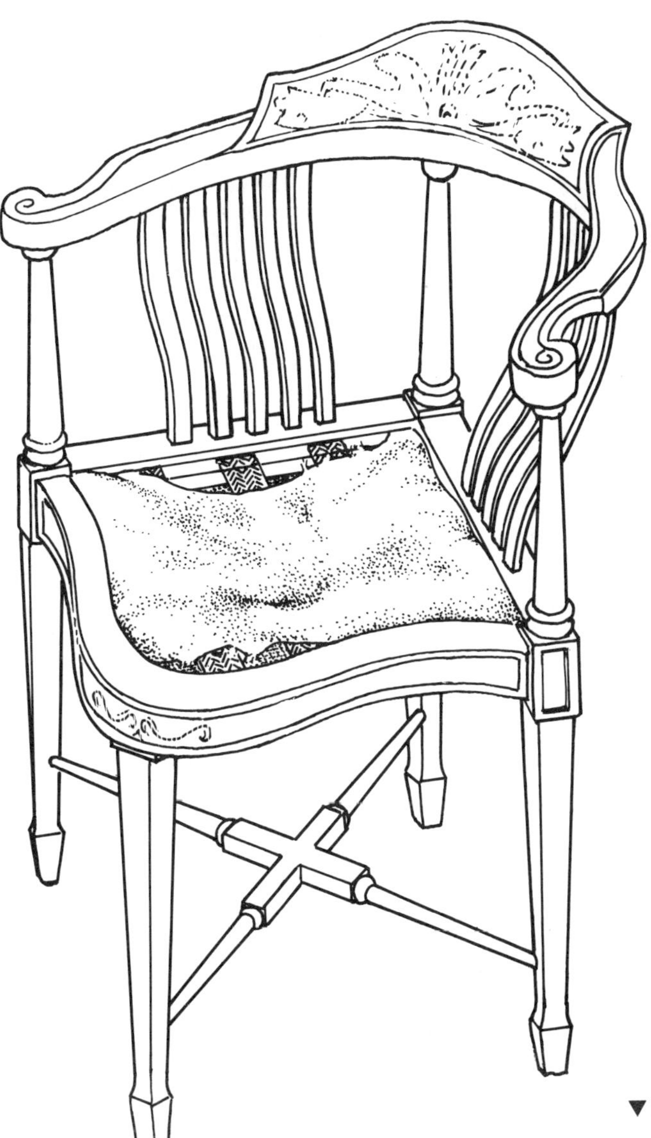

▲ **162(a)** A corner chair

▼ **162(b)** The webbing on the seat of a corner chair

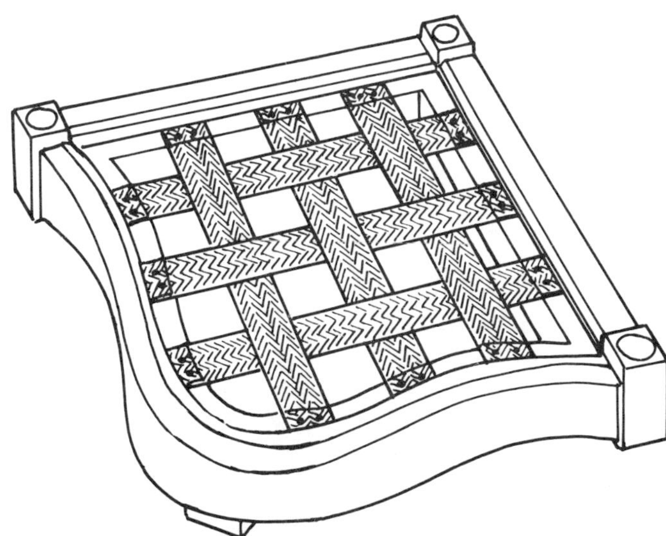

The direction of the pattern or knap of the covering material should be running from the top to the bottom of the head, and from the head to the foot—in other words lengthways—on the seat. If the back has a buttoned or plain padded top, the material can run lengthways, from the head end of course. If it is completely stuffed over, the run is from the top to the bottom. If the border is covered in a plain fabric, it can run in the same direction as the seat; if you are using a patterned fabric then it must go from top to bottom.

DROP ARMS

Most settees with drop arms or drop ends are chesterfields, but drop arms also occur on higher-backed settees of the 1920s and 1930s.

The drop arms mechanism shown in **fig. 163** has wooden ratchets and is hinged with steel back flaps. There is a better system that has steel ratchets; the whole arm swings on two bolts which should have second locking nuts to prevent them from unscrewing. There are also other types of drop arm, but these two are the most common.

In nearly all cases it is best first of all to remove the drop arm. After the back upholstery has been built up to the first stuffing stage, the drop arm can be temporarily put back to be upholstered to the correct height and a similar shape to the opposite arm. When the first stuffing of the drop arm has been completed (with roll edges), it can be removed once more while you build in the seat.

It is necessary to see that the height and thickness of the second stuffing meets the level of that of the seat when the arm is lowered, and that no gap is left between the inside of the arm and the seat when it is in the 'up' position.

The bottom edge of the covering material is fastened to the lower tacking rail of the moving arm and a scroll covering is sewn at the back of the arm and fastened to the lower part of the back. Two pieces of folded webbing are fastened on to the outside of the arm to serve as restraining and supporting straps beneath the outer covering. The back scroll material is brought round the webbing as shown and fastened at the outside with tacks at the top and bottom, then sewn down on the webbing with a running stitch. The front scroll piece is also fixed. Then the outside arm material is ladder stitched over this so that when the arm is let down, the webbing and covering collapse and fold in together.

Fig. 163 The drop end of a settee stripped bare to show the drop arm mechanism.

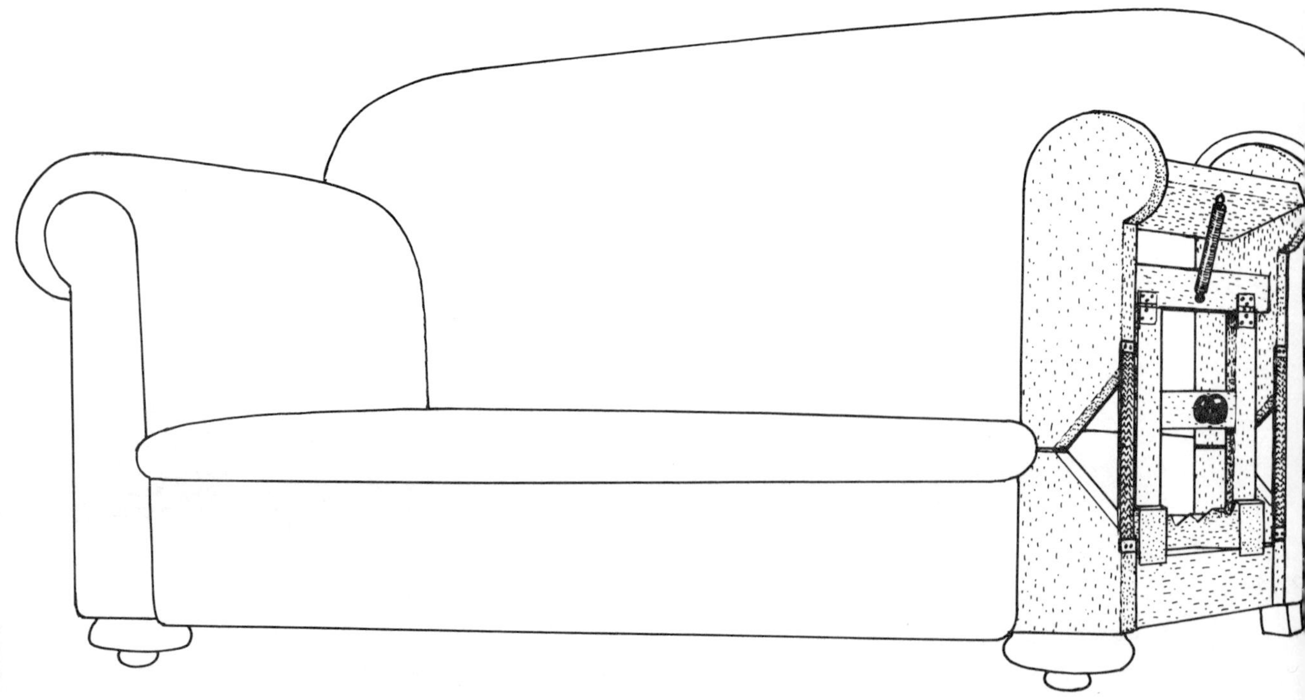

FALSE CUSHIONS

I have a notion that it is a French idea to make a chair seat look as though it has a cushion on it when, in fact, the seat is made all in one (**fig. 164a**).

A system of springs and malacca cane makes the interior for the cushion form (**b**). It is a rather peculiar system because the malacca cane is used not only around the top of the springs but also in another square frame fastened lower down on the waist of the springs to form straight edges on which to fasten the underside of the false cushions.

The covering sequence is as follows. The cushion top is covered. The base is sewn into the waist of the seat (note the mitred corners). A border is sewn in to appear as the underside of the cushion. This is padded with wadding to round it slightly. Finally, cord trimming and tassels are added.

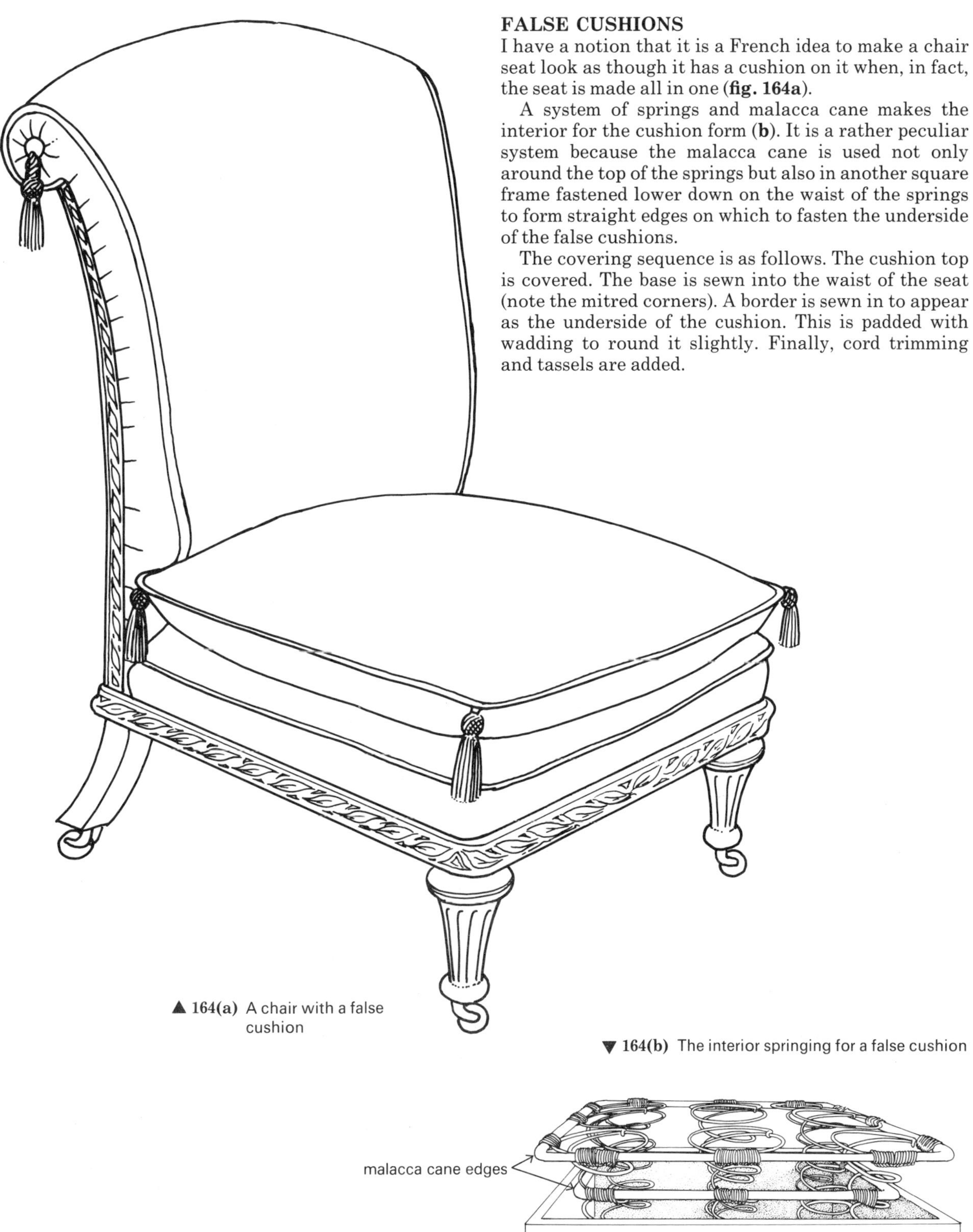

▲ **164(a)** A chair with a false cushion

▼ **164(b)** The interior springing for a false cushion

Fig. 164 Building a false cushion

Fig. 165 An easy chair with a fluted back

FLUTED-BACK CHAIRS

Although they are not all that comfortable, fluted chair backs do look attractive (**fig. 165**). Let me tell you of the mysteries of making one.

For the best results and uniform shape the back is pre-formed and then put on the chair. The filling within the flutes can be of soft foam or cotton felt. If foam is used, the back can be made up first and the shaped pieces of foam inserted afterwards. Cotton felt has to be made into the flutes as they are stitched.

First, the amount of covering material has to be measured for and worked out. If you draw a section exactly the size of the flute you can measure round this, adding 12 mm (½ in) per flute for seam sewing. The length, of course, is easy to establish, but do allow plenty of extra fabric at the top and the bottom, remembering the thickness of the filling that will roll over the top rail.

A hessian of medium weight, say 280 g (10 oz), or a strong calico will form the back lining, and this is where you have to do some setting out. Consult the sectional drawing of the flute and mark out parallel lines lengthwise on the backing cloth to the width of the base of the section drawing. Mark on the back of the covering material parallel lines at a distance equal to half the circumference of the section plus 12 mm (½ in).

Begin by sewing the covering to the backing at the left-hand side. Put line to line but stitch through a double thickness of covering so that no stitches will show. If cotton felt is to be used, cut off and roll this up into about three thicknesses. Lay one of these between the backing and the cover, then machine stitch down the next line. A piping foot is best for this task—you can then get close up to the stuffed flute. Continue in this fashion until all the flutes have been made.

If you prefer soft foam, pads of this can be cut out and shaped by brushing with a wire brush to achieve a rounded form. The pieces of foam are then wrapped round with a single thickness of cotton wadding. To insert them into the cover, take a piece of soft piping cord, tie it round one end of the piece of foam. Find a piece of thin wood about 61 cm (2 ft) long and 25 mm (1 in) thick. Make a hole at one end or just tie the

Fig. 166
A Georgian chair frame, showing the stitched edge built out to give thickness to the upholstery

piping cord there and you can use this like a giant bodkin to thread the cord through the cover and gently pull the foam and wadding through and into place.

Before we go any further, a word about the support behind this pre-formed back. Some form of springing, such as zigzag wire springs, rubber webbing or tension springs, or even soft coil springs, can be used. It is advisable to place some form of rudimentary first stuffing over the springs, to make a good, even surface.

The rest is easy, just fasten the flutes at the bottom to the underside of the tacking rail, then stretch to the top. The fastening down the sides can be done last. You will find that you can bring the tops of the flutes right over the top rail and fasten beneath the back of this, but you will have to use your regulator between the flutes where they turn over, to get rid of the fullness here.

FOOTSTOOLS

Footstools appear in many forms, but let me just mention the small Victorian footstool upholstered on a solid, square, rectangular or round base on which no webbing is needed. With this type of stool there is the problem of not being able to anchor the first stuffing with through stuffing ties. To hold the first stuffing, fasten ties of twine with small tacks in pairs across and round the stool's edge, placing two fingers beneath each loop before driving home the tacks to get the loops all to the same height.

When stitching up the edges place some wire nails temporarily through the centre of the hessian covering to prevent it from moving as you stitch. If the stool is to be buttoned, cut the stuffing right through to the base board with a tubular cutter.

GEORGIAN CHAIR FRAMES

Many late Georgian chairs were made with very square frames and they are upholstered in such a way as to keep this angular look.

The stitched edges are built out to add thickness to the otherwise thin wood. **Fig. 166** shows a frame upholstered to the first stuffing stage. When the chairs are covered, narrow borders are sewn along the edges of the arms and the top of the back and trimmed with a double line of cord.

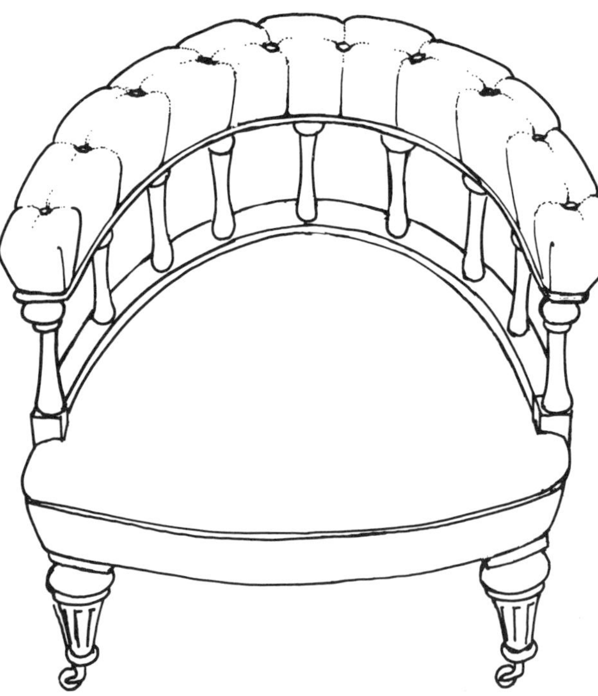

▲ **167(a)** A low drawing room chair

HORSESHOE-BACK CHAIRS

These semi-circular chairs are also known as library or reading chairs. The three most common designs of horseshoe-back chairs are shown in **fig. 167**.

In (**a**) is a low drawing room chair with a balustraded back and a buttoned top pad.

The chair in (**b**) has pierced carving instead of turned spindles in the back. This also has a higher centre part in the back and has scrolled arms. The library chair in (**c**) is larger and has a deeper, buttoned back with scroll ends.

Reupholstering the back of the chair shown in (**a**) is just a variation on upholstering a buttoned arm pad (page 167). The curve presents no problem when covering as the material is taken in at the button folds. But the first stuffing and edge building need a few notes.

The horsehair stuffing which is retained by the usual stuffing ties should be made particularly firm and made to the size and shape of the finished form. Then the scrim hessian covering will go on easily. Concentrate on keeping this tight round the outside of the curve of

Fig. 167 Three designs of horseshoe-back chairs

167(b) ▲
A slightly higher chair with carving instead of spindles

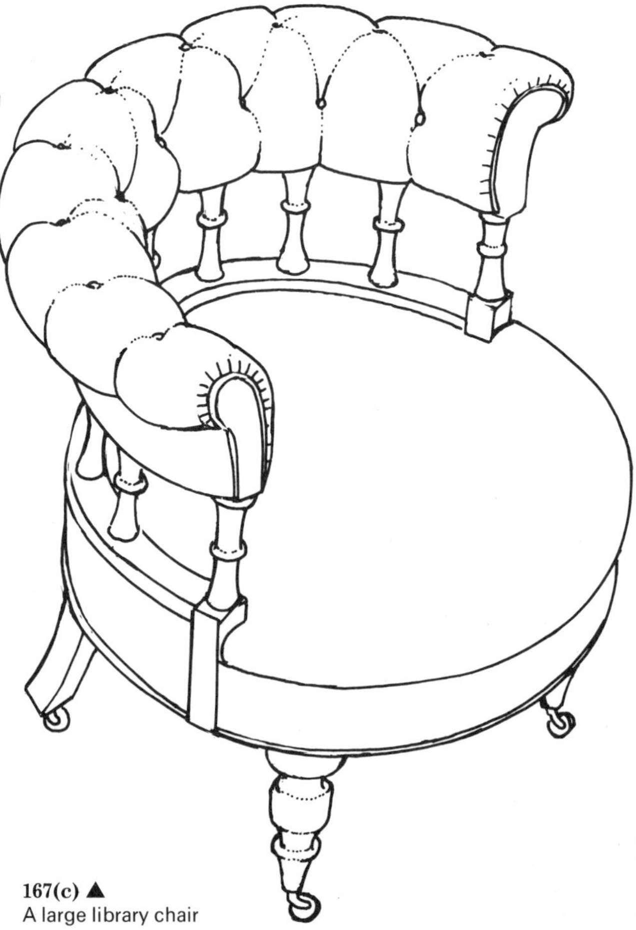

167(c) ▲
A large library chair

the back, then pleat it at about 50 mm (2 in) intervals round the inner curve. Follow threads in the weave of the scrim both on the outside and inside to keep the back parallel and of equal depth throughout. The button holes can be cut through the scrim hessian if you want them to be deeper than the second stuffing.

The top covering should be measured and set out. Take a measurement round the outside curve and make a between-button allowance of at least 12 mm ($\frac{1}{2}$ in). The chair in (**b**) can be upholstered with or without buttons. The first stuffing on this chair back is a good exercise in getting upholstery perfectly symmetrical. This back can be covered in either of two ways. You can simply first cover each arm in one piece, then cover the centre of the back and, finally, sew on separate arm scrolls.

A more elaborate way is first to cover the centre back, then border the arms, then make the arm tops and side scrolls all in one. A chair cord trimming always looks better than piping on these chairs and this can be sewn on last.

The chair back in (**c**) is probably the most comfortable, for its shape is better suited to the back of a sitter. There is only one way of effectively covering this chair back. Each between-button piece has to be cut separately and stitched together, for if you try to fold away all that surplus material at each button, on the inside curve, there will be much too much to tuck away. Careful planning and measurements have to be taken and it is best to make a test piece from a scrap of calico and try it on for size. Stitch all the sections together before you start to cover and button. The covering material round the scrolls must be very neatly pleated or gathered. A braid is used to trim here. Alternatively, a chair cord trimming for each fold can look very effective on this chair back.

KNOLE SETTEES

I am referring here to those large, square copies of the original seventeenth century type of settee. They have drop sides held up by cords and tassels and are usually trimmed extensively with wide braid and fringes.

The basic upholstery on these settees is fairly straightforward. The seats are usually of the platform type, supporting feather cushions. The back is well sprung but kept very flat and on some made at the turn of the century even the drop sides are sprung. The frame on these drop sides and at the back is built out to a good thickness with stitched roll edges (page 181) and then softly upholstered. The sides can be removed from their hinges while the seat and back are upholstered. On some of these settees the sides are upholstered completely independently and hinged afterwards, and on others they are upholstered separately to the stage where the inside is covered, then each side is fastened to its hinges and the outside covering material is taken over to cover the side and the lower fixed part of the side all in one piece.

New cords and tassels can be obtained, but they are very costly. It may be possible, if the old cords are still in good condition, to have these dyed to match the new covering. All the fixing along the top edges of the back and drop sides is done with tacks and then a wide braid is applied to hide the tacks.

The fringe across the back and on the sides can be machined on to the covering before this is put on, but I prefer to hand sew it on afterwards. The fringe around the base is sewn on so that the bottom of the fringe is level with the bottom of the settee.

LEATHERCLOTH

I can remember working with the old type of leathercloth which was a nitro-cellulose coated fabric which you had to tug, pull, stretch and even warm over a heater on cold days before you could get rid of all the creases and fullness round the sides of dining chair seats. How different today's leathercloth is. Not only is it hard to distinguish in appearance from real leather, but it behaves like soft, damp leather in that it is easily stretched and will shape itself over the most elaborately formed upholstery.

There are a few points to remember when using this leathercloth. First, make sure that there are no sharp or rough edges to the woodwork underneath, especially if it is a loose seat that you are covering. Round off all the edges with a plane or rasp and take off the sharp corners. Secondly, this leathercloth has a stockinette backing, which means that it stretches more in the width than the length, so I make it a rule to put on the leathercloth so that the run of the material is always across a seat. This gives more tension to the front edge and always looks better. Lastly, diagonal stretching is so important to get a good finish to any area of upholstered surface covered in leathercloth. Corners can be close gathered quite effectively and usually pleats can be dispensed with.

LOOSE LEATHERS (Skivers)

You can get new tooled leathers for the tops of writing tables and bureaux. Measure the area to be covered accurately and the makers will supply you with a slightly oversized leather than can be trimmed into the recess after fixing. They will also supply you with the correct adhesive for laying the leather.

The old leather and every trace of the old glue must be removed and the surface underneath should be clean, dry and smooth. Fill up any cracks or holes with plaster of Paris or a modern filler. Position the new leather and then turn it back from one side about 150 to 175 mm (6 to 8 in). Coat the bare wood that you have exposed with adhesive and lay down this part of the leather, gently smoothing it with a wide roller. Now roll back the leather from the opposite end and coat an area of the wood about 31 cm (12 in) in width with adhesive. Lay the leather over this, being careful to exclude all the air, and then roll this portion. Continue in this way until the whole leather skiver has been laid.

Trim the edges with a very sharp-pointed craft knife against a ruler or a straight edge held down on the leather to the inside of the edge (so that you can slightly undercut into the recess). You can add a little more glue along the extreme edge and press down the leather, using the flat end of a regulator to smooth the edge and make a perfect joint with the surrounding woodwork. After this give the whole area a final roll to ensure a good adhesion, and the job is done.

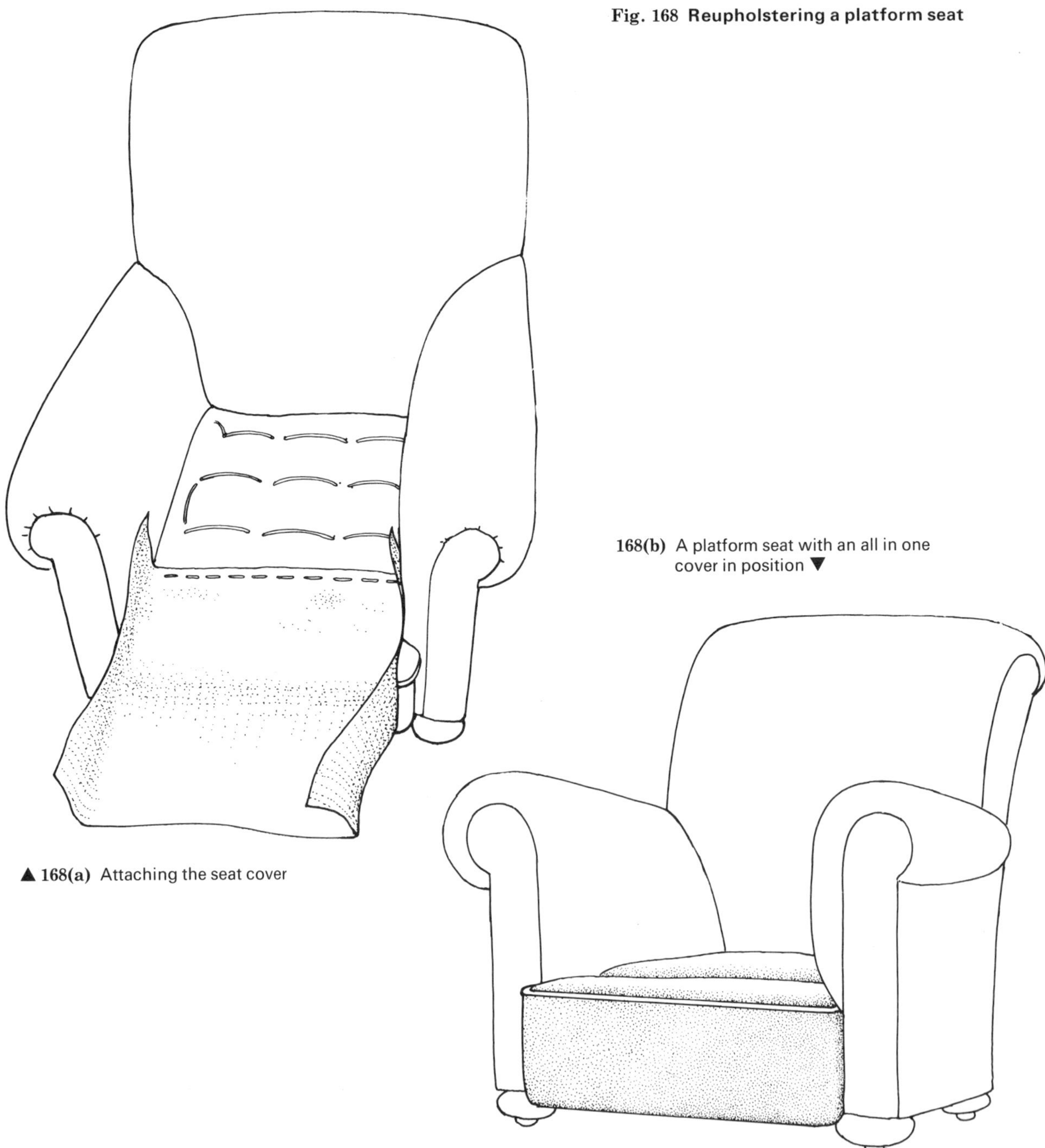

Fig. 168 Reupholstering a platform seat

▲ **168(a)** Attaching the seat cover

168(b) A platform seat with an all in one cover in position ▼

PLATFORM SEATS

The easy chair described in Chapter 7 has no separate cushion. I would like to describe here the difference in seat building when the plan is to include a cushion.

The method of springing is the same, except that the springs should be lower and laced to give a flat appearance. So use heavier gauge springs which need little tension when laced. Always keep the finished height of the seat, including the cushion, in mind for you do not want it finishing at a height that is uncomfortable.

The first stuffing is kept as flat as possible but the front edge is formed in the same way as on the chair in Chapter 7 (pages 108–112).

It is usual to cover the platform seat so that a trough is made across the seat at a distance of about 150 to 175 mm (6 to 7 in) in from the front. The purpose of this is to keep the platform flat and also, strangely enough, it helps to keep the cushion from working forward.

Using a felt tip pen, draw a line across the scrim first stuffing cover about 175 mm (7 in) from the front. Then prepare the seat cover, making this in two pieces with the seam corresponding to the line that you have drawn, and allowing plenty of length for the loft of the second stuffing. Sew fly pieces to the back and the sides and then sew the seat cover to the scrim as shown in **fig. 168(a)**, attaching the seam to the hessian at the line that you have drawn, with running stitches going right through to the spring hessian. Do not pull these stitches too tight or you will make the trough too deep.

Next, apply the top stuffing to the front and behind the trough line and tighten and fasten the cover. In this instance a separate border is to be fitted, but alternatively the border and seat cover can be made in one before fitting. The finished chair, with the 'all in one' cover in position, is shown in (**b**).

POUFFES

The pouffes that immediately spring to mind are those rather smelly camel-skin souvenirs, embossed and decorated, which are brought home by travellers to the Middle East. But I will not decry them all, for some are beautifully made with very colourful designs.

You can, of course, make up your own pouffe case from leather, leathercloth, stout fabric or a mixture of both. But the question that is always asked is, what do you fill them with? A pouffe needs to be very firmly stuffed to stand up to what is expected of it, so all those innovations for fillings that I have seen, such as torn-up newspapers, thousands of nylon tights, bushels of foam chips and small pieces of polystyrene, can be ruled out.

The good old traditional filling for pouffes is woodwool—the specially made wood shavings used for packing china and other breakables. I know that I described this in Chapter 1 as one of the fillings that you should throw away, and this is so—woodwool must be fairly new and fresh, as it gets dry, brittle and breaks up with age. However, you may be lucky if you go round to your local china shop to get some woodwool in good condition which they may otherwise just burn.

The wood shavings will need something soft surrounding them, so I would suggest that you first cut some 25 mm (1 in) plastic foam and make a complete inner lining to the case. Then you can stuff it with the woodwool, a handful at a time, working the woodwool evenly into place until the case is full. If your pouffe is one of those leather cases, cut a piece of thick hessian to just under the size of the bottom and tuck this into the bottom to cover the filling mouth. Do not rely only on the holes and thongs of leather provided to close the filling mouth; after you have laced this up, ladder stitch the join with some strong thread and your curved needle.

PRIE-DIEU CHAIRS

As their name implies, these are praying chairs, originally meant not for sitting but for kneeling on. The high T-shaped back was designed as a hand or elbow rest and the flat top is usually made wide enough to support a prayer book.

A prie-dieu chair can be made very decorative and looks good adorning the corner of a room. The seat should be very firm, the back should be straight and flat and all the stitched edges should be made very straight, fine and sharp. On some of these chairs the backs can be buttoned. A cord trimming will define the edges even more sharply.

READING CHAIRS

Reading or library chairs are also somewhat misguidedly called cock-fighting chairs. They are designed for the sitter to straddle the seat; the back then becomes an elbow rest. Some of them have a little flap book rest hinged at the back. Because these chairs are supposed to be sat on back to front, so to speak, the seat must be kept to the same height all round. And, because of its banjo shape, the seat has to have a separate border the full depth of the seat. The upholstery of the back should be good and firm to stand up to sharp elbows and quite a bit of body weight from resting arms.

RECLINING CHAIRS

Quite a number of reclining chairs have appeared in the shops over the last few years and the earliest ones are now coming into the workshops for re-covering; so you may well be faced with the prospect of refurbishing one.

They are very simple to do, except for the dismantling and reassembling of the reclining mechanism. And this should present no problems so long as you study the system and familiarize yourself with all the fixing points—and also get someone to help you to take it apart and reassemble it; it is a four-handed job. With most of these chairs everything that is upholstered comes apart, so you will be able to reupholster and cover each piece separately. Just one final important point. Do not add too much extra padding or you may find that it hampers the reclining action.

REGENCY UPHOLSTERY

The elegant Regency designs for chairs and settee frames demanded equally elegant upholstery, and it was at this time that the upholsterers perfected their foundation work. Thin linen scrim was used for covering stuffings, and edges were stitched with many rows of blind stitches and finished with pencil-thin edge rolls. The complete edges were made very square and upright, with little, if any, overhang. Edges were built out on upholstered panels in the backs of chairs, making a cameo effect within the surrounds of polished or gilded show wood. It is for stitching these panel edges that you really need that double-pointed curved 125 mm (5 in) or 150 mm (6 in) needle that I mentioned in Chapter 1 on tools and equipment. It is impossible to use a straight double-pointed needle because the show wood prevents you from putting the needle through at the correct angle. With a curved needle, it is possible to get a row of blind stitches really close to the line of fixing tacks. However, do not worry if you cannot get a curved double point, you can use a single-pointed curved needle: take it right through, turn the needle round and push it back through the same hole. You will need a curved needle to stitch the roll as well.

ROCKING CHAIRS

The model that needs an extra word or two of advice is the 1890s spindle-turned platform rocking chair. These were originally upholstered simply without much padding and they were usually covered with the thick, carpet-like 'saddle bag' velvet. I recently found one in Cornwall, and this rocking chair had in its lifetime travelled very far from home, for it was made to commemorate the Burns Centenary and on its original saddle bag covering could just be recognized a small cottage with the words, 'the birth place of Burns'.

The upholstery to these chairs can be improved upon considerably, especially the seat upholstery. The seats originally had just a webbing support from the back to the front seat rails, and the carpet bag material was stretched over this. You can see a picture of one of these rocking chairs on the jacket of the book and how I have made it so much more comfortable than it was originally. The deeper shape to the seat is formed with shallow stitched edges, the front edge roll extending well out from the round front rail. The back panel is stitched up all in one—the outside back and inside back with an inner lining of tarpaulin hessian for strength, plus a layer of wadding put in after it is made up. This back is then fastened with chair nails round the edges. The small head and arm pads can be upholstered in either of two ways. You can simply wrap around about three layers of wadding and cover them directly, sewing seams beneath the rails and trimming with close chair nails at the ends. Or, more elaborately, you can make a thin first stuffing with fine stitched edges in rings at the ends. This way certainly makes more of otherwise very thin arm and head rests.

There are other designs of platform rocking chairs that have square section frames to the seats, backs and arms instead of the completely turned frame, but these pose no special problems. The seats and backs are pin cushion (page 176) and the arm pads are usually the square, double-stuffed sort that I dealt with at the beginning of this chapter (page 167).

SHELL-BACK CHAIRS

Chairs with shell-shaped or scallop backs usually have iron frames, although I have come across earlier wooden frames.

Unlike the fluted backs. these have curved upholstered segments. And although it is possible to pre-form these to shape, it is best to upholster and cover a section at a time, beginning with the centre shape. Mark out the first stuffing hessian covering accurately, then you will be able to sew each side of the centre piece to the lines. Sew the next sections (each side of the centre) by putting in through and through stitches (page 39) with the cloth turned back. Stuff these sections and then repeat the process with the next sections. If the scallops are shallow, you can trim with chair cord between each pair of segments.

TABLES

Let's have a look at card tables first, the antique Regency or Victorian ones with the tip-over tops. The felt or baize is laid within a shallow recess. Remove all traces of the old covering and glue, fill in cracks and holes with plaster of a filler, then glue a strip of stout black or dark-coloured cloth such as platform lining over the join where the top folds. This needs to be about 75 mm (3 in) wide. If no reinforcement is put here then the baize will soon come apart. I like to cut felt or baize to the exact size of the recess before sticking it down. You can make a much cleaner cut to the edges with a straight edge on the cutting-out table than you can trying to trim into the recess after glueing, and you do not get glue squeezing through the baize round the edges. You can use a good wallpaper paste for sticking this down but I favour white P.V.A. glue thinned slightly with water and applied to the wood only, with a soft 25 mm (1 in) paint brush. When the glue is dry, say after about three hours, you can brush the surface and iron it over with a warm iron.

The more recently made card tables with folding legs have either removable side facings, which means that the cloth can be stretched over, tacked round the edges, trimmed, and the edge facings put back to hide the tacks; or they have a removable board which can be taken out, covered and replaced. Any other small tables with removable, covered thin boards that fit into recesses can be covered in the same way.

WINGS OF LARGE WING EASY CHAIRS

You can make a complete first stuffing to a chair wing covered all over in scrim and with the edge roll stitched, but if you want extra-soft upholstery—and after all a wing is often used as a head rest—then an edge can be built leaving a recess for a less dense and springy second stuffing. This is done as follows (**fig. 169**).

Apply the basic support: fix the webbing near to the back upright; fasten tarpaulin hessian at the top and front edges with tacks and sew it on to the webbing at the back. Leave the bottom edge unfastened. Draw a line 75 to 100 mm (3 to 4 in) in from the outside edge of the wing (**a**).

Cut a strip of scrim hessian or 280 g (10 oz) hessian about 200 mm (8 in) wide and sew it to this line. In (**b**) note how the strip is pleated round the curve. Throw back the scrim hessian and put in stuffing ties [(**c**); see also page 44]. Put on horsehair, packing it evenly beneath the ties (**d**). Draw over the scrim hessian and tack it on the outside to a tacking chamfer (**e**). Stitch the edge with one row of blind stitches and a roll edge [(**f**); see also pages 47–49]. The edge of the wings can join up to the roll edge of the back to form a continuous lip.

X-CHAIRS

This is a very old form of chair that usually has no real upholstery. The seat and back are covered with reinforced leather. A basic support is made for the seat by stretching four or five pieces of webbing across tightly from rail to rail, stretching good stout tarpaulin hessian over the webbing and sewing the hessian to the front and back strips of webbing. The prepared leather seat cover is then fastened over this support with large dome-headed brass chair nails. The front and back edges of the leather can be folded over the support, punched with holes about 20 mm ($\frac{3}{4}$ in) apart and 10 mm ($\frac{3}{8}$ in) in, and bound through with thongs of leather.

If the leather is of a reasonable thickness a doubled piece will be strong enough to form the back. With thinner leather, a reinforcement of hessian can be stuck or sewn between the two pieces of leather. Again, the leather is fastened to the frame with the large domed brass nails.

If the arms have to be covered, then the only padding used is two layers of wadding.

Fig. 169
Wing upholstery for an easy chair

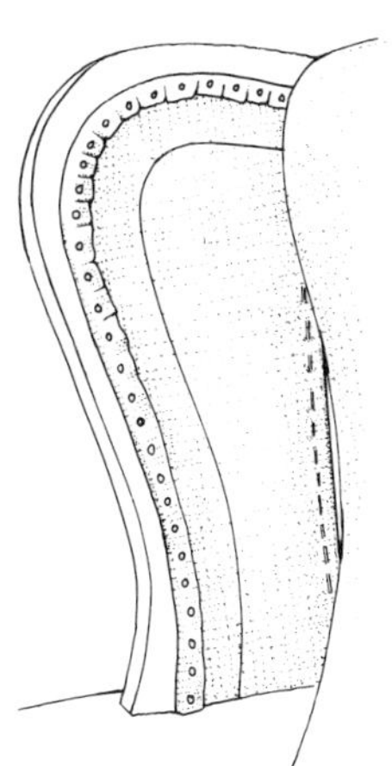

▲ **169(a)** Apply the basic support and draw a line inside the shape of the wing

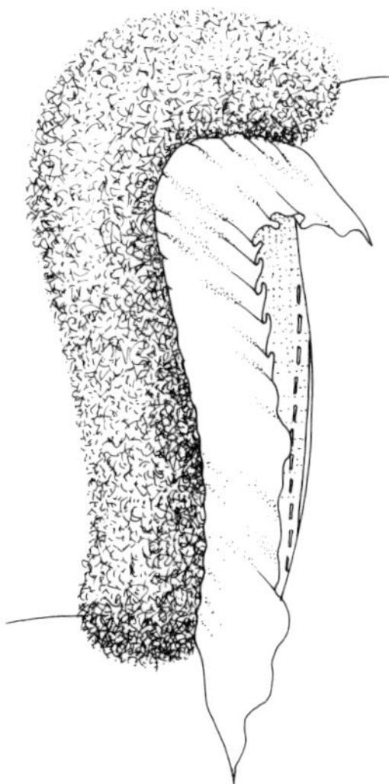

▲ **169(d)** Apply the horsehair stuffing

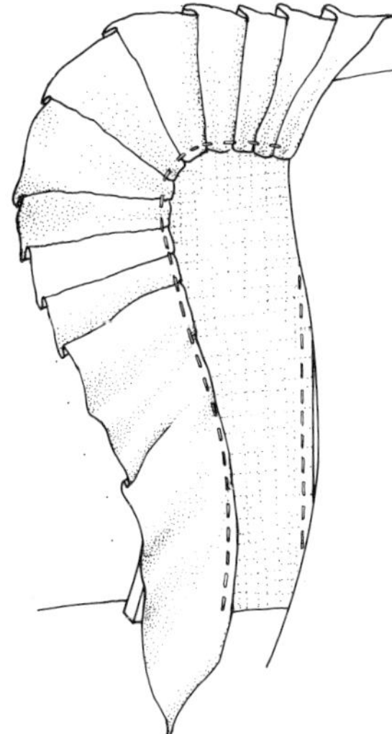

▲ **169(b)** Sew a hessian strip to the line

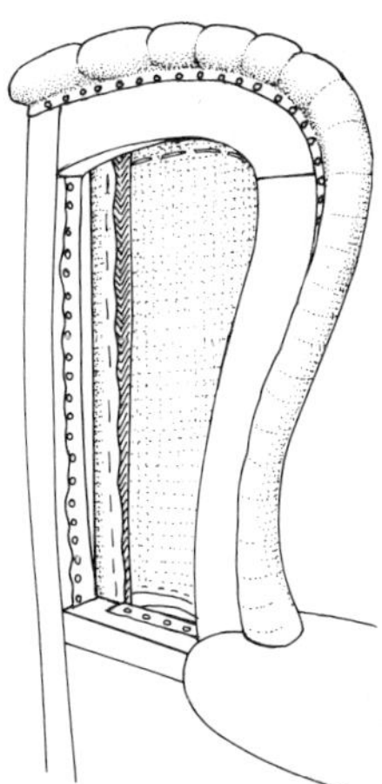

▲ **169(e)** Fasten the scrim hessian

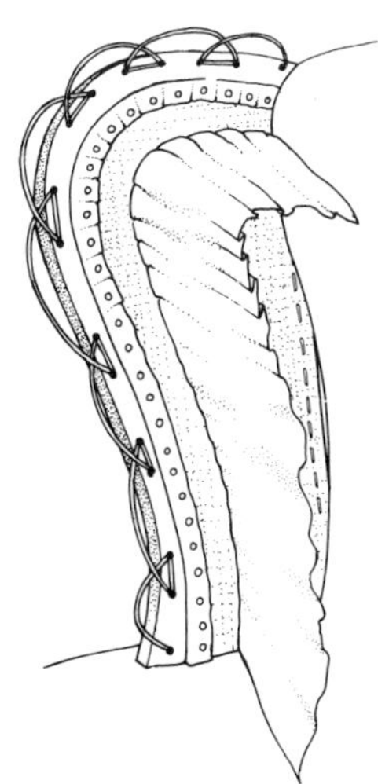

▲ **169(c)** Put in stuffing ties

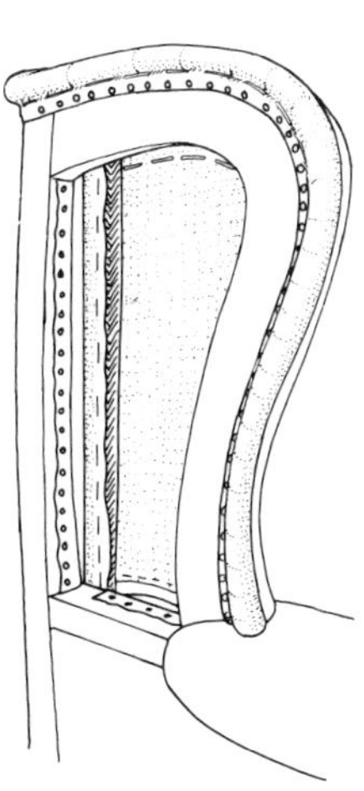

▲ **169(f)** Stitch the roll edge

Index

Numbers in **bold** refer to illustrations